In Camps

CRITICAL REFUGEE STUDIES

Edited by the Critical Refugee Studies Collective

In Camps

VIETNAMESE REFUGEES, ASYLUM SEEKERS,
AND REPATRIATES

Jana K. Lipman

UNIVERSITY OF CALIFORNIA PRESS

University of California Press
Oakland, California

Library of Congress Cataloging-in-Publication Data

Names: Lipman, Jana K., author.
Title: In camps : Vietnamese refugees, asylum seekers, and repatriates /
    Jana K. Lipman.
Other titles: Critical refugee studies ; 1.
Description: Oakland, California : University of California Press, [2020] |
    Series: Critical refugee studies ; 1 | Includes bibliographical references
    and index.
Identifiers: LCCN 2019052137 (print) | LCCN 2019052138 (ebook) |
    ISBN 9780520343658 (cloth) | ISBN 9780520343665 (paperback) |
    ISBN 9780520975064 (epub)
Subjects: LCSH: Refugees—Vietnam—20th century. | Refugee camps—
    Political aspects—20th century.
Classification: LCC HV640.5.V5 L56 2020 (print) | LCC HV640.5.V5 (ebook) |
    DDC 362.87089/95922—dc23
LC record available at https://lccn.loc.gov/2019052137
LC ebook record available at https://lccn.loc.gov/2019052138

29 28 27 26 25 24 23 22 21 20
10 9 8 7 6 5 4 3 2 1

For Eli

CONTENTS

Introduction

IN SEPTEMBER 1975, A GROUP OF DETERMINED Vietnamese men participated in an elaborate and highly choreographed political demonstration in a U.S. refugee camp on Guam, a U.S. island territory in the Pacific. Four men volunteered to have their heads shaved in a public performance of dissent. A makeshift platform served as a stage. Two men sheared the hair off each protester. The men bowed their heads as their hair fell to the ground. Dozens of supporters surrounded the men and witnessed the scene. These activists wanted a ship so they could return to Vietnam under their own command. In the background, a banner proclaimed boldly in English, "36 Hours Hunger Sit-In. Quiet & Hair-Shaving Off to Pray for a Soon Repatriation."

With the collapse of South Vietnam in April 1975, more than 125,000 Vietnamese fled the country. The U.S. government directed them to Guam for initial processing, and the vast majority soon gained resettlement in the United States. However, these protesters were different. They had also evacuated South Vietnam in its chaotic last weeks, but once on Guam, approximately 2,000 of them realized they did not want to resettle in the United States. Some had spouses and children who had been left behind, others were elderly and feared an unknown future, and still more were young men in the South Vietnamese Navy who had been at sea when Saigon fell and whose ships simply never returned to port. Their protests unnerved U.S. officials, who had not anticipated that any Vietnamese would want to return to communist-controlled Vietnam. There was no plan for them. The would-be repatriates directed their message to the American, Guamanian, Vietnamese, and United Nations High Commissioner for Refugees (UNHCR) officials who controlled their future, and they used every tool they could muster: letter writing, elected delegations, hunger strikes, sit-ins, marches, and even

FIGURE 1. Would-be repatriates have their heads shaved in an act of protest on Guam, 1975. Courtesy of the U.S. National Archives and Records Administration, Record Group 319, Box 19, declassification number 984082.

threats of violence. These men and women held their ground on Guam and insisted in no uncertain terms that they wanted to be repatriated. In a matter of months, they would succeed in forcing the hand of the United States, and most would choose to return to Vietnam.

Fast forward twenty years and turn to Palawan, an island within the Philippine archipelago with its own American colonial legacy. It too hosted a camp for Vietnamese men and women, from 1980 through 1996. During these years, approximately 40,000 Vietnamese transited through this camp, and most resettled in the United States. But not all. After 1989, not everyone gained de facto refugee status, and by 1996, approximately 2,000 Vietnamese who had been "screened out" remained in the camp. Most had been waiting there for more than five years, insisting that they were refugees and deserved resettlement in a country like the United States or Canada. The Philippines and the UNHCR disagreed. They had determined that these Vietnamese men and women had not produced evidence of political persecution, and therefore they were not refugees entitled to resettlement. By 1996, all "screened out" Vietnamese were slated for repatriation.

Like those on Guam before them, this group of Vietnamese took militant action. Over the course of the 1990s, the Vietnamese in Palawan engaged in

FIGURE 2. Vietnamese in Palawan protest the Comprehensive Plan of Action and plans for their repatriation, 1993. Courtesy of UC Irvine Libraries, Southeast Asian Archive, Project Ngoc Records.

hunger strikes, mass demonstrations, and acts of self-mutilation. There is an extensive documentary account of Vietnamese protesting within the camp with techniques that often looked remarkably like the earlier protests in 1975. In a striking 1993 photograph, a group of almost a dozen Vietnamese men and women solemnly protested inside the camp. They sat beneath a hand-made sign: "Hunger Strike for Refugee Status." Some of the hunger strikers looked directly at the camera, while others gazed away. The picture captured a melancholy moment, but the protest, including the decision to wear matching white headbands, was clearly organized and choreographed. However, in contrast to the repatriates on Guam, the Vietnamese in Palawan held the opposite goal: they rejected repatriation at all costs.

When the Philippine government organized a forced repatriation flight in February 1996, the Vietnamese camp members physically attempted to block the runway where the plane was poised to take off. The camp abutted the provincial airport, and hundreds of Vietnamese men and women flooded the airfield. Individuals cried, prayed, and protested, with the goal of stopping the repatriations with their bodies. Armed Filipino soldiers responded to the protesters with water cannons and pushed hundreds of Vietnamese off the runway. They ensured the planes, with more than eighty Vietnamese on board, could leave. The Philippine government claimed that all the Vietnamese on the plane were there voluntarily, but as one reporter commented, "At least one man was seen to be bodily carried . . . others were dragged."[1]

These images remained with me long after I first encountered them. They were evidence of Vietnamese protest in the most unexpected of places, a refugee camp on Guam right after the collapse of Saigon and an island in the Philippines twenty years later, when most people were no longer thinking about refugees in Southeast Asia. The symmetry and disjunction between these stories have propelled my work on this book ever since.

After 1975, close to 800,000 individuals left Vietnam by boat, survived, and sought refuge in camps in Malaysia, Thailand, Indonesia, the Philippines, and Hong Kong.[2] Although not the only large refugee population of the era, Vietnamese were the most visible because of the failed U.S. war in Vietnam. Newspapers, magazines, and television news broadcasts amplified stories of the war's end and of the subsequent refugee population to an American audience. In 1975, there were more than eight hundred stories in the *New York Times* alone.[3] International attention peaked again in the winter of 1978–1979, when tens of thousands of Vietnamese "boat people" took to the seas. The UNHCR dedicated unprecedented dollars and staff to the camps and programs in Southeast Asia.[4] While interest in the Vietnamese escapes and camps waned in the United States, the politics of Vietnamese refugee status and resettlement remained front-page news in Malaysia, Hong Kong, and the Philippines throughout the 1970s, 1980s, 1990s, and into the early twenty-first century.

This book probes questions that remain all too relevant today: Who is a refugee? Who determines this status? And how do the experiences of refugees resonate at the highest political levels *and* in local communities that are often imagined to be in the most peripheral of places? Unquestionably, international power dynamics shape refugee policy, but so too do specific regional pressures on first-asylum territories and activism within the camps themselves. This book argues that in order to understand refugee politics, one must look at the camps, the places that hosted them, and the people inside.

In Camps moves beyond the familiar terrain of the United States and resituates the main story in Southeast Asia, Guam, and Hong Kong. Focusing on the camps and host territories makes these places of transit and detention visible and alive. Guam, Malaysia, the Philippines, and Hong Kong all shaped the contours of international refugee policy. Each of these sites developed its own vision of humanitarianism, and their leaders sought to define themselves as being either in alliance with or independent of U.S. policy. By magnifying the places in between, the camps are no longer marginal, but rather a key stage where Vietnamese, Guamanian, Malaysian, Filipino, Hong Kong Chinese, and international actors fought over who would or would not be a refugee.

This book also pairs Vietnamese activism within the camps with the growing political networks of Vietnamese in the diaspora. Vietnamese in the camps were far from passive. They established communities, angled for resettlement opportunities, and protested when necessary, sometimes resorting to extreme measures when faced with an undesired future. Vietnamese Americans (along with Vietnamese resettled in Australia, Canada, France, and other western countries) witnessed the indefinite waiting, harsh conditions, and ultimately the individual asylum determination or "screening" and repatriation process with anger. Many had their own traumatic stories of escape, and they used their access to western media and politicians to amplify the brutality of the camps and the validity of their refugee claims. And while host countries (and colonies), UNHCR officials, and U.S. politicians generally spoke of humanitarianism, Vietnamese Americans spoke of human rights and aimed their ire at both Hanoi and the camps themselves. The camps were potent sites, because they could be conduits to resettlement or they could be used to deter, detain, and turn people back. Vietnamese in the camps and in the diaspora understood the stakes and organized.

EMPIRE, POWER, AND SOVEREIGNTY: GUAM, MALAYSIA, THE PHILIPPINES, AND HONG KONG

This book zeroes in on the camps and emphasizes the relationships between local, regional, and international politics. Resettlement countries like the United States, Canada, and Australia receive disproportionate attention in refugee crises at the expense of first-asylum sites. As wealthy majority-white countries, they were credited with benevolence and generosity for accepting Vietnamese refugees. Historian Laura Madokoro has argued that these resettlement countries cloaked themselves in the language of humanitarianism even as they restricted the majority of people fleeing persecution and, notably, have stark histories of Asian exclusion. She writes that humanitarianism "disguised, rather than replaced" structures of restriction, enabling a "myth of beneficence" and "generosity" within majority-white societies.[5] However, China, Hong Kong, Malaysia, the Philippines, Indonesia, Thailand, and even

Guam were on the front lines and hosted more Southeast Asians than any western country. As a result, many Asian leaders claimed humanitarianism for themselves.

Sociologist Yuk Wah Chan has urged academics to reorient their scholarship and consider the "Asian part" of the story.[6] Many U.S. and European-based researchers conceptualize the Asian host countries as mere way stations between flight and resettlement in the west, when in fact Asian actors played principal roles in the crisis. Contemporary media accounts and Vietnamese themselves also represented the camps as being isolated and interchangeable, seemingly anywhere and nowhere at the same time. However, the camps were not in amorphous, apolitical spaces, nor were they removed from local, national, or regional politics. In Malaysia, Vietnamese entered a country where Chinese Malaysians did not hold political power and were often suspect, while in the Philippines, the Catholic Church was a powerful ally for Vietnamese in the camps. In other words, where a camp was mattered.

Host countries and territories located camps as far from national capitals and seats of power as possible. Political leaders developed isolated islands and repurposed prison facilities, while others placed camps in close proximity to military bases, and in one instance, even close to a nuclear power plant. Places like the island of Pulau Bidong in Malaysia, the Philippine Refugee Processing Center in Bataan, and the Whitehead Detention Center in Hong Kong's New Territories were in remote, peripheral areas even by local standards. As scholars have argued, refugee camps exist uneasily within a continuum that includes humanitarian resources on the one end and prisons on the other.[7] Unlike prisoners, individuals did not have a definite sentence, and many waited without knowing how long they would live behind barbed wire. Each camp marked a place of refuge and confinement where Vietnamese waited— sometimes months, sometimes years—for status, resettlement, or return. Hosts generally stressed their humanitarian credentials and generosity even as the camps became increasingly punitive. The camps captured the paradox between migrants' mobility and detention.

Empire also mattered. Camps in Guam, Malaysia, the Philippines, and Hong Kong were all in sites of British or American empire. Despite the U.S. military loss in Vietnam, arguably its imperial nadir, the United States remained an economic and military superpower. It also remained a colonial power. Guam was (and is) a U.S. territory, acquired during the 1898 Spanish-American War and defined by the U.S. military ever since. Likewise, the United States gained the Philippines in 1898 and ruled it for more than four decades. The Philippines became independent in 1946; however, the United States continued to assert economic and military control through its overseas bases, economic influence, and its support for the Philippines' authoritarian Cold War leadership. During the Vietnamese crisis, Guamanian and Filipino leaders often hoped to gain international standing and burnish their humanitarian credentials by hosting Vietnamese. While Guamanians and Filipinos could act independently of U.S. leaders' desires, they also kept their eye on what might curry the most favor in Washington, D.C.

In contrast, the territories which became Malaysia had been British colonies (through many administrative configurations), and Hong Kong too was a British colony until July 1, 1997. As such, both Malaysia and Hong Kong looked less to the United States (and its myopic Cold War anti-communist politics) than Guam or the Philippines did. Instead, they forged independent policies, which were often hostile toward the incoming Vietnamese and contrary to U.S. ideological objectives. Malaysia was keen to demonstrate its sovereignty, and its Cold War priorities included policing internal racial divisions, defending its northern border with Thailand, and envisioning an Islamic solidarity. It was willing to host Vietnamese, but with numbers escalating, there were limits. Hong Kong also faced internal pressure to have a more restrictive policy against the Vietnamese due to the large number of mainland Chinese "illegal immigrants" who were summarily deported across its border each day. Many also feared that Chinese rule might turn all Hong Kong people into potential refugees after 1997. Malaysian and Hong Kong leaders pressured the UNHCR and Great Britain to change refugee policy at key junctures, and they acted based on domestic politics, not U.S. Cold War dictates. Shining a light on regional actors reveals how they asserted their will on the international community and navigated the complicated legacies of British and American empire.

This is not to deny U.S. military, economic, or political power in the machinations of refugee policy. Over the course of two decades, the United States was the UNHCR's largest donor, and it accepted over 400,000 Vietnamese from the camps (and more than 400,000 more through the Orderly Departure Program), far more than any other western country, with Canada and Australia following with close to 100,000 each.[8] The U.S. government accepted hundreds of thousands of Vietnamese in a departure from its immigration laws due to politics of obligation, generosity, guilt, and international expectations. And without question, all the Southeast Asian countries and the UNHCR looked to the United States to take responsibility for the resettlement of the Vietnamese. It was an American war, and so the subsequent refugee crisis was seen as an American problem. However, unlike Hong Kong, the Philippines, or Malaysia, which hosted tens of thousands of Vietnamese for an indefinite time, the United States could be selective in who it would accept. Thousands of miles away, the United States did not face the same local pressures as the host sites, and it often tried to sidestep the hard choices at hand, pointing to the UNHCR or some other entity to "solve" the problem of the camps. Social scientists have characterized this as the power of "remote control," whereby wealthier countries keep unwanted migrants at bay and develop increasingly restrictive and bureaucratic measures to exclude individuals waiting outside their borders.[9] With thousands of Vietnamese hoping to secure entrance to the United States from within the camps, one can see this development in practice. Yet Guam, Hong Kong, and Southeast Asian countries were not passive, nor powerless, and they too shaped the political terrain, which enabled Vietnamese to claim refugee status. Seen through this lens, the United States remains powerful, but it was just one player among many in the transformation of Vietnamese from refugees to asylum seekers to repatriates.

HUMANITARIANISM, HUMAN RIGHTS, AND THE END OF THE COLD WAR

UNHCR officials, Hong Kong civil servants, U.S. elected officials, and Vietnamese American activists all battled over who upheld the values of "humanitarianism" and "human rights." Although the two would seem to be natural partners, as many scholars have noted, human rights and humanitarianism are far from synonymous.[10] By the late 1980s, human rights and diasporic Vietnamese activists found that their vision of human rights would come in direct conflict with governments' more circumscribed commitments to humanitarian relief.

Humanitarianism generally encompassed rules of modern warfare, namely the care of wounded soldiers and prisoners of war, an adherence to political neutrality, and a basic bundle of protections for shelter, food, and medical care in moments of crisis. It also came to connote a politics of care for the needy, marginalized, and displaced.[11] Historically, European nations and the United States commingled humanitarian work and the civilizing mission of empire. For example, the U.S. intervention in Cuba in 1898 and the British support for Christian minorities in the Ottoman Empire both became subsumed under the umbrella of humanitarianism.[12] In this way, the language of humanitarianism was embedded in the racial and political hierarchies of imperial politics.

During the 1970s and onward, Guamanian, Malaysian, Filipino, and Hong Kong leaders all resisted this western monopoly on humanitarianism and pointed out that they provided the most care for the incoming Vietnamese. Hong Kong social workers, Filipino non-governmental organizations (NGOs), and the Malaysian Red Crescent Society sheltered, fed, and cared for tens of thousands of Vietnamese who came to their shores, seemingly without end. In fact, many saw the United States and Great Britain as hypocritical because they called for humanitarian protection for the Vietnamese even as they enforced rigid immigration restrictions. In response, Southeast Asian leaders threw the language of humanitarianism back at the UNHCR, the U.K., and the United States. Even when Malaysia pushed boats back to sea or Hong Kong detained Vietnamese in former prisons, their leaders claimed the positive attributes of humanitarianism for themselves.[13]

In contrast, human rights embraced individual political rights and a legal framework against torture, political detention, and domestic repression.[14] Scholars have demonstrated that the 1970s were a watershed for human rights activism. Amnesty International gained prominence as a grassroots movement against torture and political imprisonment, and critics of both South American dictatorships and Soviet-era communism found traction in human rights. This book analyzes how lawyers and activists called on human rights and norms from the 1980s onward. The camps drew the attention of international organizations, like Amnesty International and the Lawyers Committee for Human Rights, and Vietnamese diasporic organizations based in the United States and Australia. Vietnamese activists, students, and lawyers remained appalled and traumatized by human rights violations in postwar Vietnam, but they also became invested in refugee camp conditions and asylum claims. They did so by drawing attention to the surveillance, squalid living quarters, and minimal legal rights Vietnamese possessed within the camps. *In Camps* argues that diasporic actors called on the language of human rights not only to challenge violations within Vietnam, but to galvanize support for Vietnamese within the camps.

In short, refugee camps checked both boxes, "humanitarianism" and "human rights," in ways that could create contradictions. Vietnamese fleeing by boat needed immediate shelter and direct services. Their traumatic experiences inspired sympathy, and physical protection was part and parcel of the humanitarian zeitgeist. Caring for the Vietnamese was also an overwhelming logistical and financial challenge, and host countries and territories pointed to the extensive material and human resources they committed to the camps. However, once in camps, Vietnamese were often confined behind barbed wire and eventually engaged in legalistic asylum proceedings, needing to prove that they faced political persecution in Vietnam. The result was a standoff between UNHCR and local officials, who pointed to their humanitarian credentials, and a range of lawyers and activists who lambasted the camps as devoid of human rights. As W. Courtland Robinson, the leading scholar of the Southeast Asian refugee crisis, explained, the UNHCR valued a pragmatic humanitarianism even when it faced human rights critics from all sides.[15] Ultimately, Southeast Asian and Hong Kong leaders succeeded in pushing the UNHCR and resettlement countries to take their version of humanitarianism seriously, even as Vietnamese diasporic activists targeted them for failing to protect human rights.

The year 1989 marked a turning point for Vietnamese refugee status. At a pivotal 1989 Geneva conference, the UNHCR, host countries and territories, and resettlement countries all endorsed a new "screening" process, which turned Vietnamese from de facto refugees into asylum seekers. All Vietnamese would now have to "prove" they were refugees. If they could not, they would be repatriated back to Vietnam. The rapid decline of the Soviet Union only cemented these changes, and after 1989, Vietnamese could no longer rely on Cold War norms or U.S. anti-communism alone to establish their refugee claims.

Vietnamese who remained in camps after 1989 were stuck between political eras as much as they were trapped in the camps. The Cold War's "end" was uneven, and local specificities produced new chronologies and perspectives, particularly in regions defined by colonial histories.[16] For Hong Kong, Tiananmen Square was a far more telling event than Berlin, and the 1997 reversion of Hong Kong from British to Chinese sovereignty loomed large. Moreover, thousands of Vietnamese remained displaced, and psychologically and physically unsettled, from the 1990s well into the twenty-first century. Throughout the 1990s, thousands of Vietnamese protested in Hong Kong, others set up community organizations in the Philippines, and still, tens of thousands who had waited in the camps for years returned to Vietnam, often under duress.

This book includes the years fully entrenched in the traditional understanding of the Cold War (roughly 1975 through 1989) and more than fifteen years after its presumed "end' in 1989 (through 2005). It reveals how geopolitical changes played out in the camps, and how Vietnamese had to recalibrate their campaigns and choices in a new political era. *In Camps* shows the juxtaposition of clear turning points and the lengthy stories that uncomfortably seeped across these flashpoints. Looking at Vietnamese in camps before and after 1989 demonstrates the quickness with which geopolitics redefined Vietnamese refugee status alongside the fierce debate over the meanings of both humanitarianism and human rights.

ACTIVISM: IN THE CAMPS AND IN THE DIASPORA

Vietnamese also set the terms of protest. Far from being abject, Vietnamese were active players within the camps, petitioning for their resettlement cases, learning English, navigating camp bureaucracies, and mobilizing campaigns for and against repatriation. In turn, Vietnamese in the diaspora witnessed the increasingly brutal condition of the camps and decided to act.[17] Sizeable numbers of Vietnamese Americans, particularly young people, became politically engaged through their identification with the Vietnamese in the camps. Many had fled Vietnam just a few short years before they became college students and young professionals in the United States. Motivated by a sense of injustice and the seemingly arbitrary screening processes, members of Vietnamese American organizations developed a sophisticated politics of empathy and worked to assist those who came after them. As a result, political activism took multiple forms, from desperate and physical protests by Vietnamese within the camps to transnational campaigns that stretched from the camps in Hong Kong to the halls of the United States Congress.

This line of analysis is inspired by the development of the field of critical refugee studies, spearheaded by Yến Lê Espiritu. Espiritu has criticized the American representation of Vietnamese refugees as a redemptive story that somehow justified the violence and military intervention in Vietnam. She argues against a "rescue" narrative which posits the United States as the savior and the Vietnamese refugee as the "saved."[18] Critical refugee studies challenges assumptions of refugee gratitude, and it resists the logics of neoliberalism and American innocence and exceptionalism. Rather than separating stories of war and stories of migration, it squarely points to the U.S. war in Vietnam and its imperial violence as central to understanding refugee trajectories.[19] Scholars in the field also call for the authority of refugee voices and new ways of understanding refugee stories through creative and scholarly collaborations. They seek to showcase the multiplicity of Southeast Asian voices and jettison the representations of apolitical passivity that have been commonplace in popular and scholarly literature.[20]

Each chapter that follows includes the experiences of Vietnamese within the camps. Sometimes their actions were quiet, whether it was selling *pho* (Vietnamese noodle soup) to earn extra dollars, slipping outside the camp for a few hours, or learning how to tell the right story to gain refugee status. Sometimes Vietnamese even found moments of joy and friendship during their time in the camps. Other times they coordinated elaborate protests that could include hunger strikes and self-imposed bodily harm to draw attention to their campaigns. Their actions were militant and often politically astute. In all, their experiences disrupt an image of Vietnamese Americans as simplistically grateful or as somehow redeeming the U.S. war in Vietnam.

The Vietnamese exodus and its immediate consequences spanned more than twenty years.[21] Much of the popular literature still fixates disproportionately on the South Vietnamese who left in 1975, despite the fact that they make up a distinct minority of Vietnamese diasporic experiences.[22] The fall of Saigon is the standard starting point for works on Vietnamese migration, and in that regard, this book is no different. However, *In Camps* also analyzes the specificities of those who left Vietnam after 1975. In 1978 and 1979, the image of the "boat person" emerged on the world stage as Vietnamese fled in both small rickety boats and large merchant ships which had been organized with the acquiescence of the Vietnamese government. This population was disproportionately Chinese Vietnamese. In the 1980s, the Vietnamese emigrant population changed again when large numbers left from throughout the country, including southerners who had suffered in re-education camps in postwar Vietnam and individuals from central and northern Vietnam who claimed persecution and economic hardship. Vietnamese did not share a singular refugee experience, and instead there were temporal, regional, and ethnic distinctions.

In Camps also argues that diasporic politics became more powerful over time as the crisis stretched into the 1990s and early twenty-first century. Keeping its attention squarely in the camps, it does not investigate the politics of resettlement in the United States or other host countries. Rather, it examines how resettled overseas Vietnamese worked to advocate for Vietnamese in the camps, and it emphasizes the transnational nature of these organizations.[23] It also emphasizes that these diasporic organizations did not speak with one voice. Young, enthusiastic first-generation Vietnamese American college students led grassroots organizations, other Vietnamese American leaders grounded themselves in the politics of Washington, D.C., and still others embraced an international sensibility that included volunteer work in Southeast Asian camps. Vietnamese American activists also grabbed onto the language of human rights, and they used it to challenge violations in Vietnam and the conditions of the camps in Hong Kong and Southeast Asia. Looking at the camps deepens our understanding of Vietnamese American activism that was neither monolithic nor defined by a simplistic anti-communism.[24]

ARCHIVES, CAMPS, AND INTERVIEWS

The paradox of the refugee experience is that it is defined by both movement and stasis. Therefore the narrative of this book will move geographically through multiple sites but will also stay focused on particular camps and territories. It will move from Guam to Malaysia to the outskirts of Bataan Province and then into Hong Kong and finally back again to the Philippines. I do not attempt to analyze all the camps that hosted Vietnamese over the course of three decades, and so choices had to be made. There are key lacunae. First, *In Camps* only touches on the Orderly Departure Program (ODP), which helped facilitate migration directly from Vietnam to the United States in the 1980s and through the early 1990s. While hundreds of thousands left Vietnam through this route, those are different stories of negotiating bureaucracies and immigration processes from within Vietnam.[25] Second, Thailand, Indonesia, and other host countries like Japan and Singapore appear only fleetingly here. Thailand in particular has an important and dramatic history because of the violent conflicts in Cambodia and Laos and the immense number of "land people" who crossed into its territory. The stories of Cambodians, Laotians, Vietnamese and Southeast Asian ethnic minorities dominated these borderlands and were constitutive of the refugee crisis and ongoing warfare there. Given the long chronology and disparate geography, *In Camps* follows Vietnamese sea escapes, at the expense of including the stories of Southeast Asians who fled by land.[26]

By looking at Guam, the Philippines, Malaysia, and Hong Kong, this book also tightens the focus to colonies and independent states in the American and British imperial orbit. This framework reveals how Guam and the Philippines were more constricted by U.S. Cold War priorities than Malaysia and Hong Kong, and also how colonial territories (Guam and Hong Kong) negotiated their responses in comparison to independent states

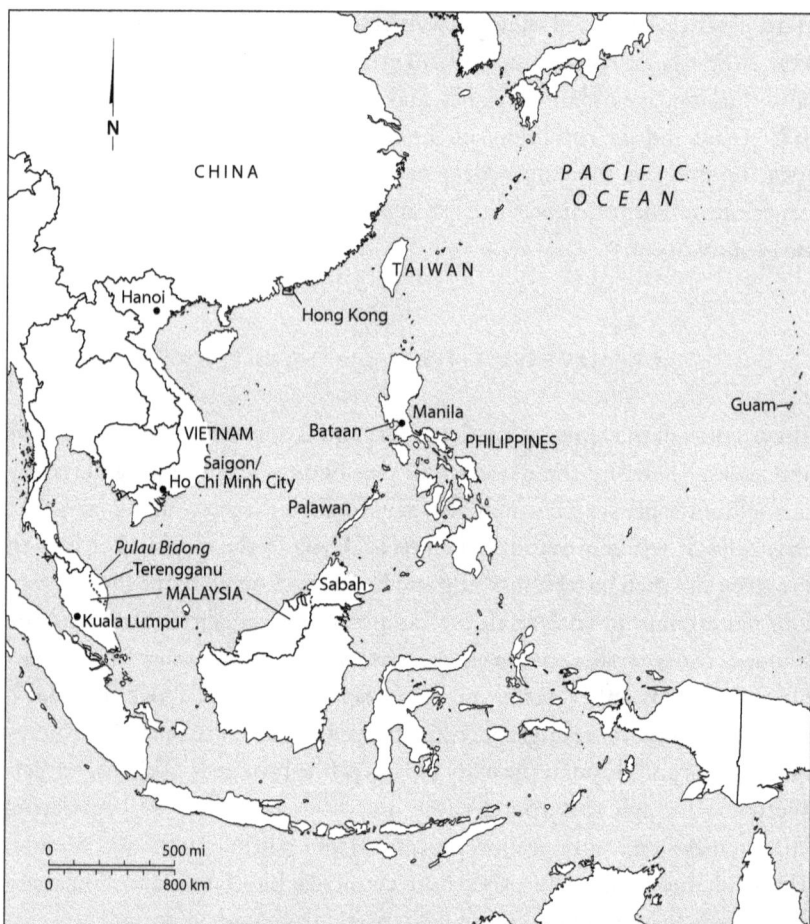

MAP 1. Southeast Asia, including Guam, Hong Kong, Malaysia, and the Philippines.

(Malaysia and the Philippines). Moreover, because of Vietnam's grip on the American political imagination, the diplomatic wrangling over U.S.-Vietnam normalization, and the importance of Vietnamese American activism, I stay focused on Vietnamese experiences.

Sources include UNHCR, U.K., and U.S. government documents, Guamanian, Malaysian, Filipino, and Hong Kong newspapers, NGO reports, ephemera, and photographs. I received hundreds of pages of declassified documents mailed to my door through Freedom of Information Act requests to the U.S. State Department and the British Colonial Office. I faced a few key limitations. One was linguistic. This book relies almost entirely on English-language sources.[27] There is an immense literature in Vietnamese and Chinese within the archives, and future scholars with better language skills than myself will be able to mine these sources.[28] I had no shortage of English-language documents to work with—in fact quite the opposite—and I argue that the documents I have accessed tell an international story and one of changing refugee policy through Southeast Asia and the United States.

I also include stories from interviews with a range of English teachers, former NGO workers, volunteers, Hong Kong government officials, and UNHCR officers, but I decided from the outset that I would not try to embark on a significant oral history project on Vietnamese experiences within the camps. For that there are several excellent books, particularly those by Stephen DeBonis, James Freeman, Carina Hoang, and Nathalie Nguyen, and the ongoing work of the Vietnamese American Oral History Project at the University of California, Irvine.[29] I draw on these works as well as others, and my interviews complemented these sources. Vietnamese men and women remain central to the arguments and analysis in this book, and their memories and testimonies reveal personal journeys and refugee advocacy in Guam, Malaysia, Hong Kong, the Philippines, and the United States.

REFUGEES: DEBATES OVER DEFINITIONS, LANGUAGE, AND THE LAW

Throughout all of the international debates, local politics, and activist campaigns was the sticky nature of language. Were Vietnamese "boat people," "refugees," "illegal immigrants," "real refugees," "economic migrants," or the strange neologism "non-refugees"? Language became fate and future. If someone received a designation as a "refugee," he or she had the right to resettle in a third country outside Southeast Asia. Individuals who did not receive this official designation had few rights at all.

In the United States, refugee policy has a history intertwined with immigration law. In Asian American history, the Chinese Exclusion Act set the precedent of exclusion and regulation from the late nineteenth century into the mid-twentieth century. In 1924, the Johnson-Reed Act restricted immigration to the United States based on national quotas and did not make any exceptions or provisions for refugees. America's restrictive immigration laws meant that the United States infamously did not accept

Jews or other Europeans at odds with the Nazi government in the 1930s or 1940s, effectively closing its doors. After World War II, the United States continued its exclusionary policies, although it did eventually accept approximately 400,000 displaced persons from the postwar European camps. The massive displacement of millions of people after the war motivated the United Nations to establish the UNHCR. The United Nations adopted the convention relating to the status of refugees in 1951. It stated that refugees were individuals who had a "well-founded fear of being persecuted for reasons of race, religion, nationality, membership of a particular social group or political opinion" who were outside their country and unwilling to return.[30] The United States did not initially sign the 1951 convention. Instead, Cold War imperatives defined American refugee policy in an ad hoc manner and when the United States could present itself as rescuing innocents from communism. Americans also focused on Europe and initially only imagined that Russians and Europeans could be worthy refugees. The political legacy and bureaucratic structures that governed Asian exclusion were not easily dislodged. The United States generally did not see Asians as refugees, even when they were fleeing communist revolution. The first exception to this rule was the 1953 Refugee Resettlement Act, which targeted postwar Europe and the Cold War but also created an allotment of 5,000 refugee admissions from Asia for the first time. Given the scope of displacement during the 1949 Chinese Revolution, this figure was numerically insignificant; however, it did create a new template whereby the "right" Asians could be rescued and enter the United States. This allowed the United States to both vet Asian migrants for ideological fealty and then celebrate them as living proof of the failure of communism. Accepted selectively and symbolically, Chinese entered the United States as refugees during the 1950s in small, highly controlled numbers.[31]

President Eisenhower admitted the first large-scale cohort of Cold War refugees after the Soviet Union's crackdown against the 1956 Hungarian revolution. However, U.S. immigration law did not permit a sudden entry of 35,000 Hungarians over the quota system, so Eisenhower turned to a loophole in the 1952 McCarran-Walter Act for executive discretion. With that authority, Eisenhower admitted Hungarians as "parolees," not refugees. In 1959, after the Cuban Revolution, Eisenhower pointed to the same provision, and Cubans too entered and could remain legally in the United States as parolees. In 1975, when the United States accepted more than 125,000 Vietnamese, the Ford administration also used this parole authority, yet again skirting U.S. immigration law through a practice of executive improvisation.[32] While the media, popular culture, government records, and the men and women themselves commonly and repeatedly referred to the Hungarians, Cubans, and Vietnamese as refugees, legally they were parolees.

Frustrated by executive control over refugee policy, Congress passed the 1980 Refugee Act. This created a framework for accepting individuals from outside the United States as refugees and a process by which individuals could petition for asylum from within the United States. The act intended to bring more order, rationality, and congressional oversight to what had been a policy defined by crisis and presidential decree. The U.S. Congress wanted to distinguish between immigrants, who gained admission through family relationships and economic sponsorship, and refugees, who could resettle in the United States because of fear of persecution in their home country. In many ways, refugees would be privileged migrants, gaining resources and support on resettlement. The key question would be, who would receive this refugee status?

In Southeast Asia, the question was no less vexed. In the late 1970s, the Malaysian, Thai, Indonesian, and Philippine governments rarely defined the Vietnamese as "refugees." Instead they were "boat people," unlawful aliens, or "illegal immigrants." The UNHCR sponsored a conference in Geneva in 1979, and there was an international agreement that all Vietnamese who fled would be guaranteed first asylum, protection, and resettlement in a third country. However, due to sluggish resettlement rates and thousands of long-stayers within the camps, Hong Kong upended the 1979 agreement in 1988. Under this regional pressure, the UNHCR instituted the Comprehensive Plan of Action in 1989. After 1989, Vietnamese would no longer be prima facie refugees; rather, they would be "asylum seekers," and they would have to demonstrate individual asylum claims in a state-run interview process. The UNHCR feared that if it insisted that all the Vietnamese were refugees indefinitely, host sites such as Malaysia and Hong Kong would stop offering anyone protection, refugee or not. Thus began the controversial process of "screening," whereby some Vietnamese were "screened in" and declared refugees, with all the rights and benefits of resettlement, while others failed in their storytelling and were "screened out."[33] Between 1989 and 1997, Hong Kong and other Southeast Asian countries repatriated over 100,000 "screened out" Vietnamese back to Vietnam.

"Repatriation" also had its linguistic politics and was the word of choice over "deportation," a far more familiar term in immigration policy. "Deportation" connotes forced removal, while "repatriation" emphasizes the individual's *patria,* or presumably natural, home country. In many circumstances, the UNHCR saw repatriation as a positive outcome by which someone could return to their country. Repatriation stood alongside the UNHCR's two other durable solutions, namely integration in a host country or resettlement in a third.[34] However, repatriation could also butt up against the idea of *refoulement,* sending an individual back to where they faced persecution, which was decidedly against UNHCR protocols and principles. This led to another round of linguistic and political fights over whether repatriation was voluntary or forced, or whether this distinction could be fudged.

Even though Vietnamese were not automatically "refugees" after 1989, the word "refugee" remained ubiquitous in the press, popular discourse, and advocacy. No matter how much the UNHCR or Hong Kong officials insisted on the more legalistic "asylum seeker," the label "refugee" stuck. For example, Clinton Leeks, a veteran member of the Hong Kong Security Branch, expressed his exasperation that "refugees" dominated American newspapers and U.S. government lingo even when the United States had strict resettlement procedures and did not accept all the Vietnamese in the camps as refugees. In a resigned voice, he concluded, "Oh well. I've seen worse," indicating that maintaining the public distinction between "refugees" and "asylum seekers" was a somewhat futile battle.[35] Of course, for Vietnamese in Hong Kong camps there was a stark difference between being a de facto refugee and being an asylum seeker who had to prove one's case.

As a writer, I feel equally stymied by the question of language. Vietnamese had to tell their stories consistently and tell them correctly in order to gain "refugee" status. Anthropologist John Christian Knudsen hauntingly called this the "screening machine," and it undermined individuals' stories, provided narrow and arbitrary definitions of "refugee," and ultimately created a gauntlet of words, whereby some stories worked and others did not.[36] In a multitude of oral histories and memoirs, Vietnamese did not call themselves "asylum seekers" or use other antiseptic terms, rather they consistently identified as refugees. In many ways, to refer to Vietnamese in the camps as anything other than refugees seems disrespectful and just another attempt by a government or international body or authority to deny their rights and narratives.

My goal is not to rejudge individuals and demarcate between the "real" refugees and the false, or to reinscribe the trauma of having a refugee claim refuted. However, referring to all the Vietnamese as refugees also ignores the changing legal landscape and the political jockeying among Southeast Asian countries, the UNHCR, and the United States over who would and who would not be admitted as refugees. To repeat the word incessantly and imagine all Vietnamese as refugees at all times is to ignore the specificity of Southeast Asian regional politics over more than twenty years. To call all the Vietnamese "boat people," which is one solution, again seems to sidestep the question and accept the designations given by various local, national, and international officials who wanted to keep them out.

This is the crux of the problem, and in many ways, this definitional question is at the heart of the book. I have no perfect solution. I try to avoid the above terms, even "refugee," as all are loaded and constantly changing, and instead refer to Vietnamese within the camps, Vietnamese Americans, and the diasporic Vietnamese community (which includes Vietnamese resettled in multiple countries). I use the terms "refugee," "asylum seeker," "illegal alien," and "boat people" when they relate directly to the documents and contemporary discourse. I do not want to affirm or undermine anyone's refugee claim or decide who did or did not meet the bar created by the UNHCR, the various nation-states and territories, or the United States. Quite the opposite: I want to drill down and explore how refugee status depended on time, place, global alliances, and local politics, while also recognizing the arbitrariness of influence, luck, and chance. By paying close attention to how Vietnamese status changed over time, I reveal the ways in which people found themselves trapped between governments, geographies, political eras, and even language.

Chapter 1 begins on Guam in 1975, with the U.S. practice of setting up camps on U.S. military bases and the unexpected story of the Vietnamese repatriate campaign. Chapter 2 moves to Malaysia, the country with the largest Vietnamese camps in 1978 and 1979. It analyzes how the presence of the Vietnamese raised alarms for Malaysian politicians, especially because of the racial divisions between the country's Malay and Chinese populations. It argues that Malaysian leaders questioned western commitments to humanitarianism and looks at how they sought to redefine humanitarianism on their own terms. Chapter 3 travels to the Philippines and the Philippine Refugee Processing Center, which promised a "model camp" complete with English language lessons and cultural orientation programs for Vietnamese and Southeast Asians on their way to the United States. The governments of Ferdinand Marcos and Cory Aquino both found value in hosting Southeast Asians in the 1980s.

Chapters 4 and 5 concentrate on Hong Kong. In the 1980s, the numbers of Vietnamese landing in Hong Kong grew, resulting in thousands of long-stayers within its camps. Chapter 4 analyzes how Hong Kong's policy grew increasingly punitive, shifting from open camps to closed camps, screening, and ultimately repatriation. Chapter 5 delves into the implications of Hong Kong's screening and repatriation program after 1989 and the growing militant protests within the camps. It juxtaposes the Hong Kong government's focus on humanitarian relief and Vietnamese American activists' determination to bring human rights violations in the camps to light. The book concludes in the Philippines, which agreed to halt repatriations after 1996 and then triggered overseas Vietnamese campaigns on how best to support this final group of "screened out" Vietnamese. Although *In Camps* trespasses in UNHCR offices in Geneva, the halls of the U.S. Congress, and college campuses with Vietnamese American student activists, the story's core remains in the Pacific and Southeast Asian camps.

．　．　．

As I was working on it, current events often seemed to swamp this book, mobilizing me to write more and faster. Between the millions of Syrians in Turkey, Lebanon, Jordan, and Europe, the hundreds of thousands of Rohingya in South and Southeast Asia, and the tens of thousands of Central Americans fleeing violence, the number of refugees and displaced people in the world is simply staggering. In 2018, the UNHCR placed the number of refugees worldwide at 25.4 million and the number of asylum seekers at 3.1 million.[37] At the same time the number of refugees was increasing worldwide, the United States elected Donald Trump as president, with his explicitly anti-refugee rhetoric, and right-wing parties that demonize Middle Eastern and African refugees gained ground in Europe. In the United States, the result was record low numbers of refugee resettlement, public displays of unabashed xenophobia, horrific tent camps along the U.S. southern border, and a constitutional imprimatur on racist, exclusionary policies.

Throughout all of this trauma and noise, I cannot help but reconsider the stories of Vietnamese in Guam, the Philippines, Malaysia, and Hong Kong. Once again, the centrality of regional actors and the precariousness of refugee status remain salient. While the post-9/11 politics differ significantly from those of the Cold War, I hope this book will resonate with the present moment in multiple, and perhaps unanticipated, ways. For example, to understand the Syrian crisis, one must begin to understand contemporary Turkish politics, Kurdish separatists, Lebanon's objectives, Jordan's monarchy, and Angela Merkel's Germany. Likewise, Central Americans claiming asylum at the U.S.

southern border cannot be divorced from histories of U.S. military intervention and support for neoliberalism in El Salvador, Guatemala, and Honduras. I hope that the attention paid to Guam, Malaysia, Hong Kong, and the Philippines here will provide a framework for understanding the interplay between refugees, imperial legacies, local politics, and international agencies.

This book also asks us to imagine regional geographies and networks. For all the flaws of the 1979 and 1989 UNHCR conferences in Geneva, they did lead Southeast Asian countries, including Vietnam, to work together and establish rules for first asylum, resettlement, and, later, screening and repatriation. The United States accepted hundreds of thousands of people from Southeast Asia, and the UNHCR worked admirably to get dozens of countries on the same page and raise sufficient funds. Critically, the wars in Vietnam were very much over and had been for years. Albeit authoritarian and a one-party state, Vietnam was stable and actively pursued the economic and political incentives it gained by working with the regional and international system. Vietnamese repatriates who returned against their will in the 1990s might have faced political harassment, trauma, and repression, but they did not face active warfare, ethnically motivated massacres, or unchecked gang or political violence. The same cannot be promised for thousands of the people who are stranded outside their countries as I write this book.

This book also urges readers not to demonize refugees, which in the 1970s and 1980s meant potential communist infiltrators or impoverished government charges, and in the present means terrorists and gang leaders. However, it also challenges readers not to depoliticize refugees. Vietnamese generally left home for political reasons, and then once in the camps, utilized multiple strategies to achieve their aims, be they resettlement or repatriation. This book is filled with examples of direct protests. It is a testament to individuals' willingness to risk everything and the failures of cages and camps to squash protests and expression, even in the grimmest of circumstances. Likewise, it reveals the ability to create a tenacious and creative political movement through transnational networks that connected people in the camps to advocates in Washington, D.C., northern Virginia, Manila, and Melbourne.

What seems unlikely to change is that people will be forced at times to flee their homes, that other countries will take them in, either begrudgingly or with generosity, and that other governments will build walls, gates, and designate isolated islands for unwanted people. Geopolitics *and* local dynamics will continue to guide hosts' responses, and activists will redefine the meaning and value of ideas like humanitarianism and human rights.

And so with that, this story begins with the well-known account of Saigon's collapse in 1975. After three decades of war, North Vietnam's troops defeated South Vietnam's forces more rapidly than even the North Vietnamese leaders anticipated. When 125,000 men and women fled Saigon, by boat, ship, helicopter, and plane, the U.S. government did not fly or sail them directly to the United States. Instead, the U.S. military directed them to Guam.

ONE

"Give Us a Ship"

THE VIETNAMESE REPATRIATE MOVEMENT
ON GUAM, 1975

IN APRIL 1975, TRAN DINH TRU, a career naval officer for the Republic of Vietnam (RVN), evacuated from Saigon along with thousands of other South Vietnamese civilians and military personnel. Separated from his wife and three children, he arrived at a gigantic makeshift camp on Guam. However, this was not his first time on the island. He had also traveled to Guam in 1972 as a naval officer for the RVN to receive technical support from the U.S. Navy. Tran Dinh Tru recalled this as a lonely time: "I was in Guam for five long months of repairs. Guam is a small island, isolated in the middle of the Pacific Ocean. I felt lost on foreign soil, and my soul always carried the burden of deep sadness." He did not realize that his next trip to Guam would be even more existential. Although he dwelt on his loneliness in 1972, in retrospect, his earlier journey seemed full of lightness and leisure compared to his second arrival on Guam. "I had taken a warship from Vietnam to Guam before, I had stood exactly where the refugee camp now stood only three years earlier. At that time, we had gone for many picnics on our rest days on this hill, which was covered with trees and located near Gab Gab Beach. Now everything had been leveled, and a camp had been erected. . . . I could barely swallow the bitterness of my fate as I was swept along with the current all the way here to the camps."[1] The first time he had been a high-ranking RVN officer, the second time he was bereft and fleeing a fallen nation.

Vietnamese did not travel directly from Saigon to the mainland United States. Since iconic images of helicopters on rooftops dominated the American press, few know that the U.S. government brought more than 110,000 Vietnamese to Guam before authorizing their entrance into the United States. The island's population numbered just shy of 100,000 residents in 1975, and so the influx of Vietnamese was massive.[2] Guam Governor

Ricardo (Ricky) Bordallo openly supported the rescue operation, and U.S. military planes and ships began landing on Guam with Vietnamese in the last weeks of April 1975. Local protests or objections would not have mattered much. Commenting on Guam's minimal autonomy, Guam Senator Carl Gutierrez noted, "Why are we arguing about this? It's all been settled by the U.S. government and we have to make the best of it."[3]

Guam became the primary staging ground for the Vietnamese evacuation, thus juxtaposing the United States' nineteenth-century imperial project with its failed Cold War objectives in Southeast Asia.[4] A Spanish possession since 1565, Guam became a U.S. territory under the 1898 Treaty of Paris, and much like Puerto Rico, it has not experienced modern political independence. Located almost 4,000 miles from Hawai'i (and almost 6,000 miles from California), Guam was under absolute U.S. military control from 1898 through 1950 (save for the years of Japanese occupation during World War II). The U.S. Navy owned and controlled Guam for half a century, and its institutions and installations fundamentally militarized the environment and culture of the indigenous Chamorro communities. With the 1950 Guam Organic Act, the U.S. government transferred jurisdiction over the island to the Department of the Interior. Even with this handover, the U.S. military controlled more than 36 percent of Guam's territory.[5] The Organic Act granted Guamanians U.S. citizenship, albeit without presidential voting rights, congressional representation, or full constitutional protections. In fact, Guamanians did not have direct elections for governor until 1970.[6] Because of high rates of military enlistment, Guam also bore the distinction of having the highest per capita casualty rate of any state or territory in the war in Vietnam. Guam's political apparatus balanced between poorly represented indigenous and local communities and extreme dependence on the U.S. government and military.[7]

This chapter tells the unusual story of the more than fifteen hundred Vietnamese on Guam who decided they did not want to resettle in the United States. For multiple reasons, hundreds of Vietnamese refused to go on to the United States. Their stories unsettled the U.S. government's rhetoric of humanitarianism and generosity. The government and media represented the U.S. evacuation at the end of the war as an act of rescue: the United States was saving those fleeing the impending communist rule.[8] Yet these would-be Vietnamese repatriates insisted that the only truly humanitarian thing to do was to help them *return* to Vietnam. Some repatriates hewed closely to anticommunist rhetoric, while others scoffed at American claims to benevolence, but they all wanted to return. The repatriates' campaign also amplified Guam's colonial status. Vietnamese repatriates realized that Guam's Pacific geography was not quite the United States. Guamanian leaders had limited authority, but they too sought to de-escalate the situation and respond to the repatriates and their own constituents. Finally, Vietnamese repatriates choreographed dramatic protests and demonstrations within the camps. Although confined and often traumatized, they became activists. Repatriates sought to pressure, signal, and communicate with the new revolutionary government in Vietnam as well as with the United States, the UNHCR, and the local community on Guam. Their refusal to be "saved" by the United States, and instead to return to Vietnam on a ship under their own command, demonstrates their political organization and unexpected but unwavering militancy.

COLLAPSE AND EVACUATION: U.S. GOVERNMENT RESPONSES

In the spring of 1975, the North Vietnamese army marched toward Saigon, and the RVN government collapsed quickly and completely. President Gerald Ford and Secretary of State Henry Kissinger scrambled to wrap up what they saw as the end game in Vietnam. This included harsh economic sanctions meant to punish and isolate the newly victorious revolutionary Vietnam and an evacuation, supported by the U.S. military, for those with close ties to the U.S. and South Vietnamese governments.

The Commerce Department froze $70 million in South Vietnamese assets held in U.S. banks right away, and the executive branch moved quickly to enforce an embargo against Vietnam. As historian Edwin Martini explains, the embargo was an extension of the U.S. policy against North Vietnam during the war, and it was executed as a punitive measure and a way to continue "the war by other means."[9] The United States was unwilling to recognize the Vietnamese government, negotiate with it, or contemplate any economic aid or support. For its victory, the U.S. government ensured that Vietnam would suffer economically in the years to come. The result was a diplomatic standoff that would only be broached in the late 1980s through areas the U.S. government deemed of "humanitarian" concern, namely, negotiations over American POW/MIAs, the immigration of Amerasians (children of Vietnamese women and American men), and ultimately the resettlement of former political prisoners.[10]

As South Vietnam's government collapsed, President Ford also requested more than $250 million for the Humanitarian Assistance and Evacuation Act to save and protect the "victims of the conflict in Vietnam." Notably, congressional representatives did not rubber-stamp this legislation. They debated the military's role, the terms of humanitarian relief, and even its potential contradiction with human rights. The bill had many supporters, including Republican and Democratic representatives, Americans for Democratic Action, the AFL-CIO, and the American Jewish Committee. However, there were critics too, namely representatives who feared the U.S. military's assistance in the evacuation would lead to re-engagement and war. Representatives Lester Wolff (D-NY), Michael Harrington (D-MA), and Donald Riegle (D-MI) all believed the bill's passage would be akin to another Gulf of Tonkin resolution.[11]

Representative Elizabeth Holtzman (D-NY) staked out her own ground. She emerged as one of the most vocal critics of the evacuation, even though she was also an advocate for refugee resettlement. An anti-war Democrat, Holtzman wanted guarantees that the United States would not admit war criminals. She repeatedly charged that through this humanitarian legislation, the United States was potentially welcoming South Vietnamese officials who were guilty of human rights violations committed in South Vietnam. She asked U.S. immigration officials if they would permit the entry of South Vietnamese who "had engaged in war profiteering, corruption, and the torture of political prisoners." Mary McGrory, a Washington, D.C., newspaper columnist, sardonically explained, "The more 'criminal' they are the more eligible they are. They [the South Vietnamese leadership] are our people."[12] Holtzman even received a letter from a Vietnamese man in France demanding that the United States deport (rather than receive) a high-ranking South Vietnamese general who had been a close adviser to South Vietnamese president Nguyen Van Thieu. He wrote, "With respect to this thief, who is the author of the downfall of the republican government in South Vietnam, I ask you, in the name of Vietnamese nationalists, to expel him from the land of America."[13] Unlike the executive branch, which painted all of the Vietnamese as deserving of U.S. support and resettlement, Holtzman parsed the difference between the humanitarian motives of the evacuation and the history of United States and South Vietnamese human rights violations.

Ultimately, Holtzman's concerns were drowned out by the far louder voices in the government and in the media that described the rescue effort as a purely apolitical, humanitarian operation on the part of the United States.[14]

Even though a majority of Americans opposed the resettlement of tens of thousands of Vietnamese, the federal government pushed ahead. The bill passed in the House (230–187) and in the Senate (75–17), but events outstripped the legislative process. It failed to come out of the conference committee and become a law before the North Vietnamese rolled into Saigon. Congressional debate became a moot point.[15] The U.S. military took a leading role in the evacuation, and despite fears, it did not result in renewed combat. The U.S. Navy assembled its ships off the coast of South Vietnam, Navy and Marine pilots manned helicopters, and the U.S. Army prepared several bases as temporary refugee camps on Guam, Wake Island, and the mainland United States.[16] The U.S. military became the primary organization responsible for transporting and housing more than 100,000 Vietnamese men, women, and children in the United States.

Dubbed Operation New Life, the large-scale undertaking capitalized on the military's vast logistical capabilities, and the U.S. military took pride in its ability to help evacuate the Vietnamese. However, Senator Edward Kennedy (D-MA) sharply noted the name's "uncomfortable ring with the old 'New Life Hamlets' or 'strategic hamlets' of the Diem years."[17] Even linguistically, Operation New Life juxtaposed military failure with military rescue.[18]

Ignoring the overlapping language of counterinsurgency and humanitarian operations, the U.S. military began preparations for a massive influx of Vietnamese men and women into the United States. The first stop was Guam.

CAMP CONDITIONS ON GUAM

In 1975, the U.S. military established a constellation of twelve camps on a mix of military bases and leased corporate facilities on Guam. The largest were located on U.S. military property. The Navy Seabees cleared "jungle land" and pitched thousands of tents on Orote Point, which soon became "Tent City," and they transformed Andersen Air Force Base into "Tin City" with rows of Quonset huts. Within weeks, the U.S. military erected close to 4,000 tents, built dozens of public showers, set up hundreds of latrines, and built massive mess halls. The military leadership also needed to think of security (fences and barbed wire), electricity, water, laundry facilities, and medical clinics for tens of thousands of people.[19] In addition to several smaller military facilities, private companies like Black Construction, J&G Construction, Hawaiian Dredging Construction, and the Tokyu Hotel also became temporary camps.[20] Perhaps most hauntingly, the Seabees converted fourteen buildings at Camp Asan into a camp for Vietnamese on the very same ground that had been used to jail Filipino insurrectionists during the early-twentieth-century Philippine-American War.[21]

When Vietnamese arrived on Guam, they underwent a reception process which included a security clearance, fingerprinting, photography, medical exams, and immunizations, and each individual received a "control number." It soon became clear, however, that the U.S. personnel on Guam could barely keep up with the logistics; they faced basic difficulties with computers, providing individuals with ID numbers, and mastering Vietnamese naming practices.[22] Lieutenant Colonel George Gonsalves, who was the deputy for refugee affairs and camp coordinator of Camp Orote from April to June 1975, explained that "current U.S. Army doctrine and training are inadequate insofar as they pertain to refugee administration and operation." He went on to argue that the U.S. soldiers he worked with on Guam simply did not possess the training necessary. "The responsibilities of the infantry battalions included functions that were in no way related to the normal missions of an infantry battalion. Infantrymen are not trained to operate baby care centers, to act as police officers in a civilian population, or to process large numbers of civilians through a refugee camp." He ended with the deadpan understatement, "Those were indeed unusual missions for infantry battalions."[23]

Guam was only a staging ground, meant for quick processing. The majority of Vietnamese spent less than two weeks there, although some waited for up to three months. Most were then transferred to a stateside camp in Fort Chaffee, Arkansas, Camp Pendleton, California, Fort Indiantown Gap, Pennsylvania, or Eglin Air Force Base, Florida. By August 26, 1975, the last flight had departed from Guam to the United States.[24]

In oral histories, Vietnamese reflected on their time on Guam with a wide range of emotions, swinging between bitterness at the U.S. betrayal of South Vietnam to pleasurable childhood memories of independence and time by the sea. Older Vietnamese remained fixated on the U.S. withdrawal. In their eyes, the vast fields of tents were not symbolic of U.S. humanitarianism, but rather evidence of the United States' fickle alliance with South Vietnam. Bruce Lam was a young soldier in the RVN army, and he had fought on the front lines since 1968. He spoke about his arrival on Guam with a younger oral history interviewer: "American[s] knew [about] the situation in advance so they could prepare to help the refugees. We lost the war because they abandoned us. You are too young to understand this, but older folks like us who served in the military once and now live in California understand the point very well. We would not lose had they not left us. They wanted to amend their betrayal by saving us and helping us to settle in."[25] While Lam went on to point out he was well fed and comfortable on Guam, he was clearly trying to educate the young interviewer that the tent city only existed because the United States was unwilling to stand by South Vietnam. Annie Thuy Tran also remembered the Americans being prepared: "Everything is ready when we land and we go down to the land. They have tent, everything is ready! I think the government, the U.S. government is ready for us, it's ready for us. . . . And we stay there for, I think, six months, something like that."[26]

Remembering their time on Guam, most Vietnamese highlighted the bureaucracy, boredom, and uncertainty of the future. For many, their days were melancholy and full of loss. Tom Phan landed on Guam on April 27. He remembered hearing the news of Saigon's fall from within Tent City. There were constant rumors, but he had harbored hopes that he would be able to return to South Vietnam. "As you know, the South Vietnam fell on April 30th, but we heard the news when we were in Guam. And I remember tears, we all cry because we all know that there's no way we can get back."[27] He explained that no one imagined that Saigon would fall so quickly. Chau Nguyen also recalled those days with a sense of futility. He explained, "In Guam we couldn't do anything, we just sleep, woke up . . . went to the mess hall for breakfast, lunch, and dinner. Then after that you just hung around, you didn't do anything all day. I remember I was just sitting around by myself, just wandering about. I was just really lost . . . I was in a daze. . . . And then someone snapped a picture [of me]. . . . If I had the picture that's what my state of mind would have been, lost. Totally lost."[28] Chau Nguyen voiced a sense of shell shock and trauma echoed by many.

Not surprisingly, few of the Vietnamese had much to say about Guam's politics or colonial history, and there was no acknowledgment of the Chamorro indigenous population. For some, Guam was just a cloudy after-thought, and the camps merged together into a single memory. A man who had been in his thirties during the evacuation barely remembered he had been to Guam: "Yeah, I forgot about the Guam thing. We were, I don't know, Guam first or Camp Pendleton, I think it was Guam."[29] Given the upheaval of Saigon's collapse and the personal tragedies that all were experiencing, this seems understandable. Confined in camps, most Vietnamese were relatively isolated and their own losses were too raw to reflect much on the island's environment. In contrast, those who had been young children remembered how the camps on Guam gave them the chance to swim, enjoy the ocean waters, and collect sea cucumbers on the shore. As one woman explained, "It sounds terrible to say this but I really enjoyed the refugee camps because we were staying in Guam and it's beautiful, it's on the water and I have always loved the water."[30] While the adults were preoccupied with their transformed circumstances and worries for the future, children's memories emphasized the freedom and independence possible in the camps.

There were also joyful family reunions on Guam. Thu Huyen remembered being separated from her father during the evacuation. She and her siblings feared he had died either in Saigon or at sea, but after a week, they reunited on Guam.[31] However, not everyone was so lucky. In stark contrast, Tran Dinh Tru inadvertently evacuated without his wife and three children. As the North Vietnamese army advanced, he was in Saigon and his family was farther south by the coast. Tran Dinh Tru evacuated from Saigon and prepared for his wife and family to escape on their own, yet despite his best efforts, the captain who was supposed to rescue his family never went ashore to look for them. Arriving on Guam alone and in despair, Tran Dinh Tru could not comprehend the tragedy that had put an ocean between himself and his family. He wanted to return to Vietnam.

He remembered his relief when he learned that the Vietnamese on Guam could register with the UNHCR for repatriation: "This news came to me like a flash of lightning, and I didn't hesitate. Instead of applying to go to America, I went directly to this office to inquire about the procedures and processes needed to go back to Vietnam. Not all of us who had been taken to Guam wanted to go to America. There were still some people who didn't want to abandon our homeland and who considered their families, their wives, and children even more precious than America." He signed up, submitted to yet another round of fingerprinting and photographing, and returned to his tent in a contemplative mood: "I could not avoid imagining the consequences of my return. I knew there would be many surprises, but I was ready to accept my fate, including the fact that I might be sent to jail. . . . So as long as I didn't die, even if the North Vietnamese put me in prison for a few years, upon my release, I could still find a way to escape from Vietnam and bring my wife and children out by boat. . . . I would risk everything to get my wife and our children out of communist Vietnam. After having made the decision to return I felt the agitation and anxiety diminish in my soul. Instead, a ray of hope shone in me."[32] Tran Dinh Tru cast his desire to return as the ultimate act of familial loyalty and anti-communism.

WHY REPATRIATE? EVACUATIONS, BROKEN FAMILIES, AND KIDNAPPINGS

As early as May 3, 1975, several Vietnamese Air Force personnel came forward and requested repatriation, and within weeks, the number of repatriation inquiries climbed to more than two thousand.[33] Like Tran Dinh Tru, approximately 80 percent of the repatriates were South Vietnamese military personnel, but most of them belonged to the military's lowest echelons.[34] The repatriates were overwhelmingly single men. Younger by a generation and most likely drafted in the war's last years, these men did not echo Tran Dinh Tru's anti-communist politics or frame their choice for repatriation as an ideological decision. A UNHCR representative on Guam explained, "[They] aren't concerned about the political change in their country. All they want to do is to get back to their families who are still in South Vietnam. Most can't believe they're really on Guam."[35] Julia Taft, the head of the Interagency Task Force on Refugees, which was in charge of the U.S. resettlement program, concurred: "They are almost all family reunion cases," she explained. Taft also admitted that many lower-level military personnel had little choice in their "evacuation." "Some of them—air force mechanics and ships' engineers—were forced to leave by superiors."[36] These men had never intended to leave Vietnam permanently, and they recounted their journeys to Guam as plagued by misfortune, misinformation, and even kidnapping.

Repeatedly, repatriates who were RVN pilots and sailors stated they had left South Vietnam in the heat of battle without realizing the finality of their actions. For example, when the North Vietnamese began bombing Saigon's Tan Son Nhut Airport, one pilot flew under orders to the U Tapao Air Force Base in Thailand. He noted that "it was as much to save the aircraft from destruction as to help the people aboard." He himself had not intended to evacuate: "Living forever in a foreign country and accepting another nationality is not my choice."[37] In a similar vein, a young sailor recounted, "I had no intention of going to the United States, but after I was aboard the ship, I was told we were headed for Subic Bay in the Philippines, and would not be returning to Vietnam." He added that his parents, brothers, and sisters were in Vietnam, and that he wanted to return.[38] The repatriates' sense of displacement and the remarkable lack of choice were recurring motifs. Focused more on family than politics, these young men presented themselves as alienated from the journey that brought them to Guam.

In the most chilling account, thirteen Vietnamese men charged the U.S. military with drugging and kidnapping them. Echoing the pilot's story above, these men repeated how dozens of RVN personnel stationed at Tan Son Nhut Airport "were so afraid that we took immediate airlift to U-Tapao (Thailand)." On arrival, their story took a darker turn. At least sixty-five men requested to return to Vietnam. In response, U.S. and Thai troops threatened to send them to jail in Thailand. At this point, fifty-two of the hold-outs agreed to go to Guam, while the remaining thirteen remained steadfast, deciding "once and for all not to go [to Guam] and being killed or having a chance to go back to our country."[39] A U.S. military officer responded to this defiance by sedating these men with Pentothal and Thorazine and then loading them, unconscious, onto a plane. When the men awoke in Guam's Tent City, they were not only psychologically disoriented, but physically dizzy and in pain. Several waited days before going for medical help since they did not trust the U.S. doctors, and the doctors, in turn, did not believe their claims until they examined their legs and saw puncture wounds and bruises.[40] On investigation, the United States admitted a U.S. officer's responsibility for the forced sedation.[41] These men cast their lots with the repatriates: "This is a true story. . . . These acts made us very concerned and frighten[ed] and moreover we no longer trust and respect the American Peace and Democracy Policy that they expand throughout the world."[42] These men expressed their sense of betrayal and lack of faith in America. If they had not been disillusioned with the U.S. military before April 1975, their subsequent experiences at the hands of panicked U.S. officers in Thailand certainly did the trick.

Along with these accounts of kidnapping and force, far more individuals chose to repatriate because of family separations. Some men and women fully intended to leave Vietnam but once stateside, rethought their decisions due to homesickness.[43] Some were separated from their families and desperately wanted to reunite with them. At least one man seems to have returned for ideological reasons. In an evocative anecdote from Tran Dinh Tru's memoir, *A Ship of Fate*, a former Viet Cong (VC) confided that he had followed the Vietnamese to the United States under orders. Seeming to justify American fears of possible communist infiltration, he was ultimately a poor spy. Tired of waiting in Ft. Chaffee with no orders or mission, he decided to return to his family and applied for repatriation along with hundreds of other Vietnamese.[44]

The rapidity of South Vietnam's collapse, the frantic nature of final military orders, and the chaotic separation of families defined the stories of evacuation. More than two thousand people initially stepped forward and applied for repatriation. Most expressed their desire to return to Vietnam because they wanted to reunite with their families. Their decision to repatriate spoke to personal and political realities that fell outside Cold War expectations. Neither the United States nor Vietnam was prepared to cope with the repatriates' demands for return. Far from being a cohesive or unified political community, what repatriates had in common was confusion, apprehension, and, soon, anger about their detention on Guam.

Consolidated on Guam in physical and political limbo, repatriates became adept political organizers. In 1975, the U.S. media overwhelmingly depicted Vietnamese through images of children, telegraphing a generic innocence and "new life" onto their bodies. In contrast, the would-be repatriates were overwhelmingly male, and their oppositional actions created a problem for American policy makers. The repatriates' highly symbolic demonstrations and destructive acts revealed a multi-pronged strategy. On the one hand, repatriates seemed to stage their protests for the benefit of revolutionary Vietnam, in order to burnish their own "revolutionary" credentials. On the other hand, their walk-outs and escalating actions expressed a growing desperation and collective frustration with Guamanian, U.S. civilian, and U.S. military officials. Repatriate leaders recognized that they needed to persuade both the U.S. officials and the Vietnamese governments of their cause and apolitical motivations; however, this was an unpredictable and precarious balancing act at best.

To further complicate matters, the UNHCR acted as a broker between the United States and Vietnam. Because of the brutal war and the American loss of face, the United States did not have a diplomatic relationship with the new Provisional Revolutionary Government (PRG) in the south or the Democratic Republic of Vietnam in the north. These two entities would formally reunify the country under a single communist government in 1976, and the United States would continue to isolate the country for almost two more decades. The UNHCR attempted to act as a neutral arbitrator which could help facilitate the repatriates' return to Vietnam. The UNHCR quickly set up procedures for those interested in repatriation. It conducted interviews and emphasized that individuals' choices were free of any coercion. UNHCR representative George Gordon Lennox stated, "This decision is theirs alone to make. . . . Nobody will ever be forced to do anything they don't want to. This should be made clear."[45] The UNHCR also advertised the possibility of repatriation to Vietnamese already on U.S. military bases in Pennsylvania, Florida, Arkansas, and California. Throughout this process, the United States repeatedly affirmed the possibility of repatriation and its belief in "freedom of movement for all people."[46] With the policy in place, hundreds of men and women came forward and registered, but for all the goodwill, U.S. and UNHCR officials seemed unprepared for the next steps.

One of the first organized demonstrations was at Ft. Chaffee in Arkansas, where approximately 180 individuals applied for repatriation. From this group, a cohort of just under 80 people publicly protested what they viewed as delays in their departure. The repatriates were nonviolent, but U.S. officials feared they could turn hostile.[47] Le Minh Tan, a forty-four-year-old former defense attaché for the U.S. military in Saigon, became the most visible and vocal repatriate leader. Calling on American strength, he insisted that if the United States prioritized the repatriates' transfer, it could happen very quickly: "We are upset and we are mad. The American government is very rich and has very, very many planes."[48] Unlike most repatriates, he framed his protest not just as a desire to return to his family, but as a rebuke against the United States. He argued, "It [Ft. Chaffee] looks like a jail. We are very sad. We want to go back [to Vietnam] immediately. We don't want to stay. I frankly say that we've been put in jail for the two months that we've been in the United States."[49] His speeches alarmed not just U.S. personnel on the base, but also many Vietnamese at Ft. Chaffee who feared the repatriates would sully their image and create resentment in the American public. In response, a second Vietnamese protest organized *against* the repatriates. Their signs proclaimed, "We are grateful to Americans," and "We ourselves look to freedom."[50] Using the political rhetoric familiar to them, the counter-demonstrators labeled the repatriates as Viet Cong "agents." In a 1977 history, Pham Kim Vinh, a Vietnamese writer who resettled in the United States, argued that communist infiltrators, and Le Minh Tan in particular, played on people's homesickness and encouraged repatriation for its propaganda value.[51] Le Minh Tan responded sharply to these charges: "If we were communists we would never come to the United States, or if we were communists we would stay in the United States and send information back to Vietnam. . . . We are not Communists. We just love our country and want to return."[52]

Le Minh Tan's rhetoric and the counter-demonstrators' liberal use of "communist" may have raised some eyebrows among U.S. officials. Likewise, it is not surprising that the counter-demonstrators demonized the repatriates as Viet Cong. While few of the repatriates identified with the revolutionary government or had been members of the National Liberation Front (or VC), the communist/anti-communist dichotomy was the political framework—albeit an imperfect one—which had defined the terms for Americans and South Vietnamese for more than a decade. Le Minh Tan's own denials may also have appeared somewhat suspect. For Americans, many of whom had always distrusted their South Vietnamese counterparts, Le Minh Tan may have seemed an all-too-familiar figure, a troublemaker (or, more ominously, a VC) masquerading as a friend. Regardless, the U.S. military worried that violence could escalate on repatriate flights to Camp Pendleton and Guam, and it authorized U.S. Air Force security police to carry sidearms on board. Armed and on the alert, they were instructed to "maintain order" if repatriates initiated any political demonstrations in flight.[53]

The Americans' fears of unrest proved well founded and over the course of the summer, the would-be repatriates' protests on Guam escalated. In a petition to the UNHCR, the repatriates emphasized that they had "not lost a country, rather a new regime has taken over the government." With this turn of phrase, they distanced themselves from those who mourned the collapse of South Vietnam. Instead, they wanted to "help with their country's reconstruction."[54] They matched this loyal rhetoric with bold visual images, namely the prominent display of a painting of Ho Chi Minh. During one protest, repatriates stood at attention under the large portrait and a banner declaring, "Tinh Than Cu Ho Chi Minh Bat Diet," or "The Spirit of Ho Chi Minh Lasts Forever."[55] Particularly anomalous given its presence on a U.S. military base in 1975, the image of Ho Chi Minh could be seen as a direct rebuke of the United States and the U.S. war in Vietnam. However, it's more likely that the Ho Chi Minh painting acted as an easily legible signal directed at Vietnam. In all probability, the goal was to convince the communist Vietnamese government that the repatriates would be willing and loyal members of the new society in Vietnam.

In Tran Dinh Tru's memoir, he wrote explicitly about the Ho Chi Minh portrait and his own shame in its prominent display. Tran Dinh Tru stood apart in both age and rank from the majority of the repatriates, and he identified strongly with his family's Catholicism and anti-communism. He criticized the strategic use of Ho Chi Minh's image: "I don't know whether these paintings represented his [the artist's] own opinion or the opinion of those standing behind him, pulling the strings. Nonetheless, he was able to weigh

FIGURE 3. Vietnamese repatriates displaying a banner of Ho Chi Minh, 1975. This strategic use of Ho Chi Minh's image was controversial within the camp. Courtesy of the U.S. National Archives and Records Administration, Record Group 319, Box 19, declassification number 984082.

the pros and cons for himself, and he must have thought that if he produced this procommunist artwork, he would not meet with the same vicissitudes back in Vietnam as the rest of us." He tried to make sense of what he saw as a lack of integrity: "Some people are just opportunists. Any given society always has people who wait for an opportunity and seize it. Even here, among souls tormented by their longing to return, one could see that a number of people worked to score points with the communists even before they returned. No one dared to criticize them, even when they engaged in excessive and loathsome acts, because they ultimately had reasons of their own."[56] While frustrated, ashamed, and critical, Tran Dinh Tru understood that many of the repatriates hoped to signal their loyalty to the new revolutionary government, regardless of their actual political beliefs. They knew that the burden would be on them.

Repatriates also aimed many of their actions at American and Guamanian leaders. The repatriates believed the United States had the power to return them to Vietnam and was simply stalling. Upon his arrival on Guam, Le Minh Tan immediately organized a two-day hunger strike.[57] Two hundred and fifty individuals participated, and the military reported that it served meals to only twenty women and children in the camp.[58] In one memorable photograph, an elderly couple posed holding a hand-written sign declaring simply, "We Are on Hunger Strike."[59] The juxtaposition of their aged bodies and faces with the defiant sign lent a moving image to the repatriates' cause.

The repatriates also orchestrated numerous demonstrations and "walk-offs" to make their campaign visible to Guamanians off the base. For example, Le Minh Tan led 251 repatriates out of the camps. They carried their belongings in bags and boxes and seemed prepared to leave the base permanently. One repatriate wore a t-shirt with the ominous slogan "Kill Us or Send Back" emblazoned across the front.[60] Violating the U.S. military perimeter, the repatriates upped the ante. Marshals and police responded with nightsticks and mace, herded the repatriates onto buses, and isolated Le Minh Tan from the group.

The following day a second group of two hundred repatriates marched out of the camp with their hands tied behind their backs to symbolize their imprisonment. They protested in front of Shakey's Pizza, the island's largest pizzeria, in full view of rush-hour traffic, again wearing t-shirts with political slogans. Five hundred more repatriates marched out of the camp at Black Construction Company with red ribbons and signs that read "We Are Not Prisoners of War." These protests were notable for their coordination and focus. The repeated comparison to POWs, alongside the deliberate move out of the camps, highlighted not just their readiness to return home, but their anger at the Americans. One camp leader, who until that point had spoken to the press in both French and English, now insisted in speaking only in Vietnamese. Another repatriate leader and former air force major said he "and his fellow campmates were treated like prisoners."[61] The protests gained momentum as repatriates nimbly pressed American officials' buttons and pressured U.S., UNHCR, and Guamanian officials to act.

The U.S. responded to these coordinated protests by consolidating all of the repatriates at Camp Asan, where they could be monitored and policed on military property.[62] Now clearly detained and under suspicion, the would-be repatriates vacillated between militant tactics and attempts at gaining public sympathy. The protests created dissension within the group, with a more moderate cohort urging greater diplomacy and patience, while a more aggressive faction advocated violence. These divisions were evident from the competing signs erected within the camp. One sign urged politely, "Dear Guamanian and American People, Our desire is only to go home. We don't want to disturb you and to be lost your sympathy that would be reserved for us. Please understand that how painful we are now and try to support our repatriation," while another billboard threatened less amiably, "Hunger strike until die."[63] One man threatened to slice off his own finger in protest and write a letter to President Ford in his own blood.[64] Another individual threatened to self-immolate, a highly potent image that invoked the anti-Diem Buddhist demonstrations of 1963.

Vietnamese repatriates also made good use of their English-language skills, displaying signs and banners within the camps and writing letters to the local newspapers. Protesters' facility with English spoke to their former ties with the U.S. military. Perhaps the repatriates' most powerful use of English was in their appropriation of "POW" to their own ends. As one sign stated baldly: "We Are Not POWs."[65] And while it was true that Vietnamese repatriates were *not* POWs, their confinement and camp life struck a nerve with Vietnamese and American personnel alike. The military made a concerted effort to demilitarize the refugees' living situations, but the fences, military security, and indefinite waiting all made the distinctions between a refugee camp and a POW camp slimmer than the U.S. military may have liked to admit. Moreover, Vietnamese repatriates labeling themselves as POWs was a rhetorically powerful move. Quite distinct from the POWs Americans welcomed home in 1973, Vietnamese repatriates inverted

Americans' understanding of rescue and positioned themselves as the captives and the U.S. military as the captor.

As repatriates escalated their protests, the UNHCR and Guam both found themselves in a precarious state between the United States and Vietnam. The UNHCR wanted to retain its credibility as a neutral international organization that could work with the United States and with Vietnam. Its sense of humanitarian mission valued the physical safety of the Vietnamese and their protection above all else. The UNHCR was sympathetic to the repatriates' demands; however, it could only support the repatriates' return if the Vietnamese government cooperated and agreed to accept them without reprisals. Throughout the summer of 1975, UNHCR officials made multiple visits to Hanoi and Saigon, inquiring about the possibilities and procedures for repatriation. At first Vietnam seemed open to at least a small number of repatriates, and the UNHCR proactively submitted applications in the hopes of a quick resolution. However, after a matter of weeks, it was clear Vietnam was not pursuing the repatriate question with any speed. In fact, the government held up individual applications, did not respond to repatriates' requests, and if anything, became less receptive to repatriation over the course of the summer.[66] Instead, Vietnam demanded direct negotiations with the United States and refused to communicate formally through the UNHCR or a third country. It either wanted to avoid the repatriate question entirely, or it hoped the repatriates might be used as a wedge to compel the U.S. government to recognize the new government diplomatically. Internal conflicts between military and civilian factions were competing in South Vietnam, and given hunger, environmental devastation, economic upheaval, and huge casualties, the repatriates remained very low on the priority list. In addition, Vietnam feared that the U.S. "has infiltrated the repatriates with covert agents."[67] The UNHCR believed its hands were tied. It had tried to broker an amicable agreement with Vietnam, and it had failed.

The Guam government also worked to find a solution, which in its eyes involved making sure the Vietnamese repatriates were no longer on Guam. Guam had welcomed and hosted tens of thousands of Vietnamese, but by the summer, its patience was wearing thin. Less concerned about humanitarian niceties or the UNHCR's protocols, Governor Bordallo wanted the

Vietnamese off the island. Bordallo was not unsympathetic to the Vietnamese repatriates, and in many ways, their aim, to return to Vietnam, dovetailed with his own, the removal of the Vietnamese camps in Guam.

Initially, there had been mixed reactions on Guam to the huge influx of Vietnamese. There were fears that the Vietnamese might stay and overrun the islands "like Miami was with the Cubans," or that it would drain Guam's limited economic resources.[68] It was also clear that the U.S. government was calling the shots, and Guam had little autonomy over the repurposing of the island as a massive camp. Guam's *Pacific Daily News* published a letter to the editor that complained, "Our local government officials and others have the least role and definitely no say.... We are being forced to play the major league game of the big leaguers in International Politics and the big boys in Washington are using some of our local government officials to further bail them out of their untold political failures in South Vietnam."[69] Despite these critiques, some politicians hoped the operation would improve Guam's economy through new government contracts, and others hoped it would demonstrate "the true value of Guam" to the U.S. administration.[70] Guam's government also hoped its cooperation would raise the island's profile stateside. As Senator Tommy Tanaka explained: "Guam can really do something positive to help these people who have been banished from their land.... And if we act in a responsible manner, maybe we can improve our image with Washington officials."[71] Governor Bordallo emphasized the role local Guamanians played in supporting the Vietnamese. "We owe these strife-torn human beings from Vietnam the best we can offer in terms of our responsibilities as citizens of the United States of America." He noted the military community's work, but he also pointed to the volunteer efforts and donations of hundreds of local Guamanian people.[72] Senator Ernesto Espaldon added, "When you hear about the hundreds of local people volunteering to help, you know that Guam is behind the evacuation, at least in a humanitarian sense."[73] In this way, Governor Bordallo recognized that Guam's position could help burnish the island's humanitarian reputation, and ideally improve its economy and score points with the U.S. government.

However, as the repatriates' discontent simmered, Bordallo became increasingly frustrated by his own limited authority. Guam's cooperation and goodwill did not seem to result in any great advantage with the U.S. government, and he feared the repatriates could remain on Guam indefinitely. He also worried that ongoing unrest would hurt Guam's reputation as a tourist destination and lead to reduced revenues. Bordallo's earlier goodwill had reached its limit. By the time the repatriates were marching out of the camps, Bordallo threatened to take the matter into his own hands: "The lives of the people of Guam are in jeopardy. Immediate action is imperative . . . the repatriates advised me that they will initiate a series of violent acts at the risk of their lives if they are not moved to Vietnam immediately. . . . If I do not receive word from you concerning this matter within 48 hours, I shall proceed unilaterally with the latter alternative."[74] The U.S. response to Bordallo's independence was curt, to say the least. Secretary of State Henry Kissinger urged Bordallo to limit his meetings with the repatriates, since he had no power to grant their demands.[75]

Guam's Speaker of the House Joseph Ada seemed personally insulted by the repatriates, and he too wanted a solution where the Vietnamese could be thrown out of Guam. He characterized the protests as "an affront to the hospitality which has been freely offered them," and he chastised them for not being grateful for Guam's role as a humanitarian host. In Resolution No. 133, Ada formally proposed the repatriates be removed to Wake Island, an even smaller and more remote unincorporated territory in America's generally forgotten Pacific archipelago. Ada argued that the repatriates posed a safety hazard to local civilians and a threat to Guam's international reputation. The Guamanian Senate concurred and voted twenty to one overwhelmingly in favor of this proposal.[76] However, this near unanimous vote to forcibly deport the repatriates in fact underscored the Guam government's lack of sovereignty. The Interagency Task Force on Refugees, an unelected federal task force, shot down the "Wake option" as untenable.[77]

Governor Bordallo landed on another solution: give the repatriates a ship to return to Vietnam under their own power.[78] In Tran Dinh Tru's memoir, he attributed the idea of a ship to the repatriates themselves.[79] For both the repatriates and the Guamanians, the idea quickly gained allure. It would allow the Vietnamese to return to Vietnam, it would remove them from Guam, and it did not need approval from the Vietnamese government or the UNHCR. It neatly solved the problem for Guam. The repatriates added that many were skilled seamen. U.S. officials did not automatically say no. It was UNHCR officials who tempered their optimism. They were noncommittal and promised only to pass the idea on to the high commissioner.[80] The UNHCR was concerned that if the United States acted unilaterally, it would put the repatriates at risk of being persecuted in Vietnam on their return. Guamanian politicians were stymied, and the repatriates continued to wait.

"DO NOT PLOT TO . . . IMPRISON US IN FORGETFULNESS"

By the end of August, 1975, the repatriates' protests hit a fevered pitch. Desperate for action, they moved from hunger strikes and sit-ins to even more extreme measures. Two to three hundred of the sixteen hundred repatriates staged a protest that became violent, complete with rock throwing and Molotov cocktails. At its climax, repatriates burned down two barracks within the camp and destroyed military property. In response to the melee, U.S. Marshals resorted to tear gas, and the U.S. military ordered a U.S. Marine Action unit on alert. By the end of the night, repatriates had injured four U.S. Marshals.[81] The U.S., Guamanian, and UNHCR officials were desperate for a resolution.

The repatriates' rhetoric verged on the violent, and they spoke out against the United States loud and clear. One elderly Vietnamese man threatened suicide. Calling on "Mr. Gerald Ford!" and "Mr. Henry Kissinger!" he explained that the only humanitarian response would be to let the repatriates return to Vietnam.[82] Others had no patience for America's humanitarian claims and blamed the U.S. for the bloodbath in Vietnam. If there had not been a war, there would be no refugees. Anticipating the arguments that would be made by scholars in the field of critical refugee studies decades later, some of the repatriates viewed Operation New Life as yet another failed U.S. initiative. In a strongly worded letter, they stated, "If the U.S. did not interfere into Vietnam's internal situations since 1956, there would have been no Vietnamese killed innocently! . . . If the senseless war caused by U.S. planners did not happen, how completely united Vietnam would have been developing its economy during the past two decades? To drop the final curtain for a clumpsy [sic] drama, the U.S. planners planned the evacuation program called 'Operation New Life.'" Unlike other accounts, which applauded American generosity, this letter questioned the assumption that Vietnamese would be welcomed into U.S. society, particularly as a non-white minority: "But can those 100,000 Vietnamese refugees appropriately respond to their 'NEW LIFE' in a very different Society? Or are they just becoming a new kind of colour-people among the colorful American Society?"[83] These repatriates clearly did not feel "rescued" by the United States, and their language marked a general skepticism of American racial liberalism. They did not want to be a minority in a foreign country.

Other repatriates challenged the American goals of humanitarian rescue, noting their months-long wait in enclosed camps and the separation of their families. They believed their return to Vietnam would be the proper humanitarian gesture. Two repatriates drove these points home in the impassioned essay "What Do We Want from Washington." First, they criticized their living conditions on Guam and "being cooped up behind iron-fences of the U.S. inhumane concentration camps." Second, they called into question the humanitarian credentials of Operation New Life. While they admitted that the American public deserved credit for its generosity, they also explained that the operation had traumatically separated hundreds of families: "Talking about 'Operation New Life,' people of the world will think of the great hospitality and open arms of American people who are welcoming miserable Vietnamese families from 'refugee camps' in some states of the USA ... we sincerely congratulate these golden hearts of American people for their support aids in helping exiled Vietnamese in this country. However, do American people need to reconsider the policy of the US government in the plan called 'human mission' that evacuated called 'humanitarian' while it separated many 'refugees' from their families and pushed them into the most dramatic circumstances?"

After casting aside U.S. aspirations of humanitarianism, the repatriates' language became more threatening. They charged the U.S. government with war crimes in Vietnam and noted that if the Americans could fly a man to the moon, they should be able to send two thousand people to Vietnam. Whether their arguments were instrumental or ideological, their conclusion was clear and somewhat terrifying: "We want the US government to carry out either of the following two things: First, send 2000 people of us all back to Vietnam immediately. Second: if the first thing could not be done, kill all of us with its own weapons. . . . Do not plot to send us to the wild Wake Island or to any unknown place else imprison us in forgetfulness."[84]

U.S. military officers were nervous. Faced with overt threats of violence and suicide, the military no longer saw the Vietnamese as passive recipients of aid, but instead feared they might remain under U.S. custody or carry out their threats. U.S. Rear Admiral Kent J. Carroll weighed the possibility of committing federal troops to quell civil unrest under a plan code-named Operation Garden Plot.[85] However, Guam's colonial history and isolated geography confounded him. Garden Plot authorized military control over a domestic civil disturbance, but military protocol clearly stated that it could not be launched without explicit presidential approval. Hamstrung by Garden Plot's need for presidential review, Carroll argued that the "normal civil disturbance rules cannot be easily applied to Guam." He wanted more autonomy and continued, "Garden Plot procedures are not appropriate for emergency situations in U.S. territories." In essence, the U.S. simply did not have a game plan for a civil disturbance on Guam because it had never considered it could face one. The FBI did not include Guam in its purview, nor did the CIA, thus there was essentially no legal framework for intelligence gathering on Guam or in the camps.[86] Carroll repeatedly urged his colleagues in Washington, D.C., to grant him the authority to order troops into the repatriate camp if hostilities flared again. In the end, Carroll's superiors refused his requests. They recognized the possible media and international fallout if U.S. troops came into direct conflict with the Vietnamese on Guam.

In order to prevent the feared rioting within the camp, President Ford finally embraced the ship option. He agreed to grant the Vietnamese full access to the *Viet Nam Thuong Tin*, a merchant ship that could hold over two thousand passengers. The Vietnamese responded with celebration. The photos on the front page of the *Pacific Daily News* showed jubilant, shirtless young men rushing out into the night and jumping in the air.[87] As an experienced naval captain, Tran Dinh Tru agreed to captain the ship. At the most basic level, the repatriates succeeded in their mission; they had adeptly pressured the U.S. government to give them a ship. Presumably weighing their options and evaluating the potential public relations disaster of all-out rioting, indefinite detention camps on Guam or Wake Island, or forced removal to the continental United States, the U.S. government had finally conceded the "ship option" was its best course of action. Over the course of the next three weeks, Vietnamese sailors worked on the ship with enthusiasm, conducted sea trials, and packed needed food and water stores for thirty days.[88] The ship option was a somewhat improvised and desperate decision, but the United States made it with the goal of supporting the repatriates' stated dreams of return.

The UNHCR refused to throw its support behind the ship option because it could not guarantee the well-being of the repatriates on arrival. Although it was frustrated with the Vietnamese government's intransigence and hostility toward the repatriates, it could not give its blessing to their unauthorized return. The UNHCR feared violent reprisals if the U.S. acted alone. Vietnam framed the repatriates' return and the ship option as an infringement of its territorial borders and a violation of its nascent sovereignty and power. Angered that the United States refused to recognize its new government or negotiate directly, Vietnam denounced the repatriate ship as a "sinister scheme." "This is a new crime against the Vietnamese people. The PRG calls on the patriots now forced to live abroad to be aware of the bad intention of the United States, and to unite with one another to protect themselves and the nation's sovereignty against all wicked actions of U.S. imperialism. The PRG formally demands that the U.S. government stop settling the question of 'refugees' in its own way."[89]

Vietnam characterized the event as an "adventurous and irresponsible action. . . . The U.S. government has made a big mistake by acting unilaterally and arbitrarily in the matter."[90] In conversations with the UNHCR, Vietnam expressed fear that the U.S. government was using the repatriates as a ploy to return CIA agents to its territory.[91] While seemingly paranoid and unsympathetic to the repatriates' claims, Vietnam was in a fragile state and skeptical of any U.S. action. It had experienced years of U.S. military violence and CIA-led plots. In short, Vietnam argued that the United States was forcing a marginal, and potentially subversive, population on its borders and violating its own right to determine who could and could not enter the country.

However, the U.S. government and the repatriates themselves decided it was worth the risk. In order to best protect the repatriates, the United States ordered its officials to "play down the U.S. role" and remain on the sidelines. It wanted to avoid any appearance of U.S. control and allow the operation to appear fully Vietnamese. Because Vietnam viewed the repatriates with great suspicion and as tainted by the U.S. imperialists, there was to be no "formal, send-off ceremony" or fanfare from U.S. or Guamanian representatives. Any final event was to be "strictly a repatriate show."[92]

While the repatriates prepared for return, U.S. officials publicized Vietnam's aggressive statements within the camp. They wanted repatriates to be fully cognizant of the Vietnamese government's public animosity toward their cause.[93] The repatriates were not blind to the possible consequences of their return. As one of the repatriate leaders explained, "If we have to wait for Hanoi's approval, then who knows when we can return? We are living here every day, every hour, thinking about our families, our wives, and our children. We cannot prolong this state of perpetual limbo. We want to make our own decisions, and the solution that we have chosen is very simple. . . . We are willing to accept any consequences, including death or imprisonment."[94]

Willing to take any risk, this man probably could not imagine the network of brutal "re-education camps" that would terrorize thousands of South Vietnamese military veterans for more than a decade.

Before the repatriates boarded the ship, the U.S. provided them with one last chance to change their minds and travel to the United States rather than Vietnam.[95] U.S. officials feared that the constraints of Camp Asan had forged an "uncommon solidarity" among the repatriates, and they wanted to provide one final "bail-out" option for repatriates who "secretly may want to remain" and go to the United States. Approximately twenty-four hours before departure, individuals would encounter an elaborately staged final "counseling session" complete with secret rooms and doors.[96] Twenty-eight people, including protest leader Le Minh Tan, changed their minds and opted not to board the *Viet Nam Thuong Tin* and instead went to the United States.[97]

In total, 1,546 Vietnamese boarded the boat. In an almost comical conclusion, the repatriate leaders had forgotten the portrait of Ho Chi Minh, which they wanted to display on the ship. U.S. marines promptly retrieved the picture and carried it to the ship, creating the rather unseemly picture of U.S. marines side by side with Ho Chi Minh. A public affairs officer intercepted the embarrassing photo-op, ordered the Marines to drop the painting, and asked the repatriates to bring it on board themselves.[98]

On October 17, 1975, the ship left Guam without a named port or a guarantee that it would be allowed to land on Vietnamese soil. When the ship arrived in southern Vietnam in November, the government imprisoned the repatriates in a Vietnamese military camp near Nha Trang. It then transferred the repatriates into the network of brutal re-education camps mapping southern Vietnam. Tran Dinh Tru remembered being taken ashore and interrogated. Vietnamese officials charged him, as the captain, with leading an American plot against Vietnam. They believed he was a CIA plant and would not accept that his sole motivation was family reunification. He was demeaned as a "puppet soldier" and forced to listen to speeches about how the Vietnamese had defeated the "imperialist" United States and "chased the Americans out of Vietnam forever."[99]

Ironically, and tragically, the repatriates in fact became prisoners of war. Their earlier protests that they were not POWs transformed into the sad reality that the reunified government of Vietnam classified them as former enemies and suspect citizens. To the best of my knowledge, the Vietnamese government placed all the repatriates in re-education camps.[100] Thus, the

FIGURE 4. Vietnamese men boarding the *Viet Nam Thuong Tin* to return to Vietnam, 1975. Courtesy of the U.S. National Archives and Records Administration, Record Group 319, Box 19, declassification number 984082.

repatriates traveled from a U.S. detention camp on Guam to the network of euphemistically named re-education camps in Vietnam, which were better characterized by hard labor, starvation, and torture than by any "education."[101]

In Tran Dinh Tru's memoir, he recounted spending more than twelve years in a forced labor camp in Vietnam. Based on my sources, it is impossible to know how long other repatriates were interned in Vietnamese re-education camps. While Tran Dinh Tru may have been punished more harshly due to his being the ship's captain, the re-education camps were generally characterized by starvation diets and arbitrary brutality. After the first six months' imprisonment, the revolutionary government allowed him to write to his family, and his wife began sending periodic supplies to support him in prison. Six years later, the government permitted his wife to visit him at a re-education camp in the north. Tran Dinh Tru felt horrible about the hardship and expense of her trip, because the resources she was sending him meant his children had less to eat. He wrote extensively about forced labor, starvation diets, constant surveillance, and communist "re-education." "We lived in a strange world, like insects, like birds, like wild animals. We lived without being allowed to distinguish between right and wrong. Our clothes were mere tatters patched up, and we toiled in the cold under the barrel of AK-47s. Even when I was in a deep sleep, I had nightmares. Horrendous dreams. When I woke, I was drenched with sweat. But when I was wide awake and opened my eyes, I looked straight at my current life and saw the spectacle around me. It was even more horrendous than my nightmares."[102]

He concluded his memoir with regret. He had not fathomed that by the late 1980s, Vietnamese would be allowed to leave Vietnam, nor had he imagined that Vietnamese Americans would be able to send remittances to their families. These were possibilities he could not have anticipated:

I wish I had not returned. By now, I would have established a new career in America and had the ability to send money home to help my wife and children. The communists had begun to allow relatives living overseas, including America, to send money and supplies back to their families in Vietnam. By the time I learned about this, it was already too late. When I made up my mind to return, I had never expected that such a thing could happen. I had drawn on my earlier experience from 1954. Between 1954 and 1975, families in North Vietnam and families in South Vietnam had no contact. Yet this history did not repeat itself a second time. That is fate. How can humans escape their fate?[103]

Tran Dinh Tru was released from the re-education camps in February 1988, and he finally reunited with his wife. Three years later he applied to the Humanitarian Operation program, a 1990s immigration program which facilitated re-education camp survivors' resettlement in the United States. In 1991, Tran Dinh Tru left Vietnam for the United States, this time with his wife and children.

If the history of the Vietnamese repatriates refuted an American rescue narrative, it also cannot be read as a triumphant rejection of U.S. imperialism or a romanticized revolutionary victory. In fact, repatriates' tenacity and successful protests resulted in one of the war's lesser-known tragedies, as Tran Dinh Tru's story testifies. On Guam, away from their families the repatriates made choices with the knowledge available at the time. Their choices were fraught with anger, hope, despair, good luck and bad.

· · ·

The repatriates' campaign tested the parameters of humanitarianism for the United States, Guam, the UNHCR, and the repatriates themselves. The repatriates' militant protests clearly unsettled the United States. The U.S.-led evacuation was an attempt to pair military failure with humanitarian rescue, and the repatriates' refusal to follow the expected script of gratitude and passivity cracked this veneer. The repatriates turned the language of humanity and humanitarianism right back at the United States. With blistering attacks against the U.S., many charged that the only possible humanitarian action would be to allow the Vietnamese to return and reunite with their families. It's worth noting that the U.S. government listened. It did not force the Vietnamese to the mainland or to an indefinite camp; rather, it sought to resolve the situation by responding to the repatriates. For all the U.S. violence and callousness in Vietnam, in this instance, it attempted to fulfill the repatriates' stated desires.

Guam found itself in between. As a U.S. colony, it had little leverage, and its local government generally acquiesced to being the proverbial welcome mat to the United States. Guam had to accept a massive number of people quickly, and publicly, the local government echoed the U.S. rhetoric of rescue. However, Guam also faced its own pressures, and it did not want to be an indefinite detention camp. Guam's isolation and distance from the mainland made this a legitimate concern, and its elected leaders were adamant that the repatriates would not remain on Guam. These would be the same concerns first-asylum sites like Malaysia, Indonesia, Hong Kong, and Thailand would soon echo. Southeast Asian and Pacific leaders bristled at the extent to which they were expected to be generous and humanitarian on behalf of the United States. Within limits, Guam's politicians worked to pressure the U.S. government to find a solution, any solution, which would remove the Vietnamese from Guam. Guamanian officials passed resolutions, met with repatriates, and worked to make the U.S. government respond to the potential crisis. Governor Bordallo was particularly enamored with the ship option, and Guam's Pacific geography made this a tenable plan of action.

Finally, the repatriates' campaign was breathtaking in its militancy and passion. Far from being passive, hopeless, or vacant recipients of aid and goodwill, the repatriates displayed an impressive array of political skills and organizing strategies. The photographs of Vietnamese standing beside images of Ho Chi Minh or shaving their heads—on U.S. military bases, no less—remain stunning. Their activism succeeded in convincing the United States that they should be allowed to return to Vietnam under their own power. Some of the repatriates, like Tran Dinh Tru, made their choices out of family devotion and their own vision of anti-communism. A few returned to contribute to the new revolutionary government, and probably the majority returned as young men who had not chosen to evacuate for themselves. Their stories highlighted the repatriates' personal attempts to elude the Cold War's stark binary divides between communism and anti-communism and simply to go home. Ultimately, and tragically, they failed to escape these dichotomies, and instead faced an insecure and vengeful revolutionary Vietnam.

The repatriates were only a small number of those who suffered in the years following reunification. In 1975, the Vietnamese government imprisoned thousands of former South Vietnamese military personnel in re-education camps. The repatriates were far from the only ones punished because of their ties to the Americans. Then, in 1976, the new government moved thousands more who had been loyal to the South Vietnamese government or involved in capitalist urban enterprises to euphemistically named New Economic Zones.[104] In addition, by 1978, the Vietnamese government began a concerted campaign against its large ethnic Chinese Vietnamese minority. With various populations facing repression— former South Vietnamese military personnel, Chinese Vietnamese, and those in the upper and middle classes—Vietnamese began to escape the country both by land and by sea. At first, the numbers were relatively modest, but by 1978, they had ballooned into the tens of thousands, with Vietnamese arriving daily along the coasts of Thailand, Malaysia, Hong Kong, the Philippines, and Indonesia. By December 1978, there were tens of thousands of Vietnamese in Malaysia alone, waiting and hoping to resettle in the United States or another western country.

To "Shoot" or to "Shoo"

VIETNAMESE IN MALAYSIA, 1975–1979

ON JUNE 5, 1979, MALAYSIAN DEPUTY PRIME MINISTER Mahathir Mohamad lashed out at reporters who suggested Malaysia had not been sufficiently humanitarian or generous in responding to the thousands of Vietnamese who had landed on its shores. In December 1978, it sheltered 75 percent of the people fleeing Vietnam by sea. By June of 1979, there were approximately 76,000 Vietnamese in Malaysia's overcrowded camps, mostly clustered in the northeastern state of Terengganu.[1] The Malaysian political establishment feared that without a radical change, Vietnamese would keep landing on its shores, and with no assurance of final resettlement elsewhere, would remain indefinitely in Malaysia. To discourage future boat landings and create a deterrent force, Malaysian police and immigration officers towed rickety, often leaky boats out to sea, pushing Vietnamese on to Indonesia, the Philippines, or anywhere other than Malaysia.

Mahathir's comments pressed the point: "Our patience is fully extended. If 500,000 immigrants tried to land in Britain, they might probably shoot them. We've already been accused by *Newsweek* of shooting illegal immigrants, so we might as well do it and justify their accusation. We are being nice and humane, but what do we get? Nothing. So why bother?"[2] Mahathir's frustration broke all polite or diplomatic pretenses, and Mahathir reiterated his threat to shoot at incoming Vietnamese at a public meeting the following week. The media response was immediate. The *New York Times* and other international outlets repeated that "shoot on sight legislation" could be forthcoming, and Mahathir's strong words succeeded in capturing international attention.[3]

A regional Malaysian newspaper interpreted Mahathir's comments somewhat differently. It suggested the threats were intentionally provocative, meant to create a crisis and move American and European politicians, and not to be taken literally. "Shooting on sight? Here Datuk Mahathir may find his threat too easily turned into a bluff, because Malaysian servicemen are not of that ilk. They are not going to shoot defenseless people—and Datuk Mahathir knows it."[4] In this reiteration, Malaysian journalists chafed at any suggestion that the military would carry out violence against unarmed Vietnamese. The Malaysian English-language newspaper *New Straits Times* was generally more sympathetic toward a tough policy: "Between shooting, which is unacceptable, and shooing, which is ineffective, there lies a murky territory of unsatisfactory solutions." The paper also stoked fears that the Vietnamese were themselves communist agents: "Camps are now scattered on beaches up the whole length of the coast. Any reasonably recourseful (sic) communist agent could slip out of such camps, and there is no guarantee that some have not already done so."[5] Prime Minister Hussein Onn brushed this aside and refuted Mahathir's comments as hyperbole, and Home Minister Ghazali Shafie suggested Mahathir meant "shoo, not shoot" in "mock admonishment."[6] That said, the harsh rhetoric had done its trick and accelerated pressure on the UNHCR leading into the 1979 Geneva Conference.[7]

Mahathir's initial comments were in fact more oblique and interesting than simple threats to shoot Vietnamese at sea. In his pique, Mahathir compared the U.K.'s vision of humane action to Malaysia's, and he found the U.K. wanting. Already famous for making outrageous statements and championing Malay nationalism, Mahathir voiced his animosity against the incoming Vietnamese and their incompatibility with his vision for Malaysia *and* his rejection of the British—and by extension, the west's—monopoly on humanitarianism. Far from viewing them as humane, he saw Britain, the United States, and the UNHCR as hypocritical, and he saw little advantage in Malaysia's hosting the Vietnamese. More to the point, Mahathir called into question the politics of humanitarianism in the late 1970s.[8]

This chapter argues that Malaysia ultimately pushed the UNHCR and resettlement countries, including the United States, to change their refugee policies. Unlike Guam, Malaysia was no longer a colony or under British rule. It acted independently of the U.K., and most certainly of the United States, and as a former colony, the government fiercely defended its borders and sovereignty. At this time, the UNHCR defined all the Vietnamese as refugees, but the Malaysian government did not. Malaysian hostility included a nationalist animosity against foreigners common to most nation-states. In particular, this was intertwined with anxieties about the place of Chinese Malaysians and the history of communism in postwar Malaysia. These two dynamics shaped the Malaysian government's reception of the Vietnamese, whom it categorized as "Vietnamese illegal immigrants" and *not* as refugees. While Mahathir's comments crossed many lines, he was not alone in believing the real responsibility of humanitarianism lay primarily with the Americans, the British, the Australians, the Canadians, and the UNHCR.

Between 1976 and 1979, the Malaysian government executed a contradictory and uneven policy, providing shelter to approximately 120,000 Vietnamese while simultaneously expelling thousands more to unknown futures and potential death. The Malaysian government established a network of camps along its eastern coast, the largest and most infamous being on the small island of Pulau Bidong.[9] In the end, Malaysia hosted tens of thousands of Vietnamese despite its deep reservations. The Malaysian Red Crescent Society took a leading role, providing emergency services, food, clean water, and invaluable assistance locating family members and sponsors. In an effort that was far less publicized, Malaysia also welcomed more than 90,000 Filipinos fleeing the southern Philippines in the early 1970s.

At the same time, Malaysian immigration forces brutally forced Vietnamese boats back to sea. In 1979, the Malaysian Navy pushed off close to four hundred boats, which carried in the realm of fifty thousand passengers.[10] The unwritten understanding was that individuals who reached Malaysian shores could stay, while boats that confronted Malaysian patrols were routinely "pushed" on their way. Malaysian police may not have actually shot at Vietnamese (although there are accounts that on occasion they did), but it was common to tug precarious boats back to international waters. The UNHCR pressured the Malaysian government to stop pushing boats back out to sea, and it fought to secure the right of first asylum for all Vietnamese. In contrast, the Malaysian government forged its own path and never signed the 1951 UNHCR Geneva convention on refugees. It would allow thousands of Vietnamese to stay in isolated camps, but it would do so on its own terms, and the Vietnamese would not be allowed to remain in Malaysia.

The crisis in Malaysia also pushed the American government to recalibrate its own practice of humanitarianism. The Office of Human Rights and Humanitarianism, established during the Ford administration, largely focused on the resettlement of Vietnamese in the United States. The U.S. accepted more than 125,000 Vietnamese in 1975 and President Jimmy Carter allowed approximately 32,000 more to enter in 1978, all through executive prerogative.[11] There was no U.S. refugee law. However, these resettlement numbers did not come close to meeting the need as Vietnamese waited for months in camps throughout Southeast Asia in 1978 and 1979. Scholars Laura Madokoro and Ayako Sahara have demonstrated how this discrepancy between the burdens on first-asylum sites and resettlement countries underscored hierarchies in which majority-white western countries appeared more benevolent and generous than places like Malaysia and Hong Kong, even as they too kept Vietnamese at bay.[12] The United States admitted set numbers of Vietnamese and gave preference to those with preexisting ties to America. The United States' humanitarianism and resettlement policies were conditional, and Malaysia repeatedly asked why it had to accept all Vietnamese as refugees when the United States could be selective.

Vietnamese also remained politically active in their desire for speedy resettlement in the west. In contrast to the repatriate campaigns on Guam, during the 1970s, Vietnamese did not mobilize protests within the camps in Malaysia. They feared if they were labeled as troublemakers they would risk their chance of resettlement in the wealthier western countries in which they hoped to live. In oral histories and letters to the UNHCR, they alternately noted their frustration, anger, and gratitude to the Malaysian government, and their fears of being pushed off. However, most waited, if not patiently, and nothing comparable to the militant activities on Guam took place in Malaysia in the 1970s. In addition, many Vietnamese who had already resettled in the United States wanted to help those who were still seeking escape from Vietnam. They became activists, initiating letter-writing campaigns and lobbying the UNHCR and the United States to move faster on resettlement for those stuck in camps. Vietnamese Americans also began to coalesce into organizations, and the Indochina Refugee Action Center was one of the first national NGOs with Vietnamese American leadership. Its goals included advocating for higher resettlement numbers in the United States, providing social services, and creating new opportunities for Vietnamese through the resettlement process. It became a player in Washington, D.C., and in Geneva, and its ability to forge relationships with U.S. politicians and the UNHCR developed a platform for Vietnamese organizations.

Diasporic Vietnamese harnessed the language of human rights to condemn Hanoi's policies and advocate for Vietnamese fleeing the country. By the late 1970s, the language of human rights had penetrated political and popular culture in the United States. As scholars like Mark Bradley have argued, the confluence of decolonization, the rise of Médecins Sans Frontières and Amnesty International, and the visibility of anti-Soviet dissidents and victims of Latin American dictatorships meant that human rights entered the American vernacular. Historian Barbara Keys has argued that both Democratic and Republican politicians used the language of human rights to try to redeem U.S. foreign policy in the years following the Vietnam War.[13] This was also an era of Cold War détente and of President Jimmy Carter's personal identification with human rights. However, for Vietnamese in the diaspora, there was a single target: the Socialist Republic of Vietnam, Hanoi's communist government. Throughout the late 1970s, tens of thousands of South Vietnamese suffered in the network of "re-education camps," or forced labor camps, throughout the country. Vietnamese in the diaspora argued that those imprisoned in the camps deserved refugee status. If antiwar activists had condemned the U.S. war in Vietnam because of atrocities and human rights violations like the My Lai massacre, now southern Vietnamese were using the language of human rights to condemn the new revolutionary communist government and its brutal postwar regime. In 1979, Vietnamese in the diaspora endorsed the UNHCR's humanitarian mandate—saving and protecting Vietnamese fleeing the country—and articulated their own vision of human rights. For the time being, humanitarianism and human rights could coexist with ease, and Vietnamese in the camps and in the diaspora looked to the UNHCR for protection and support. However, this presumed compatibility between the two would fray in the years to come.

Finally, the Malaysian police did not have to "shoot" for Vietnamese to know their lives were at stake. Malaysia's refugee policies and definition of humanitarianism played out across the lives of Vietnamese men and women, and unknown numbers perished at sea. The Malaysian government did admit tens of thousands of Vietnamese in the late 1970s, but it was unwilling to accept Vietnamese without limit and without guarantees of resettlement elsewhere. By 1979, Malaysia succeeded in changing the status quo and pressuring the UNHCR and the west to expedite and improve the resettlement process, minimizing the burden on itself and other first-asylum countries.

COLD WAR MALAYSIA AND THE CHINESE VIETNAMESE EXODUS

In the years immediately following the fall of Saigon, Malaysia became an important host country. In 1975, the first group of forty-seven postwar Vietnamese landed in Malaysia. Largely cared for by the Malaysian Red

Crescent Society, they remained for only a brief stay before resettling in the west. At the same time, Malaysia resettled 1,500 Cham, a Muslim minority within Cambodia, demonstrating its willingness to cooperate and assist individuals at risk in Southeast Asia.[14] For the next few years, the number of people fleeing Vietnam remained modest. This pause between 1975 and the huge onslaught in 1978 and 1979 can be attributed to changes within Vietnam. First, the Vietnamese government imprisoned large numbers of RVN officers in re-education camps, like the ones where Tran Dinh Tru suffered after his return from Guam. Many men remained imprisoned during these transitional years, restricting the number of obvious dissidents and individuals seeking to flee. The camps began to release some of the lower-ranking men by the late 1970s, leading to higher numbers wanting to escape the country. In addition, the Vietnamese government attacked private enterprise and relocated thousands of people from the commercial sector to remote agricultural "New Economic Zones." In 1978, the government also began a concerted campaign against its minority Chinese Vietnamese population, uprooting their businesses and "encouraging" them to leave the country.[15] After North Vietnam's victory, diplomatic relations between Vietnam and China reached a violent nadir. Vietnam's invasion of Cambodia and cooperation with the Soviet Union precipitated a brief but bloody war between the two countries.[16] Between 1978 and 1979, more than 250,000 Chinese Vietnamese were relocated to southern China, making China, somewhat ironically, an unheralded major resettlement country.[17] These combined forces meant that after 1978, thousands of Vietnamese had an immediate incentive to leave, and in the case of the Chinese Vietnamese, the Vietnamese government often facilitated their removal through a combination of pressure and graft.

The escapes were almost universally traumatic. Experiences varied, from individuals who fled with groups of friends and family, to individuals who joined strangers on small boats, to Chinese Vietnamese who bribed their way onto large ships, often in concert with the Vietnamese government. For those escaping, the stress of persecution and dislocation within Vietnam and fear of death and dehydration at sea were often compounded by physical and sexual violence at the hands of pirates. Their numbers climbed quickly, however, and due to geographic proximity and sea routes between southern Vietnam and Malaysia, Malaysia became the most frequent landing site for the Vietnamese "boat people." Beginning in the fall of 1978, several thousand Vietnamese began landing in Malaysia each month, and by the end of the year, there were approximately 48,000 Vietnamese waiting in camps throughout Malaysia.[18]

The Vietnamese landing on Malaysian shores were disproportionately Chinese Vietnamese. An ethnic minority within Vietnam, this population triggered specific fears and anxieties in Cold War Malaysia, which had its own large Chinese population. In Malaysia, the ruling United Malays National Organization party defined its raison d'etre as representing what it saw as indigenous Malay people, as opposed to Chinese, Indian, and other minority communities in both peninsular and eastern Malaysia (the provinces of Sarawak and Sabah on northern Borneo). The political tensions between Malay and Chinese populations dated back to the colonial era, when the British recruited thousands of Chinese workers and created economic and racial competition between the two. These divisions intensified during and after World War II, which saw greater numbers of Chinese identifying with the communist-led Malayan People's Anti-Japanese Army and Malay leaders cooperating with the Japanese occupiers. When the war ended, the Malayan Communist Party (MCP) remained largely identified with the Chinese population, and Malay leaders pressured the British colonial government to maintain Malay privileges in the postwar order. From 1948 until 1960, there was a violent guerilla war between remaining MCP-identified guerillas and the colonial government, the so-called Malayan Emergency. The government crushed the guerilla movement, and the remaining fighters retreated to the Malay-Thai border. Fighting persisted in the northern border region until the last guerillas surrendered in 1989, keeping the fear and threat of communism alive in Malaysia long after the MCP was no longer a viable alternative to the government.[19]

Malaya gained its independence from Great Britain in 1957, and in 1963, Singapore and the provinces of Sarawak and Sabah combined to form a new Malaysia. Singapore soon left the federation, but the eastern provinces remained Malaysian. Historians have noted that with independence, a bargain was struck which delegated the political realm and civil service positions to Malays and the commercial sphere to the Chinese. Islam became the official state religion and Malay the official language, and the government offered economic incentives and political advantages to Malays. Chinese received Malaysian citizenship but few opportunities to join the government. When racial violence resulted in riots and the deaths of anywhere from 200 to 2,000 people on May 13, 1969, it shook the country's precarious stability.

In its wake, Mahathir and his brand of Malay nationalism came to prominence. Mahathir was the most important Malaysian politician of his generation. Born into a middle-class but non-noble family, he entered parliament in 1964 as a member of the ruling party, the United Malays National Organization (UMNO). Mahathir made a name for himself as a vocal champion for Malays, or *bumiputeras,* who composed approximately half of the population and disproportionately occupied the lower echelons of the country's economic strata. Political scientist Khoo Boo Teik argued that in the aftermath of the inter-ethnic violence in May 1969, Mahathir became a "living symbol of Malay nationalism." His support for "Malay supremacy" came at the expense of the Chinese (who made up approximately 35 percent of the population) and Indians (roughly 10 percent), and it rejected a Malaysian identity based on more complicated racial, religious, and national identities.[20] UMNO's creation of systematic preferences for Malays in civil service jobs and government contracts was central to its New Economic Policy. In 1976, Prime Minister Hussein Onn selected Mahathir to be his deputy prime minister, and Mahathir would go on to dominate Malaysian politics with a mix of charisma, authoritarianism, Malay chauvinism, and modernist economic policies.[21]

Thus, to many eyes, the Chinese Vietnamese population threatened to unbalance the Malaysian government's preferred demographics. It also tapped into a historic Malay hostility against its Chinese population, one that was, somewhat ironically, identified with both a commercial elite and communist radicalism. The Malaysian government saw the Vietnamese as suspect and burdensome and not part of its Cold War vision for the country.

In November 1978, the freighter *Hai Hong* arrived on Malaysian shores carrying roughly 2,500 Vietnamese on board who were disproportionately Chinese Vietnamese.[22] Smugglers located in Southeast Asia arranged for thousands of Chinese Vietnamese to leave by large ships such as the *Hai Hong,* demanding gold from people desperate to leave, paying kickbacks to the Vietnamese government, and creating a mutually profitable system of bribes and trickery. As one journalist explained, "First they [the Vietnamese government] get rid of reactionary elements . . . you know, officers and intellectuals. Second they get gold, and third they push the problem to other countries."[23] As a result, the Vietnamese government gained millions of dollars and the removal of an undesired population.[24] In the case of the *Hai Hong,* the ship had changed hands multiple times in a dodgy way, and the captain claimed, somewhat weakly, that thousands of Vietnamese had forced their way on board when it had engine trouble. There were rumors that the ship owners and Vietnamese officials walked away with five million dollars.[25]

The Malaysian government forced the freighter to remain offshore, and it declared that the individuals on board were not refugees and could not land.[26] Ultimately the crisis was resolved thanks to resettlement offers by the United States, Canada, and France, but the incident with the *Hai Hong* prompted the Malaysian government to take a more aggressive stance against the Vietnamese, and it formed the Federal Task Force on Vietnamese Illegal Immigrants, or Task Force VII.[27] The government did not accept the United States' or the UNHCR's representation of the Vietnamese as deserving Cold War refugees. Even though most Vietnamese in the camps self-identified as anti-communists, and this is definitely how U.S. officials envisioned them, Malaysian politicians doubted these claims. The Malaysian government might have been in an ongoing guerilla war with MCP militants and been virulently anti-communist, but it still sought to define anti-communism on its own terms. Its Cold War objectives did not mean automatic support or sympathy for the Vietnamese, particularly Chinese Vietnamese.

In many ways, Malaysian hostility toward the Vietnamese seems contradictory given the government's fierce and staunch anti-communism. Malaysia had been a founding member of the Association of Southeast Asian Nations (ASEAN), which formed as an anti-communist regional alliance during the U.S. war in Vietnam.[28] Malaysia had also established diplomatic relations with South Vietnam, and it feared domestic communist movements. The *New Straits Times* consistently praised the government's war against communist infiltration, and throughout the late 1970s it regularly published progovernment articles heralding the military's successes against the guerilla "reds." The Malaysian government argued that the Vietnamese landing on its shores in the 1970s drained the resources of the country's security forces, and as a result, the military had fewer men to fight communists in the north. The *Far Eastern Economic Review* reported on the government's renewed vigilance on the Malaysia-Thailand border, "Malaysian army officers are complaining that they cannot maintain military pressure on the MCP because their forces are increasingly being required to man dozens of outposts along the country's east coast, to look out for incoming Vietnamese refugees."[29] The Malaysian government stated that protecting the Vietnamese was hindering the fight against communism, rather than an example of anti-communist politics.

In addition, Malaysians repeatedly cast suspicion on the Vietnamese as potential subversive agents. This was reinforced by the large number of Chinese Vietnamese. Were the Vietnamese really fleeing communism, or were they coming to infiltrate Malaysia? The *Far Eastern Economic Review* reported that the government feared Hanoi was intentionally "planting" agents among the "so-called refugees."[30] A Malaysian letter to the editor put it succinctly: "The communist underground in Peninsular Malaysia, led by Chin Peng, was and still is dominated by the Chinese. The idea that Chinese are communists is embodied in the minds of the Malays. They form an equation: Chinese = communists, Chinese = refugees, therefore, refugees = communists."[31] The government argued for constant vigilance and even suggested that many of "those who were running away" had supported the Viet Cong.[32] In an unsolicited letter to the UNHCR, a Chinese Vietnamese man looked to the international organization for protection. He explained that on landing in Malaysia, he was confronted by government officials who identified him and his boat-mates as potential communists rather than as refugees. He wrote: "On the evening that we arrived the Malaysian Government at Terengganu grumbled at us: 'Why do you all run away after your country has become independent? Didn't you all welcome the communists? Do you think it's legal to steal into Malaysia like this?'" The author continued, "When they cursed us in this mindless manner it was difficult for us to find words. . . . If we didn't love freedom dearly then why should we go through these terrible misfortunes in order to escape?"[33]

The Malay-language weekly *Mastika* amplified these anxieties. Rather than positing Malaysia as an anti-communist safe haven, journalist Yahaya Ismail worried that there were spies embedded among the Vietnamese. If these suspected agents were able to make contact with the MCP at the Malaysia-Thailand border, Malaysia would face a significant threat.[34] The *New Straits Times* also suggested that the Vietnamese could be communist agents.[35] A reporter who went to Terengganu found that locals were suspicious of the Vietnamese. One fisherman believed that "the boat people are well informed because there are communist agents among them who have come to subvert Malaysian security." He continued, "I am 30 years old and I've never handled a weapon. But the Vietnamese—even five-year-olds know how to use guns. Now their own war is over, they have gone to Thailand and they are fighting China." He also implied that the thirty-six Vietnamese who had gone "missing" from the camp were subversives spreading communism, rather than impatient men who decided to try their luck back at sea or in another camp.[36] The Malaysian government recognized that these suspicions were unfounded, and it even published materials to temper these fears and educate Malaysians that the Vietnamese were neither spies nor invaders. It acknowledged that there were Malaysians, even politicians, "who think these illegal refugees are communists, simply because they come from a communist country." Yet Home Minister Ghazali insisted this "speculation" was wrong. Still, the government's need to reassure its citizens indicated just how deeply the Vietnamese triggered local anxieties.[37]

Other Malaysian reporters downplayed reports of communist infiltration and instead chastised the Chinese Vietnamese for not having adapted to Vietnamese society. Following this line of critique, *Mastika* described the Chinese Vietnamese as ethnic chauvinists. "These ethnic Chinese Vietnamese are elitists in that communist country who could not change the luxurious lifestyles they enjoyed prior to the fall of Saigon. . . . They are also unwilling to abandon their wealth and easy life in order to work under the hot sun of the economic zones [NEZs] to fulfill the needs of the communist zones." The reporter concluded, "These ethnic Chinese Vietnamese were known for their strong Chinese-ness and unwillingness to sacrifice their culture, which has no place in communism." Rather than praising this anti-communist fervor, he emphasized the "Chinese-ness" of overseas Chinese in Southeast Asian countries, which kept them separate from the majority population (and which would have had even heavier resonances in Malaysian domestic politics). The reporter concluded the crisis was a Vietnam-driven plot to create unrest and destabilize its neighbors.[38]

Other *Mastika* writers speculated even further about the implications for domestic Malaysian politics. "Peking hopes to support overseas chauvinist Chinese who play important economic roles in Thailand, Malaysia, Singapore, and Indonesia. . . . The problem of the illegal immigrants, the majority of whom are ethnically Chinese, must be looked at in a grand design perspective. This will cause new tensions in race relations in Malaysia and relations between Malaysia and Peking in the future."[39]

In other words, the Chinese Vietnamese couldn't win in Malaysia. Either they were potential communist agents or they were capitalist elites, unwilling to assimilate to Vietnamese life. Although in practice, the Malaysian government treated all incoming Vietnamese as illegal immigrants and did not discriminate against those who were Chinese Vietnamese, Malay journalists in Kuala Lumpur at least etched domestic racial politics into the crisis. In this configuration, the Vietnamese could be communist agents, chauvinists who refused to assimilate, or a fifth column by which China might interfere in local matters.

In contrast, the Malaysian Chinese-language press was fairly quiet on the Vietnamese question. The Malaysian Chinese Association, part of UMNO's governing coalition, condemned Vietnam for its "horrendous ethnic cleansing," and the Chinese-language newspaper *Sin Chew Jit Poh* criticized the expulsion of the Chinese Vietnamese as a "racial policy."[40] However, Yahaya Ismail hypothesized that both the Malaysian Chinese Association and the opposition Democratic Action Party "feel that this issue is very sensitive" and might "burn the spirits" of Malaysia's multiracial society "if they tried to fight for these illegal immigrants."[41] Democratic Action Party leader Lim Kit Siang did protest Mahathir's "shooting" comments.[42] He believed if the Malaysian government followed through with "shooting" the Vietnamese, Malaysia would "lose its soul" and gain a "cold-blooded" reputation, which would be even worse than Vietnam's notoriety.[43] However, Lim Kit Siang generally supported the government's desire to find an international solution to the crisis, and he adhered to the language of a universal humanitarianism.[44]

In Vietnamese American and Vietnamese Australian memories of Malaysia, there is only discrete and fragmentary evidence about the distinct experiences of Chinese Vietnamese. These fleeting examples are evocative and point to stories of unstable identities in postwar Vietnam. For example, in activist-scholar Carina Hoang's collection of oral histories, she includes an unusual example of a Vietnamese man who surreptitiously "became" Chinese Vietnamese in order to facilitate his migration. He remarked that in May 1979, it was easier for Chinese to leave the country, and he did not want to "sneak out" as other Vietnamese did. "My family spent their last savings on my fare, a fake birth certificate, and a counterfeit Chinese National identification."[45] In this case, an ethnic Vietnamese falsified his papers and became Chinese in order to speed up his departure; however, this did not endear him to the Malaysian police. The Malaysian military shot at his boat to prevent it from landing, and he eventually reached a camp in Indonesia.

In another oral history collected by Carina Hoang, she records the complicated history of Hai Au, a Chinese Vietnamese who explained his political double life. Hai Au was a member of Saigon's Chinese ethnic minority, and he was also an elite member of the Communist Youth Party. He did not change or buy a new identity but instead was a party member *and* an active member of an underground anti-communist group. Formed in 1977, his organization secretly spread information about the new revolutionary government's prejudice against Chinese Vietnamese. Under cover, he would bring leaflets with anti-communist messages to high schools, spreading counter-propaganda to fellow Chinese Vietnamese students. He fled in 1978, "running for my life" because of this political activity.[46] In this story, several points converge, demonstrating the precarious situation of Chinese Vietnamese and the Malaysian government's suspicion. Here was a Chinese Vietnamese who was a member of the Communist Party, potentially reinforcing negative stereotypes and fears of infiltration. However, it was precisely his former party loyalty, and subsequent subterfuge, that compelled him to escape. While Hai Au's claims to political persecution sound credible, his story is more slippery and complicated than the story of a South Vietnamese military officer who suffered in a re-education camp and had always been publically anti-communist. Recognizing only a simplistic division between communist and anti-communist identities, most politicians (American, Vietnamese, and Malaysian) had difficulty accepting the duplicity and multiple identities that communist societies often produced, and as such, the reality of a Communist Party member being the very individual needing refuge. For Malaysians reluctant to accept any large number of non-nationals, the fears that these migrants could be communist infiltrators reinforced ethnic and political fears that already ran deep in Malaysia.

And for many Vietnamese, the threat of Malaysian push-offs was real. After surviving what could be a perilous sea journey, Vietnamese then had to make their way to shore. Mahathir gained notoriety for threatening to "shoot" Vietnamese at sea, but prior to this outburst, there were numerous stories of Vietnamese facing hostile naval police. Malaysian police routinely towed Vietnamese boats back to sea. Vietnamese responded by scuttling their boats, hoping this would lead to their rescue, or they would sail off and then try landing again at another beach. The UNHCR noted that by late 1979, Malaysian officials had pushed off almost half of the incoming boats. Malaysia had no obligation to admit all illegal immigrants who landed on its shores, and it had the sovereign right to maintain its borders. Moreover, the government claimed it only sent off seaworthy boats. As a result, there was often a game of cat and mouse between the Vietnamese and the Malaysian police. In Carina Hoang's oral history collection, Jean Luc remembered that the Malaysian authorities would not let his boat land, even though it had severe engine problems. The police "haul[ed] us out of their territorial waters and cut the tow rope." Rather than risk a longer journey in the troubled boat, the captain returned in the evening. All the people on board swam to shore under the cover of darkness. Jean Luc himself stayed in Malaysia for several months and then resettled in Washington State.[47]

There is substantial evidence of harassment by Malaysian police and a high level of arbitrariness that determined who eventually reached a camp and who did not. For example, in one memoir, Miss Yee, a Chinese Vietnamese woman, remembered reaching Terengganu: "We approached it with hope and excitement. A patrol boat headed towards us from the harbor with a man holding a machine gun in it." The passengers on her boat were joyous and applauded, only to be met with an official firing shots into the air. He barked at them in English and Chinese and denied them landing rights in Malaysia. According to Miss Yee, the official mocked them, noting that the UNHCR was not there, so "no one would know or care if we died in that place." The Malaysian official was correct: the boat was internationally invisible and vulnerable. Under his threat, Miss Yee's boat returned to sea and made two more failed attempts at landing. Finally, a Malaysian fisherman acted on his own accord, outside official channels, and allowed her boat to follow him into the harbor: "We felt like a lost child that has found its mother."[48] Miss Yee's story spoke to the hostile Malaysian policy and the very real danger of being returned to sea and left to the elements. And yet her narrative also testifies to the empathy of a Malaysian fisherman. Here was a story of individual compassion in the face of governmental hostility.[49]

In another example, Malaysians aided families and boats that landed along the coast. A family of Chinese Malaysians vacationing on a beach in eastern Malaysia came across a Vietnamese family whose boat had washed ashore. The local family gave the Vietnamese some cash and invited them to share lunch and dinner. These Chinese Malaysians warned the Vietnamese group that they should destroy their boat if they wanted refuge. The Vietnamese followed this advice and succeeded in being accepted into a camp. Not only this, but the money from the Malaysian vacationers enabled their group to improve their standard of living once they reached the refugee camp on Pulau Bidong.[50]

Through these anecdotes and stories, several points become clear. First, the Malaysian authorities pushed off hundreds of Vietnamese boats and administered a brutal policy. The terror and risks of meeting a hostile sea patrol were real, and untold numbers of Vietnamese drowned at sea. Second, Malaysian hostility to the Vietnamese was compounded by the large percentage of Chinese Vietnamese who sought refuge at this time, and many Malaysian politicians viewed the Chinese Vietnamese with additional suspicion. Third, the Malaysian government and the Malaysian Red Crescent Society (MRCS) also provided shelter for tens of thousands of Vietnamese in camps. This too should not be forgotten. Finally, individual Malaysians could offer aid and advice and become conduits for refuge. Arbitrariness and individual luck could mean the difference between entry into a camp and being sent back to sea.

PULAU BIDONG AND THE POLITICS OF WAITING

Pulau Bidong was not the only camp in Malaysia, but it became the most crowded and the most visible. In order to run the camp, the Malaysian government needed the MRCS to be firing on all cylinders. It needed to be able to quickly procure food and fresh water for thousands, and it needed to welcome high-profile visitors like Ed Bradley from CBS's *Sixty Minutes* and U.S. Congress members. The Malaysian government argued that it sheltered more Vietnamese than any other first-asylum country and that it did not receive enough credit from the UNHCR or western resettlement countries for this burden.

The Vietnamese remembered their days in the Malaysian camps as being full of lethargy and black markets, and unlike Guam in 1975 or camps after 1989, the goal was endurance, not protest. The UNHCR funded the camp with donor dollars, the largest donor being the United States, which contributed $58 million between 1975 and 1979 to the UNHCR's overall budget of $112 million.[51] Even this was not enough. In Malaysia alone, the UNHCR estimated its expenses reached $20 million in 1978 and then more than doubled to over $45 million in 1979.[52] With costs high and no end in sight, Pulau Bidong became the prime exhibit of the desperation of both the Vietnamese and the Malaysian government. Pulau Bidong was an island camp approximately two and a half hours by boat from the regional capital of Kuala Terengganu. There were multiple camps up and down the Malaysian east coast, but Pulau Bidong stood out for its size, its isolation from the local population, and its overcrowded and often desperate conditions. The camp was in the northeastern state of Terengganu, which had potential as both a tourist and an oil-producing region. However, these boosterish plans remained unrealized, and being far from Kuala Lumpur, it remained relatively underdeveloped, with a per capita income of approximately $500 a year.[53] Unlike much of urban Malaysia, Terengganu was relatively homogenous, with an

FIGURE 5. Photograph of Pulau Bidong published in *Mastika,* a popular weekly Malaysian magazine. The original caption described the Vietnamese as "illegal immigrants," replicating the government's language. *Mastika,* August 1979. Courtesy of Utusan Melayu (M) Bhd.

overwhelmingly Malay *bumiputera* population, powerful sultans, and a conservative Muslim tradition, and it would become the base of UMNO's rival Malaysian Islamic Party. In this rural region, political opposition leaders charged that the capital was "deliberately" bringing Chinese Vietnamese to eastern Malaysia to increase the number of Chinese in the region.[54] While there is no evidence of this being the case, this sentiment spoke to the tensions between the provinces and the capital. By the end of 1978, the number of Vietnamese on Pulau Bidong hovered between 30,000 and 40,000 people, making the island the second largest "city" in the region.[55]

Pulau Bidong was overcrowded and full of stink, shit, and garbage. Fresh water was in short supply, and sewage facilities were a constant problem. American officials noted the open sewers and trench latrines, and rats were endemic within the camp. One described the camp thus: "After a week of heavy monsoon rain and cold winds, large areas of the camp are mired in mud. Human excrement and trash are strewn throughout the camp attracting swarms of flies. Three to four thousand recent arrivals are sleeping on the beach with little shelter and no sanitary facilities."[56] A reporter emphasized the polythene plastic that served for shelter and the omnipresence of nasty odors and black flies that never left the compound.[57] Thousands of rats

FIGURE 6. This image captures the makeshift camps' high density and the ubiquitous plastic tarps used for shelter on Pulau Bidong. *Mastika,* August 1979. Courtesy of Utusan Melayu (M) Bhd.

invaded the island, and the MRCS sponsored rat-killing contests. During a ten-day campaign, the Vietnamese killed more than 14,000 rats, with an eleven-year-old winning a special prize for killing the most (205).[58] There was also a "Monkey House," or jail, for "troublemakers," who could be imprisoned without trial in this extra-judicial space. Despite the filth, the Vietnamese organized themselves and tried to minimize the stench and sanitation risks. They elected camp leaders, developed communication networks, and went about making the camp more livable by conserving kerosene, digging pit latrines, and discouraging people from defecating on the beaches.[59] The UNHCR and Malaysian officials encouraged Vietnamese self-management, since it added to camp security and organization without additional costs.

For Vietnamese, Pulau Bidong was a place of limbo, a way station to endure before final resettlement in a third country. In memoirs and oral histories, Vietnamese pointed to the harsh juxtaposition between the camp's crowded and filthy conditions and the lush tropical setting. Similar to younger people's positive memories of Guam's beaches and unstructured days, Vietnamese could also view Pulau Bidong as a place of beauty. This stood in sharp contrast to its reputation as an overcrowded slum. For example, Thuy Trang Lai recalled, "I was now on the beautiful Pulau Bidong island, with its lush tropical trees, white sand beach, and blue sea. Also hundreds of huts made from tree branches, plastic sheets and palm leaves. The beautiful environment, the stillness of the Malaysian island and the heavy monsoon rain triggered me into the reality that I was in a foreign place far, far away from my family."[60] In her oral history, shared with Carina Hoang,

Thuy Trang Lai intermingled her memories of swimming and exploring Pulau Bidong's mountains with the ubiquitous plastic tarps and makeshift huts. Vietnamese often lived under blue plastic tarps, while others went to the hills and constructed temporary shelters, the luckiest, those with access to gold, bought sturdier houses from those who were leaving.

Oral histories also noted the development of an informal economy within the camp, which relied on entrepreneurship and a black market. Thai Quoc Ha described the island as a beautiful place with an active cultural and economic life: "You know the most amazing thing is how a culture formed on that isolated island. You can see it right in front of your eyes because I came to Pulau Bidong in November 1978, one of the very first people there. So actually when we came to Pulau Bidong, the beachfront was pretty much empty. So we chose our spot and built our things, and it just got more and more people. And throughout the months, you see the formation of the local market. We saw the formations of *mấy cái quán cà-phê* [some coffee shops], and *văn nghệ buổi tối* [cultural productions in the evening] and the whole thing. It was really, really amazing."[61] Thai Quoc Ha's account is fairly romantic and starry eyed, but he was not wrong that the island's economy was key. Vietnamese established small shops and cafes within the camp, and there was a robust and clandestine black market, which the UNHCR and Malaysian police did their best to control.

The UNHCR channeled most of its resources to the MRCS, which was the principal organization caring for and managing the camps. The MRCS did its best to provide food, shelter, and basic services, becoming the best-known voluntary organization in Malaysia. When Vietnamese thanked Malaysia for providing shelter, they directed many of their words of gratitude to the MRCS. A Vietnamese camp leader wrote, "We would also like to take this opportunity to express to you—chairman and officers of MRCS. The deepest gratitude of the Vietnamese who have risked everything to escape from the cruelty of the inhuman communist prison, who have been rescued and well taken care of materially as well as spiritually by you. The image of officers in shirts printed with a Red Crescent is so familiar and dear to us."[62] One of the most valuable services the MRCS provided was "tracking" family members and distributing remittances. This was a time-intensive process, and remarkably successful. Overseas relatives would write to the MRCS, searching for family members they hoped had escaped and reached safety. The MRCS would send field officers into the camps and track down recent Vietnamese arrivals, finding them for their family members in the United

States, Canada, Australia, and other resettlement countries. Reuniting these families was one of the MRCS's most tangible successes. Once reconnected, the overseas families would send remittances and often sponsor their relatives, and the MRCS would facilitate these exchanges.[63]

The MRCS also provided basic foodstuffs, such as rice, cooking oil, and sardines to the Vietnamese waiting in the camps. To do this it needed local support and supplies. It hired fishermen to courier food and water back and forth to Pulau Bidong (work which often paid more than their regular fishing). It also bought fresh food and building supplies from local farmers and companies to supply the rations needed for the tens of thousands of Vietnamese on Pulau Bidong. As a result, money flowed into the Terengganu region, and many businesses and farmers had the chance to profit. However, others complained that the MRCS and UNHCR contracted with suppliers from regions further afield, or even from Thailand, and people in Terengganu pointed to the sharp spike in local prices, particularly for beef.[64] In conversations in Terengganu, older fishermen told me that they remembered friends clandestinely going to Pulau Bidong to sell fresh fish at inflated prices. Fishermen would anchor their boats near the island, and Vietnamese would meet them in the water. Swimming in the dark, they would exchange fresh produce for Vietnamese gold. The Malaysian police actively arrested and even shot at these black market fishermen, but to many, it seemed worth the risk. They could earn 500 percent above the market price.[65] One Malaysian politician argued that the inflated prices were hurting the people of Terengganu, where prices of essential commodities had more than doubled since the landings began: "A kati of certain fish which used to cost 60 cents is being sold to the boat people for $1.80 thus automatically pushing up prices of the local population. Even a box of matches which should cost five cents is being sold to the Vn for fifty cents."[66] The black market signaled the inability of the UNHCR and the Malaysian government to fully control the perimeter of the island.[67] Conversely, it also revealed daily, and clandestine, interactions between Malaysians in Terengganu and Vietnamese in Pulau Bidong. While the government worked to ensure the two populations remained separate, placing the camp on an isolated island far from shore, even there, commerce continued, and with it an unspoken, illicit partnership to reap fresh food and profit.

The black market also revealed an inverted hierarchy. While the Vietnamese were "illegal immigrants" to the Malaysians and "refugees" to the UNHCR, in both cases, they were designated as a population to be contained and cared for. And yet the Vietnamese were often wealthier than the rural people in Terengganu. Many Vietnamese who fled in 1978 and 1979 were from the professional classes and urban areas in southern Vietnam. A Vietnamese Buddhist nun explained she didn't resent the local bribes necessary to buy things on the black market, because "we knew they [the Malaysian police] were poor and needed the extra income."[68] Tran T.D. also expressed sympathy for the Malaysian guards and officials, recognizing the difficulty of controlling the black market and negotiating between the Malaysian population and the international actors. Despite some frustrations, he noted, "I had no complaints about my life. Malaysian officials and policemen seemed to be willing to help us, but we had to understand that the refugee problem was very delicate and difficult for them to handle, and we couldn't have all that we wanted or needed."[69]

The UNHCR paid the bills, contributing millions of dollars to the Malaysian government and MRCS for the well-being of the Vietnamese, but it also ceded control of the camp's daily operations. UNHCR officers who wanted to visit Pulau Bidong, negotiate with Terengganu security officials, or influence national policy had to tread lightly. Malaysia, a former colony, was now a sovereign state, and it guarded its independence and autonomy. As the high commissioner explained, "By itself the UNHCR can neither grant asylum, nor provide resettlement, nor any durable solution." It was only through consultations, meetings, international conferences, and regional agreements that the UNHCR could set the groundwork for humanitarian policies.[70] The UNHCR was in a precarious position, needing to coax the Malaysian government to provide refuge to more and more people, but with few incentives available to persuade Malaysia to cooperate.

This was the UNHCR's first major involvement with an Asian refugee crisis, and it risked its credibility and prestige to protect the Vietnamese. As Gil Loescher, the leading historian of the UNHCR, wrote, the 1978–1979 Southeast Asian crisis created a "seemingly endless international commitment," which would "dominate the attention and resources of the UNHCR until the mid-1990s."[71] The UNHCR's chief goal was to provide first asylum to the Vietnamese and basic living conditions as they waited for relocation to western resettlement countries. It opposed all push-offs, and its goal was to rescue and support the thousands of Vietnamese taking to the seas.[72] The UNHCR had a very small staff in Malaysia, and it needed the government's cooperation at every turn. It deemed its mission a mixed success. While it funded the MRCS and provided millions of dollars in support, the Malaysian government still towed away or pushed off hundreds of boats.[73] The UNHCR had failed to compel the Malaysian government to protect all incoming Vietnamese, and it realized that most of its power came through moral persuasion and the imprimatur of the United Nations.

U.S. officials routinely complained that the UNHCR did not have the personnel or political strength to enact its programs, and they were incensed at the latitude granted Malaysian politicians and security guards to "shoo off" Vietnamese with impunity. Americans also criticized the "intolerable conditions" in the camps and the UNHCR's inability to manage the "deteriorating" situation.[74] In 1978, a U.S. official damned the UNHCR in Malaysia as stretched too thin and barely competent: "UNHCR does not have a single officer on East Coast with knowledge of basic community development and public health techniques necessary to facilitate orderly transition of large numbers of disorganized refugees into a viable camp community. Even the regularly assigned Terengganu UNHCR sub-office chief is now on much-needed leave to Switzerland, and his replacement is quite inexperienced. . . . Clearly the UNHCR personnel in region are simply spread too thinly." The U.S. took a dig at the staff and urged the UNHCR to hire "competent" officials. At the same time, the United States recognized the overwhelming scope of the situation, noting that the UNHCR was "creaking with overload."[75]

Vietnamese within the camps believed that the Malaysian, UNHCR, and U.S. officials were all playing politics with their lives as more and more people waited in places like Pulau Bidong. As one Vietnamese recalled, "Many people had an unfounded fear that the island [Bidong] would sink into the sea, and disappear completely with the weight of all the people. I felt as if the planet had stopped, and had forgotten about us. Yet nothing happened, we weren't cast off the island, for as my husband said, the Malaysians were only playing a psychological game to pressure other counties, when they said they would send the refugees back to sea."[76] At the time, gratitude was generally reserved for the MRCS, which provided direct aid and served the important function of finding family members.[77] For Vietnamese who made it ashore and to a camp within Malaysia, the best strategy was to navigate the interview process and wait for resettlement. Most hoped to resettle in the United States.

The United States wanted Malaysia to accept all the incoming Vietnamese and for the UNHCR to provide the bureaucratic infrastructure. However, this did not mean that the United States agreed to resettle all the Vietnamese in the camps. The Malaysian government questioned the United States' commitment to human rights and resettlement of non-white Asian migrants. Malaysian political scientist Zakaria Haji Ahmad wrote in 1979, "The United States, contrary to all its rhetoric about human rights, seems to have been shuffling its feet with regard to the resettlement of the refugees. The U.S. policy seems to be rather ethnocentric. If the Vietnamese had been or are Europeans and other Caucasians or Jewish, perhaps countries like Malaysia would not have refugee problems of the present magnitude on their hands."[78] To the Malaysian government, this was the rub.

HUMANITARIANISM DEBATED: THE U.S. CONGRESS, NGO ACTIVISM, AND MALAYSIAN UNILATERALISM

In 1979, a bipartisan U.S. congressional delegation traveled to Malaysia for a first-hand fact-finding mission. For many in Congress, a sense of obligation to South Vietnam outlived the country's legal existence, and Hanoi was the clear enemy, profiting from the large bribes and exit fees extorted from those who fled. This bipartisan bunch included Hamilton Fish (R-NY), Billy Lee Evans (D-GA), Elizabeth Holtzman (D-NY), Henry Hyde (R-IL), Robert Dornan (R-CA), and Richard Kelly (R-FL). Representative Fish chastised the Hanoi government for racketeering in refugees. He supported new legislation which would increase the numbers of Vietnamese the United States could admit each year, numbers well over the 1965 Immigration Act quotas.[79]

Anti-war congress members like Representative Holtzman shared Fish's sense of urgency and commitment to the Vietnamese. Holtzman had been elected in 1972 as one of the youngest Democratic representatives in Congress after Watergate. Holtzman became a fierce presence early on, opposing the U.S. war in Vietnam and U.S. policies in Latin America and using the language of human rights to condemn former and current U.S. allies in Southeast Asia and the western hemisphere.[80] In Pulau Bidong, Holtzman turned her fury on both the UNHCR and Malaysia, calling conditions in the camps "deplorable." She saw "some 30,000 neglected refugees living on survival rations without medicine or milk. Over 70% of the children were suffering from scabies. There was a shortage of drinking water and no water was available for washing." She added that the UNHCR was understaffed, boats broke down regularly between Terengganu and Bidong, and the camps offered a quality of life far below the local Malaysian standards.[81] Holtzman also pointed to the specific anti-Chinese prejudice within the Malaysian government, which resulted in its seeing the incoming Vietnamese as "garbage." Holtzman believed U.S. diplomats in Kuala Lumpur needed to be more aggressive and convince Malaysian leaders to cut the "red tape" and improve conditions. She also faulted the UNHCR's inadequate accounting systems, and she feared that the U.S. was not getting its "money's worth" for all its contributions. Finally, the State Department needed to take a firmer stance, "internationalize the problem," and make other countries like Australia, Great Britain, and Japan carry more of the financial and resettlement burden.[82] Resettling the Vietnamese could not be solely on the Americans.

The congressional delegation's visit magnified the tensions between the United States and the UNHCR. The U.S. representatives repeatedly argued that the UNHCR's staffing was too sparse and it was unable to monitor the worsening situation in Malaysia, while the UNHCR charged that the United States was not resettling Vietnamese fast enough and sloughing off the problem on other donor states. While both were committed to a politics of humanitarianism, each felt as if it was left holding the ball.

Just as the UNHCR struggled with an immense mandate and limited resources, the United States also found itself in a compromised position. It was ideologically committed to providing refuge to the Vietnamese, and it blamed Hanoi for the root cause of the exodus, but it did not want responsibility for resettling everyone in the camps. Congress members feared the political fallout at home if they could not "show that the world community is assuming a greater share of these burdens."[83] The United States wanted Canada, Australia, the U.K., and Japan to assist with resettlement in greater numbers. The trick was how to get them to do so. To further complicate matters, unlike the case with Guam in 1975, the United States could not dictate Malaysia's policies. U.S. diplomats admitted that the Malaysian government is as "sensitive as we are to the humanitarian issues involved, but they will become increasingly restive with United States and/or UNHCR pressure to do more on caring and feeding of refugees as long as they believe the international community's response on resettlement remains inadequate."[84] U.S. officials were not wrong in this assessment. The Malaysian government was increasingly frustrated with the United States. The United States insisted on a lengthy interview process within the camps and then selected Vietnamese for resettlement based on their previous relationships with the U.S. military and government in South Vietnam. To many, this seemed far more like a standard immigration procedure than a refugee resettlement program based on desperation and fear of persecution.

The U.S. government agreed to admit an additional 25,000 Vietnamese and Cambodians in June 1978, and it upped the number to over 45,000 by the end of the year.[85] The U.S. sent immigration officers to Pulau Bidong and other Southeast Asian camps to interview Vietnamese and select the ones for resettlement.[86] Vietnamese who arrived in Malaysia first registered with the UNHCR. Next, the United States required a three-tier interview procedure, with each case investigated by a Joint Voluntary Agency officer (typically someone from a non-governmental agency that helped shepherd cases and locate sponsors); a State Department refugee officer; and finally, an Immigration and Naturalization Services (INS) officer, who made the ultimate determination.[87] There were a finite number of spots. The U.S. government created a priority system, with Category One reserved for those with close relatives already in the United States, Category Two for former employees of the U.S. government, and Category Three for those "closely associated with U.S. policies or programs," including the former South Vietnamese government or armed forces. There was also a Category Four for individuals who did not fall into Categories One through Three and had not been accepted by a third country but still had "obvious compelling reasons" for humanitarian parole.[88] In general, the Joint Voluntary Agency workers were the most sympathetic, helping guide Vietnamese through the system and find placements, while the INS acted as gatekeepers. As early as 1978, the United States used the word "screening" to describe the interviews.[89] This would become much more controversial after 1989, but at this juncture, the UNHCR promised that all the Vietnamese would be treated as refugees and resettled in a third country. The question would be which one and when.

Like Malaysian politicians, President Carter faced domestic flak for letting in more Vietnamese during a time of economic crisis, but Malaysia and the UNHCR both kept the pressure on the United States to expedite interviews and resettlement. The United States increased its quotas, but it never agreed to accept all the Vietnamese in the camps. As a result, the number of resettlements did not catch up with the number of incoming Vietnamese. There was a palpable fear that the camps might never be emptied.

Malaysian officials became increasingly nervous that the United States and international community did not have a plan. How long would Vietnamese be in Malaysia? Malaysian politicians questioned the United States' commitment to resettlement and latched on to President Carter's public identification with human rights. The United States might say it championed "human rights," but it only accepted "those refugees with families or those with qualifications which will enable them to earn a living in the United States." Malaysians resented this doublespeak. "In this light will Malaysia have to bear the burden of putting up the old and aged who can no longer work? . . . Where will these people go? Are we supposed to build old people's home for them? America does not want them. Neither Australia."[90] Home Minister Ghazali also noted the crossover between President Carter's rhetorical commitment to human rights and the expectations that the United States would resettle all the Vietnamese. As long as Carter "maintained his human rights campaign and promoted his country as 'the promised land,' Malaysia would continue to be 'bombarded' with this influx."[91] Malaysian politicians also charged that they received no credit for the support they were already providing. As the finance minister vented, "Not only are our humanitarian efforts not appreciated but countries [that] are not affected by the problem continue to criticize us for not taking in more illegal immigrants."[92]

This pressure precipitated some of Mahathir's more xenophobic and noxious language. He argued with venom that Malaysia did not have to accept Vietnamese indefinitely. Malaysia had already offered shelter to more than 100,000; there needed to be a limit. Minister Ghazali complained that the U.S. labeled the Vietnamese as "refugees" in one breath while enforcing normal immigration procedures in the next. He argued, "If they are really refugees, why are these Vietnamese being subjected to normal immigration procedures? Genuine refugees are accepted without condition, instead of being screened to see what abilities or special skills they have."[93] Although speaking in different registers, both Mahathir and Ghazali chafed at charges that Malaysia failed to act in a humanitarian way.

Perhaps the Malaysian government's most brazen claim was that the Vietnamese push-offs *were* humanitarian. Ghazali reiterated descriptions of the camps' horrific conditions as a reason to send the Vietnamese on to other shores. He explained, "The action taken against the illegal immigrants [Vietnamese], including driving them away, was based on law and on humanitarian grounds."[94] The Malaysian Navy was willing to help the Vietnamese, but not by providing refuge. Instead, the Malaysian patrols would fix Vietnamese boats, ensure they were seaworthy, and then send them on their way: "It is not our intention that these boat people should perish. It is also on humanitarian considerations that we were unable to accommodate them in our overcrowded camps. . . . As the boat was in good condition and had adequate provisions, it was requested to leave Malaysian waters and proceed with its journey."[95] This was the fate of hundreds of boats in 1978 and 1979. To most outside Malaysia, these push-offs were the antithesis of humanitarian action. Ghazali's linguistic machinations reveal the Malaysian government's frustration and the very malleability of the language of humanitarianism.

To Malaysian politicians, the UNHCR and United States were offering up a double standard, one whereby the United States could pick and choose its refugees while Malaysia was required to offer asylum to all without a foreseeable end. Calls for humanitarian actions by the UNHCR and the United States seemed to be just another reiteration of colonial structures and legacies. The UN and the U.S. called for the Malaysian government and population to be patient and to provide refuge and care even as western nations were selective and slow (at least in Malaysian eyes) in their resettlement processes. Although not explicitly, this language of humanitarianism harked back to a colonial era when Europeans rescued Christian minorities from persecution and travails in the Ottoman Empire. With tens of thousands of Vietnamese on its shores and the MRCS working full force, the Malaysian government resented being seen as somehow outside the humanitarian circle. It also feared that without pressure, the U.S. would abdicate its responsibility, and Malaysia would be stuck with thousands of people it didn't want and who frankly didn't want to be there.

Moreover, the Malaysian government insisted it did provide resettlement and refuge. First, it resettled 1,500 Muslim Cham from Cambodia in the 1970s.[96] Second, and with greater demographic consequences, it also welcomed more than 90,000 Filipinos who were fleeing the wars in the southern Philippines, permitting them to resettle in the eastern province of Sabah. In 1972, Ferdinand Marcos's government proclaimed martial law as a necessary measure to combat a "secessionist" movement in the southern Philippine islands. Rather than creating order or quelling dissent, Marcos set the stage for greater domestic violence, particularly in Mindanao, and Philippine forces engaged in regular and active combat with what soon became the Moro National Liberation Front. The fighting in Mindanao was fierce. More than one million Filipinos were internally displaced by the violence between 1972 and 1977. Filipino Muslim civilians remembered the war as "one of acute loss"; they had been forced to leave their land and their farm animals (hence their livelihoods), and almost all had lost a close relative to the violence.[97] Between 90,000 and 150,000 Filipinos fled and relocated to Sabah.

Within less than a decade, Filipinos accounted for 10 to 20 percent of Sabah's population.

Unlike the Vietnamese in peninsular Malaysia, the state government in Sabah did not push off the Filipinos, but rather allowed them to remain. Malaysia did not formally categorize them as refugees, but in every UNHCR report from Malaysia, UNHCR officials counted the Filipinos as the second major refugee population they were monitoring, after the Vietnamese. UNHCR dollars assisted in building housing and roads, providing job training, and helping the Filipinos establish small businesses.[98] Filipinos gained working papers in Sabah, and no efforts were made to deport or repatriate them. The Malaysian government generally viewed Muslim Filipinos as religiously and culturally akin to *bumiputeras*. Sabah was distinct from peninsular Malaysia, and the ruling party had to compete with indigenous non-Muslim ethnic groups. By permitting the Filipinos to stay, it arguably hoped to consolidate the ruling Muslim political party in Sabah.[99]

On the international stage, the Malaysian government pointed to the Filipinos as another concrete example of its humanitarian practices. At a United Nations meeting in December 1978, Minister Ghazali spoke out for greater international support and sympathy for Malaysia, which had accepted an unprecedented number of Vietnamese. Malaysia needed western resettlement countries to take the lead, and fast. However, he prefaced his comments by noting that "it was also important not to forget other and earlier groups of refugees in South East Asia, particularly . . . the group of 90,000 refugees in Sabah who retained the hope of returning one day to their homeland, once conditions were favorable."[100] Likewise, the Malaysian ambassador in Thailand explained, "It cannot be said that Malaysia has not been responsive to the plight of refugees." He added, "We have accepted as genuine refugees nearly 100,000 persons who are now being resettled in various parts of Malaysia. . . . We have done more than our share in shouldering the burden of the refugee problems."[101] Both were speaking of the Filipinos who fled the conflict in Mindanao and Marcos's authoritarian government. The government officials emphasized that Malaysia's policies toward the Filipinos in Sabah were largely unheralded by the international community.

By 1979, the Malaysian government had little patience for what it saw as the limited nature of the United States' commitment to humanitarianism. As the host country with the largest Vietnamese population, Malaysia was not content to acquiesce to U.S. desires. Through harsh policies, push-offs, and increasingly hostile language, it signaled its unwillingness to cooperate with the UNHCR and United States unless new guarantees were put in place. Malaysia would be in control of its borders, its territory, and its own humanitarian policy.

GENEVA, 1979: INTERNATIONAL CONFERENCE ON INDOCHINESE REFUGEES

Mahathir's 1979 "shooting" comment was interpreted by almost all observers to be intentionally provocative and a play to force international action. Thailand and Hong Kong were also at tipping points; Thailand was pushing people back, and Hong Kong believed it was overburdened with incoming Vietnamese. On June 17, 1979, British Prime Minister Margaret Thatcher wrote a terse letter to the UNHCR, pointing to the detrimental consequences of long-term camps in Hong Kong and calling for an international conference to end the crisis.[102] The United Nations responded, and the result was the 1979 International Conference on Indochinese Refugees, the largest international conference to date on Southeast Asian refugees. Although there had been several international meetings prior to this one, the July 1979 meeting in Geneva succeeded in creating a new framework which would hold for the next decade. It brought together representatives from first-asylum, resettlement, and donor countries and, importantly, Vietnam itself. More than sixty-five governments met in Geneva over July 20 and 21, and the goal was a regional solution which would reduce the burden on Southeast Asian partners and develop funding streams and resettlement placements from wealthier countries.[103] With the memory of refugees in Europe and the Holocaust still in living memory, the conference pitted competing claims to humanitarianism against each other, while Vietnamese in the diaspora began to harness the language of human rights as an increasingly effective tool.

Going into the conference, the Malaysian media was skeptical that European leaders recognized the burdens on their peninsula and bristled at criticisms aimed at the country's presumed lack of humanitarian values. One journalist expressed little patience for a European lecture on how Malaysians could improve their humanitarian credentials: "If the Geneva conference turned out to be a lecture on humanitarian principles (for Malaysia) and asking us to do exactly the things which I ask them (the resettlement countries) to do . . . and they are unwilling to do, then I shall tell them to jump."[104] In fact, he continued, if the west was serious about humanitarianism, it would accept all the Vietnamese, without screening, selection, or interviews. Home Minister Ghazali concurred that it was western nations, not Malaysia, that were wanting in humanitarian actions: "This [the selection process] is why the camps are packed and this is what has led me to assume that Western countries are not genuine in their humanitarian outlook but are only looking at their own national interests."[105] Ghazali did not want to be "rude" to the Americans in Geneva, but he had in fact lost patience.[106] "The Geneva conference has helped us make the point that it is not we who are responsible for our shooing policy. It is those who are unable or unwilling to give us a guarantee that temporary asylum means temporary asylum."[107] Malaysia had already fulfilled its humanitarian responsibilities, and it was time for the UNHCR and the west to step it up.

The UNHCR succeeded in getting the parties to the table, and because of much preliminary work, the conference succeeded in brokering a deal. First, Vietnam agreed to prevent boat departures, and most importantly it agreed to stop enabling large numbers of Chinese Vietnamese to leave. By closing the proverbial doors, Vietnam tacitly admitted it had encouraged the exodus. It also agreed to stop the wholesale selling of exit visas and the collection of bribes, which had profited the new government and rid it of a potentially disruptive population. Vietnam also agreed to the establishment of an Orderly Departure Program so Vietnamese could apply to leave Vietnam from within the country rather than risking their lives at sea. This mechanism was fairly limited in the early 1980s, but later in the decade it would become a significant pathway for Vietnamese still in Vietnam to apply for resettlement in the United States.[108] Second, the United States agreed to double the number of Vietnamese it would admit from 7,000 to 14,000 a month, for a total of 168,000 people a year. This enabled a faster rate of resettlement and spurred Canada, Australia, France, Germany, and Great Britain to raise their quotas too.[109] Third, the UNHCR secured agreements from first-asylum countries like Malaysia to respect the principle of first asylum. The UNHCR wanted guarantees that Thailand, Indonesia, Malaysia, Hong Kong, and the Philippines would not push off boats. It promised these countries it would find final placements in third countries outside Southeast Asia for all the Vietnamese. While Malaysia and other first-asylum countries still hedged, continuing to assert that their generosity was temporary and voluntary, the 1979 conference effectively maintained Malaysia's commitment to the principle of first asylum and minimized the push-offs, although it did not eliminate them altogether.[110]

Western nations like the United States also looked at the Geneva conference as an opportunity to take a meaningful stand for humanitarian protection, albeit on their own terms. In the 1970s, several U.S. leaders invoked the specter of the Holocaust and America's failure to protect Jews fleeing from Nazi Germany as a clear precedent to the situation in Vietnam.[111] Rather than compare the Vietnamese to the Cubans who fled that country following Fidel Castro's rise to power (and who also defined themselves through anti-communism), Vice President Walter Mondale compared them to European Jews. In his opening remarks in Geneva, he cited the 1938 Evian conference, at which Europe and the United States "failed the test of civilization."[112] Notably, Israeli Prime Minister Menachem Begin extended this analogy with World War II Europe, but he did so to critique the Geneva conference. He argued that past conferences, like Evian, had been stalling measures. He demanded immediate action for the Vietnamese: "The Government of Malaysia has publicly declared its intention to expel them [the Vietnamese] to the open sea, where they face the peril of drowning or death by exposure. This horrific tragedy must be prevented in this, our generation of the Holocaust. I respectfully submit to you that such a Conference would be an exercise in futility. As a Jew, I cannot forget the useless Conferences at Evian and Bermuda whose end results were the non-saving of even one Jewish child out of the one and a half million Jewish children who were dragged to a wanton death."[113] Begin dismissed the value of Geneva and offered up an additional two-hundred resettlement placements in Israel.

The Palestine Liberation Organization (PLO) lashed out at Israel, accusing it of hypocrisy for making grand presentations on the humanitarian issues at stake for Vietnamese while refusing to admit the tragic scope and violation of Palestinian territorial rights. The PLO's anger was twofold. First, it turned its ire against the UNHCR for prioritizing Vietnamese above Palestinians and once again delaying the Palestinian question for another day. Second, it offered a scathing critique of Israel's refugee policy as "a cynical and blatant propaganda gesture on the part of a state, which deliberately caused the exodus of hundreds and thousands of persons out of their homeland."[114] As scholar Evyn Espiritu has noted, refugee politics registered in Israel and Palestine in a particularly pointed way, as Israel lauded its welcoming of Vietnamese even as Palestinians lived at best as second-class citizens, in camps or under occupation.[115] In an even more fraught example, a Singaporean suggested that a deserted Pacific island be repurposed as a Vietnamese resettlement camp. Far from the PLO's critiques, he romanticized

Israel's origins and asked, "If the Israelis could transform arid deserts into thriving communities, there is no reason why the idea of settling these unfortunate people on an uninhabited island in the Pacific could not be made a living reality."[116] If Israel could work, why not Wake Island or Midway Atoll? In all these disparate cases, the politics of the Holocaust, World War II, and Israel's nationhood shaped the international discussion over refugee policy and humanitarianism a generation later.

With the convening of the 1979 Geneva conference, Vietnamese in the diaspora also entered as active players with their own vision of human rights and humanitarianism. In 1979, most Vietnamese looked to the UNHCR as a protector and ally. In letters to the UNHCR and U.S. officials, Vietnamese Americans thanked the UNHCR and the United States. For example, a group of "Free Vietnamese" in Hawai'i came together and wrote to the UNHCR and "prayed for its success" in its humanitarian mission. This group did not condemn Malaysia, but rather cast its anger firmly against Hanoi. It hoped Vietnam would solve the "refugee problem" at "its fundamental level."[117] However, there was a significant divide between the UNHCR and many Vietnamese Americans over whether to even include Hanoi in the conference. The UNHCR believed Hanoi's involvement was essential. It needed to work with the Vietnamese government to control its borders and stop the mass numbers leaving, who were doing so with tacit if not official permission. The Vietnamese government's participation was essential to the three-legged stool that made up the Geneva conference agreements: stem the tide from Vietnam, offer first asylum in Southeast Asian camps, and secure resettlement placements in the west. Without cooperation from the Vietnamese government, the UNHCR believed it would not get cooperation from the first-asylum countries.

In contrast, many Vietnamese in the diaspora protested any rapprochement with Vietnam, and they did so through the language of human rights. Front and center in this discourse was a denunciation of Hanoi and the communist government. As one man wrote in French, to invite Hanoi was like inviting the oppressors to speak for the oppressed.[118] Another group of Vietnamese, resettled in Orange County in Southern California, wrote to the UNHCR right before the opening of the conference. Recognizing an international audience, they too called on the example of the Holocaust to give weight to their claims—"We are grateful for your effort to save Indochinese refugees"—however, this language of gratitude quickly morphed into fury at Hanoi and the inconceivability of it being part of the

FIGURE 7. Vietnamese in the diaspora demonstrate support for the 1979 UNHCR Geneva conference. Their banner reads, "Let us pray for the success of the United Nations conference on refugees in its humanitarian mission." Many of the individuals are waving the flag of the Republic of Vietnam (the South Vietnamese flag). UNHCR Archives, Fonds 11, Series 2, 391.39, Volume 3.

international conversation: "*but!!!* . . . As long as the present mad rulers in Hanoi stay in power the Indochinese exodus will continue just like the Jewish holocaust ended only after the fall of Hitler. We need help in ridding our homeland of the criminals who are as vicious and coldblooded as any Nazi storm-trooper. Indochina presently is just a vast prison, and human being[s] [are] treated as animals. If these atrocities continue we expect millions people are going to die."[119] Vietnamese new to the United States were strong in their emotions and joined the political fray. Their letters speak to the balancing act of supporting the UNHCR's mandate in Southeast Asia and condemning Hanoi. They hoped refuge and rescue could be achieved for Vietnamese still trapped in Vietnam and Southeast Asian camps without giving legitimacy to the Vietnamese government.

Vietnamese activists also landed on the language of human rights as a way to reach an international audience and lobby the UNHCR and the U.S. government. They drew on the legibility and credibility of American anti-war protesters. Anti-war activists such as Joan Baez, Ed Asner, Cesar Chavez, and Norman Lear joined Vietnamese Americans in condemning Hanoi. In a large published advertisement, with Baez's name prominently displayed, the signatories attested that "it was an abiding commitment to fundamental principles of human dignity, freedom, and self-determination that motivated so many Americans to oppose the government of South Vietnam and our country's participation in the war. It is that same commitment that compels us to speak out against your [the Socialist Republic of Vietnam's] brutal disregard for human rights. As in the 60s we raise our voices now so that your people may live."[120] The ad showcased the names of many prominent American liberals and leftists, but the handwritten, unpublished petition that accompanied it in the UNHCR archives included a long list of Vietnamese names. Many Vietnamese Americans might have distinguished themselves from anti-war protesters, arguing for the righteousness of the South Vietnamese cause, but here, they ignored their differences. To speak to an international and American audience as well as a Vietnamese one, former opponents of the war provided even greater justification of the Vietnamese Americans' claims of human rights abuses.

In still other instances, diasporic groups called for human rights and humanitarianism in the same breath. A group of Vietnamese Americans in Portland, Oregon, wrote a collective letter to the UNHCR calling on the United Nations to punish Hanoi for its policy of "discrimination and oppression." Pointing to specific examples of imprisonment and torture, the letter writers called out Hanoi for violating human rights. At the same time, the Vietnamese American organization urged, "The free countries who had been allies of South Vietnam for 20 years should, for humanitarian reasons, provide resettlement to the refugees."[121] The letter writers easily moved from the U.S. support of South Vietnam to the United States' responsibility to resettle Vietnamese stranded in Southeast Asian camps. The language of humanitarianism, allying itself with protection, lay side by side the eviscerations of Hanoi's postwar policies and Vietnamese Americans' claim to human rights.

The diasporic population's ability to wield this language would grow over time as Vietnamese Americans developed domestic and transnational organizations. In the wake of the 1979 conference, the Indochina Refugee Action Center (IRAC) became one of the first nationally focused nonprofit organizations with Vietnamese American leadership.[122] Starting out as a refugee advocacy, support, and networking organization, IRAC sought out leadership among recently resettled Vietnamese, Cambodians, and Laotians in the United States. It supported Mutual Assistance Associations and the inclusion of Vietnamese Americans in the resettlement process. A former professor from the University of Saigon, Le Xuan Khoa, came to the United States in 1975 and rose through the ranks to become IRAC's executive director in the early 1980s. He explained that IRAC was an "advocacy group working closely with policy makers in the areas of refugee protection, admission numbers and budget for refugee resettlement." Over the years, he worked closely with the State Department and U.S. Congress members on humane and durable solutions to refugee crisis situations.[123]

Just one of many Vietnamese American organizations that would grow in the 1980s, IRAC became a close partner with the UNHCR in the late 1980s and early 1990s. Growing out of the 1979 conference and intimately tied to refugee resettlement programs throughout the country, Le Xuan Khoa stood apart from many of the Vietnamese activists who wished to isolate Hanoi. Instead, he reflected, "I realized that the refugee problem could not be resolved merely by humanitarian assistance. There must be a political solution. You need to deal with the root cause, and that's in Vietnam. After the border war with China in 1979, Vietnam felt strongly that it needed to normalize relations with the United States." Le Xuan Khoa believed that Hanoi used the refugees as political pawns to gain leverage with the United States. He explained it was necessary for IRAC to try and "influence both governments with a dual approach: increasing admission numbers to the U.S. and improving human rights conditions in Vietnam."[124]

While IRAC did not play a role in the 1979 conference, it would become an important political player in the years ahead. Looking at the desperation, fear, and uncertainty in the camps, many Vietnamese Americans identified with those in limbo, and they wanted to do more to help those seemingly stranded in Malaysia, Hong Kong, Indonesia, and Thailand. It was often just a matter of chance that separated those in the United States from those still fleeing Vietnam. In 1980, Nguyen Huu Xuong, a chemistry professor at the University of California, San Diego, founded Boat People SOS. This organization would grow and change significantly over the next decade, but in its original iteration, it raised money to fund rescue missions for Vietnamese boats at sea. As he explained, "Ninety percent of the Vietnamese people in the United States . . . are boat people themselves. . . . They want to do anything they can to help those people. They don't want the new people to suffer like they did before."[125] Over time, these organizations, including IRAC and Boat People SOS, would grow stronger and separate political strategies would emerge.

The result was a complex, and sometimes transnational, relationship between Vietnamese activism within the camps and U.S.-based Vietnamese organizations. Vietnamese Americans would learn how to influence U.S.

elected politicians, the State Department, and the UNHCR. In 1979, many Vietnamese Americans trusted the UNHCR and its commitment to humanitarian protection. However, as the years went by, many became skeptical, and even hostile, to the UNHCR's vision and policies, and they increasingly called on the language of human rights to express their displeasure.

The 1979 international conference did succeed in recalibrating the fine balance between the UNHCR, host countries like Malaysia, and the United States. Although there continued to be stories of push-offs from Malaysia, it agreed to remain a country of first asylum, and Pulau Bidong remained an active refugee camp through the early 1990s. A Malaysian diplomat explained it this way: "It is not a question of denying humanitarian rights. . . . In fact, we have not denied humanitarian rights."[126] Here was a neologism: "humanitarian rights." By merging human rights and humanitarianism, the Malaysian diplomat seemed to unconsciously create a new concept. In his pledge, he reaffirmed the Malaysian government's claim to be upholding humanitarian norms. However, he also demonstrated the way in which human rights and humanitarianism competed for attention in the late 1970s, and the multiple ways UNHCR officials, Malaysian and American politicians, and Vietnamese, in camps and in the diaspora, could interpret them.

A FRAGILE BALANCE

The 1979 Geneva conference succeeded in ensuring that all Vietnamese who sought first asylum would be treated as refugees, and that the UNHCR would guarantee them resettlement outside Southeast Asia. The 1979 conference put a deal in place. Malaysia, Thailand, Hong Kong, the Philippines, and Indonesia agreed in principle to offer first asylum; the U.S., Japan, and other western countries upped their contributions to the UNHCR; and the United States, Canada, Australia, the U.K., and northern European countries agreed to increase their resettlement numbers.[127] By 1980 there were 231,000 Vietnamese in the United States (a combination of the 1975 arrivals and those resettled from the camps).[128] From a perspective of protection and resettlement, the UNHCR had been able to work deftly with multiple actors and broker a regional solution.

For Malaysia, the 1979 agreement was a measured success and assertion of its sovereignty. On a certain level, it had pushed off and won. Malaysian officials held fast to their ability to define refugees and humanitarianism.

While horrifying Vietnamese Americans in the diaspora and frustrating UNHCR officials on multiple continents, Malaysian politicians like Mahathir Mohamad and Ghazali Shafie insisted the country *did* enact humanitarian policies. While no one else saw the push-offs as humanitarian, Malaysia argued it had the right to control its own borders and that it could not pile more people into its already overcrowded camps. Malaysian officials insisted that this would be a violation of humanitarian practice. Malaysian politicians argued that the Vietnamese crisis had pressed the government far past any reasonable humanitarian obligations or expectations, and they challenged any western nation to act in a more humane manner. While not always explicit, Malaysia's refusal simply to acquiesce to the UNHCR's mandate spoke to humanitarianism's longer history of colonial legacies and European roots. Malaysia would control its own borders.

At times, journalists and local officials also recast Vietnamese within the Malaysian racial landscape as Chinese Vietnamese and as potential communist infiltrators, speaking to the specificity of Malaysia's own Cold War politics. The government's insistence on classifying Vietnamese as illegal immigrants was an expression of public exasperation colored by both xenophobia and pragmatism. While the government ultimately treated all the incoming Vietnamese the same, regardless if they were Chinese Vietnamese or ethnic Vietnamese, these dynamics shaped national and local perceptions. More quietly, Malaysia defined Muslim Filipinos as worthy of rescue and resettlement. This was a case of Islamic solidarity and political opportunism, but one which deftly redefined humanitarianism and refugee politics on the Malaysian government's own terms.

Of all the nations involved, Vietnam pivoted the most, and its agreement to stop facilitating thousands of departures eased the crisis. Its willingness to change and compromise was intertwined with its own postwar goals of acquiring a seat in the United Nations, gaining recognition from the west, garnering support for its occupation of Cambodia, and minimizing diplomatic fallout from its war with China. With hundreds of thousands of Chinese Vietnamese already purged from its cities and northern regions, it was ready to cut a deal with the UNHCR and the ASEAN nations. Vietnam remained ideologically committed to the Communist Party and to its own independence, but in an age of détente and diplomatic rapprochement between the United State and China (and the U.S. and the Soviet Union), it was willing to work within an international framework. It also desperately hoped for U.S. dollars to stabilize its postwar economy.

Vietnamese in the United States also began to find their political voices. Through letters and petitions to the UNHCR and the U.S. government, Vietnamese Americans began what would be an almost three-decade-long campaign to support the refugee claims of Vietnamese and their quick resettlement in the west. Diasporic Vietnamese developed organizations through which they could pressure U.S. politicians and international entities like the UNHCR, and these would only grow in strength and diversity as the years progressed.

The United States also recalibrated its approach. With President Carter's agreement to accept more Vietnamese in 1979 and 1980, the United States accelerated its resettlement programs. The sense of emergency, ad hoc nature of refugee resettlement, and executive privilege also motivated legislators to write new laws governing refugee admissions. In 1980, Senator Edward Kennedy sponsored the Refugee Act, which regularized U.S. refugee policy and allowed a set number of refugees to enter the United States each year. This was Congress's way of claiming authority and oversight over U.S. immigration and refugee policy, and congress members like Elizabeth Holtzman fought to ensure the act did not equate refugee status with anti-communism. Holtzman also matched the humanitarian impulse of refugee protection with her commitment to human rights, and she insisted that the law's provisions excluded those who had committed atrocities and human rights abuses. However, implementation remained under the purview of the INS within the State Department—in other words, within the executive branch. The INS retained its preference system, which meant that the United States selected Vietnamese based on ideology and past relationships, rather than on their risk of immediate political persecution. Although the 1980 Refugee Act formally decoupled American refugee policy from the Cold War, in practice, Cold War prerogatives continued to drive admissions and status.[129]

The 1979 conference also established two new "processing centers," one on the island of Galang in Indonesia and a much larger camp in Bataan in the Philippines. The goal was to move people out of Malaysia and other first-asylum countries faster. After 1980, Vietnamese in first-asylum camps selected for resettlement in the United States (as well as much smaller numbers headed for Germany, and Norway) would next go to a processing center. Those headed for the U.S. would then take part in a six-month English language and cultural orientation program in Indonesia or the Philippines. Only then would they resettle in the United States. In addition, individuals who exited Vietnam directly through the Orderly Departure Program would also go to the processing center in the Philippines. Malaysia supported these provisions, but its officials worried about what would happen to the Vietnamese *not* selected by the United States. They also rightly saw this as U.S. immigration policy on the cheap. The *New Straits Times* tartly commented, "The United States has apparently taken the odd position that it will guarantee 'no residue' with regard to the proposed new Filipino resettlement centre, but not to Malaysia's camps. As cockeyed is the apparent U.S. view that among the important reasons why it could not agree to Malaysia's proposal for processing centres on American territory is because it would be ten to twenty times more expensive to process the boat people there than in Southeast Asian camps."[130]

The selection of the Philippines as a place for Vietnamese refugees mirrored and complicated the Malaysian government's own acceptance of Filipino refugees in Sabah. The Malaysian government and the UNHCR helped resettle this population, allowed the Filipinos to work, and generally encouraged their presence, as it reset the ethnic and political balance in this far eastern province. If Malaysia welcomed Filipinos as refugees in Sabah, the Philippines welcomed the Vietnamese in a designated camp meant to ease the burden on first-asylum countries. Many of those fleeing Southeast Asia in the 1980s would find themselves on an extended journey; the UNHCR and the United States required them to spend six months in the Philippines before they could go to the United States. The camp in Bataan would be a model camp.

THREE

A Model Camp

IN 1986, NGOC ESCAPED VIETNAM ON A FISHING BOAT with forty-four other individuals. Leaving Vietnam after the 1979 Geneva conference, he was guaranteed first asylum and resettlement if he succeeded in surviving at sea and reaching land in Southeast Asia. Ngoc was a thirty-five-year-old navigator, and presumably through his skills and good weather, his boat reached Malaysia. In Malaysia, Ngoc received protection, and like most, he was then transferred to the Philippine Refugee Processing Center (PRPC). Once there, he believed he was just a few months away from resettlement in the United States. The PRPC offered English and cultural orientation classes, and it was the final hurdle facing Vietnamese seeking a new home. However, Ngoc's journey hit a major obstacle. According to Ngoc, a fellow Vietnamese in the camp accused him of being a communist. This changed his fate and postponed his flight to America indefinitely. He expressed his despair and disbelief at the situation: "I have never been a communist. I despised the communist. That is why I left Vietnam. I am very, very sad." Stuck at the PRPC indefinitely, Ngoc found informal employment, establishing a coffee shop near his barracks and working for a Filipino money changer buying gold from other Vietnamese within the camp.[1]

Ngoc's story is elusive. There is no further record of the accusations made against him, their veracity, other charges, or whether he ultimately resettled in the United States or remained in the Philippines. It is also unusual. Vietnamese who made it to the PRPC were on their way to America. Very few found themselves trapped in limbo like Ngoc.[2] However, his story remains pertinent. The PRPC, for all its trappings of benevolence and its English-language classes, was still a space of transit. Vietnamese were not yet in the United States, and the PRPC remained a camp in between.

From 1980 through 1994, roughly 400,000 Vietnamese, Cambodians, Laotians, and Southeast Asian ethnic minorities passed through the Philippines before resettling in the United States.[3] The camp's tenure originated during Ferdinand Marcos's authoritarian, anti-democratic regime, and it spanned Corazon "Cory" Aquino's 1986 People Power victory, which ousted him from office. The camp remained in operation through the mid-1990s. Despite the cataclysmic changes in Philippine politics, both Filipino leaders believed the PRPC illustrated their commitment to humanitarianism.

On its face, the PRPC was a strange experiment. Almost every element of it seems curious.[4] It was not constructed in a moment of crisis like the camps on Guam or in Malaysia. Instead, the initial reason for the PRPC was to alleviate the crowding in the first-asylum camps. The idea was to move Vietnamese who had been accepted by a resettlement country out of Malaysia, Indonesia, Thailand, or Hong Kong more quickly and minimize the political pressures on these places by transferring people to the Philippines. However, as the number of Vietnamese subsided throughout the region and the Orderly Departure Program (ODP) accelerated, the PRPC reframed its mission and became a training or processing center, defined by English-language and American cultural orientation classes taught primarily by Filipinos. The vast majority of the Vietnamese would stay at the PRPC for roughly six months before proceeding to the United States.[5] Anthropologist Carol Mortland explained that the Philippine PRPC staff and the U.S. government found a common goal in providing cultural training classes *before* resettlement in the United States, hoping to "transform" the Vietnamese into good Americans.[6] The U.S. was far and away the largest donor to the UNHCR, and by all accounts, it was less expensive to provide these services in the Philippines than in the United States.

The PRPC was very much a way station, and this chapter too acts as something of an interlude, examining how the Philippines found opportunities to benefit from hosting the PRPC. During the 1980s, the 1979 Geneva conference agreements more or less held. There were fewer push-offs from first-asylum countries, the UNHCR guaranteed that all the Vietnamese would eventually be resettled, and the United States accepted significant numbers of people from Southeast Asia. The United States admitted 100,000 Southeast Asians in 1981, 64,000 in 1983, and 50,000 in 1984 through the 1980 Refugee Act.[7] Quite distinct from Guam, which had no choice but to accept thousands of incoming Vietnamese, and the Malaysian government, which resented the expectation that it would protect thousands more, the Marcos government found a sweet spot whereby the Philippines could placate U.S. interests *and* assert its sovereignty. The PRPC worked to the advantage of the Philippines, both for its national leaders, who wanted to improve the country's international reputation, and at the local level, for Filipino teachers and social workers who often found meaningful work and even friendship through the PRPC.

This was a time of significant domestic change in the Philippines, and the popular movement against Ferdinand Marcos dominated the mid-1980s. On the world stage, Prime Minister Margaret Thatcher in the United Kingdom and President Ronald Reagan in the United States reinvigorated classic Cold War divisions. Marcos's willingness to volunteer Philippine territory for the camp placed him staunchly on the side of the west. Vietnamese in the camps were assumed to be anti-communists, fleeing an oppressive state. They might wait months or years in a first-asylum camp, and when they had been accepted by a third country, they were transferred to the PRPC. The goal was then simply to wait and tolerate the time in the Philippines before starting their lives in the United States. Therefore Vietnamese protested far less at the PRPC than they did on Guam or they would in Hong Kong and other Southeast Asian camps after 1989. Instead, the most notable political activity emerged not from Vietnamese within the camp, but from Filipinos fighting against the Marcos regime outside the PRPC.

BATAAN: "A CITADEL OF PEACE"

In 1980, a Philippine promotional brochure heralded the opening of the Philippine Refugee Processing Center in Bataan, declaring, "Bataan, once a citadel of war, is now a citadel of peace." With this flourish, the Philippine government transformed a place defined by war and violence into a place of peace and a "balm" for the world's conscience.[8] The PRPC allowed President Ferdinand Marcos to project his government's humanitarian credentials at a time when he was under attack by domestic and international human rights critics. Marcos went so far as to appoint his wife, Imelda Marcos, as the formal head of the PRPC, closely identifying the success of the camp with his own family and political power. By protecting Vietnamese, the Marcos government aligned itself with humanitarianism and refugees and thereby downplayed its own internal repression and persecution of domestic critics.

This Philippine turn to humanitarianism was not new. U.S. and Filipino politicians and business boosters previously heralded "Operation Brotherhood," which sent thousands of Filipinos to South Vietnam. Historian Simeon Man argued that U.S. imperialism took advantage of Filipino "humanitarian and militarized labor" to showcase the possibility of beneficent American colonialism and legitimize the U.S. presence in Southeast Asia.[9] Geographer James Pangilinan offers another take. Pangilinan challenges historians to reimagine a Filipino ethos of humanitarianism that emphasized Catholic notions of care as an "alternative basis" for resistance, transnationalism, and asylum.[10] Unlike critics who view humanitarianism purely as a tool of empire, Pangilinan sees a generative possibility in humanitarianism and south-south solidarities that should not be rejected out of hand, but rather should be analyzed in specific settings, such as Philippine refugee camps. The tension between a cynical opportunistic humanitarianism and deeply felt notions of care persisted in the PRPC, where Marcos took advantage of the camp to minimize the concerns of human rights critics, even as local Filipino teachers and social workers developed deeper, often substantive relationships with Vietnamese waiting for resettlement.

During the 1979 Geneva conference, the Marcos government agreed to host a transit station for Southeast Asians en route to their final resettlement destinations. In doing so, it won kudos from the UNHCR and the United States for alleviating the burden on its Southeast Asian neighbors. UN Secretary-General Kurt Waldheim characterized the Philippine proposal as a "breakthrough," and Vice President Walter Mondale praised it for catching "the imagination of the world."[11] The Philippines initially offered a camp with a capacity for 7,000 residents, then quickly upped its offer to a 50,000-person facility. While the PRPC never reached this density, it processed approximately 400,000 people, with a peak population of 17,000 living at the camp at any one time. The United Nations agreed to provide a hundred percent of the funding for the camp and a guarantee that there would be no "residual problems," namely, unsettled Southeast Asians lingering in the Philippines.[12] The permanent resettlement of all refugees *outside* of the Philippines was the key international guarantee that secured the Marcos government's pledge. The Philippine government welcomed tens of thousands of Southeast Asians, as long as they promised not to stay.

The Philippines could afford to be more generous than its regional neighbors because the number of Vietnamese landing on its shores and requesting asylum was always significantly lower due to its distance from Vietnam. For example, from 1975 to 1997, approximately 51,000 Vietnamese sought refuge in the Philippines, compared with 254,000 in Malaysia.[13] For these individuals who came on rickety boats, the Philippines established a first-asylum camp on the island of Palawan (the subject of chapter 6). Palawan functioned much like the camps in Malaysia, Indonesia, Hong Kong, and Thailand; Vietnamese would wait there for an international placement, generally achieved through a process facilitated by the Joint Voluntary Agency and INS officials. Once they received a placement, they too would be transferred to the camp in Bataan.

At first glance, Ferdinand Marcos fit the mold of many U.S.-supported right-wing dictators during the Cold War. Like all such dictators, Marcos was never a puppet, and along with his wife, Imelda, he became a key client of U.S. military and economic aid. For the United States, his strident anticommunism and ability to project strength were more important than his proclamation of martial law and erasure of democratic government.[14] Marcos won the Philippine presidency in 1965, and he became the first reelected Philippine president in 1969.[15] He consolidated his power through appeals to populism, celebrity personalism, large-scale infrastructure projects, and targeted, albeit minimal, challenges to traditional Philippine elites. He also continued the tradition of crony capitalism, patronage, and corruption, which created both dependence and complicity at all levels of government. By 1969, and through the early 1970s, economic and political instability was the norm in Manila. The International Monetary Fund required the Philippine government to devalue the peso, and the result was rapid inflation in the prices of basic necessities, which exacerbated deep historic inequities in the economy. Opposition to the Marcos government included the conservative-bound elite, a growing student movement, the working class, and a reorganized Communist Party of the Philippines and its military wing, the New People's Army (NPA). Political violence intensified with attacks on student activists, bombings at political rallies, and an increasingly trained, albeit still nascent, NPA. In addition, Muslim separatists in Mindanao posed a threat to Marcos's authority in the south. In 1972, the Marcos government declared martial law. The government arrested over a hundred people, including Benigno "Ninoy" Aquino, his leading opponent, silenced the independent press, and closed the legislature.[16]

Martial law in the Philippines did not initially incite a popular revolt against the government, and in fact, many Philippine residents in Manila welcomed the order and promises of economic and political stability. Marcos dubbed his platform "The New Society." However, the Marcos regime also arrested approximately 67,000 Filipinos on political grounds, eliminated the free press and habeas corpus, and vigorously prosecuted opponents.[17] The

Philippines received far less attention from human rights activists in the United States than dictatorships in Latin America, but Filipinos in the United States coordinated a transnational campaign against the Marcos regime.[18]

The United States' reliance on the Philippines as an anti-communist bulwark and its military bases in the country meant it was unlikely to threaten Marcos's authority. In fact, the U.S. government doubled its military aid to the Philippine government in the early 1970s. President Jimmy Carter placed more pressure on the Philippine government to release opposition leader Ninoy Aquino, who faced a death sentence, but once he was released for health reasons in 1980, the Carter administration scaled back its demands. In addition, between 1977 and 1979, the Philippines and the United States renegotiated the Military Bases Agreement, a sore point for Philippine nationalists but one which the Marcos government was able to leverage for greater U.S. military and economic aid to the tune of $500 million.[19]

In this context, the Marcos government found great value in providing refuge for thousands of Southeast Asians, particularly since doing so identified the government with humanitarianism and thereby deflected attention away from human rights abuses.[20] Historian Barbara Keys has identified how the U.S. government often accelerated the everyday slippage between human rights and humanitarianism in the late 1970s. The newly established U.S. Bureau of Human Rights and Humanitarian Affairs focused most of its energies on the Southeast Asian refugee crisis, making this bureaucratic entity "less a human rights advocate than a humanitarian relief office."[21] In other words, the U.S. government lumped together human rights and humanitarianism, making the distinction between the two less legible to the public. The Marcos government took advantage of this lumping and the apparent, if inaccurate, proposition that human rights and humanitarianism were synonymous.

By hosting the PRPC, the Marcos government cast itself on the side of "humanitarianism" and brought it closer to its sibling, "human rights." In the process, the PRPC aided the Marcos government's relationship with the United States. The U.S. government repeatedly applauded the Philippines for its role. On the PRPC's second anniversary, U.S. Embassy officials celebrated the Philippine government's "emphasis on this humanitarian undertaking" and the personal involvement of President Marcos and First Lady Imelda Marcos: "We feel that the successes of the PRPC are indeed worthy of praise. What is more, the Center's operations have made it a plus in the Philippines' relations with ASEAN partners, with the region in general, and with the U.S."[22] The UNHCR affirmed that the PRPC was a "matter of national pride" to the First Couple and the government of the Philippines.[23] Many of the men and women I met in the Philippines also noted that Imelda was a frequent visitor in Bataan, and she identified herself personally with the PRPC.[24] The Marcos government's cooperation with the United Nations also allowed it to shine as a developing nation which embraced the UNHCR's priorities and mission. To further muddle the relationship between human rights and humanitarianism, the Marcos government appointed General Guandencio Tobias to manage the PRPC, creating a direct line between its military involvement in Vietnam and its care for refugees in the Philippines.[25] Imelda Marcos was the formal head, but General Tobias, a veteran of the Philippine Army, oversaw the PRPC's day-to-day operations. General Tobias had served in World War II and fought against the domestic Huk guerillas. He also had direct experience in South Vietnam; he had commanded the Philippine Civic Action Group in 1966 in Tay Ninh province.[26] Despite considerable opposition to the war within the Philippines, it was one of the few countries to join the United States in Vietnam (the others being South Korea, Australia, New Zealand, and Thailand). Marcos used his support for the American war to garner funds and favors from the U.S. government, and the Philippine Civic Action Group was a key part of that equation.[27] In South Vietnam, General Tobias commanded two thousand Filipinos, who ostensibly provided development and humanitarian aid, including infrastructure and medical programs, to the countryside.[28]

General Tobias brought his military sensibility to the PRPC, and many Filipino former staff members noted the camp's martial character. They recalled Tobias's strict discipline and expectation that staff would follow orders. At the same time, he garnered a great deal of respect for his professionalism, and he ensured Vietnamese received the services and support they needed. Tobias's experiences in Vietnam also created ideological linkages between the Philippines's support for South Vietnam and its decision to host refugees.

The Marcos government's call on humanitarianism also resonated with the Philippines' close identification with Catholicism. The Philippines is a majority-Catholic country and one where the Church hierarchy holds tremendous sway. In this context, the Catholic Church's own rhetoric of humanitarianism and anti-communism combined to give legitimacy to the government and the PRPC. In 1981, Imelda Marcos invited Pope John Paul II to visit the

PRPC during his trip the Philippines. The Pope performed a mass in an open field at the camp, and he connected Vietnamese stories of escape and redemption to the journey of Jesus Christ.[29] It is hard to image a higher profile event than a visit and blessing from the pope. The PRPC positioned the Philippines as a generous, compassionate, and humanitarian nation, albeit with the expense of the camp resting squarely on the UNHCR and its principal donor, the United States.

The United States also assumed it would exert influence over the PRPC. Although the United States had "no official function" in the PRPC's administration, the U.S. fingerprints (or thumb) were all over it.[30] In the initial phase of the PRPC, the United States committed the greatest dollar amount, $14 million in 1980 alone, followed by Japan, with a $5 million contribution, and West Germany at $3.3 million.[31] The vast majority of Vietnamese and Southeast Asians directed there would be resettling in the United States, and the cultural training program was geared to integrating into life in America. The United States put up all of the funds for the English-language and cultural orientation instruction. It justified the costs by arguing it was cheaper to host the language and training program in the Philippines than it would be in the United States.[32] Given the influx of U.S. dollars, U.S. officials often believed they had the right to monitor the PRPC's expenses and influence PRPC operations.[33] In addition, Joint Voluntary Agency staff (contracted by the State Department) were responsible for finding sponsors for Vietnamese in the United States, and U.S. officials kept regular tabs on the camp. This created a structure whereby the donor countries (in particular, the United States) provided dollars and the UNHCR administered funds, but neither was in direct control of the PRPC.

The Philippine government remained steadfast that the camp would be under its authority. The U.S. might be the largest donor, but as a former American colony and an independent country only since 1946, the Philippines closely guarded its sovereignty. Marcos insisted the PRPC would remain under Philippine control, and whenever the refugee operations reached their conclusion, "All facilities would be turned over to the [Philippine] government for use for quote humanitarian, social, and economic purposes unquote."[34] The Philippine government would appoint the chief camp administrator, who would be responsible for the PRPC's successes and failures and who would have the authority to hire and fire Filipino staff and control the funds: "The [Filipino] Administrator must have the authority to decide on all matters affecting such operations. He is accountable only to the

Philippine Government."[35] While consultation with the UNHCR was ideal and often expected, the UNHCR did not have veto power over any matter within the camp. California State Representative Art Agnos (future mayor of San Francisco) was in fact "surprised and somewhat dismayed" when he learned the U.S. did not have more influence over the camp, given the millions of dollars invested.[36] However, the Philippine government stood firm and did not cede any formal sovereignty over the PRPC.

As a result, there were numerous tensions between the UNHCR's desire to rein in costs and stay under budget and the Philippine government's authority to make unfettered decisions regarding contracts and local services. The UNHCR was financially responsible for every aspect of the camp: improving local roads; supplying water, electricity, and drainage systems; constructing camp housing; and providing health, educational, and recreational amenities.[37] All of this was extremely expensive. At the same time, the UNHCR did not have independent funds and relied on donor nations, namely the United States, Japan, West Germany, and Norway. The UNHCR cited the "very sensitive nature of the Filipinos, [to] any direct or indirect criticism of their policies or any query on money matters." Such critiques or suggestions "could easily give offence and lead to tension in the relationship between UNHCR and the Government of the Philippines." The Philippines was only willing to cooperate on its own terms. The UNHCR concluded, "The situation is delicate and any faux pas on the part of UNHCR could endanger this smooth relationship."[38]

The UNHCR couldn't afford to be picky, and throughout the 1980s, it worked cooperatively with the Marcos government. The UNHCR's mandate was to implement the regional agreement and provide protection to Vietnamese fleeing by land and sea. Given the financial and political pressures on countries like Malaysia and Thailand, the Philippines was a welcome partner, and there were only the most coded critiques of Marcos's human rights abuses in the UNHCR reports. For example, in the 1981 Annual Report, the UNHCR Manila Branch Office relayed that its relationship with the Philippine government remained "on the whole very good during 1981," and in particular, it thanked "Mrs. Imelda Romualdez-Marcos ... in her capacity as Chairman of the Task Force on International Refugee Assistance."[39] The 1983 report echoed these sentiments, saying the "attitude of the Philippine Government towards the refugees from Indochina has from the outset been a humane and generous one."[40] It was not in the UNHCR's interest to challenge the Marcos government's human rights abuses or policy of martial law; quite the contrary, the UNHCR was thankful for the Marcos government's willing and public cooperation on the refugee issue.

While it might seem paradoxical, the Marcos government worked with the UNHCR and the international community even as it repressed internal dissidents. The two policies were not mutually exclusive. Hosting the PRPC allowed the Marcos government to signal to the Carter administration and the U.S. Congress that it was willing to work with the international community on humanitarian issues and simultaneously deflect concerns about its human rights abuses. The Philippines also made the unusual decision to sign the 1951 UNHCR Convention in 1981. It was (and to this date remains) the only country in the region to do so. This was a significant act, and it set the Philippines apart from the region's overall hostility to refugees. Unlike Malaysia and Thailand, which were likely to "push off" Vietnamese seeking shelter and refuge, the Philippines never towed boats out to sea and instead celebrated its care of Vietnamese and Southeast Asians.

INSIDE THE CAMP: "HAPPY REFUGEES"

The PRPC stood apart from other Southeast Asian camps for its relatively plush conditions and its material comforts. UNHCR officials and journalists referred to the PRPC as the "Hilton," because it boasted concrete floors, secure housing, decent food, and medical care.[41] It was "arguably among the most expensive [refugee camps] ever constructed" and was relatively "luxurious," complete with "landscape architects, gardeners for neighborhood beautification, and so forth."[42] The UNHCR justified the high standard of living and attention to detail because unlike other makeshift camps, refugees at the PRPC "were being prepared for their lives in more developed nations," and so "services and facilities provided at the PRPC would indeed be at a level higher than in other refugee facilities."[43] During its nearly fifteen-year existence, the PRPC was a veritable international village, complete with UNHCR officials, former Philippine military officers and camp administrators, international NGOs, American teachers, Filipino teachers and market vendors, and families and individuals from Vietnam, Laos, and Cambodia.

From the point of view of the UNHCR, the PRPC was for "happy refugees" about to resettle in the United States, Norway, or West Germany, in stark contrast to the Vietnamese still lingering in camps in Malaysia,

Thailand, Hong Kong, and Indonesia. As a UNHCR report concluded, "The PRPC is a way-station, a processing centre, for basically healthy, happy refugees nearing the observable end of their ordeal and the final commencement of new lives after resettlement. . . . It need do only what needs to be done, and in that it is succeeding admirably well."[44]

But who were these "happy refugees"? For Vietnamese, the PRPC marked a time of waiting, which often seemed needless, as they were making their way to the United States. There was great diversity among the Southeast Asians, with Vietnamese in the majority, sizable populations from Cambodia and Laos, and ethnic minorities from all three countries. Much like first-asylum camps in Malaysia and other Southeast Asian countries before 1989, most Vietnamese at the PRPC typically opted not to cause much disruption. In fact, quite the opposite. There were few protests within the PRPC, particularly given the levels of boredom and frustration people experienced waiting for resettlement.[45] Vietnamese generally saw the PRPC as a place to be tolerated. The goal was resettlement, and if they were at the PRPC, they were almost there. Rocking the boat, protesting, or agitating for better conditions would only lead them to be seen as troublemakers and delay their resettlement. The *Christian Science Monitor* reported that "As for the refugees, many would just as soon skip the program—and the six months it consumes—and go directly to the United States."[46]

The camp itself included more than a hundred bunkhouses organized into ten different neighborhoods, a hospital, school buildings, mess halls, and numerous cafeterias. Building what was essentially a small city, officials also needed to ensure working drainage lines, sewage lines, electricity grids, and water supplies, all of which needed regular upkeep and maintenance.[47] Vietnamese, Cambodian, and Laotian communities built a range of temples, memorials, and burial grounds, and the PRPC sponsored numerous cultural activities and musical performances to celebrate the range of Southeast Asian identities and traditions. Archival photos and the current on-site museum attest to active classrooms, vocational activities, and youth programming. In addition, the PRPC recruited Southeast Asians within the camp to hold leadership positions, representing their "neighborhoods" or barrack blocks and working with Filipino officials to administer the camp. The goal was to benefit from internal Vietnamese, Cambodian, and Laotian leadership, facilitate communication between the Southeast Asian communities and the PRPC administration, and efficiently govern the thousands of people within the camp's perimeter.

The PRPC required that those in the camp take classes in English as a second language (ESL) and cultural orientation, and this occupied a significant portion of each day. Filipino and American teachers worked together to implement a curriculum largely developed and directed by the International Catholic Migration Commission. English classes and the cultural orientation program provided information about everything from the basics of U.S. currency to the layout of an American kitchen, reading the want ads, and American measurement standards. Southeast Asian recipients of all this aid also had to participate in a work credit program, or "voluntary" labor, for two hours each day. The "Monkey House" was an extralegal prison where administrators could isolate "troublemakers" and detain those who broke camp rules, which ranged from minor offenses like drinking to more serious ones like violent crime or domestic abuse. There were more than a dozen voluntary organizations providing social services, including the World Relief Corporation, the Philippine National Red Cross, Caritas Manila, Philippine Baptist Refugee Ministries, Mormon Christian Services, the Center for Assistance to Displaced Persons, and Community Family Services International. Several former PRPC teachers and scholars criticized the camp for trying to "transform" the Vietnamese into Americans, training them to be racialized low-level workers in the United States, and for operating as a "total institution."[48] While there is some merit to these critiques, for most Vietnamese, the PRPC was a camp to be endured and one that hardly succeeded in substantially altering their culture or identity.

Vietnamese American oral history collections include limited commentary on the PRPC, and participants often expressed fond memories, particularly in comparison to the other Southeast Asian camps.[49] In general, Vietnamese only spoke of the PRPC in passing and without great detail. For example, in the Vietnamese American Oral History Project at the University of California, Irvine, more than two dozen participants mentioned the PRPC, but very few spoke about it other than to say it was a point of transit between an earlier, more traumatic camp and the United States.

When Vietnamese Americans did look back on the PRPC, it was often positively. Paul Chi Hoang was just a young boy at the camp, and he remembered "doing a lot of things there was fun, playing with kids, going around."[50] Others noted their improved living conditions and the opportunities for entrepreneurship at the PRPC, in contrast to Pulau Bidong. Binh Le recalled greater openness at the PRPC and more interaction with the "native population" (the Filipinos), but for him the most important element of the PRPC seemed to be his ready access to pork, which had been unavailable in Malaysia due to Muslim prohibitions. "They could beat you to death if they caught you eating it. I missed having pork so much. Three years without pork is a long time when you've been used to having it. When we got to the Philippines and were given pork, it was the greatest thing." He also added, that his time in Bataan "seemed short because we knew for sure that we were going to America and could relax and focus on school."[51] Nhan T. Le spoke even more warmly about her months in the PRPC. She recounted her time in a positive and romantic tone: "We had to study about United States culture and the English language for six months before we could leave. . . . I received rice and other food supplies once every two days and always had more than I had had in the other camps. . . . I felt like I was moving up in the world. There was a waterfall where everyone could go swimming. Bataan was the most memorable place for me because it was the place I told my husband that I was pregnant with our first child."[52]

For both the interviewers and perhaps the subjects themselves, dwelling on the camp experience was not the goal of most of these recorded oral histories. In general, the dramatic escape from Vietnam and the challenges of resettlement were paramount, overshadowing the interim memories of the PRPC. At a remaining religious shrine, an engraved stone stated ambiguously, "Don't Worry, It Will pass, Everything Does."[53] The details that do emerge demonstrate the Vietnamese men and women's English-language skills *before* they even reached the camp. Hoang Dai Hai noted, "They taught us all the basic things like how to use a map, how to use a phone book, how to go to interview, all kind of stuff. My English was good enough so I was a translator, T.A. like an assistant of teacher back then. I will be translating lesson to Vietnamese because the teacher was Filipino. They speak in English, and I translate into Vietnamese."[54]

Some of the Vietnamese were less sanguine about their time in the PRPC. However, there was a certain level of resignation in their testimony. The PRPC became one more hoop they had to jump through to make their way to the United States. Anthropologist John Christian Knudsen's 1983 survey of the PRPC documented how the Vietnamese he spoke with generally expressed a sense of "meaninglessness of their present existence." He surveyed Vietnamese in a range of camps, and even given Bataan's educational programming, he believed that it was not immune from Vietnamese men and women's sense of forced passivity and living in "a limbo state."[55] In short,

Vietnamese oral histories generally glossed over the PRPC, and the overall impression is one of boredom and wasted time.[56]

There are a few first-person accounts which further unsettle the camp's self-presentation as a place of cultural preparation. One of the most pointed testimonies is in a collection by Joanna C. Scott, an American who first visited the camp in 1985. She interviewed two dozen Vietnamese, Lao, and Cambodian men and women while they were still at the PRPC, and there is a rawer and more documentary dimension to their interviews, which are not colored by twenty years of memory and forgetting. Nguyen Thi Yen Nga was a Vietnamese woman who became friends with Scott and visited her home twice in Manila. After she was discovered outside the camp's periphery, the camp tightened its security; she was not supposed to leave unauthorized. However, just a few weeks later, she visited Scott again. When questioned about how she had escaped the camp despite the more stringent rules, she said, "We are all experts at escaping. That's how we got there in the first place."[57]

Unlike the subjects of the oral histories collected two to three decades later, Nguyen Thi Yen Nga resented many of the English and cultural classes she had to attend, and she expressed these frustrations in terms of class and privilege. She had been a stewardess with Vietnamese Airlines, her siblings had studied abroad in France, and she was from a wealthy family. Her parents emigrated to France in 1982, and she left Saigon with her husband through the Orderly Departure Program in 1985. She resented having to go to the PRPC for six months before she could travel to the United States. "I could not persuade them otherwise even though all the family speaks English and we had worked with the Americans before 1975. We tried to get the time shortened, but it was no use." The PRPC was a substantial decline in her standard of living; she was accustomed to "modern conveniences" and had to learn how to light a charcoal fire and cope with limited supplies. She also noted the frustrating nature of learning American culture from Filipino teachers: "The Filipinos teaching us American cultural orientation have never been in America and don't know anything about it. Many refugees have visited America and lived there to study or do military training. When they tell the Filipino teachers that they are mistaken in what they tell us, the teachers fly into a rage." She concluded, "We have to understand that the Filipinos are also very poor and need to feed their families. At least, when we have suffered through our time here, we will go to the United States. We have hope. They have none, so we can only pity them."[58]

In this brief account, Nguyen Thi Yen Nga hit on the inverted hierarchies that persisted at the camp. On the one hand, the Filipinos had far greater authority and liberty than the Vietnamese. They were teachers, administrators, and support staff, and they could enter and leave the camp as they pleased. However, it was the Vietnamese and not the Filipinos who had access to the United States. In Vietnam, it took financial resources (and often bribes) to organize an escape or navigate through the bureaucratic exit process, and so it was often wealthier Vietnamese with more resources who were able to leave. In this example, one can see her class status and her sense of superiority over the Filipino teachers and camp workers. She, for one, rejected the idea that she was the recipient of Filipino humanitarian aid, and instead believed she was helping the Filipinos.

From the point of view of the U.S. government, one of the central benefits of the PRPC was the low cost of its English-language and cultural orientation programs. The program acted as a mini-development program within the Philippines, while at the same time, Filipino teachers could be cheap labor for the U.S.-driven refugee program. As a 1981 U.S. government report stated, "Basing the program in Southeast Asia represents considerable savings, according to the State Department. . . . State Department officials expect additional savings from the decision to rely heavily on local, national teachers."[59] A former American ESL teacher and critic of the PRPC, James Tollefson argued that Filipino teachers earned only one-tenth of what an ESL teacher in the United States would earn.[60] Within the camp, American teachers generally had supervisory positions even when they had less training in English language pedagogy than their Filipino counterparts.

Many of the ESL teachers at the PRPC had been Peace Corps volunteers, thus moving from one U.S.-directed development project to another. Gene Boggs had been a Peace Corps volunteer in North Africa. On his return to the United States, he worked in a legal aid office in Richmond, California. He heard about a job in the PRPC from a friend who was teaching English there, and so Boggs and his wife decided to take the plunge and move to the Philippines. His friend had promised that the duties were light and the money was good. Although he had less experience than most, Boggs became a supervisor because he was an American. He explained that most of the Filipino teachers had been working in the camp for a year, and so the program ran "on autopilot." Boggs only remained at the camp for seven to eight months, a relatively short stay compared to many of the long-term teachers, but he was impressed with the Filipino teachers' skills and professionalism. He explained that "the

Filipino classroom teachers were highly educated, and they were meticulous in their pedagogy. . . . They had lesson plans planned to the nth degree—and they were very conscientious—but I think they had to put up with a lot of indignities as well, and they were doing it because it was good money."[61] Given that at its peak there were approximately a thousand Filipino and American staff on site, the PRPC could generate remunerative jobs for Filipinos and substantial savings for the U.S. government.[62] For Filipinos the pay was far better than that offered by most Philippine-based positions. Essentially, the PRPC acted as a development program and motored the local economy.

The Philippine government, the UNHCR, and the United States framed the camp as a humanitarian gesture and a way to ease the transition from refugee camp to resettlement. In practice, it minimized the financial and political burdens on first-asylum countries, and perhaps more importantly, on the United States, and it infused U.S. dollars into the Philippines. In many ways, the PRPC had a greater long-term impact on the Bataan region and the Filipinos who worked there than on the Vietnamese within the camp.

OUTSIDE THE CAMP: SUBIC BAY, EXPORT
PROCESSING ZONES, THE MORONG NUCLEAR POWER
PLANT, AND THE NEW PEOPLE'S ARMY

Bataan is one of the few Philippine place-names with any currency in American popular history. In American memory and culture, Bataan is synonymous with the Bataan Death March and the brutal fighting in the Philippines during World War II. Bataan conjures notions of heroism and Philippine-American solidarity, rather than a rural Philippine province with deeper histories of U.S. colonialism.[63]

After World War II, Bataan remained relatively underdeveloped and struggled economically. Its landscape was militarized not only by the legacies of World War II, but also the U.S. occupation between 1898 and Philippine independence in 1946. Theodore Roosevelt established the Subic Bay naval station in the Bataan region in early 1901. Before World War II began, the U.S. had promised to grant Philippine independence in 1944. World War II changed that trajectory and both countries' conceptions of security. The Philippines did become an independent country in 1946, but it did so agreeing that the U.S. could continue maintaining its military bases. Despite wrangling over extraterritorial jurisdiction, the two signed a bases agreement in 1947, which granted the U.S. military ninety-nine-year leases over twenty-two sites, including Subic Bay.[64] As scholar Vernadette Vicuña Gonzalez notes, the heroic memorialization of the Bataan Death March stands in contrast to the imperial, and tawdrier, histories of the Subic Bay naval station and Clark Air Force base.[65]

In 1970, Bataan province had just over 215,000 people, most of whom were employed in the agricultural sector, and the small town closest to the PRPC, Morong, had only 6,738 residents.[66] Morong was located just south of the U.S. naval base; however, despite this proximity, most people in the area gained access to the base via Olongapo, the main commercial and economic nexus for U.S. military personnel and Filipino workers. Subic Bay also played a direct role in the U.S. war in Vietnam, providing a staging base for the U.S. air war, much to the consternation of anti-war Filipinos and anti-war GIs.[67] The PRPC's proximity to Subic Bay underscores a longer trajectory of U.S. military power and U.S.-Philippine cooperation during the U.S. war in Vietnam.

During the 1980s, Subic Bay was not easily accessible for PRPC staff or the Vietnamese, many of whom might have had earlier contact with U.S. military officers. Filipinos and Americans stationed at the PRPC had to traverse the mountainous region, circling an interior route for more than two to three hours, if they wanted to visit the base or Olongapo. Very few of the Americans or Filipinos I spoke with mentioned Subic Bay or its prominent role in the region's economy or the years of military dependence on the United States. However, Gene Boggs, the U.S. English teacher who taught at the PRPC in 1989, remembered multiple trips to Subic Bay, often with Vietnamese Amerasian students for whom he had gained passes. He remembered taking advantage of the Baskin-Robbins ice cream shop, the PX, and first-run movies, none of which were available at the PRPC. In particular, he recalled an endless loop of Cher's "If I Could Turn Back Time" music video on the overhead television monitors. The irony of the base's military legacy was not lost on Boggs. Here he was, an English teacher for Vietnamese fleeing a failed U.S. war, but on weekends he could visit the Subic Bay officer's club: "It was a breathtaking scene. . . . You could just imagine Admiral Dewey or Douglas MacArthur doing the same thing . . . looking out at this beautiful scene . . . with an incredible spread for Sunday brunch."[68]

A bit farther afield, the Philippine government also launched its first Export Processing Zone (EPZ) at the southern tip of the Bataan peninsula. The EPZ offered an economic counterpoint to the U.S. military footprint in Subic Bay, approximately 100 kilometers away.[69] Following the lead of

MAP 2. Bataan, location of the Philippine Refugee Processing Center.

Taiwan, Singapore, and South Korea, the Philippines set up the EPZ and welcomed in foreign companies to open light manufacturing plants such as Integrated Shoe, Intercontinental Garments, and other textile companies. In the vanguard of neoliberal approaches to economic development, EPZs were another way to attract foreign capital with the promise of low-wage labor and minimal regulation. Foreign companies would often rotate through the Bataan EPZ, with almost equal numbers leaving and coming each year, but local boosters still touted its long-term benefits for the region.[70] For example, Officer-in-Charge Romeo C. Dizon commented that "the Zone is still in its infancy, but its revenue 'reservoir' has from the beginning revealed a futuristic posture. I am highly optimistic over its continuous striking viability."[71] The Bataan EPZ included plans for an elementary school for workers' children, and the government envisioned it to be a long-term development investment. However, as many scholars have noted, these free-trade enclaves had limited abilities to improve local economies, and they have often maintained imperial networks and dependency through the guise of neoliberalism.

Subic Bay and the Bataan EPZ were not the only projections of technological, economic, and military power in Bataan. In 1973, Ferdinand Marcos decided to launch construction of a "showcase" nuclear power reactor six kilometers from the town of Morong.[72] According to the Philippine newspaper *Malaya,* the Bataan Nuclear Power Plant was the "most expensive single project under ex-President Marcos' 20-year rule." Its total cost of $2.1 billion was unprecedented, and it resulted in substantial government debt.[73] Antinuclear groups confronted Westinghouse, the American firm behind the facility, concluding, "Sorry, big W, you cannot fool us anymore."[74] The plant was mired in crony politics, corruption, and bribery from the start, with Westinghouse paying Marcos in-law Herminio Disni almost $80 million in construction fees, and Marcos taking a healthy slice off the top.[75] In 1984, more than 3,000 Filipinos marched to Balanga, the regional capital, just sixty kilometers from the PRPC.[76] Protesters emphasized the dangers of radiation and the inherent risks in situating a nuclear plant in an earthquake- and volcano-prone region. Professors from the University of the Philippines added that Philippine nuclear scientists "lacked experience" to operate such a plant.[77] Catholic clergy sided with the activists: "We are for life whose quality is not compromised by so-called progress in nuclear technology."[78] The anti-Marcos movement was gaining ground in the 1980s, and the nuclear power plant became a flashpoint for anti-government protests, bringing together outrage over political corruption and nuclear safety.

Notably, in none of the local reporting do any of the journalists, advocates, or anti-nuclear activists even mention the PRPC and the tens of thousands of Vietnamese, Laotians, and Cambodians nearby.[79] Rather, former U.S. teachers noted, in passing and somewhat comically, that they utilized the power plant regularly because it was the only place where they could make reliable national and international phone calls. When they wanted to make long-distance calls, they would mount bicycles or motor scooters and head off to the plant. The nuclear power plant as telephone booth could hardly seem more surreal.

Finally, pervading this militarized landscape was the Marcos government's military campaign against the communist-affiliated New People's Army.[80] In the UNHCR documents related to the PRPC, this proximity to guerilla welfare is almost, although not completely, invisible. On February 17, 1987, just shy of one year after Marcos fled to Hawai'i, the UNHCR documented that "twenty to thirty armed rebels entered Morong town and occupied the municipal town. Some fighting was reported and two policemen wounded, rebels left after one hour which coincided with arrival of military reinforcements. PRPC not rpt not affected but we [are] checking report . . . Additional unconfirmed report states two refugees briefly taken hostage near PRPC by armed men on 14 or 15 February but quickly released . . . will revert when details are known."[81] This is the only mention of the NPA fighting to penetrate the thousands of pages on the Philippine camps in the UNHCR archive.

In direct contrast to the UNHCR documents, the *Bataan Star* was rife with articles and stories about the NPA. A sampling of headlines included "Rebels Gaining Strength Here," "Military Scores Big Blow in Campaign against the NPA," "Drive against NPA in Full Swing," and "Invisible Government in Rural Area Bared." In these accounts, the battle between the government and the NPA was front and center and clearly drove much of the daily news.

In casual conversations and interviews with men and women who worked in the camp, the NPA was a known quantity and part of the political landscape. However, everyone I spoke to agreed that the NPA never violated the camp's perimeter or security, and there is no documentary evidence to the contrary. Presumably, the NPA did not want to draw attention to themselves or attack the refugee camp. It seems that it was not worth the risk, government assault, or international attention.

Thus, the PRPC was situated in a constellation of military struggles and colonial legacies. The Philippine government masked the contested politics of the region through the implementation of a massive humanitarian project, heralded by such institutional and transnational players as the UNHCR and the Catholic Church. While Bataan was sparsely populated, Subic Bay, the EPZ, and the Bataan Nuclear Power Plant stood as major institutions of state power—the U.S. military on the one hand and the corporate and technological aspirations of the Marcos government on the other. The PRPC complemented this trifecta of international symbolism by elevating the humanitarianism and development promised by both the U.S. military and the Philippine government.

The camp thus did a great deal of work for the Philippine government. It acted as a beacon of humanitarianism and a local economic investment in an impoverished region. However, a closer look at the geography also revealed longer histories of U.S. military occupation and the Marcos government's neoliberal and nationalist ambitions. When it came to the PRPC, the UNHCR and the United States both downplayed, and often outright ignored, these broader political realities, and instead remained steadfastly focused on the camp.

CULTURAL ORIENTATION AND NOSEBLEEDS

The Philippine government insisted on its sovereignty, but for the Filipinos who worked in the PRPC, it was an international environment and English was the lingua franca. One social worker explained that the PRPC "was a different world."[82] Many articulated their own vision of humanitarianism, one based on their personal experiences teaching English or counseling traumatized families. It was an opportunity to work in an international setting and gain skills and professional respect, and many cited it as a career highlight and the foundation for lasting international connections. Still others chafed at the PRPC's identification with humanitarianism when there were so many domestic abuses of power. These competing stories complicated the government's more antiseptic vision of humanitarianism and demonstrated how Filipinos understood the relationship between their work, the American cultural resettlement project, and the Philippine government.

Many Filipinos emphasized the PRPC's location *in* the Philippines as one of its greatest benefits. In an era of economic instability, the PRPC jobs were professional, relatively well-paid positions in which Filipinos did not have to go abroad as guest workers. Beginning in the 1970s, the Marcos government aggressively launched overseas guest worker programs as a way of funneling desperately needed dollars and hard currency into the Philippines. The Marcos government celebrated those who worked overseas and sent their dollars to relatives in the Philippines as "national heroes."[83] By 1980, when the PRPC opened, 214,000 Filipinos worked abroad.[84] Several people told me they worked at the PRPC because they did not have to leave the country to make a decent salary. Instead they had the opportunity to work with an international community *within* the Philippines.

The PRPC allowed many Filipino teachers to gain professional experience, participate in rewarding work, and gain a sense of satisfaction from their students and an international community. Nida Ermita Magallanes studied at Saint Isabel College, where she trained to be an English teacher. She was also an early volunteer with the Center for Assistance to Displaced Persons, a Catholic voluntary agency spearheaded by Vietnamese national Sister Pascale Le Thi Triu, who dedicated herself to the Vietnamese in the Philippines. The Center for Assistance to Displaced Persons would become the most important voluntary agency in the first-asylum camp on Palawan, and it would create ties between Vietnamese in the diaspora and the Philippines. Magallanes decided to go to Palawan in 1986 because she "was a very adventurous person," and she wanted something more exciting than teaching in the provinces. Her warmth and enthusiasm were palpable. A career teacher with a great deal of energy, she spoke glowingly about her work in the camps and her Vietnamese students. She remarked on how her students would welcome her into their bunks and feed her tea and *banh mi* sandwiches. In the decades following the camp closures, she maintained ties with her students, and many later visited her in the Philippines. Magallanes reflected:

> I'm so proud to be a part of the Vietnamese journey. . . . It's not their fault that they became refugees, but it will be our fault if they continue to be a refugee all the rest of their lives. . . . This is a chapter in my life, I'm so proud of, sharing with my siblings and with my nephews and nieces and with my own son. . . . I was part of the Vietnamese life as far as education is concerned. I was of help to them, learning English, even if for a short time.

She also developed lasting connections with Vietnamese, and she has reunited with former students on Facebook and even made a trip to Hanoi as a tourist.[85]

Filipina women professionals also had the chance to advance their careers within the PRPC in a way that would not have been possible in other sectors.

Luwalhati Pablo was a social worker with Community Family Services International, a voluntary agency founded in the Philippines which promoted mental health services within the camp. Pablo explained that the PRPC could be a "man's world," and the UNHCR and American officials were almost exclusively white men. As a Filipina woman, she remembered that Community Family Services allowed her to develop her authority and come into her own professionally. She was also proud of the fact that Filipinos ran the PRPC and that she had trained countless Vietnamese to be para-professional social workers. It was a "feather in the Philippines' cap," and it proved what Filipino social workers could do.[86] In my conversations with Filipina women who worked at the camp, many echoed these stories of pride, professionalism, and accomplishment. The PRPC provided them the opportunity to work within an international apparatus, which advanced their status, and provided the emotional satisfaction of supporting a community that needed their skills.

Working with an international staff could also have its challenges. Another Filipina social worker at the PRPC remarked that she too took pride in her work: "I was proud to be part of that history of the Vietnamese." She believed it gave her integrity and commitment, and it taught her to remain focused on her clients and a mission, rather than simply the hours and pay of a regular job. Witnessing Sister Pascale's dedication carried over into her future endeavors. She learned what it was like to work for a cause and how to be a professional. That said, it could be stressful. She also grew tired of always having to work in English at the PRPC. "I wanted ... to speak Filipino," she remembered. "I am tired of speaking English ... so I said my nose is bleeding," using the popular Filipino phrase about how speaking English too much caused pressure in one's head, and thus a nosebleed.[87] In many ways, the individual Filipino teachers and counselors created substance for the Marcos government's platitudes of humanitarianism. They advocated for individual families, provided comfort for their sojourn at the PRPC, and even established lasting friendships. Here was a new articulation of humanitarianism at the granular level.

However, President Ronald Reagan's support for Ferdinand Marcos and his anti-democratic practices also dominated the early 1980s. These neocolonial ties created dissonance in some Filipino teachers' memories, and in at least one case, dismay that there was a "refugee processing" camp borne out of the United States' failed war in Vietnam, now in Bataan. George Chiu and Susan Quimpo met at the PRPC in the mid-1980s. Chiu was an English teacher, and Quimpo taught in the cultural orientation program. In 1983,

George Chiu remembered that he was looking for a job the year "Ninoy was murdered." Because of the political upheaval, the economy was in shambles and there were few jobs for recent graduates. He began teaching English at the Palawan camp, and like Magallanes, he remembered it as "an adventure." He had fond memories of his time with the Vietnamese and his ability to spend hours at the beach.[88] In 1985, he transferred to the PRPC, where he continued teaching ESL. There, he met his future wife, Susan Quimpo. Quimpo was from an activist anti-Marcos family. Like Chiu, she chose to work in the camp because she needed a job. She was a full-time political activist, but her savings had run out, and she needed a steady income. The PRPC offered steady work, but "I felt horrible about having to work there, simply because I saw the U.S. government, foreign interventions, and wars of aggression as the enemy."[89] She came to the job with resentment and skepticism, and out of economic necessity. In contrast, Chiu did not view the camp as the manifestation of the U.S. empire or the political detritus of the U.S. imperial war in Vietnam, but rather an opportunity to demonstrate Filipino hospitality and humanitarianism. Ultimately, both Chiu and Quimpo developed close friendships with Filipino and American co-workers and enjoyed working with the Southeast Asian students; however, Quimpo remained more critical of the overall project. At the end of our conversation, both Chiu and Quimpo seemed surprised by their divergent perspectives.

Quimpo's critique rested on the camp's U.S. funding, the U.S. imperial war in Vietnam, and the Philippine government's relationship with the United States, but on a day-to-day basis, she also hated the curriculum she was expected to teach. She had never been to the United States, and she was tasked with teaching the Vietnamese about what to expect when they resettled in America. She saw the curriculum as "silly" at best.[90] Quimpo felt "horrible" about teaching American culture. She remembered that she was supposed to teach about American life, which she felt was reduced to western toilets and a modern oven. She believed the PRPC teachers couldn't talk about real life, and that problems related to racism and poverty were never incorporated into a curriculum that focused on toilets, social security cards, and the post office. She thought the ESL curriculum was better than the cultural orientation program, maintaining that the latter was "awful." "The refugees were never told about poverty, crime, and racism in America." She ended by saying that when she did move to the United States several years later, "none of that knowledge applied, even to me."[91] She, at least, never accepted the image of the U.S. government as a benevolent actor.

Quimpo was correct that the ESL and cultural orientation classes were ideological.[92] The curriculum displayed both a desire to relate to Southeast Asian students and a didactic nature, which is not surprising given the pedagogical function of the camps.[93] English-language readers created by the International Catholic Migration Commission matched simple vocabulary with striking illustrations. Some of the ESL readers were reinterpretations of Vietnamese folk tales, presumably to help students connect to the reading and learn basic vocabulary within a familiar framework.[94] Other readers focused on life and transitions to the United States and American culture. In *The Fourth of July*, Vietnamese learned about American customs like cookouts, hot dogs, and hamburgers, and "of course ice cream."[95] In *Pocket Money*, students were taught how to earn extra cash in the United States. The main character, Moua Thong, is a student at Westview Adult School. He responds to a help-wanted sign for yard work in his neighborhood, interviews for the position, and gets the job: "Moua Thong was very happy."[96] Other stories' messages were a bit more ambiguous. For example, *Thao Gets a Haircut* starts off with Thao getting a spiky mohawk at the local barbershop. He likes the new style but soon learns that a "punk haircut" makes it much harder for him to get a job. His uncle laughs at him, sits him down, and shaves his head. The reader ends with Thao skimming his fingers over the freshly shaved stubble with a disturbed look on his face.[97]

The critique that the curriculum avoided questions of racism and discrimination was not entirely accurate. Some of the ESL readers offered dark pictures of life in the United States and the reality of racism, violence, and crime that Vietnamese might confront. In *Who Is My Friend*, readers meet sisters Tuyet and Linh Veng, teenagers who arrived in the United States in 1987. In the story, based on a true case from Pennsylvania, the sisters face harassment in their local public high school, and the ESL reader's illustrations display the girls on the floor, with American teenagers laughing and taunting them. The hero of the story is a sixteen-year-old African American student, Mamie Kellam, who comes to the Vietnamese girls' defense. Kellam "pities" the Vietnamese girls, and she reports the incident to the principal. The story ends with Kellam winning the "Anne Frank Youth Award" for "helping people she did not know."[98] In this story, the African American teenager is the central protagonist, teaching the Vietnamese students a lesson about racial discrimination and implying that they should consider themselves to be racial minorities like Kellam herself. It's not clear how the young Vietnamese girls in Pennsylvania understood this experience, and in an

FIGURE 8. This ESL reader does not shy away from the hardships recent Vietnamese arrivals might experience in the United States. Here a group of students mock and push two Vietnamese girls to the ground. *Who Is My Friend?* © International Catholic Migration Commission.

interview with the *Philadelphia Inquirer,* Tuyet Veng said she just wanted to forget the incident.[99] She did not articulate a story of racial solidarity or perseverance.

In an even more ambiguous example, an ESL reader evocatively titled *Too Much Freedom* also took its story from recent U.S. headlines.[100] Students were introduced to the history of Sang Nam Chinh, a teenage boy who left Vietnam in 1977 and resettled in Los Angeles. The reader portrays him as a poor student who quit school and threw his English-language book in the trash can. He had a few service jobs, as a busboy and a delivery boy, but was attracted to the gang world. Along with several other gang members, he robbed a jewelry store in 1984, and a police officer was shot at the scene. The denouement was stark: "Now he is in jail. He may be put to death." The illustrations show him in a cell, speaking with a woman behind a metal grate. The reader goes on to ask, "Why did Nam get in trouble? His sister, Mui, says

FIGURE 9. This ESL reader's text explains, "Why did Nam get in so much trouble? His sister, Mui, says, 'There is too much freedom in America.'" *Too Much Freedom* © International Catholic Migration Commission.

there is too much freedom in America." In this instance, freedom is not a positive attribute associated with wealth, education, or anti-communism, but rather with drugs, violence, and access to guns. This cautionary tale was based on the events of a Los Angeles robbery. In the end, Sang Nam Chinh was not sentenced to death; instead, a California jury sentenced him to life without parole. According to the *Los Angeles Times,* jury members took his refugee experiences into account when they decided not to impose the death penalty. Throughout the case, witnesses testified to his "childhood amid the violence of Vietnam and later of his time as a barely literate farmhand whose family sent him to an uncertain future as a refugee rather than have him stay and be pressed into military service against Cambodia." One juror justified the decision, noting, "The fact that he was young at the time [of the robbery] and he came from a childhood in South Vietnam, that he was a refugee for sometime . . . "[101] These "easy readers" did not shy away from examples of

American racism, discrimination, or the trauma of the legal system. Instead, they stood as warnings, teaching Vietnamese that they were about to enter a world where they would be racialized minorities.

This grim didactic lesson was in sharp contrast to many Vietnamese individuals' prior social standing. Notably, many Vietnamese came from privileged backgrounds, and this could invert the hierarchy of caretaker and cared for within the camp. Vietnamese might be refugees, but that did not mean they were universally bereft or from impoverished backgrounds. For example, Vietnamese often gave gifts to the Filipinos, allowing for exchange and creating a more complicated politics of charity and aid. Susan Quimpo remembered that when the Vietnamese completed their six-month program, they would often give gold rings to the Filipino teachers. When she and George Chiu decided to get married, they had very little money, but after working at the PRPC, they had so many gold rings that they decided, "Show me your rings, and I'll show you mine, and let's just find something that fits, you know, and so those were our wedding bands."[102] Most importantly, Vietnamese would also be going to the United States, and the Filipino staff remained in the Philippines.

The PRPC offered a higher standard of living than was typical for rural regions in the Philippines. For the Philippine government, it was important that the PRPC did not vastly outstrip the quality of life of Filipinos living nearby in Morong. It also did not want the UNHCR "refugee money" to be spent conspicuously on "items which might be considered luxurious."[103] Philippine administrators like General Tobias were sensitive to potential local resentment and the need to ensure Morong benefited from the camp as well. Tobias actively advocated for higher wages for Filipinos who worked for the PRPC, and he resented that their salaries were notably lower than the NGO and international salary scales.[104] To help alleviate some of the discrepancies, local Filipinos were allowed to use the medical facilities at the PRPC. When I was in Morong, I was able to locate birth and death certificates of Filipinos who were born and died in the PRPC. As the best medical care in the region (outside of Subic Bay, which remained off limits), the PRPC offered a radically improved health care system for men and women in Morong.

The PRPC English teachers and social workers I spoke to who were college educated repeatedly stated that if they had not been working at the PRPC, they would have been working abroad. For Filipino workers from Morong, the options were generally the PRPC or the nuclear power plant. Many people I spoke with in Morong remembered the positive effects of the PRPC on the local economy and the professional opportunities it created.

Working at the PRPC provided marketable skills, namely improved English-language abilities and greater experience working with foreigners. One woman remembered applying for positions at both the PRPC and the nuclear plant; the PRPC offered her a job in the food services group first. She soon worked her way up to become a procurement officer, and her job was to purchase food and rations from throughout the region to feed all the incoming Vietnamese. Buying fruits and vegetables was part of the PRPC's local outreach, and farmers were paid in cash. Her own salary was far greater than she could have earned elsewhere in Morong.[105]

The PRPC embodied competing meanings of humanitarian care. For the Vietnamese, staying at the PRPC meant taking classes, jumping through bureaucratic hoops, making friends with teachers, sometimes getting into trouble, and more than anything else, waiting. For the United States, the camp meant it could offer English classes and one final vetting process outside its borders and at a discount, and for the UNHCR, it offered the chance to create a model refugee camp with far more amenities and support than the often physically and psychologically miserable camps in Malaysia and Hong Kong. For the Philippines, the PRPC provided a showcase of its sovereignty, international acumen, and humanitarianism. For teachers and administrators, it offered a place to find valuable, rewarding, and remunerative work. It also acted as a quasi–development project in a poor region, funneling thousands of pesos to local Filipinos through salaries, contracts, and procurement. These cross-purposes persisted even as domestic Philippine politics turned upside down and the 1986 Yellow Revolution toppled the Marcos government.

In our conversation, it seemed that for Susan Quimpo, the camp was almost a footnote in her life story. She had worked at the camp but had not reflected on it in years. Instead, her participation in the anti-Marcos revolution and her involvement in Filipino politics and culture were all-important and superseded her work at the PRPC.[106]

TIMES OF CHANGE: 1986 PEOPLE POWER REVOLUTION

In 1986, Cory Aquino's People Power overtook the Marcos government. For the Philippines, this was a turning point in its postwar politics, and it ushered in a moment of optimism for democracy, as well as a challenge to the United States government. However, for teachers, administrators, and

Vietnamese within the PRPC, daily life and the administration of the camp did not change dramatically. When it took power, the Aquino government also found value in the PRPC's association with humanitarianism, and it reframed the camp within its own narrative of anti-Marcos politics.

Not surprisingly, the Filipino staff knew changes were afoot in Manila, and radios across the camp tuned in. George Chiu remembered becoming fixated on the radio as the street demonstrations escalated. During the five days when demonstrators occupied Epifanio de los Santos Avenue (EDSA) and Luneta Park in Manila, there were almost no ESL lessons:

> So it went on for five days, and what I remember distinctly was, there were several false alarms that Marcos had left, but the real one came maybe around five or six in the evening, and we were already in our billets, and suddenly it was announced on the radio. There was a collective, you could hear the whole camp erupting, right? It was all by radio. What we did was we all left our billets . . . we were hugging each other, and then before you knew it, spontaneously, we had a procession and we went to the church [within the PRPC].[107]

Even if Imelda Marcos was the camp director, there was enough anti-Marcos sentiment within the camp for Aquino's victory to be honored with a Catholic mass. Nida Magallanes pointed out that the revolution did not directly affect the Vietnamese. She was working in Palawan at the time, and she remembered many Vietnamese asked her questions about what was happening in Manila. She too emphasized the importance of radio: "They felt for us Filipinos . . . at the height of EDSA, People Power, they were listening to the radio."[108] The Vietnamese were anxious about the political instability, but Magallanes reassured them they would be okay.

With the new government, there were almost immediate changes at the PRPC for the Philippine staff. First, the military leadership, which had been headed by General Tobias, shifted to a civilian administration under Herman Laurel, who had been an Aquino supporter. This meant the camp's militarized command and structures diminished after 1986. According to most written and oral accounts, General Tobias had run a tight ship, and the camp ran smoothly under his command. As the reins were transferred from Tobias to Laurel, the UNHCR voiced concerns that the Aquino government was discharging an effective administrator for political reasons.[109] In the media, *Malaya* journalist José Burgos criticized the Aquino government for "merrily replacing incumbent officials." Burgos argued that Aquino should not jettison all of the Marcos-era appointees, and he singled out Tobias for his service, experience with the

Vietnamese refugees, and tenure with the Philippine military in Vietnam. He added, "Some people, I understand are eyeing the Tobias post, without realizing that the job does not partake of a political 'spoils' and that running the Center calls for a unique kind of experience and expertise. . . . President Cory should tell her people to keep politics out of the Refugee Center."[110] Despite this endorsement of Tobias, Laurel soon replaced him within the camp.

For the Vietnamese, little if anything changed, and most would not have noticed any changes that did occur because they were only in the camps for six-month stints. Many of the Filipino PRPC staff saw it as an opening for greater professional opportunities. Under Laurel, there was more room for staff participation, more benefits, more training, electric typewriters, and staff recreation. In other words, it was less like a military operation. One Filipina staff worker worked in the PRPC across the two administrations and felt positively about both: under Tobias, she learned discipline, how to meet deadlines, and the "proper way of writing," while the post-1986 bosses "were more like our friends" and there was less of a generation gap between the administrators and workers.[111]

On a policy level, the Aquino administration continued Philippine support for the PRPC. It worked closely with the UNHCR and the United States, and it too found political value in the symbolic work of the PRPC. The Aquino government accepted and repeated the Marcos government's faith in Philippine humanitarianism, albeit with an anti-Marcos twist. Most notably, the minister of foreign affairs under the Aquino administration, Raul S. Manglapus, had himself been a refugee during the Marcos era.[112] Manglapus very pointedly connected his own experiences to the experiences of the Vietnamese. On the eighth anniversary of the PRPC, Manglapus visited the camp and spoke evocatively about his flight from the Marcos government and political persecution:

I am not a stranger to being a refugee. I was a refugee from the previous government in our country. My family had to escape from the Philippines through Malaysia, through Sabah. And who are those who helped my family in their escape? Now that Marcos is safely in Hawaii, I can reveal that secret. It was the UNHCR.

Not only my family but many more Filipinos escaped the dictatorship in this country in order to find a place where constitutional freedoms would be available so that they might speak out for freedom in their country. And now after 13 and a half years of refuge in the United States, I am back and, as one can see, I am back in political power in this country.[113]

This was a remarkable speech because of Manglapus's identification with the Vietnamese and his revelation of his experiences in Sabah and his "fight for freedom" and "democracy." He connected his own personal story as a refugee from the Marcos dictatorship to that of the Vietnamese fleeing Vietnam and Southeast Asia. He also implicitly included Malaysia's regional role in accepting Filipino refugees. Blurring the ideological lines and Cold War binaries, Manglapus situated himself, and the Aquino government, on the side of refugees.[114]

FROM CAMP TO CAMP

The late 1980s saw substantial changes in the camp's demographics due to the acceleration of the Orderly Departure Program (ODP) within Vietnam and the implementation of the 1989 Comprehensive Plan of Action. The ODP had been in place since the 1979 Geneva conference, and it created a mechanism whereby Vietnamese could apply to exit from within Vietnam and avoid the dangers of escape by sea. In practice, it was a highly bureaucratic and fickle process, and Vietnamese had to convince Vietnamese and U.S. officials to issue the required paperwork for emigration. The process was plagued by bureaucratic delay and barriers to diplomatic relations (e.g., U.S. State Department officials were based in Bangkok rather than Ho Chi Minh City), and the program stalled in the early 1980s. However, by 1987, internal reforms in Vietnam, congressional legislation, and State Department protocols had jump-started the program. These combined changes expedited legal departures through the ODP in 1988 and 1989 and into the early 1990s. Vietnamese Amerasians (children of Vietnamese women and American men) became the most visible population to benefit from the improved ODP coordination. Many of these young people (generally adolescents by the late 1980s) became veritable "golden tickets" out of the country, and wealthy families would "adopt" Amerasians to create "fake families" and facilitate their own migration.[115] In addition, thousands of Vietnamese, particularly those with the economic and political wherewithal to bribe officials and navigate both countries' bureaucracies, could depart Vietnam without having to risk escape by sea.

For Vietnamese exiting through the ODP program in Ho Chi Minh City, the next stop was the Philippines. They were still required to go to the PRPC in Bataan for six months before resettling in the United States. Vietnamese

Amerasians could be disaffected, and they received a great deal of attention due to their physiognomy and, often, their history of psychological abuse. In oral history collections, Vietnamese Amerasians describe the PRPC as a place where they continued to suffer abuse and violence (both self-inflected and from others within the camp).[116] Many social workers and journalists attributed the increased levels of violence and instability within the PRPC in the 1990s to the influx of young Amerasians. As a result, there were two distinct populations within the PRPC in its final years: Vietnamese from first-asylum camps who had faced the trauma of sea escape, and Vietnamese who came directly from Vietnam through the ODP. A social worker from Morong remembered divisions between the "boat people" and those who came through the ODP. She noted that the boat people saw themselves as "survivor[s]."[117] They had risked their lives and gained refugee status, a route they believed had been more arduous than the bureaucratic immigration process from within Vietnam. By the early 1990s, Amerasians and Vietnamese who left through the ODP far outnumbered those from first asylum camps, thus changing the PRPC's demographics.[118]

Most Vietnamese activists in the diaspora remained focused on the poor conditions of the first-asylum camps and the trauma of re-education camp survivors who could not leave Vietnam. The PRPC was not a site of significant Vietnamese activism within the camp or a target of diasporic activism outside of it. In the 1980s, the Indochinese Refugee Action Center assisted those who came to the United States and integrated them into local communities, Boat People SOS continued to facilitate rescues at sea with international partners, and the Families of Vietnamese Political Prisoners Association (FVPPA) developed deep networks in Washington, D.C., to advocate for those who suffered in re-education camps. The Humanitarian Operation program went into motion to prioritize these re-education survivor cases in the early 1990s.[119] At this point, there was talk of first sending former political prisoners to the PRPC. This got the FVPPA's attention.

In 1992, the U.S. government floated a proposal to send released re-education camp prisoners to the PRPC, just like most other Vietnamese en route to the United States and resettlement. The State Department authorized an assessment of whether former political prisoners would benefit from the PRPC's cultural and English-language programs, since most received a mere six hours of cultural training before flying to the United States. Perhaps not surprisingly, voluntary agencies already working in the PRPC were more likely to support this program, while Vietnamese American organizations based in the United States did not. There was a consensus that former political prisoners needed more resettlement support, English-language instruction, and job training, but it was not clear how best to do this. The service providers who opposed additional training in the PRPC "primarily objected" to the location "outside the U.S. and to its use of non-American teachers."[120] FVPPA leader Khuc Minh Tho could not fathom how anyone could recommend that re-education camp survivors spend yet more time in a camp, no matter how benevolent. In a meeting with State Department personnel, the FVPPA leaders were blunt: "The camp is in the Philippines; and the Philippines is not the United States." More to the point, the proposed plan would send survivors of re-education camps into yet another camp system: "The camp causes bitter and unpleasant memories as they reflect on the time spent in reeducation.... They should not have to spend months in the Philippines to learn the United States system."[121]

The FVPPA mobilized its resources and reached out to allies in the Philippines to make sure former political prisoners were not sent to the PRPC. Khuc Minh Tho urged Sister Pascale, founder of the Center for Assistance to Displaced Persons, to call on her political alliances and ensure that the Philippine government did not contract with the United States to expand the PRPC's programming for re-education camp survivors. Her pitch was straightforward. Vietnamese former political prisoners had spent, on average, ten years in camps; they wanted to come directly to the United States. They did not want to go to another camp.[122]

Sister Margarita Tran Binh, who was also affiliated with the Center for Assistance to Displaced Persons, criticized the U.S. proposal for the PRPC as well. She voiced a more global critique of the camps, including the PRPC in the Philippines: "Living and working side by side with the refugees since 1980, I do not consider refugee camp a healthy environment for anyone. In refugee camp, the refugees are being subjected to rules and regulations which are more strict than those in normal society.... What do refugees usually gain in the refugee camp? If not dependency, fear, apprehension, humiliation ... and what do they lose? If not their dignity, self-esteem, self-reliance, self-confidence, and human rights." She explained there were "countless problems" the former political prisoners might confront in the Philippines, and if they transited through the PRPC, their arrival in the United States would be delayed. This was particularly poignant for those who had survived re-education camps. Why would they be sent to yet another camp? "None of them wants to stay one more day in the camp unless they have to. Our ex-political prisoners have been suffocated from freedom in many re-education camps. Why do we want to prolong their agonies?"[123] Like Khuc Minh Tho, Sister Margarita was criticizing the idea of placing those who had survived re-education camps in yet another camp. And yet her lament could also apply to Vietnamese at large. She did not view the camp as a chance for acculturation or improvement, nor did she wax nostalgic about the Philippines' humanitarian role. Rather, the PRPC was a delay, a possible roadblock, and a setting which fostered dependency and the loss of rights for all.

In their critique of the PRPC's efficacy for re-education camp survivors, these diasporic Vietnamese activists unintentionally questioned the legitimacy of the PRPC's overall mission. Who did the camps benefit? The PRPC had been set up to alleviate pressure on first-asylum countries such as Malaysia, Thailand, and Indonesia, and it enabled the United States to better control the number of Vietnamese entering that country. Of course, many former re-education camp survivors would already have gone through the PRPC. Men who suffered in re-education camps in the 1970s and 1980s, and when released fled to Malaysia or Hong Kong, would have been sent to the PRPC as a matter of course as part of the 1979 Geneva protocols. For many, their journey to the United States tracked an archipelago of camps, from re-education camps in Vietnam, to first-asylum camps in Malaysia, Thailand, Indonesia, and Hong Kong, and only then to the PRPC in Bataan. While unquestionably far better than the re-education camps and the first-asylum camps, the PRPC was still another camp, another place to navigate, tolerate, and wait.

Critically, Marcos used his cooperation with the UNHCR to accentuate his humanitarian credentials and the Philippines' international importance, even as he turned on his domestic enemies and committed gross human rights violations. In the process, millions of U.S. dollars entered the Philippines. Even after 1989, the PRPC's ideological, educational, and economic functions remained fairly constant, and the Philippines continued to be identified as a safe haven for refugees because of the PRPC. Marcos's gambit worked, and the PRPC became an odd yet telling node on Vietnamese journeys from Vietnam to the United States, and one that the Aquino government continued to honor. The PRPC remained open until the mid-1990s, after which the government transformed it into the Bataan Technology Park, with hopes it might become a tourist site.[124]

The Philippines also positioned itself as the opposite of Hong Kong. Starting in 1982, Hong Kong placed Vietnamese in closed camps run by prison guards, while the PRPC showcased English classes, excellent medical facilities, and importantly, a promised ticket to a western country. Hong Kong would become identified with barbed wire, closed camps, violent protests, and ultimately, forced repatriation. Hong Kong also did not have the neocolonial relationship to the United States that the Philippines did. By the late 1980s, the British colonial government and Hong Kong Chinese officials implemented policies which would fracture the 1979 regional agreement and lead to individual asylum screenings and the Comprehensive Plan of Action. Not every Vietnamese would be considered a refugee in Hong Kong, and many would be forcibly returned to Vietnam.

This chapter began with Ngoc, a Vietnamese man who had come to the hard reality that the PRPC was in the Philippines. His story is unusual because it is inconclusive, but as time progressed, more and more Vietnamese in camps in Malaysia, Indonesia, Thailand, and Hong Kong found they were no longer seen as refugees just because they were Vietnamese. Like Ngoc, their claims of being refugees would be challenged and subject to scrutiny, with authorities probing into their political identities and their economic circumstances. In no place was this truer than in Hong Kong.

FOUR

Hong Kong

DETERRENCE, DETENTION, AND
REPATRIATION, 1980–1989

ON JUNE 16, 1988, TWO OVERCROWDED BOATS holding seventy-eight Vietnamese arrived in Hong Kong harbor. Children dominated the group, with more than half being under the age of fifteen. The boats had set sail from central Vietnam, and the adults fully expected Hong Kong to grant them asylum and resettlement in a third country under the terms of the 1979 Geneva conference. This cohort arrived on June 16, one day after Hong Kong instituted a new screening policy. On June 15, 1988, the Hong Kong government announced it would no longer identify all Vietnamese as refugees. Instead, if Hong Kong officials determined that an individual faced persecution in Vietnam, he or she would be granted asylum and allowed to wait for a resettlement placement. If, however, the Hong Kong officials were *not* convinced, the Vietnamese individual would be detained and repatriated to Vietnam. Hong Kong officials estimated that only 10 percent of the Vietnamese were "genuine refugees."[1] And the message was not subtle. Hong Kong Secretary for Security Geoffrey Barnes declared, "The message we want to get across is, 'Do not come here; you will only face years of detention.'"[2]

Truong Viet Doi, a Vietnamese woman on one of the ill-timed boats, looked "bemused" on hearing she would not gain automatic asylum. Her husband had fled to Hong Kong two years earlier and resettled in Canada. She had planned to follow his path and join him in Edmonton. Nguyen Dai Tuan, a fisherman also aboard the boat, made two statements, foreshadowing the ambiguous and often overlapping histories of economic deprivation and political persecution: "We had to flee because rice has become too expensive back home," he said. He then concluded that he was a "genuine refugee" and he "would face political persecution if sent back."[3]

In the late 1980s, Hong Kong upended the UNHCR protocols hammered out in 1979 and effectively transformed Vietnamese from de facto refugees into asylum seekers. Unlike Guam and the Philippines, which were beholden to the U.S. government's prerogatives, Hong Kong was more akin to Malaysia. Hong Kong was still a British colony, yet like Malaysia, it did not rely on U.S. dollars or clientelism, and it wanted to do everything in its limited power to end the number of Vietnamese entering Hong Kong.

The Vietnamese influx coincided roughly with the end of Britain's ninety-nine-year lease over the New Territories and the negotiations to return Hong Kong to Chinese rule in 1997. Borders and refugee rights were not merely academic topics. Debates over these issues resonated within Hong Kong because of the local population's lack of full British citizenship, the growing restrictions against mainland Chinese border crossers, and the fear that Hong Kong Chinese themselves might become refugees after 1997. Hong Kong became emboldened to act unilaterally despite initial reservations in the U.K. and opposition from the United States. Hong Kong officials, both British and local Chinese civil servants, felt pressure to close the Vietnamese camps before the 1997 handover.[4] A colony with little formal authority, Hong Kong nevertheless managed to rewrite regional refugee policy, with serious ramifications for Vietnamese, first-asylum sites, resettlement countries, and the international standards of protection.

Throughout the 1980s, Hong Kong set the stage for the more aggressive and often controversial policy of repatriation. Historian Hong Kiu Yuen argues that between 1975 and 1979, Hong Kong's colonial status constrained any autonomous response to the incoming Vietnamese, and instead the British government used Hong Kong's asylum policy as an act of "proxy humanitarianism." In other words, the British could appear humanitarian through sheltering Vietnamese in Hong Kong without actually resettling more than a nominal number of Vietnamese within the U.K.[5] After 1980, Hong Kong increasingly maneuvered within the colonial framework and pushed the U.K., and the UNHCR, to accept what were initially seen as controversial policies, such as closed camps, individual screening, and repatriation. Hong Kong's assertiveness also allowed Great Britain, under Margaret Thatcher's leadership, to sidestep and obfuscate its own responsibility for these more punitive policies. Rejecting the notion that only the UNHCR and western nations could dictate what was humanitarian and what was not, Hong Kong decided to set its own course. This included closed camps or detention centers, individual screening, and ultimately, repatriation.

The UNHCR and the U.S. government both found themselves in a sticky place. The UNHCR supported repatriation in principle, *if* it could guarantee safe return to an individual's home country. This was a big if, and since 1975, there had been a tacit understanding within the UNHCR and first-asylum governments that Vietnamese would not be subject to repatriation. This assumption also hinged on Vietnam's refusal to accept repatriates or cooperate with the UNHCR; however, Vietnam's own economic and political practices were changing in the mid-1980s as it experimented with market reforms and sought recognition from the United States. The UNHCR had to choose between cooperating with Hong Kong's new screening mechanism or scrambling and cajoling the other first-asylum countries to keep the old 1979 framework in place.

For the U.S., Hong Kong's closed camps eerily mirrored U.S. practices in the Caribbean, particularly the acceleration of detention as a deterrent strategy against Haitians.[6] While Hong Kong officials often drew these connections, U.S. policy makers were mum. They refused to endorse a policy which denied refugee status to Vietnamese, who were former U.S. allies, or countenance their return to a communist country. The United States remained wedded to a quickly calcifying Cold War anti-communism, even as Hong Kong was looking ahead. Hong Kong had to contemplate its future under China's sovereignty, and ironically, closing the camps and initiating repatriation flights were among the only policy matters British, Hong Kong, and Chinese politicians agreed on.

The 1980s also saw the escalation of Vietnamese activism within the camps and in the diaspora. Facing the threat of repatriation (and increasingly prison-like conditions), Vietnamese within the camps began to protest, which took the form of hunger strikes, petitions, demonstrations, and internal unrest. In turn, students at the University of California, Irvine, located in Orange County—home to the largest Vietnamese community in the United States—mobilized their own resources to support Vietnamese in Hong Kong camps. In 1987, they formed Project Ngoc, and many would volunteer in Hong Kong. Students witnessed the protests and harsh camp environment, bringing their first-hand experiences back with them to the United States. Organizations like the Indochinese Resource Action Center (IRAC) and Boat People SOS also raised their voices, particularly when repatriation was on the table, and they found ways to lobby and influence policy makers in Washington, D.C. and Geneva.[7]

Between 1980 and 1988, events in Hong Kong reshaped who would be granted refugee status in the region and who would not. Hong Kong experimented with closed camps and deterrence policies. Its colonial status, relationship with China, and the Sino-British negotiations shaped how Hong Kong defined and viewed the politics of humanitarianism, refugees, and subsequent policies toward the Vietnamese. Vietnamese within the camps and the diaspora protested, advocated, and lobbied for their rights and protection more than a decade after the fighting between the United States and Vietnam had ended. Hong Kong argued that not all Vietnamese were refugees, and instead insisted that they must be screened on an individual basis. This set Hong Kong's own territory-specific vision of security and humanitarianism in motion, one that might be limited but would become a template for the region.

BRITISH CITIZENS, COLONIAL SUBJECTS, CHINESE
MIGRANTS, AND REFUGEES: HONG KONG
MIGRATION POLICY 1949–1980

Migration defined Hong Kong's twentieth-century population. Numbering as low as 650,000 in 1930, the population reached three million in 1950 due to the high number of Chinese fleeing the revolution.[8] By 1975, Hong Kong's population was 4.65 million, and in 1988, it topped 5.6 million.[9] Unlike migration to Malaysia or the Philippines, Hong Kong's demographic changes were potentially overwhelming.[10] As a result, it was impossible for Hong Kong to see the growing numbers of Vietnamese in the territory in isolation from the mounting restrictions on Chinese migrants. After 1980, the Hong Kong government promptly sent back any mainland Chinese who surreptitiously tried to cross into the territory, while it offered Vietnamese first asylum and the chance to resettle in the west.[11] The two policies stood in stark contrast to each other, and both unfolded against the backdrop of the Cold War and debates over refugee identity.

The British acquired Hong Kong Island in January 1841 under the Convention of Chuenpi during the First Opium War, and in 1842, the Treaty of Nanking solidified British rule over the island. In 1860, the British gained control over Kowloon, and in 1898, Britain entered a ninety-nine year lease with China to govern the New Territories (an additional 365 square miles).

During the nineteenth and early twentieth centuries, Chinese traveled and resettled back and forth between Hong Kong and Guangdong Province with relative ease, until the onset of World War II. Prompted by civil war and the Communist victory in 1949, more than 700,000 Chinese fled to Hong Kong, accounting for almost a third of the colony's population by the early 1950s. In 1954, the UNHCR sent a delegation led by Norwegian Edvard Hambro to investigate whether this massive influx of Chinese fell under the UNHCR's mandate. It was the first time that the UNHCR claimed an interest in non-European refugees. Britain was a signatory of the 1951 UNHCR Convention governing refugees, but it did not extend these protections to its colonial possessions. The People's Republic of China denied that the Chinese migrants were "refugees" wishing to escape a communist government. At the same time, China took the opportunity to criticize the British government's poor services and insufficient support for this very same population. To complicate matters even further, the Republic of China (ROC) on Taiwan held the official seat for China in the United Nations, and so in a narrow legal sense, Chinese "refugees" in Hong Kong had a government to which they could turn, that of the ROC. These combined factors meant that Chinese migrants never legally gained refugee status, but since they shared a common language, culture, and often, family networks with the people in Hong Kong, the Hong Kong government assisted in integrating them into the local economy. The colonial Hong Kong government framed this problem in its official publications as "a problem of people," in this case, Chinese people.[12]

A small cohort of Vietnamese did seek refuge in Hong Kong during the U.S. war in Vietnam, but they did not enter as refugees. Dozens of Chinese Vietnamese men left Saigon to evade the South Vietnamese draft and the war that had engulfed the country, and they integrated easily into the Cantonese-speaking territory.[13] This population was too small to garner much bureaucratic attention. Far greater was the number of Chinese pouring into Hong Kong in the wake of the Cultural Revolution.

The upheaval, violence, and chaos of the Cultural Revolution generated the conditions whereby thousands tried to escape China, and many set their sights on Hong Kong. Although the Cultural Revolution sparked left-wing, anti-British agitation within the colony, for many, it legitimized British rule as a preferred alternative to the People's Republic.[14] During these years, the border between Hong Kong and mainland China remained relatively open, and thousands crossed into Hong Kong and stayed. Chinese who resettled in Hong Kong were not persecuted, detained, or deported. This practice changed in 1974, by which point the Cultural Revolution had ebbed and the U.S. had initiated diplomatic relations with China. These macro-political changes and growing economic pressures made the colonial government less inclined to welcome incoming Chinese migrants out of humanitarian motives.[15] In 1974, Hong Kong Governor Murray MacLehose initiated a new "reach base" policy. If Chinese migrants made it across the border and into Hong Kong undetected, they would be allowed to stay; however, if they were stopped at the border by Hong Kong security, they would be deported and promptly sent back to China. The UNHCR expressed "concern" that individuals covered by the 1951 protocol might be returned to China, a practice akin to refoulement, but the UNHCR did not publicly criticize Hong Kong's decision.[16]

This 1974 practice of border control laid the groundwork for Hong Kong's subsequent migration policies, and it foreshadowed the later controversy over unfair screenings and forced repatriations of Vietnamese. The colonial government recognized it had to pay lip service to the possibility that some Chinese migrants might have a claim to refugee status, noting that it never committed to returning "*all*" illegal immigrants.[17] The Foreign and Commonwealth Office initially noted that Hong Kong officials would individually examine all cases. In principle, there was an interview process, but the Hong Kong government did not want to be too vocal about it, for "to do so would allow would-be illegal immigrants to prepare their stories accordingly."[18] Governor MacLehose added that if "it was publicly announced that genuine refugees would not be sent back, then everyone would claim refugee status."[19] This internal conversation would echo in the future when Hong Kong immigration officials doubted Vietnamese refugee claims, and the pressure mounted on migrants to tell a legible "refugee" story.[20] In most documents, government officials referred to the Chinese as "illegal immigrants" or "II's," and in practice, the Hong Kong government returned Chinese back across the border to China en masse.

Also foreshadowing later debates during the Vietnamese crisis, British officials dismissed human rights organizations as meddling and unpragmatic. Numerous NGOs, including Amnesty International, the American Council of Voluntary Agencies for Foreign Service, the International Rescue Committee, and Lutheran Immigration and Refugee Services, expressed their dissent.[21] The British Red Cross Society questioned the blanket removal of Chinese border crossers; it wanted to safeguard the rights of individuals seeking political asylum.[22] Many British politicians had no such compunctions.

Lord Goronwy-Roberts noted he had "little faith in organisations such as Amnesty International" and "no brief for draft dodgers."[23] Another British official noted, "The evidence for any increase in the severity of punishment for returned illegals is very thin, and based entirely on hearsay." In other words, he did not believe Chinese turned back at the border faced any reprisals. His concerns instead were political and about bad publicity. The government had to be vigilant, as Amnesty International was "already making noises."[24]

Finally, Taiwan-based organizations and politicians were the harshest critics of the new policy, and their rhetoric and tactics foreshadowed what would become vigorous Vietnamese diasporic campaigns in the 1980s and 1990s. These spokespeople condemned the British government for its weakness in the face of communism and for ignoring the purported western notions of humanitarianism. For example, the Association of the National Assembly of the Republic of China wrote to the British Parliament that the new policy was "equivalent to sending lambs into the mouths of wolves, an act tarnishing the reputation of your country. We urgently request you to adhere to Britain's consistent humanitarian policy and stop this repatriation in the name of justice."[25] The Free China Relief Association employed even stronger language, arguing that due to "population pressure," "the so-called 'Beacon of Freedom' has turned overnight into an 'Execution Ground' for the freedom seekers.... Could anything make people more shocked and indignant!"[26] These organizations simultaneously scoffed at notions of British moral superiority and tried to use these same claims to compel the Hong Kong government to protect and resettle incoming Chinese. British hypocrisy was twofold; it failed in its responsibility as a benevolent colonial power that was presumably "civilizing" the east, and it failed to meet its ideological responsibilities in the Cold War fight against communism. Vietnamese diasporic activists would call on similar language in the years to come. Yet despite these vitriolic statements, the British government argued that popular opinion within Hong Kong was on its side. The strongest objections would come from Taiwan, but "these will, of course be disregarded."[27]

The "reach base" policy persisted through 1980, at which point the Hong Kong government tightened its migration policy for a second time. Hong Kong repatriated more than 150,000 Chinese between 1974 and 1980, but this number was dwarfed by the more than 460,000 who crossed the border undetected and settled in Hong Kong. Most of the Chinese who made it into downtown Hong Kong or Kowloon found employment, assimilated quickly, and often reunited with relatives. Hong Kong officials feared that these numbers would only continue to grow, and they blamed illegal immigrants for increased government spending on social welfare programs and a rise in crime. Taking a harder line, the Hong Kong government announced that after October 23, 1980, all illegal immigrants who entered the territory could be arrested and deported, even if they had made it safely across the border and "touched base." This was a one-hundred-eighty-degree reversal of policy and custom. The government also would now require that "all persons resident in Hong Kong . . . [have] to carry proof of identity at all times."[28] Although there was a long history of registration and identity cards, this would be the first order that individuals must carry identification with them. It empowered immigration police to deport anyone without a Hong Kong ID card. Government officials noted that there were pitfalls to the proposal, namely the creation of a newly profitable black market for identity cards; however, they remained confident that a majority of people in Hong Kong supported increased controls on migration.[29] According to sociologist Agnes Ku, the 1980 policy played a significant role in creating cultural and legal distinctions between Hong Kong Chinese and "mainlanders."[30]

Hong Kong's crackdown against unauthorized Chinese migrants coincided with the large number of Vietnamese fleeing their country in the late 1970s. In accord with the 1979 Geneva agreement, Hong Kong accepted all incoming Vietnamese, and the UNHCR promised them resettlement in a third country. The result was a two-tiered system, and one in which Chinese were de facto illegal immigrants and Vietnamese were de facto refugees. Tory MP Peter Blaker justified the division: "The Hong Kong government has displayed active humanitarian concern for the tens of thousands who last year reached the territory in small boats from Vietnam. These people are internationally recognized as refugees. They should not be confused with the many thousands who each year illegally cross the border from China to Hong Kong."[31] With this flourish, Blaker upheld the practice of offering Vietnamese first asylum and eventual resettlement in a third country. Yet many Hong Kong Chinese wondered why Vietnamese could remain in camps and resettle in the United States, Canada, and Australia, while their own relatives could not legally remain in Hong Kong. People in Hong Kong also could not view the Vietnamese camps in isolation. Rather, the Vietnamese camps coexisted in a landscape defined by years of Chinese migration, and more recently, migration restrictions and deportations. As a result, Hong Kong Chinese grew to resent the policy discrepancies and began advocating for a more consistent policy: first closed camps, and then, repatriation for the Vietnamese.

Between 1975 and 1980, more than 80,000 Vietnamese landed in Hong Kong, and initially Hong Kong offered one of the more liberal camp settings in Southeast Asia, particularly compared to Malaysia, Indonesia, and Thailand. In 1975, the *Clara Maersk,* a Danish ship, brought 3,743 Vietnamese to Hong Kong, and between 1976 and 1978, the number of Vietnamese in the territory remained modest, never topping more than 5,000 at one time. The numbers escalated dramatically in 1979, when the massive and organized exodus of Chinese Vietnamese led to the region-wide crisis. In Hong Kong, more than 68,000 Vietnamese arrived in just the first few months of 1979.[32] With the 1979 Geneva conference, Hong Kong agreed to be a place of first asylum, guaranteeing that it would not "push off" incoming Vietnamese and would offer refuge until Vietnamese were resettled in a third country.

Between 1979 and 1982, approximately, 30,000 Vietnamese arrived in Hong Kong and waited. The largest camp was Kai Tak North, located in the heart of Kowloon, a busy residential and industrial area. Densely populated with rows of warehouse-like bunkhouses, crowded and unsanitary, the camp housed Vietnamese in cramped quarters and surrounded by high fences. In oral history collections, Vietnamese Americans referred to the Hong Kong camps as "concentration camps" as a matter of course, and they emphasized the daily roll calls, which made them feel like prisoners.[33] Comparatively, Hong Kong's camps were more open than similar facilities in Thailand and Malaysia, but even the Hong Kong camps could cause a great deal of psychological stress. Norwegian anthropologist John Christian Knudsen documented the damage to the Vietnamese inhabitants' mental health, their wasted time, and the sub-par educational and recreational activities.[34] For example, Hung Luu remembered that Sham Shui Po, a camp in Kowloon, was truly "miserable," and the officers would all "treat you like refugee."[35] Of course, Hung Luu was in the camp precisely because he claimed to be a refugee, but his offhand comment emphasized the dismissive and negative ramifications of this very category. To be seen as a refugee was an invitation for confinement and material deprivation.

Unlike those in Malaysia, the Hong Kong camps were initially "open." The government not only allowed but expected Vietnamese to leave the compounds and work in Hong Kong in order to pay for their subsistence. During these years, Hong Kong's economy was growing due to the rapid expansion of light manufacturing. There was a need for more factory workers and cheap labor, and Vietnamese stepped into these jobs and earned hard currency. There was even an employment agency within the camp that acted as a liaison between Vietnamese and local manufacturers.[36] The UNHCR estimated that by 1982, hundreds of the families in the open camps were "self-supporting when it came to food."[37] Woo Chan Chan recalled that it was easy to find a job, especially in the electronics industry. She worked in factories alongside Hong Kong workers, commuting back and forth between the factories and the camp. Woo Chan Chan reminisced about how much she enjoyed exploring Hong Kong: "Saturday, oh was a lovely day! We got up quickly in the camp and dressed neatly. That was the day we all wanted to go to town! Some wanted to go shopping, others visited their relatives who lived in Hong Kong, and still others preferred to travel around Hong Kong, and see all the places near it. I was one of this number." Her reference to the possibility of relatives within Hong Kong underscored older networks of diasporic Chinese communities and the ability of Chinese Vietnamese to speak Cantonese with the local population. Still, Woo Chan Chan was not immune from Hong Kong's growing animosity against the Vietnamese. She added, "One Saturday when my friend and I were walking down the road, we heard a Hong Kong person shout angrily at us: 'Go back to your country.'"[38]

Hong Kong's camp demographics included substantial numbers of Chinese Vietnamese, southern Vietnamese, and northern Vietnamese, resulting in a heterogeneous population with competing claims for refugee status and resettlement. As detailed in chapter 2, in 1979, a significant number of Chinese Vietnamese left Vietnam under duress. Those who made their way to Hong Kong often spoke Cantonese and had family connections in the territory. Indeed, close to 14,000 Chinese Vietnamese resettled permanently in Hong Kong before 1983. In the 1970s, approximately 70 percent of the Vietnamese in Hong Kong were Chinese Vietnamese, and like Woo Chan Chan, they could more easily navigate and explore Hong Kong because of their facility with the language.[39] However, with the end of the military conflict between Vietnam and China, the numbers shifted heavily toward ethnic Vietnamese. In 1983, Chinese Vietnamese made up about 55 percent of the camp population still waiting for resettlement, and the incoming Vietnamese after this date were almost all (90 percent) ethnic Vietnamese.[40]

Because of its geography, Hong Kong admitted far more Vietnamese from central and northern Vietnam than other first-asylum sites did. Hong Kong officials, U.S. officials, and Vietnamese themselves frequently remarked on the animosities between northern and southern Vietnamese within the camps and the need to separate Vietnamese by region due to infighting. More materially, the U.S. government privileged Vietnamese from southern Vietnam for resettlement. The northern Vietnamese had been the "enemy," so the U.S. generally dismissed their refugee claims and refused to resettle them. This meant that Hong Kong developed a larger "long-stayer" or "hard-core" population of unsettled, waiting Vietnamese than other first-asylum countries. The growing number of Vietnamese long-stayers also magnified the contradiction between Hong Kong's increasingly restrictive policy against Chinese migrants and its more generous policy toward Vietnamese.

There was still an even more complicated group commonly labeled by authorities as "ex-China Vietnamese illegal immigrants," or ECVIIs. During the 1978–79 political and military conflict between China and Vietnam, more than 200,000 Chinese Vietnamese fled Vietnam by land, and China resettled this population in rural areas near the border. When Chinese Vietnamese stranded on collective farms learned that people fleeing from northern Vietnam were finding refuge in Hong Kong, they too decided to make the trip and try the same path to the west. The UNHCR and Hong Kong authorities categorized these Chinese Vietnamese as Chinese rather than Vietnamese and deported them back to China as they did other undocumented Chinese border crossers. Chinese Vietnamese coming from China would then lie about their boat journeys, trying to establish that they had originated from northern Vietnam, not China. UNHCR officials often remarked that the ECVIIs were among the trickiest cases, because it was hard to parse where people were coming from. In the end, the ECVIIs had few avenues of recourse, and they were rejected by Hong Kong and resettlement countries.

The Hong Kong government worried it would be left with long-stayers, or what it more disparagingly referred to as "residue," equating the lingering population with a sticky substance that would not leave and could not be rubbed out. These long-stayers could be from northern Vietnam, or they might have refused one country's placement offer in hopes of another one, or they simply might not have met the political and economic criteria desired by the resettlement country.[41] The United States continued to select the Vietnamese it wanted, namely those who had served in the Republic of Vietnam's military or government or worked for the United States. Few Vietnamese from central or northern Vietnam could make these claims. The U.K. also offered limited resettlement opportunities. In 1979, Margaret Thatcher pledged to resettle 10,000 Vietnamese, but after meeting this initial quota, Britain's commitment dropped to the mere hundreds per year. In 1985, the U.K. resettled approximately 500 families. In 1986 this number dropped to 464 Vietnamese, and the number remained low, with 468 resettlements in 1987.[42] As historian Laura Madokoro has argued, majority-white resettlement countries like the U.S., U.K., Australia, and Canada often accepted symbolic numbers of Vietnamese to demonstrate their humanitarian bona fides, while in fact limiting numbers based on their ideological (in the case of the U.S.) and economic (Canada and Australia) potential.[43] For Hong Kong, this meant that even though only 3,485 Vietnamese entered the territory in 1982, there were still close to 10,000 Vietnamese in the camps.[44]

The UNHCR expressed frustration that many Vietnamese did not accept their first placement and often tried to "wait it out" for resettlement in the United States. This was one of the risks of the open camps; the conditions were not dire, so individuals did not mind waiting. In a backhanded acknowledgment of racial discrimination and the challenge of acculturation, one UNHCR official added that Hong Kong was often a friendlier locale than most resettlement sites. He reflected that "given the fact that they are self-supporting in a society where they feel relatively secure (indeed often more secure than in a more alien country of final asylum) Hong Kong refugees have tended to develop a selectiveness with regard to resettlement offers."[45] In other words, Vietnamese were willing to wait in Hong Kong.

These macro forces were already well under way when a disturbance within Kai Tak North sparked Hong Kong's decision to force all future Vietnamese into closed camps. On April 30, 1982, violence broke out in the camp, and more than a thousand people were involved in fights that lasted through the first days of May. Riot police arrested 176 Vietnamese and confiscated homemade weapons. More than twenty people were injured. Although there was a tendency to chalk these conflicts up to fights between northern and southern Vietnamese over the April 30th anniversary of the Fall of Saigon, or Reunification Day, close observers argued that anxieties about refugee status played just as significant a role. Hong Kong security officers noted that northerners believed they faced discrimination from resettlement countries. In contrast, southerners adopted a "righteous and superior attitude," saw themselves as "true refugees," and believed the northerners were "interlopers" who hurt the southerners' own chances of resettlement.[46] Other observers pointed to economic competition between Chinese Vietnamese and ethnic Vietnamese and the relatively better economic opportunities for Cantonese-speaking Vietnamese in Hong Kong.[47]

In response to these conflicts and growing frustration with the Vietnamese population, Hong Kong instituted a harsher policy of "closed camps" on July 2, 1982. This began an era of "humane deterrence." Closed camps would be run by the Correctional Services Department (CSD), or more colloquially, the Prisons Department, and Vietnamese would no longer be able to leave the camps for work or other purposes. The logic went as follows: If Hong Kong confined Vietnamese in closed camps, rather than allowing them to work in Hong Kong, it would act as a deterrent, and fewer Vietnamese would seek refuge within Hong Kong. Those who had arrived before July 1, 1982, could remain in open camps until resettlement in a third country. Any Vietnamese arriving on July 2, 1982, onward would be held in a closed camp. Deterrence was arguably far more important than the "humane" aspect of the policy, although Hong Kong officials were always quick to defend their commitment to first asylum. Calling on its Britishness, Hong Kong maintained it would not prevent landings and send boats off, like Malaysia and Thailand were apt to do. Hong Kong simply would no longer promise the opportunity to work outside or leave the camps, and in the process, the camps became even more like jails.

"Humane deterrence" would only work if Vietnamese in Vietnam knew they would be held in closed camps in Hong Kong. In order to speed the message along, the Hong Kong Security Branch suggested that all letters being mailed to Vietnam be clearly stamped "Chi Ma Wan Closed Centre," so that relatives receiving the missives would be warned about the camps. A Mr. Lok from the immigration department urged more direct language. He suggested astutely "that most Vietnamese would not know what a 'closed centre' was but they would surely understand what a 'prison' was."[48]

The CSD took over the management of the closed camps, and so it was professional prison officers who managed them. The government defended the decision to place the CSD in charge as a matter of efficiency and expediency. It argued that only the correctional department had the skills to control large numbers of people in enclosed spaces. The camps remained overcrowded and unsanitary, and Vietnamese families now had little to do except wait. Adults could no longer find work in Hong Kong's thriving economic sector, children often knew nothing of grass or open spaces, and corrections officers policed the space and maintained order. There were basic English-language classes and social services programming, which the UNHCR characterized as offering a low standard of instruction.[49] In Chi Ma Wan, Vietnamese were held tantalizingly close to the water, with beaches visible from behind the wire. The punitive nature of the camps was intentional. One Vietnamese man explained, "A camp is a camp you know. . . . They treat us like detainees . . . criminals."[50]

In a 1983 Hong Kong television report on Chi Ma Wan, the anchor noted that the new life of the Vietnamese was no freer than the old. One Vietnamese explained, "Hong Kong is really very kind, but we have no freedom, no rights." In this formulation, Hong Kong's "kindness" could not equate with rights. Clinton Leeks, the Hong Kong security director, described the situation as "walking on [a] tightrope."[51] If the policy was too harsh, the Hong Kong government would face criticism from the international community, but if there was "too much humanity," the camps would not act as an effective deterrent.

Anthropologists, journalists, and non-government organizations all attacked Hong Kong for the closed camps, but the government remained adamant that its policy was humane and necessary.[52] In 1984, the British Refugee Council condemned Hong Kong for its prison-like treatment of Vietnamese: "The fact that the refugee camp at Cape Collinson is in effect a prison within a prison makes it an unsuitable site. . . . Refugees are not criminals in need of correctional treatment."[53] Oxfam came to similar conclusions: "The overwhelming impression of all closed camps is that they are prisons. They are surrounded by tall fences and there are uniformed officers everywhere."[54] In some regards, prisons were seen as preferable: "Even a prisoner in Stanley Prison knows the length of his sentence and has the chance of being released early for good conduct. The refugees, who have committed no crime, do not know how long they will have to stay in prison and can do nothing to advance their release."[55] Norwegian anthropologist John Christian Knudsen, who conducted extensive fieldwork in multiple trips to Hong Kong, was also highly critical of the Orwellian ramifications of "humane deterrence" and the similarities to prison camps.[56]

In order to combat some of the negative publicity associated with the closed camp policy, the Hong Kong government developed its own public relations materials. The Hong Kong Security Branch hoped an illustrated booklet would set out its side of the story *and* compel western countries to expedite their resettlement policies.[57] The pamphlet, titled "No Exit," would serve two functions. First, it would emphasize that Hong Kong had fulfilled its humanitarian duties and reached its limit. Second, it would appeal to leaders in western countries, highlighting poignant stories from Vietnamese within the camps, with the goal of stimulating resettlement offers. As Security Officer Clinton Leeks noted, the booklet should be a powerful "lobbying

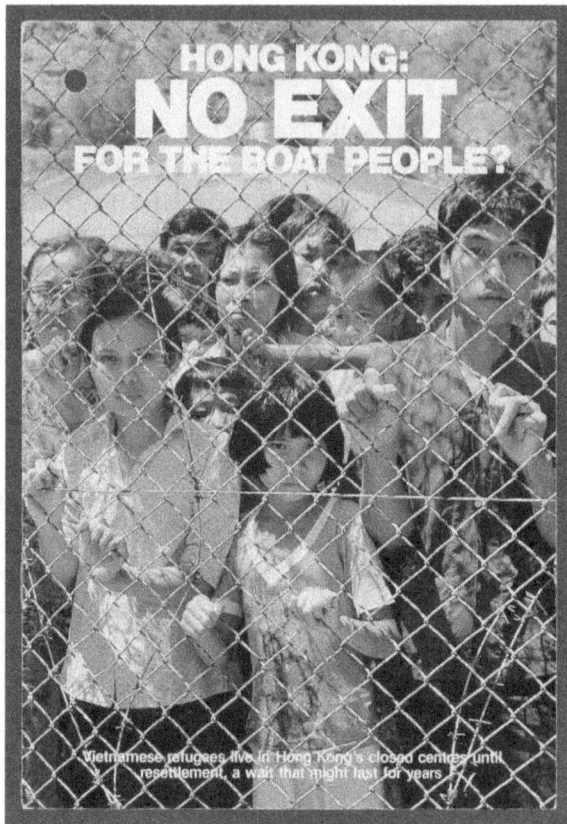

FIGURE 10. Hong Kong government publication developed with the hope of persuading other countries to resettle the Vietnamese waiting in the camps. This publication was also translated into French and German. Hong Kong Public Records Office, Government Records Service (政府檔案處歷史檔案館).

tool."[58] In the editing process, the officials were attentive to detail and optics, for example, requesting that the term "camps" be replaced by the more neutral "centres."[59] They also debated how to best use images from within the camps. Hong Kong security officials worried that photographs of camps ringed by barbed wire might backfire and cause greater criticism rather than sympathy for Hong Kong's situation. One officer bluntly noted, "The front picture brought to mind immediately the dreadful pictures one sees every now and then of Auschwitz. What do you think?"[60] The Hong Kong government ultimately published 10,000 copies of the pamphlet; yet try as they might, the officers themselves seemed cognizant that images of the camps invoked detention facilities more than they did Hong Kong's humanitarianism or generosity.

In spite of these critiques, the Hong Kong government remained firm; it had fulfilled its humanitarian obligations and only the CSD had the capacity to control the camps.[61] Hong Kong CSD officers repeatedly argued that life in the camps was not like the experience of being incarcerated: "The [Oxfam] report [Vietnamese Refugees in Hong Kong: The Way Forward] refers to closed centres as 'prisons.' In fact, the only resemblance between a closed centre and a prison is that both places are used for the confinement of people. In all other respects the closed centres are operated under a totally different regime with the refugees given as much freedom as is practically possible within the confines of their place of enforced residence."[62] In an oral history with historian Carina Hoang, Mak Pak Lam, a former prisons officer, explained, "The Prison Department was professionally well-trained. . . . It was not an easy matter with [such] a large number [of people]." He added that the department knew how to manage people in confined facilities, and the Vietnamese at Kai Tak numbered 8,000: "Just imagine how we supplied food—it was not a small matter." The logistics were considerable, and they needed to be able to offer enough food, bathing water, and drinking water, and to clear human waste out of the camps. He believed the task was too complicated for volunteers or a civilian branch to oversee, and "that's why [the] prison [department] 'reached out its hand' to receive the boat people."[63] The CSD officers had to allow the Vietnamese to move around within the camp, even if they were behind barbed wire. In this way, it was much different than a prison, where inmates could be forced into their cells. However, the enclosed space and long days with little to no activity could lead to fights, physical and sexual assaults, and political protests, and so CSD officers found it extremely challenging to maintain order. The conundrum was how to uphold the language of humanitarianism while also detaining people indefinitely in miserable conditions. Despite the linguistic gymnastics and individual goodwill, to most Vietnamese and outside observers, the camps seemed very much like prisons.

The British blamed the United States for this particular late-colonial headache. The United States maintained that all the Vietnamese deserved resettlement but then implemented a selective process, which effectively categorized only a minority as "refugees." The INS instituted a complicated and bureaucratic infrastructure within the camps, consisting of multiple interviews where an applicant faced possible rejection at each stage, particularly if they expressed economic reasons for leaving the country. In practice, a minority of Vietnamese in Hong Kong cleared the INS's threshold for refugee resettlement in the United States.[64] Thomas Wu, the superintendent of the Hong Kong camps, described that after being rejected by the United States, "The women cried and the men were speechless. Some were hysterical."[65] By the early 1980s, Hong Kong officials estimated that the Americans refused close to 90 percent of the applicants from Hong Kong because "they do *not* consider them to be refugees." However, those individuals remained in the camps indefinitely with the presumption of resettlement elsewhere. "Hong Kong is restrained in its treatment of them by the fact that the UNHCR does consider them to be refugees."[66]

The U.S. government believed that the remaining Vietnamese in Hong Kong should be a British and *not* an American responsibility. In the early 1980s, the U.K. accepted only token numbers of Vietnamese, and Thatcher's conservative government remained firm that it would not accept more. A U.S. official relayed to his British counterpart that "Hong Kong was seen by the world as a British problem, and leaving aside questions of morality, it was idle to pretend that either Her Majesty's Government or the Hong Kong Government could afford to sully its reputation by turning refugees out to sea."[67] In other words, the Americans threw Britain's benevolent colonial obligations back at them and almost taunted them with the need to uphold western humanitarian norms. They went on to point out that the U.K. should accept more Vietnamese itself before trying to pressure the United States on resettlement. British MPs resisted this line of argument, insisting that since the Americans had lost the war in Vietnam, the Vietnamese were primarily an American problem. Labour MP Donald Anderson stated on a trip to Hong Kong that "Britain only had a secondary responsibility" for the Vietnamese, because the United States and France had "colonial and historical experience[s] in Vietnam."[68] Competing over who had the *least* colonial responsibility for the Vietnamese became an Anglo-American contest. Both countries argued that the other was the imperial power left holding the bill, and in this case, the integration of thousands of Vietnamese. This made Hong Kong, as one British official put it, the "pig in the middle."[69]

Left to their own devices, and with thousands of Vietnamese lingering in camps, Hong Kong officials stuck with the closed-camp policy and the rhetoric of humane deterrence. They also began to speak openly of repatriation, voluntary or otherwise.

In 1987, Hong Kong Secretary for Security and Legislative Council (LegCo) member David Jeaffreson stated that Vietnamese repatriation was his preferred plan, committing a so-called gaffe when he expressed these opinions to the press.[70] "In principle" all newly arrived Vietnamese should be screened—and those who were not "genuine refugees" would be repatriated since they were only "economic migrants." Galvin Young, a journalist in Hong Kong, explained Jeaffreson's remarks as equal parts "digs" at the U.K. and a sop to Hong Kong's popular sentiment. The Chinese language press "hailed the move as practical and effective," with some public figures reportedly jumping for joy at the formal statements on repatriation.[71] Assistant Secretary for Security Ken Woodhouse added that repatriation would lead to a "durable solution," and other Hong Kong officials thought "it would only need a couple of plane loads, landing back in Vietnam to have the deterrent effect they're looking for." These colonial officials wanted to act, and they argued London was slowing them down because they were not yet "satisfied" that Vietnam would respect the needed human rights conditions.[72]

Hong Kong colonial officials had been toying with the idea of repatriation since 1982. However, they were told repatriation was a "non-starter," since the UNHCR and the "free world" generally regarded the Vietnamese as refugees.[73] The UNHCR opposed repatriation, as did London. Still, the Hong Kong officials remained optimistic that "if talks failed on involuntary repatriation, [they] might at least produce something for voluntary repatriation."[74] The fantasy of voluntary repatriation imagined that Vietnamese waiting in Hong Kong would choose to return to Vietnam on their own volition.

Within Great Britain, "voluntary repatriation" had a very particular connotation, associated with the rise of Enoch Powell and the conservative movement in postwar Britain.[75] The idea emerged in Britain in the 1960s as a xenophobic response to the rising numbers of non-white immigrants from former colonies in the West Indies and South Asia who were quickly changing the U.K.'s demographics. As early as 1965, the Conservative Party incorporated voluntary repatriation into its party platform.[76] Powell, the face of the party, promoted voluntary repatriation as a means to eject former colonial subjects from the polity, and his anti-immigrant rhetoric emphasized the value of an all-white England. In 1968, he delivered the "Rivers of Blood" speech, which cemented his anti-immigrant, anti-black political ideology. The *Times* of London noted that Powell gave anti-immigrant policies "a clothing of respectability." He also substantively changed the terms of debate. Politicians no longer argued over immigration restriction or "how to treat" new immigrants; rather, the emphasis was on "how to get them out."[77] Public opinion polls in the U.K. demonstrated that a consistent majority of British citizens supported government efforts to offer "voluntary repatriation" to "colored immigrants."[78] Powell's emphasis on the "voluntary" nature of his proposals belied the foundational belief that non-white immigrants did not belong in Great Britain.[79]

In other words, "voluntary repatriation" was a term loaded with colonial and anti-immigrant baggage. It traveled into the language of Hong Kong bureaucracy with little comment or connection to its 1960s anti–West Indian and anti-black politics. This layered etymology and British context remain unremarked upon in the Hong Kong, British, and UNHCR records. However, its sanitized usage was telling as the idea of "voluntary repatriation" circulated from the British mainland to its colonial outpost. Advocates for repatriation began testing the waters in the early 1980s, but they faced resistance from multiple quarters, including the UNHCR, London, and the United States.

The UNHCR argued that repatriation to Vietnam was off the table. The Vietnamese government had categorically refused to accept repatriates and viewed those who left as "traitors who had refused to help build the country." Although there might be "some possible softening" of this position, the UNHCR did not see any major changes in the early 1980s.[80] Vietnam still maintained an extensive network of "re-education" camps, and as long as Vietnam threatened to punish returnees, the UNHCR refused to take part in any repatriation scheme.

The Hong Kong government then put pressure on the U.K. to take a more aggressive stance against the Vietnamese. This was an instance of a colonial government working to get around its limited authority and convince the metropole to change course. Hong Kong officials wrote to London urging the government to treat incoming Vietnamese just as it did Chinese: "We believe the door should and can be shut." From their perspective, the Vietnamese and the Chinese were all "illegal immigrants."[81] They also noted that the camps were overcrowded, resettlement rates had slowed, and there was "little sympathy among Chinese in Hong Kong for Vietnamese." Repatriation was the answer. Hong Kong's colonial government found a relatively sympathetic hearing in the Foreign Office with staunch Thatcherite Lord Belstead.[82] However, London was hesitant to take any action without the support of the UNHCR. From the Foreign Office's perspective, the number of Vietnamese was manageable and hardly a burden in the greater scheme of Hong Kong's growing population. The Foreign Office also cautioned that the U.K. should not get too far out on a limb or support repatriation until the UNHCR "accepted that the boat people were economic migrants, not refugees."[83]

Already under attack for its closed-camp policy, London did not want Hong Kong to "set the pace" and implement a repatriation program or break with the 1979 agreements.[84] First-asylum countries (such as Malaysia and Indonesia) had closed camps, so Hong Kong's change was not out of step with the region. However, going further with repatriation would jeopardize the international reputation of Hong Kong and, by extension, of the U.K. The risks simply did not outweigh the benefits. Even floating the idea of repatriation could harm the U.K.'s standing. For example, if the U.K. broached the subject with Hanoi, it could "risk a leak," and "put us in the doghouse publicly even if we have in practice taken no decisions on involuntary repatriation."[85] London also shushed Hong Kong legislative councilors who had announced that economic migrants would be repatriated after a certain date. "We need to ensure that there are no more public statements of this kind."[86] London concluded that it had to rein in the Hong Kong government. Hong Kong remained a British colony, and repatriation was off the table because of the "humanitarian considerations and legal difficulties."[87]

For the Americans, repatriation was not even a consideration. Although its own acceptance rates had declined, U.S. ideological commitments to anticommunism and the United States' wounded pride prevented it from contemplating returns to Vietnam. In the 1980s, the United States did not have diplomatic relations with Vietnam, and it primarily aimed to punish and isolate the country. The Reagan government remained almost monomaniacal in its pursuit of MIAs and POWs. The Vietnamese held a place akin to that of Cubans during the 1980 Mariel boatlift; even economically and racially undesirable people fleeing a communist country had ideological value to the Carter and Reagan governments. The U.S. government could not fathom or condone a policy which would return people to a communist country, particularly one which challenged U.S. power. In addition, with the Joint Voluntary Agency and INS officers in Southeast Asia and Hong Kong, the United States could limit who it would and would not accept. Finally, the

United States did not want the Vietnamese government to get any "kudos" or be able to "make political mileage" out of repatriation.[88] In other words, the U.S. rejected repatriation not because it opposed deportation regimes, but because it did not want Vietnam to win any points or acknowledgment as a legitimate place of return.

Hong Kong officials were not so fixated on anti-communism. They could not afford to be. After 1997, Hong Kong would revert to Chinese sovereignty.

THE BASIC LAW: BRITISH COLONY TO CHINESE SPECIAL ADMINISTRATIVE REGION

Overshadowing the debates over Vietnamese refugee status was Hong Kong's pending transfer from British to Chinese sovereignty. For Hong Kong, this was the main event. Since the fall of the Qing dynasty in 1912, China had renounced the "unequal" treaties which had ceded Hong Kong, Kowloon, and the New Territories to Great Britain in the nineteenth century. However, choosing not to force the point, China did not directly challenge the U.K., even during the 1949 revolution. As China reached a rapprochement with the west in the early 1970s, Great Britain was no longer an imperial power, and its interest (and ability) in maintaining its final colonial holdings had waned. In contrast, Deng Xiaoping believed that China could benefit from Hong Kong's financial growth, shed the indignities of the colonial era, and showcase the possibility of reincorporating territory under the "one country, two systems" model. In a monumental meeting for Hong Kong's future, Prime Minister Thatcher and Deng Xiaoping signed the Joint Declaration in December 1984 agreeing that all of Hong Kong would revert to Chinese sovereignty on July 1, 1997. Hong Kong would have a "high degree of autonomy" for fifty years after that.[89]

Under colonial rule, the U.K. had offered Hong Kong very little in the way of democracy. It was telling that Hong Kong was not one of the signatories of the Joint Declaration, and Hong Kong satirists likened it to an arranged marriage in which the bride (Hong Kong) had no choice in her groom.[90] Hong Kong was a Crown colony with an appointed British governor up until 1997. The governor appointed both the Executive Council and LegCo from the administrative elite and business sectors. There were no elections before 1984. The only real checks on the governor's power were the British parliament, the press, and the cooperation of the civil service. The colonial government opened up the civil service to Hong Kong Chinese after World War II, but because there was never any illusion that Hong Kong would become an independent nation, like other former colonies, Britain did not institute democratic reforms. With 1997 looming, Britain faced pressure to implement democratic structures as a hedge against Chinese communist control and to protect Hong Kong's economic system. However, even these were modest. In 1985, there were elections for roughly half of the LegCo seats, but these were through indirect elections, and only members of district boards and professional constituencies could vote. The first direct elections for LegCo members did not occur until 1991. China sought to continue the British colonial practice of consolidating executive power without direct elections and resisted British efforts to democratize Hong Kong at so late a date.[91]

Many Hong Kong Chinese worried about their own political future after 1997. In 1981, the British Nationality Act changed the terms of Hong Kong Chinese's relationship with Great Britain. More than 2.5 million were now only "British Dependent Territory Citizens," and the British government established numerous barriers against migration to the U.K.[92] However, even with these restrictions, more than 600,000 Hong Kong Chinese left the territory after 1984, settling in Australia, Canada, the United States, New Zealand, Singapore, and the U.K. Elite Hong Kong Chinese with international connections hoped their personal and family ties would ease their ability to emigrate and adopt a new nationality, even if they ultimately returned to Hong Kong. These options were simply not open to the majority of Hong Kong's working-class population.[93]

With large numbers of people in Hong Kong looking for an exit plan, there was a growing resentment against the Vietnamese and their presumed right of resettlement in the west. It was impossible to divorce the Vietnamese camps from Hong Kong's anxieties about the future, which one official characterized as a "malaise."[94] The colonial conundrum was manifold. Because of its British legacies and commitments, Hong Kong needed to preserve at least a veneer of humanitarianism, and the Hong Kong government held the line against sending boats back to sea. At the same time, the end of the British colonial era created new possibilities for Hong Kong politicians, and Hong Kong Chinese LegCo members took the lead in demanding harsher measures against the Vietnamese. By flexing their political muscles, they demonstrated an independence from London and Geneva, and the U.S. held little sway. Hong Kong would not push boats back to sea, but it would push the UNHCR and the international community to embrace repatriation.

In the shadow of the existential negotiations over Hong Kong's transfer from British to Chinese sovereignty, the Vietnamese camps took on an outsized role. Hong Kong politicians knew that they had at least the tacit support of the U.K. and China for more aggressive policies against the Vietnamese. With so many unknowns and points of dispute, here was one issue where the U.K. and China found consensus: closing the camps before 1997. The issue also made strange bedfellows of Hong Kong's pro-Beijing and pro-democracy activists. The majority all agreed on repatriating the Vietnamese. With this knowledge, Hong Kong politicians took matters into their own hands, symbolically tore up the 1979 Geneva agreement, and made repatriation a reality.

The UNHCR initially underestimated Hong Kong's tenacity and willingness to undo almost a decade's worth of regional cooperation. Hong Kong was a colony, after all. As journalist Catherine Napier noted, "Hong Kong is, to a large extent, powerless to act because it's Britain which decides the colony's foreign policy and Britain has said it's not prepared to consider revising the policy of first asylum."[95] According to Fazul Karim, the UNHCR representative in Hong Kong, "Hong Kong, unlike other countries, has little political clout. All that LegCo could do was to make some noise."[96] However, LegCo, led by Rita Fan, appointed in 1983 and a fixture in Hong Kong's political scene before and after 1997, made noise, and more. Fan was the head of LegCo's Ad Hoc Group on Vietnamese Refugees, and she became the most vocal advocate for forcible repatriation and the closure of Vietnamese camps in Hong Kong.[97]

Demanding action and resolution, LegCo members voiced some of their sharpest anti-imperial critiques against the U.K. over the stalled Vietnamese policy. LegCo members urged the U.K. to take immediate action. Between 1982 and 1987, the number of Vietnamese in the camps hovered around 10,000 people, and it only dipped below 9,000 briefly in 1986.[98] The Vietnamese question became one of the most contentious and visible issues in the Hong Kong media, and British officials saw it as part of Hong Kong's "birth pangs of public politicking."[99] LegCo member and social welfare advocate Hui Yin-Fat characterized the British as "perfidious," saying he believed Britain was forcing Hong Kong to shoulder the burden of Britain's so-called humanitarian values, even as Thatcher's government refused to admit more Vietnamese out of domestic political considerations, including an upcoming election. For "self-salvation," Hui Yin-Fat argued, Hong Kong needed to enact policies similar to those implemented at the U.S.-Mexican border.[100]

In 1987, Hong Kong LegCo members even threatened to go directly to Vietnam and bypass the British Foreign Office in their attempts to force a solution. A direct challenge to British colonial rule, this created "an immediate rush of blood to the head in the British Foreign Office. Only Britain could negotiate on behalf of the colony of Hong Kong."[101] Rita Fan argued that Britain should just "let Hong Kong settle the problem as we see fit."[102] Fan lashed out at the United States too: the United States refused to resettle most of the Vietnamese left in the Hong Kong camps *and* opposed mandatory repatriations. She criticized the U.S. position as "hypocritical" and "illogical." She noted that the U.S. would not accept most of the Vietnamese waiting in Hong Kong because the INS had not accepted them as "refugees," while at the same time, the U.S. insisted that Vietnamese remain in Hong Kong until they repatriated voluntarily. She had no patience for this: "It is already difficult for the people of Hong Kong to accept that they must operate what amounts to a U.S. immigration control point on America's behalf. It is impossible for them to accept that those not accepted by America should somehow acquire a right to live indefinitely in Hong Kong."[103]

Chinese-language newspapers supported LegCo and argued that the Hong Kong government should ask Hanoi to "take back the Vietnamese."[104] The financial costs were also real. Hong Kong contributed roughly 122 million Hong Kong dollars (8.5 million British pounds) per year to running the camps.[105] When the number of Vietnamese escalated sharply for the first time in years, with almost 7,000 arrivals in the first half of 1988, LegCo leaders amplified their calls for repatriation. Fan chastised the "well-intentioned visitors from the western world," who she argued could not solve Hong Kong's problem and who refused to accept more Vietnamese.[106] Hong Kong Chinese resented the idea that Hong Kong should be left with the burden of the camps and long-staying Vietnamese only so that Britain's conscience could rest easy and it would not lose prestige in "the eyes of other Western nations."[107] On the one hand, Fan's campaign against the Vietnamese had an element of xenophobia and more than a hint of anti-refugee sentiment. In these ways, her language and policies mirrored her constituency's desire to remove the Vietnamese writ large. On the other hand, Fan was articulating a specific vision of humanitarianism that reflected the stalemate of refugee resettlement in the 1980s. If the United States (or other western countries) were not prepared to resettle Vietnamese, then were they condemning these boat people to years of life in limbo, behind barbed wire, in Hong Kong?

The assistant secretary for security believed repatriation would lead to a "durable solution" and act as a deterrent in a way that the closed camps had not. These colonial officials wanted to act, and they argued London was slowing them down out of concern for human rights violations in Vietnam.[108] The pressure worked. Foreign Secretary Geoffrey Howe visited Hong Kong in June 1988, and on return to London, he and Prime Minister Thatcher decided to give Hong Kong the go-ahead.[109]

On June 15, 1988, the Hong Kong government overturned the 1979 Geneva conference presumption of refugee status and instituted a new policy on its own authority outside the UNHCR framework. In Hong Kong, Vietnamese were now asylum seekers. LegCo announced that after June 16, Hong Kong would be a port of first asylum (it still would not "push off" boats), but now its immigration officers would interview all incoming Vietnamese. If they determined the Vietnamese in question had a refugee claim, the individual would be placed in an open camp and wait for resettlement in a third country. If the Hong Kong officers did not find a refugee claim, the Vietnamese would remain in a closed camp and then be repatriated to Vietnam. Hong Kong justified this shift as placing it in line with how all "illegal immigrants" were treated "anywhere in the world."[110] The government contended that Hong Kong was not an outlier; in this new equation, it was simply acting to defend its borders, like any other territory. The first unlucky boatload of Vietnamese arriving on June 16, 1988, did not know the rules of the game had changed.

THE UNHCR: INITIAL RESPONSES TO SCREENING AND REPATRIATION

Vietnamese within the camps immediately resisted the new policy. Thousands arrived after the fateful June 15 cutoff, and they demonstrated within the camps. For example, Vietnamese held on the island of Hei Ling Chau initiated a hunger strike to protest their new classification as illegal immigrants. They also asked for the UNHCR's help to prevent their repatriation and to halt talks between Hong Kong and Hanoi.[111] This cohort still viewed the

UNHCR as a potential savior and advocate. Well-known organizations such as Refugees International, Amnesty International, and IRAC all expressed strong reservations about Hong Kong's plans for screening and repatriation, and they too lobbied the UNHCR.[112]

The UNHCR was in a bind. Hong Kong, and by extension the U.K., wanted the UNHCR's imprimatur on its new policy; however, the UNHCR was not willing to give it right away. The UNHCR supported repatriation in principle, but it was hesitant to implement it in the Vietnamese case. Doing so would set off radical changes in Southeast Asia, and it feared repercussions for returnees in Vietnam. The UNHCR was also furious that Hong Kong had acted independently and outside the 1979 framework. Hong Kong had moved out in front of the UNHCR on screening and repatriation policies. "Despite our request for more time and need for consultation, UK/HK took this decision unilaterally and without giving UNHCR requested time for current efforts to bear fruit."[113] The UNHCR refused Hong Kong's invitation to participate in the initial press conference, as it scrambled, noting that "'no comments' will not do."[114]

UNHCR officials vacillated between wanting to keep their distance from Hong Kong's policy, which they saw as dangerously close to refoulement, or, alternately, wanting to be involved so that they could influence the process as much as possible. Arguments against involvement included deep concerns over the UNHCR's credibility and international reputation. Legal officer Ghassan Arnaout warned that if the UNHCR cooperated with Hong Kong, it risked being left with "appalling" camps and running afoul of the UN's minimum rules for the treatment of prisoners. It also could end up participating in a screening process it did not control, and which rejected "95% of arrivals, irrespective" of their claims. "Extreme caution should be exercised concerning UNHCR's participation in screening *at this point*."[115] More publicly, Simon Ripley, a former UNHCR monitor, resigned. He believed the UNHCR's standing as a humanitarian organization was at stake, and he wrote a stinging op-ed in the London *Times* insisting that the UNHCR "must challenge governments where injustice is done, not condone it."[116]

Sergio Vieira de Mello, the new UNHCR director for Asia, took the opposite tack. He argued that there needed to be an endgame in Southeast Asia. If not, the UNHCR risked having regional partners like Malaysia, Thailand, and Indonesia jettison the principle of first asylum.[117] There were already reports of Thailand pushing boats off and not granting asylum. Vieira de Mello, who would go on to have a long career at the UN until he was killed while on a mission in Iraq in 2003, became the leading proponent of accepting Hong Kong's policy change and retooling it for the region under UNHCR auspices.[118] He saw this pivot as critical to regional credibility and a pragmatic response to exhausted host countries and changes in the Cold War. In a sympathetic biography, Samantha Power, the former U.S. ambassador to the United Nations, wrote that Vieira de Mello was well aware of repatriation's controversial nature, but believed that "If we [UNHCR] don't find a compromise, we will permanently kill asylum."[119] Since the early 1980s, the UNHCR's own internal reports suggested only about one-third of the Vietnamese easily found resettlement placements as "refugees." Those remaining were categorized as fishermen, professionals, and students, and they were just waiting.[120] The UNHCR was not required to provide protection for all migrants, and it wanted to find a way to close the camps.

Vieira de Mello urged the UNHCR and international community to accept screening and repatriation as a necessity in keeping with the UNHCR's principle of refugee protection. Rather than marginalizing Hong Kong, the UNHCR ultimately cooperated with, and then accepted, the new formula of first asylum, individual screening, and ultimately repatriation for those who were not deemed refugees. The UNHCR would assist Hong Kong in developing criteria for refugee status and would monitor the interview process. It also succeeded in convincing Hong Kong officials to change language like "screening" and "illegal immigrant" to suit "UNHCR phraseology," instead using preferred terms like "status determination."[121] Next, the UNHCR facilitated regional meetings with Hong Kong, Thailand, Indonesia, the Philippines, and Malaysia throughout the fall of 1988.[122] In December 1988, the UNHCR entered into a memorandum of understanding with Vietnam to help facilitate voluntary repatriations, an essential piece of the puzzle. This was a game-changer. The Vietnamese government agreed not to prosecute or discriminate against those who returned, and just as importantly, it would permit UNHCR monitors into the country to verify these promises.[123] Southeast Asian countries held a regional planning meeting in March 1989 at which they established a new set of principles for determining the status of Vietnamese and endorsing repatriation. The other first-asylum countries followed Hong Kong's lead and set cutoff dates, implementing mandatory individual asylum screening for all Vietnamese who arrived after March 14, 1989.

There was considerable consternation within the UNHCR about Hong Kong's muddled policy and warnings about avoiding Hong Kong's "pitfalls," for example, its tendency to screen out the vast majority of Vietnamese.[124] Despite the risks, Vieira de Mello saw promise in the new policy of status determination and repatriation, and his international negotiating efforts culminated in a June 1989 meeting in Geneva. Hong Kong had succeeded. It had set in motion a new policy which would become a blueprint for the region. Vietnamese would no longer be de facto refugees—now they would be asylum seekers.

THE COMPREHENSIVE PLAN OF ACTION: FROM REFUGEES TO ASYLUM SEEKERS

The 1989 Comprehensive Plan of Action (CPA) embraced the central tenets of Hong Kong's goals of screening and repatriation. With the CPA's implementation, Vietnamese would be asylum seekers, rather than de facto refugees. More than seventy countries signed the agreement in Geneva in June 1989. First, it protected the standard of first asylum. All the original 1979 signatories agreed that they would not push off boats, but would allow migrants to land and be screened. Second, the CPA established a practice of asylum screening whereby immigration officers would interview Vietnamese and determine whether or not they met the threshold for refugee status. If so, they would be "screened in," and the UNHCR guaranteed them resettlement in a third country. If not, they would be "screened out." The language for what happened next was left deliberately vague. The agreement stated that "every effort will be made to encourage the voluntary return of such persons." If "voluntary repatriation" did not work, "alternatives recognized as being acceptable under international practices would be examined."[125] As historian W. Courtland Robinson noted, all parties recognized this was just code for forced repatriation. Ironically, the only two countries opposed to forced repatriation were Vietnam and the United States.[126] The CPA managed to legitimize and sanction repatriation through finessed euphemisms and by kicking the proverbial can down the road. The language of "voluntary" repatriation would be a sticking point for almost a decade, and Hong Kong would continue to press for repatriation, voluntary or otherwise, of all unsettled Vietnamese. The UNHCR and international NGOs had initially viewed Hong Kong's experiment as too extreme and contrary to humanitarian principles, but now the UNHCR and Southeast Asia's regional players codified Hong Kong's initiative.

One of the key reasons the Comprehensive Plan of Action could move forward was because Vietnam was at the table. The dynamics of the Cold War were changing. Le Duan, general secretary of the Vietnamese Communist Party, died in 1986, setting in motion a set of economic reforms and new leadership. Simultaneous with the Soviet Union's turn to *perestroika* and *glasnost*, Vietnam experimented with its own acceptance of capitalist markets through the policy of *doi moi*. Vietnam had also begun withdrawing from Cambodia, satisfying one of the United States' key conditions of engagement. In other words, by 1989, Vietnam wanted diplomatic ties and economic relationships with the international community and the west, including the United States. To this end, Vietnamese diplomats promised that they would not punish Vietnamese who returned voluntarily, making repatriation a feasible policy: "For humanitarian reasons we accept all voluntary repatriates with the financial assistance of the international community and they will not be punished though they have departed illegally."[127] Vietnam also agreed to better police its shorelines and improve the Orderly Departure Program (ODP), which allowed Vietnamese to apply for refugee status and resettlement in the United States from within Vietnam. The ODP was bureaucratic and rife with corruption and administrative hurdles, but it allowed both Vietnam and the United States to select and manage who could leave and be resettled without the risk of death at sea. American and Vietnamese officials had been working together on matters of shared "humanitarian interest," including Amerasians, re-education camp survivors, and POW/MIAs since the mid-1980s, and it was through these issues that the U.S. and Vietnam maintained communication and inched their way toward normalization.[128]

The United States wanted to have it both ways: it refused to accept all the Vietnamese as refugees, but it remained adamantly opposed to repatriation. During the 1980s, the United States continued to adhere to its Cold War ideological priorities, routinely offering asylum to Cubans and Soviet Jews but rejecting Haitians and Central Americans out of hand as "economic migrants."[129] Vietnamese were fleeing a communist country, as were Cubans and Soviet Jews, but they were also non-white, often poor, and from agricultural backgrounds, and so less desirable, like Mexicans, Central Americans, and Haitians. INS officials routinely denied Vietnamese asylum cases, agreeing with Hong Kong officials that a growing number of Vietnamese were "economic migrants" and not refugees. The INS, true to its history, saw its job as one of control and restriction. In contrast, Congress members often criticized the INS's distinction between economic migrants and political refugees. For example, Representative Stephen Solarz (D-NY) argued the Vietnamese were more akin to Jews fleeing Europe in the 1930s: "I do not accept the fashionable wisdom of the day which holds that these are people who are really economic migrants. My impression is that the great majority of these are just as much political refugees fleeing from repression as the tens of thousands who have preceded them over the course of the last fifteen years."[130] Solarz sponsored a congressional resolution going into the 1989 Geneva conference urging the State Department to refuse to "legitimize the principle and practice of forced repatriation" as being contrary to "American values." Representative William Broomfield (R-MI) seconded Solarz, and he argued that Southeast Asian host countries must recognize "they have a responsibility to the victims of communism." He spoke against "any form of forced repatriation."[131] This split between the INS administration (under the executive branch) and congressional leadership resulted in a paradoxical, and ultimately untenable, U.S. position. [132]

In Geneva, the United States spoke out against forced repatriation. Deputy Secretary of State Lawrence Eagleburger stated, "The United States will remain unalterably opposed to the forced repatriation of Vietnamese asylum seekers."[133] However, the United States was largely alone on this count. Representative Broomfield's call to Southeast Asian allies' commitment to Cold War ideology was no longer compelling more than ten years after the U.S. defeat in Vietnam and in light of the rapid economic changes in the Soviet Union and Vietnam. Moreover, the United States' imperial and economic ties did not hold sway even among its anti-communist allies, such as Malaysia, Indonesia, and most importantly, the U.K. Only the Philippines, a former American colony, proposed yet another holding center to keep repatriation at bay.

The British did not shy away from the CPA's implied logic: forced repatriations would be necessary. Hong Kong was not to be bound by American prerogatives or its ideological fixedness. Foreign Secretary Geoffrey Howe stated bluntly, "Voluntary repatriation is no answer." Only 150 of 40,000 Vietnamese in Hong Kong had opted for voluntary repatriation, and the U.K. was committed to negotiating with Vietnam so it could send people back.[134] The U.S. could control who it admitted and who it did not, but the U.K. would not have its hands tied by American anti-communism. Hong Kong would go forward with its plan to repatriate thousands of Vietnamese.

By the end of the 1980s, there were more than half a million Vietnamese in the United States.[135] They had formed community organizations and nascent political lobbying groups, and the UNHCR also hoped to work with the Vietnamese American community as partners. However, the CPA's commitment to individual screening and repatriation was extremely controversial. With the 1989 Geneva conference, Vietnamese activists in the diaspora became the loudest voice against the CPA and forcible repatriation; some tried to influence the UNHCR to improve the implementation, while others rejected the new policy and aimed their anger at Hong Kong and the UNHCR.

IRAC leader Le Xuan Khoa remembered working with the UNHCR in the months leading up to the 1989 Geneva conference: "We wanted to be part of the solution. We didn't just want to be helped. We wanted to participate in the process and help resolve the situation ourselves."[136] Because IRAC was able to position itself as a partner with the UNHCR, Le Xuan Khoa was able to funnel reports, information, personal examples, and recommendations to UNHCR officers. For example, IRAC had relationships with individuals who had lived in North and South Vietnam and who could testify about the "factual background in human rights" and support the refugee claims of the Vietnamese in the camps.[137] IRAC mobilized 145 Indochinese organizations to sign a collective document, which they submitted to the UNHCR, protesting any steps toward the "involuntary and the so-called 'voluntary' repatriation" proposed in the CPA. This included organizations as far afield as the National Vietnamese American Voters' League in Oklahoma City, the Union of Pan Asian Communities Counseling and Treatment Center in San Diego, and the Vietnamese and Friends Association of Knoxville, Tennessee.[138] IRAC's involvement in resettlement programs throughout the United States enabled it to develop a national network, which succeeded in reaching the conference rooms in Geneva.

Through the process, Le Xuan Khoa became close friends with Sergio Vieria de Mello, and this entrée allowed IRAC to have some influence over the process. Le Xuan Khoa insisted on IRAC's independence; it was not a foreign government, and it was not dependent on the UNHCR. Rather, IRAC could serve as a valuable mediator that "provide[d] a genuine voice for the refugees." Le Xuan Khoa had mixed feelings about the CPA's final formula. He pointed to some "positive components," including jump-starting the Orderly Departure Program (which had been largely moribund before the late 1980s) and "real voluntary repatriation." However, he balked at the screening process, which he believed was often "corrupted." "We [IRAC] were not happy with the screening process. We were not fully in agreement with the CPA, but we saw it as a step toward a humane solution." Despite these reservations, Le Xuan Khoa was something of a realist. He wanted Vietnam's authoritarian, communist government to change, but he was also an advocate for diplomatic normalization. He knew that other Vietnamese American nonprofit organizations were more critical of the UNHCR and the CPA. "That's understandable. In the 1980s, anti-communism was still very strong." He added that many took an extreme position, such as returning to fight communism, which he did not believe was practical. "In order to resolve the refugee problem, we needed to be wise and have a vision for that." He explained Vietnamese Americans shared a similar goal, change in Vietnam and support for the refugees, but that they had different approaches.[139] IRAC would work with the U.S. government, the international community, and the UNHCR.

Along with national NGOs like IRAC, Vietnamese American college students, particularly those in Orange County, California, began to organize and advocate for Vietnamese within the camps. Project Ngoc at the University of California, Irvine, became the most prominent of these advocacy groups.[140] Van Thai Tran, a student leader, explained, "Morally, we could not sit on our hands and do nothing. We were once former refugees ourselves not so long ago. We just had to jump up and take advantage and scream and yell and do whatever we can so these governments will hear us." Van Thai Tran called on his personal experience as a refugee to explain his passion and political activity, and he even traveled to Geneva to protest the CPA.[141] Advocating for Vietnamese within the camps became a defining experience for a core subset of Vietnamese within the diaspora, and many became particularly invested in the camps and asylum hearings in Hong Kong. Their personal experiences with the camps created affective ties, and many Vietnamese Americans became fierce critics of Hong Kong and the CPA's screening mechanism. And they adamantly opposed repatriation.

In their campaign against the CPA, Vietnamese Americans deployed human rights language against Hanoi, and for the first time, against the UNHCR. Organizations as far afield as the Vietnamese Buddhist Association of Sacramento and the Paris-based Comité d'aide aux réfugiés denounced Hanoi and demanded that the UN protect human rights and Vietnamese seeking refugee status in the west.[142] Vietnamese American organizations also used their knowledge and personal experience to protest plans for repatriation. In one notable petition, the Indochinese community in Westminster, California, cited the imprisonment of the 1975 repatriates from Guam on the *Viet Nam Thuong Tin* as an argument against the CPA. Leaders from the Hmong, Laotian, Cambodian, and Vietnamese American communities in Orange County joined together to denounce screening and repatriations, and they scoffed at the idea that "voluntary" repatriations were voluntary, arguing that returnees were "most likely induced by the threats of indefinite detention by the host governments and by the harsh living conditions of the camps."[143]

With the UNHCR's endorsement of the CPA, Vietnamese Americans no longer saw the UNHCR as a protector, and they turned their animus against it. This anger would only escalate in intensity as Hong Kong moved to repatriate "screened-out" Vietnamese. Many of these activists turned to U.S. lawmakers to intervene, sending faxes to President George H. W. Bush, calling on him to "reaffirm your long-held stand against forced repatriation."[144] While they were unsuccessful at changing the terms of the CPA, Vietnamese American organizations like Project Ngoc and, later, Boat People SOS, would soon send volunteers, money, and lawyers to Hong Kong's camps and challenge the implementation of the CPA after 1989.

ALTERNATE HONG KONG CHINESE VIEWS ON THE VIETNAMESE

In Hong Kong, the 1988 policy and the 1989 CPA demonstrated Hong Kong's ability to influence international refugee policy on its own terms, despite its colonial status. Hong Kong's own experiences with Chinese migration and deportation, alongside the uncertain transition to Chinese sovereignty, affected its turn to repatriation as the answer to the Vietnamese camps. In particular, Hong Kong Chinese politicians resented the idea that Hong Kong should be more "humanitarian" than western countries. Hong Kong also defended and defined its interests quite apart from U.S. objectives. If the Philippines worked hand in hand with the United States and agreed to act as a way station before resettlement, Hong Kong had no such long-term economic, political, or colonial ties to the United States. Its ties were to Great Britain, and soon China. Few in Hong Kong were interested in American sentiments of responsibility to former allies or calls to uphold anti-communist objectives. Instead, the Hong Kong government looked to its practice of deporting Chinese migrants and kept a keen eye on its not-too-distant future under Chinese sovereignty. Even as a British colony, it forged ahead and pressured the UNHCR to change its definition of who would be a refugee and who would not.

While by all accounts the majority of people in Hong Kong supported the harsh new policies, there were outliers who spoke out in support of the Vietnamese. For example, a group of sympathetic Hong Kong Chinese university students wrote to the UNHCR and argued that the Vietnamese could potentially help Hong Kong meet a labor shortfall. They dismissed the notion that the Vietnamese posed a threat to the colony and declared Hong Kong's Britishness as the reason Hong Kong needed to maintain the first-asylum policy. Any violation would "undermine all past, present, and future principles that Britain stands for. . . . The refugees cannot be blamed for their predicament. They are literally in the hands of politicians."[145] A set of Hong Kong law students criticized the screening process as antithetical to the "basic principles of British justice."[146] In both cases, the students believed that the repatriation campaign contradicted the British colonial promises of civilization and the rule of law.

Using an alternate line of argument, some Hong Kong Chinese savaged any pretense of democracy or representative government in Hong Kong. These critics also condemned the new policies of repatriation. In a letter to the UNHCR, one woman complained that the Hong Kong government was not representative and so could not act on behalf of the Hong Kong people. "There are no representatives of Hong Kong people, and it is wrong for local councilors to profess they act on behalf of Hong Kong people in the application of policies, especially toward the boat people. . . . There is no mandate of Hong Kong people. . . . Hong Kong people do have compassion and caring. Do not let our officials pretend to the world at the Geneva conference that we do not!"[147] Another resident seconded this sentiment in his own letter to the UNHCR: "At no time during the Geneva conference will the Hong Kong delegates be able to claim that the people of Hong Kong want forced repatriation as a solution to the refugee problem. The delegates will only be representing the Hong Kong government, which itself is NOT representative of Hong Kong people."[148] This disaggregation of the Hong Kong government and Hong Kong people was a clear rebuke of Hong Kong's British colonial status and lack of democratic norms. While they were in the minority, these students and letter writers rejected the notion that the British or Hong Kong governments represented their interests, and they did so by using anti-colonial language and by supporting protection for Vietnamese.

Emily Lau, at the time a reporter for the *Far Eastern Economic Review* and later a pro-democracy LegCo member herself, saw LegCo's preoccupation with the Vietnamese to be a distraction, one that allowed administrators to mobilize public opinion without addressing the key issues of the Basic Law and Hong Kong's transition to Chinese sovereignty. In an interview with the BBC, she commented,

> I think the Hong Kong government has been very successful in stirring up many members of the Legislative Council, many Chinese members, to come out and oppose the refugees. And I see that as a big diversion from the very important matters of the day. I mean, we have quite a number of refugees coming here, but it is not the biggest problem. And for some political reasons, other people are diverting attention from the real issues, and that is the implementation of the Joint Declaration, the drafting of the Basic Law, and they want to talk about something else like refugees, which is not I think by any stretch of the imagination, the most pressing problem in Hong Kong.[149]

Lau's commentary was prescient, and she explained how the Vietnamese had become a politically popular target.

For Vietnamese who landed in Hong Kong and other locales throughout Southeast Asia, the 1989 CPA reversed their chances at resettlement for good. Hong Kong's local politics had forced the hand of the UNHCR. The changing dynamics of the Cold War meant that Hong Kong and the west had jettisoned an easy equation between anti-communism and refugee status. Hong Kong remained in the spotlight as everyone waited to see how the internationally sanctioned policy of screening and repatriation would play out on the ground. Hong Kong leaders would carry out the new policy. Meanwhile, Vietnamese in the camps and in the diaspora were not willing to accept these changes without a fight.

FIVE

"*Protest against Forced Repatriation!*"

HUMANITARIANISM AND HUMAN RIGHTS
IN HONG KONG, 1989–1997

ON DECEMBER 12, 1989, THE HONG KONG government choreographed the first forcible, involuntary repatriation of fifty-one Vietnamese. Carried out secretly at 3:00 a.m., more than one hundred Hong Kong Correctional Services Department (CSD) officers in full riot gear removed nine men, sixteen women, and twenty-six children from a holding camp. According to media reports, the families were "crying and screaming," and many held signs declaring, "We would rather die than return to Vietnam." The UNHCR was not there to monitor the operation, because Hong Kong did not inform them about it. There was "No, repeat, No, prior notice of operation."[1] The CSD insisted its officers did not use force, but they did have to resort to physically loading the unwilling Vietnamese onto a plane. It was clear to all that the repatriations were not voluntary by any standard. It was the first forcible repatriation in Hong Kong's attempt to implement the Comprehensive Plan of Action (CPA) and remove "screened-out" Vietnamese from its territory.

Outrage was immediate. U.S. elected representatives, the U.S. State Department, Amnesty International, human rights NGOs, and Vietnamese diasporic organizations all condemned Hong Kong's actions. Senator Claiborne Pell (D-RI) characterized the forced repatriations as a "disgrace," and Senator Mark Hatfield (R-OR) wrote to the Hong Kong governor to demand that he "immediately cease the forcible repatriation.... Human decency demands no less."[2] Robert Winter, the director of the U.S. Committee for Refugees, argued that the Hong Kong operation violated asylum seekers' human rights.[3] Anti-war activist Joan Baez spoke out against the forced repatriations and was the lead signatory, along with dozens of Vietnamese Americans, in a paid advertisement that read, "When armed guards are used to move unarmed defenseless women and children against their will, into a plane, and to return them to a land which they had just risked their lives to escape, this is as clear a use of force as can be imagined."[4] Vietnamese Americans threatened a boycott of Cathay Pacific, Hong Kong's flagship airline.[5] Pope John Paul II even singled out the Hong Kong government for criticism in his weekly homily.[6] Despite this onslaught of negative publicity, Prime Minister Margaret Thatcher brushed off the international criticism with aplomb: "Illegal immigrants have to be returned to their country of origin." She also placed her government on the side of the Hong Kong population, which supported the repatriations at rates close to 90 percent.[7]

Governor David Wilson himself defended the policy as necessary to maintain Hong Kong's first-asylum policy: "In Hong Kong, we have taken in, housed, fed, and clothed over 170,000 asylum seekers from Vietnam. We are proud of this record and we wish to preserve it. But if no distinction is made between genuine refugees and those who do not meet the internationally agreed criteria, the system will collapse under the weight of numbers."[8]

After years of talking about screening and repatriation, Hong Kong had finally put these practices into motion. Word spread quickly that it was going to be more difficult to gain refugee status, leading to a rush of Vietnamese departures. In 1988, more than 18,000 Vietnamese landed in Hong Kong, and in 1989, that numbered topped 34,000. After the June 1989 Geneva conference, there were approximately 55,000 people in Hong Kong's camps.[9] Hong Kong leaders had applauded the CPA as a success and an endorsement of its 1988 initiative; however, not surprisingly, the roll-out was far more convoluted and controversial in practice. First, the Hong Kong government developed an asylum hearing process that often resulted in arbitrary decisions, and second, it had to organize repatriation flights. Vietnamese within the camps and in the diaspora resisted both the screening process and repatriation through the legal system and through militant protests. The result was messy, emotional, and sometimes gut wrenching. Throughout it all, the Hong Kong government insisted it upheld the value of humanitarianism, while critics countered that the screening and repatriations violated human rights.

The unexpected end of the Cold War propelled changes at a quicker clip than most countries could have imagined when they initially hammered out the CPA's protocols in March 1989.[10] The subsequent international conference in Geneva in June 1989 convened just days after the Tiananmen Square massacre. China's crackdown on democracy activists in Beijing served as a warning to those who wanted to preserve a degree of liberalism and autonomy within Hong Kong after 1997. The government brutality demonstrated China's commitment to authoritarian single-party rule. Many Chinese fleeing punishment and persecution after Tiananmen Square escaped through Hong Kong.[11] In the days after June 4, Hong Kong people protested in the streets, and the Hong Kong stock market dropped by more than 20 percent. As one shopkeeper explained, "In the past, I never wanted to leave Hong Kong. My whole life is wrapped up here . . . but look what has happened in Beijing. The leaders are butchers, they're animals. How can I remain here after 1997?"[12] Given this specific sense of uncertainty and insecurity within Hong Kong, the Vietnamese camps raised questions related to citizenship and refugee status that touched a raw nerve.

Hong Kong's colonial status as a *British* colony also made it a particularly visible and potent symbol, magnifying the contradictions of colonial promises and the rhetoric of humanitarianism. In the wake of the December 1989 forced repatriation, the archbishop of Canterbury wrote to Governor Wilson to express sympathy at Hong Kong's dilemma. "Hong Kong suffers the misfortune of being what it is where it is, and there is an excess of hypocrisy in the air."[13] The "what it is where it is" indicated Hong Kong's now-anomalous position as a British colony in East Asia. British politicians emphasized the double standard facing Hong Kong and resented the international attention. Many maintained that deporting illegal immigrants was par for the course and they did not deserve all the negative publicity. Organizations like the British Refugee Council repeatedly urged the U.K. to accept more resettlement cases, but the U.K. accepted only a paltry number of Vietnamese after 1989. Margaret Thatcher was quite clear that this was a problem *outside* of the U.K.

In contrast, U.S. politicians remained far more committed to Cold War anti-communism than Hong Kong or British officials, but here too the international dynamics were changing. The late 1980s and early 1990s witnessed a move toward normalization, and President Bill Clinton's decision to lift the U.S. embargo and restore diplomatic ties with Vietnam would demonstrate how the Cold War calculus that had driven the U.S. into war in Vietnam no longer held true. Improved relations also opened the door for tacit U.S. acceptance of Vietnamese repatriation and a turn to a more normalized immigration process for all Vietnamese. U.S. politicians wanted to have it both ways. Most opposed forced repatriation, but they were also ready to wind down the preferential practice of admitting large numbers of Southeast Asians into the United States, and they looked positively at renewed diplomatic relations and

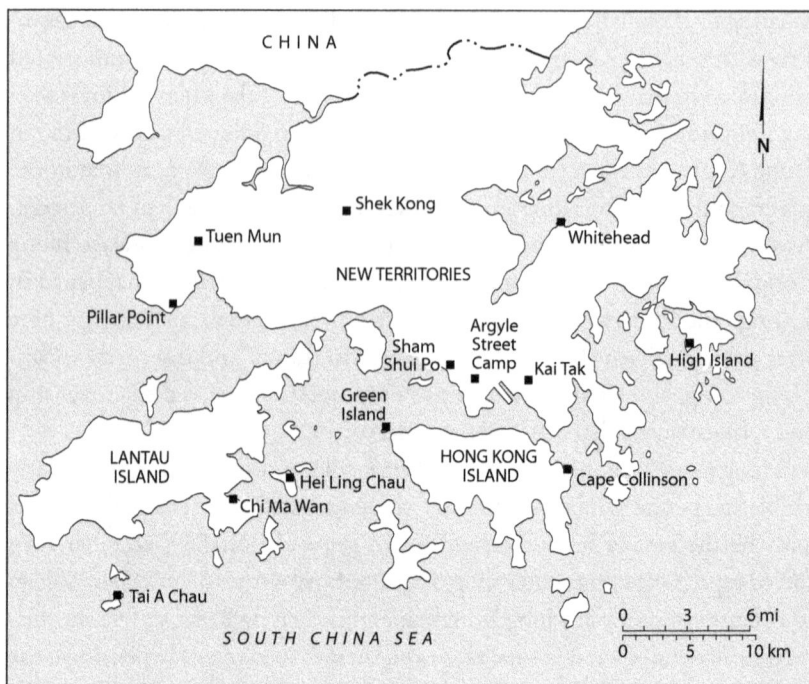

MAP 3. Hong Kong, open and closed camps. This map depicts the primary camps in which Hong Kong held Vietnamese between 1975 and 2000.

investment in Vietnam. The battle over repatriation, and particularly forced repatriation, played out in this new geopolitical landscape.

The CPA and Hong Kong's screening and repatriation practices mobilized Vietnamese in the diaspora. This was a watershed moment for Vietnamese American activism, and the dire camp conditions in Hong Kong and the very real practice of repatriation created a crisis-like atmosphere, and often a sense of personal identification. Vietnamese American organizations forged strong alliances with elected officials, and others sponsored lawyers in the Hong Kong camps. Going beyond signing petitions and writing letters, Vietnamese Americans even traveled to Hong Kong, witnessed the camps for themselves, and returned to share their stories. Many Vietnamese Americans also embraced the language of human rights. In the 1970s, most Vietnamese American organizations rallied against human rights violations in Vietnam and condemned the re-education camps and New Economic Zones. Now, human rights violations included suffering in communist-controlled Vietnam *and* indefinite suffering in Hong Kong, including arbitrary screening, miserable camp conditions, and forced repatriations. Vietnamese within the camps, Vietnamese Americans, and international human rights activists attacked Hong Kong and the UNHCR (and not just Vietnam) on all these counts.

Throughout it all, Hong Kong officials and the UNHCR defended screening and repatriation. There was little Hong Kong officials could do to sugarcoat the practice. The act of dragging people out of camps and forcing them onto airplanes was physical, brutal, and dramatic; however, Hong Kong officials remained firm and the UNHCR backed them up. Humanitarianism meant initial protection, shelter, and an interview process, it did not guarantee resettlement for all. In the Vietnamese camps in Hong Kong, humanitarianism and human rights were no longer close cousins, but instead fierce competitors. The Comprehensive Plan of Action and its logic of repatriation set the language and politics of humanitarianism in opposition to the language and politics of human rights.

INSIDE THE CAMPS AND THE SCREENING PROCESS

The CPA's major innovation was to set up an interview process whereby all Vietnamese who arrived after the regional deadlines had to "prove" their refugee claims of persecution to immigration officials. This was a radical change, and it forced all incoming Vietnamese to tell the right story if they hoped to be resettled in the west. In addition, there were two parallel bureaucracies. Hong Kong Immigration officers made an initial determination, and Vietnamese could appeal unfavorable decisions to the Refugee Status Review Board (RSRB), also staffed by Hong Kong personnel. The UNHCR also managed an independent appeal process, and it could grant refugee status to individuals who had been rejected by the RSRB.

Anthropologist John Christian Knudsen documented the haunting cases of Vietnamese who were "screened out" in Hong Kong in 1991, and his writings remain among the most poignant and bitter accounts of the camps. In *Chicken Wings: Refugee Stories from a Concrete Hell*, Knudsen paints a desperate picture of the Hong Kong camps, the prison-like conditions, and the terror of a "chicken wing," the colloquial camp term for a negative decision from the Hong Kong RSRB and UNHCR appeal process. If one received two "chicken wings" or denials, one would have to fly home. Knudsen described the asylum determination process as a post-modern "screening machine" which forced Vietnamese to produce legible stories and evidence to support their refugee claims. Vietnamese needed to produce the perfect "story," which often meant hiding the complexity, particularity, and tragedy of their personal experiences.[14]

The singular purpose of the CPA was to deter future migrants. To do this, the Hong Kong government needed to limit the numbers granted asylum and give little hope for resettlement. Each Vietnamese faced an intake interview with a Hong Kong immigration officer, and typically there was no lawyer present. This initial interview held great weight, and it set a template for the individual's case.[15] To further complicate matters, there were multiple levels of translation, with translators facilitating Vietnamese-Cantonese exchanges in this proceeding, and then with the immigration officers translating the interviews into English for the written report. The UNHCR could monitor the interviews, but due to its small staff, this happened in only a small subset of cases. Hong Kong officials geared their questions toward southern Vietnamese experiences, asking for the individual or family's ties to South Vietnam and any experiences in re-education camps. If the immigration officer believed there was enough evidence for a refugee claim, then he or she could grant asylum at this point. Hong Kong officials rejected most cases, and generally Vietnamese were not provided with any explanation for the decisions. Amnesty International reported that in 1988 and 1989, Hong Kong "screened in" only 3 percent of the asylum cases at this stage.[16]

"Screened-out" Vietnamese could then appeal to the RSRB. In 1988 and 1989, by all accounts the RSRB rejected the vast majority of Vietnamese asylum cases. The RSRB did not permit the individual or his or her lawyer to attend the closed meeting. The RSRB determined whether or not the immigration officer had overlooked any evidence, and if so, it could grant asylum status. This happened in very few cases. The RSRB granted refugee status to approximately 7 percent of these appeals, for a total of 10 percent "screened in."[17] The RRSB initially did not provide written reasons for its decisions. Some critics questioned the RSRB members' credentials, noting that most members were from the private sector and had no expertise in immigration or refugee policy.[18] Others feared that the RSRB jobs were simply highly paid patronage positions.[19]

The UNHCR provided a final level of review, which to many Vietnamese and Vietnamese Americans made it an enemy equal to the Hong Kong government.[20] If an individual's appeals before the RSRB failed, he or she could then bring the case to the UNHCR for a mandate review. In this final review, the UNHCR could independently grant asylum outside of Hong Kong's

RSRB process. Working on the ground in Hong Kong, UNHCR bureau officer Robert Van Leeuwen recognized the screening process's imperfections, but he sought to improve, not jettison it. He defended the asylum determination hearings and hoped they would gain legitimacy. He recognized that Hong Kong's seemingly arbitrary decisions opened up the UNHCR to charges of violating its humanitarian mandate, but he held firm and endorsed "the explicit humanitarian spirit of the CPA."[21] By definition the asylum determination hearings meant that some individuals would be screened in and others would be screened out and declared not refugees. Van Leeuwen hoped that the UNHCR could provide enough protections, transparency, and safeguards so that these decisions would be accepted.

Human rights lawyers decided to challenge Hong Kong's screening process, and they took the Vietnamese cases to court. While these cases were winding their way through the legal system, Hong Kong agreed to pause forced repatriation flights. In the first major case, the lead plaintiff was Do Giau, a young man in his twenties who arrived in Hong Kong in July 1988, and thus after Hong Kong's cutoff date. His father had served in the French army in the 1950s and then the South Vietnamese army. Also a village chief, he had arrested local communists. When the North Vietnamese defeated the South, Do Giau claimed his father had been "tortured and 'publicly humiliated.'" The new government forced nine-year-old Do Giau to move to the New Economic Zones and undertake the life-threatening work of removing live land mines. Do Giau refused to join the military and was arrested in 1987. After this, he fled and sought asylum in Hong Kong.[22] During his immigration interview, Do Giau claimed that he was forced to work in the informal sector and could not secure a government job due to his family background, but the immigration officer recorded that he had worked for a state-run rice factory. This discrepancy became the key sticking point.[23] Do Giau's lawyers emphasized that the failure was one of both language and inquisitiveness. Hong Kong immigration officers had translated the initial interviews from Vietnamese to Cantonese, but they then submitted the written reports in English without reading them back to Do Giau for verification.[24] The trilingual loop inadvertently emphasized Hong Kong's colonial status, whereby lower-level civil servants operated in Cantonese, but the higher-level administrators and RSRB members needed English-language documents. Along with the mistranslation, the implication was that if Do Giau had a government job in a rice factory, then he could not have a legitimate claim to persecution. This also mirrored Amnesty's critiques that immigration officers failed to ask follow-up questions or show any curiosity about their subjects. Instead, they tended to rephrase the key question "Why did you leave Vietnam and why do you not wish to return?" to simply "So, you left Vietnam to seek a better economic life?"[25]

Hong Kong Judge Barry Mortimor decided in favor of Do Giau and explained that the RSRB had erroneously destroyed pieces of the applicant's file and the translation had been faulty. Given this, Judge Mortimer stated that the "applicant never received a fair deal in all the circumstances." However, the court also affirmed the RSRB's procedures in principle as "fair."[26] Rather than declare Do Giau a refugee outright, the court opened the door for another review and procedural protections. Do Giau was "jubilant" at the decision, but also anxious about the fact that he was not granted refugee status, but rather just a new hearing.[27] U.S. lawyer Arthur Helton saw it as a victory for refugee rights: "The decision was technical and narrow, legally speaking, but politically it will have enormous consequences." At the same time, Hong Kong officials were relieved. Security officer Clinton Leeks saw the case as a minor rebuke but ultimately as an endorsement of the RSRB and a "vindication" of Hong Kong's screening procedures.[28] He also traveled to Vietnam to witness the repatriates' reintegration process and claimed, "I am more certain than I was before I left that our screening system is as far as possible identifying the relatively small number who are genuine refugees and is correctly screening out a large number who aren't refugees and who quite frankly never would be."[29] In the aftermath of the Do Giau case, Hong Kong agreed to allow Vietnamese to seek legal advice and be accompanied by a lawyer at hearings, and the court ordered the RSRB to issue written decisions.[30]

Through this case, the courts sanctioned the screenings and the attendant repatriations for those "screened out." Human rights organizations remained skeptical and vigilant. Amnesty International reiterated that the Hong Kong refugee determination procedure could not be trusted. It could not identify all "those who would be at risk of human rights violations if returned to Vietnam."[31] Likewise the Lawyers Committee for Human Rights issued a report in 1992 concluding that while the Hong Kong RSRB might meet "minimum international standards," it continued to be "grudging and hostile" to genuine refugees.[32] The Lawyers Committee documented numerous stories where it believed refugee claims had been ignored. However, the Lawyers Committee and Amnesty International, like the UNHCR, did not oppose repatriation in general, just the repatriation of *refugees*. This placed activist lawyers in a bit of a bind. Their arguments rested on legal grounds, individual rights, and procedural protections. This meant that if Hong Kong could fine-tune its asylum process and if Vietnam agreed not to persecute those who returned, Hong Kong and the UNHCR could argue that they were acting in line with human rights standards.

Given two avenues, the RSRB and the UNHCR mandate review, activist lawyers worked both angles. With a good lawyer, an individual was more likely to succeed in his or her appeal and thus hold repatriation at bay. Outsized personality Pamela Baker became the expatriate Hong Kong lawyer most closely identified with the Vietnamese refugee claims. A Scottish woman with six children, she moved to Hong Kong in the early 1980s after she and her husband separated. As a British citizen, her path followed a somewhat circuitous colonial route, from her childhood in Cape Town, South Africa, to higher education in England, and after her divorce, to her work in Hong Kong's legal aid office, which she initially chose "for an adventure really." After she witnessed "awful decisions coming out" of the RSRB, she dedicated herself to providing legal assistance in the camps and founded Refugee Concern Hong Kong.[33] Refugee Concern's high profile, legal tenacity, and good sense of publicity made UNHCR officials worried. They believed Refugee Concern's stridency and "false hope" would ultimately "undermine what we are trying to achieve on behalf of tens of thousands in Hong Kong's detention centers."[34] In other words, Refugee Concern got in the way of efficient screenings and repatriation.

Along with public advocacy, Refugee Concern acted as a scrappy law firm, representing individual clients through the screening process and fighting against repatriation. Throughout the 1990s, Baker and Refugee Concern emphasized due process and abysmal camp conditions, and their efforts succeeded in gaining refugee status for scores of clients. Refugee Concern published investigative reports and a regular newsletter that exposed the harsh conditions within the camps and the stories of individual Vietnamese who had been "screened out." A regular presence in the English-language media, Baker gained considerable publicity and shone a spotlight on much of the misery and arbitrariness within the system. She also succeeded in being a constant irritant to the UNHCR.[35] For example, in November 1993, more than five thousand Vietnamese at the Tai A Chau camp marched within the camp in protest of the "unjust" screening process. Baker backed their claims 100 percent, stating, "The basis for screening is that all Vietnamese are liars and that at least 90% are not refugees. . . . There are some Vietnamese who know that they are refugees and they sure as hell aren't going to go back."[36]

Baker's strident language and opposition to the screening process made her few friends in the Hong Kong bureaucracy or the UNHCR.

Critics of the screening noted the precariousness of the interview process and the necessity of telling the "right" story. The most legible cases involved Catholic South Vietnamese men who had served in the ARVN military and then faced years in re-education camps.[37] Cases, even compelling ones, that did not follow this script were far more likely to be rejected. For example, Amnesty International documented the case of a Protestant Vietnamese man who was working in Czechoslovakia during the 1980s on a socialist guest worker exchange program. While in Central Europe, he became an advocate for Vietnamese workers' rights and active in a dissident movement. As a result of his political activities, he was arrested in Czechoslovakia and then again in Vietnam. He fled Vietnam and arrived in Hong Kong just days after the CPA cutoff date for automatic refugee status.[38] Amnesty pointed out that his story seemed to be "absolutely clear cut," however, Hong Kong immigration officers rejected his case. He had been a Vietnamese guest worker in a socialist country, and not a veteran of the South Vietnamese Army. Hong Kong immigration officers did not know what to do with his story, and they rejected his case.

Likewise, a disproportionate number of the Vietnamese who arrived in Hong Kong in 1988 and 1989 were from northern Vietnam. This was largely due to geography and sea routes, with Hong Kong's closer proximity to northern Vietnam, while the majority of southern Vietnamese landed in Malaysia, Indonesia, Thailand, or the Philippines. Hong Kong officials believed that northern Vietnamese were coming for economic reasons, and they implied that only southern Vietnamese could be "real refugees." The United States too came to this conclusion, and as a rule, it did not resettle northern Vietnamese. These practices assumed that all northern Vietnamese supported the communist government, and that the communist government would not oppress anyone from the north, a dubious assumption if one was actually interested in countering communism. In addition, the Hong Kong media repeatedly characterized northern Vietnamese as violent and prone to antisocial norms. Conflicts between northern and southern Vietnamese garnered a great deal of attention, and Hong Kong journalists repeatedly depicted northerners as the instigators. These reports never suggested that the antipathy between northerners and southerners might have been because of southerners' disproportionate ability to find resettlement options and be "screened in."

One testimony by an artist and playwright from northern Vietnam revealed these contradictions. This dissident artist wrote eloquently in English from High Island Detention Centre, and he recounted his years in the North Vietnamese army and the Cultural Information Agency. In this missive, he disavowed his years in the Communist Party in the name of artistic truth: "The culture and letters and arts only serve people's lives, it rises their spirits and recreations. It couldn't serve for the political circulation of any political party. . . . I was a art person." He went on to describe how he hoped to get around the censors, and then began to tape-record his dramas so they could be circulated secretly. Eventually the Communist Party caught up with him, and he fled in 1989 to avoid imprisonment in a re-education camp. His timing could not have been worse. Arriving after the CPA cutoff, he was confined to a camp and failed his screening interview. Refusing voluntary repatriation, he was in a Hong Kong camp for five years. He continued to act, draw, and develop plays within the camps, but he also stressed the CSD's brutality during a 1994 protest, and the resultant injury to his three-year-old. He explained, "Vietnam should respect the human rights, especially Vietnam should have to defend radical thought art workers and their art results. I am an artist with human-conscience."[39] This poignant account spoke to a northern Vietnamese artist's initial identification with the communist nationalist project, his change in political loyalties, and his desire to create political art, which he managed to do in hostile environments in Vietnam and Hong Kong. However, his story failed to compel the Hong Kong hearing board. We do not know if this is because there were inconsistencies, or if his calls to human rights and his artistic vision rang false, or if it was simply because as a northerner he was not legible as a refugee. Regardless, his words spoke to the fraught spaces within the camp and the vulnerability of thousands of Vietnamese trapped within the screening process.

By the early 1990s, Hong Kong immigration officers had "screened in" 11.6 percent of cases. Throughout Southeast Asia, Hong Kong offered the lowest rate of asylum.[40] Human rights activists had achieved more due process protections through Hong Kong's legal system; however, they had not ended the screening process or the plan for repatriation. For Vietnamese who were "screened out," the camps became identical to detention centers. Vietnamese waited for months on end, first for their appeals, and if these failed, for the feared flights back to Vietnam. The result was a tense and sometimes violent environment, where Vietnamese protested their detention as a violation of human rights, and Hong Kong people countered that they were providing humanitarian protection and doing the best they could.

PROTEST IN THE CAMPS

For activists, human rights violations permeated the detention and screening system. The camps became volatile spaces where personal vendettas and political movements could spark violent aggression from the CSD. American lawyers such as Arthur Helton argued that the very nature of the prolonged detention violated human rights.[41] Steve Muncy, a social worker and NGO director, documented the Hong Kong camps' pervasive "process of dehumanization and depersonalization," marked by barbed wire, high fences, steel bars, and isolated locations. Muncy described how Vietnamese lost almost all control over their daily lives, and he criticized the Hong Kong policy as simply "warehousing." The result was an environment which accelerated mental health declines at "poor" and "alarming" rates.[42]

Vietnamese within the camps were also conscious of the changing Cold War politics. They did their best to use the language of human rights to their own advantage. In July 1989, just weeks after the Geneva conference, which endorsed the CPA, Vietnamese in the Hong Kong camps met with UNHCR officials. They were understandably anxious, but they also had a good sense of the politics at hand. For example, one asked, "How can the United Nations let us be forced back? What about Human Rights?" Another individual challenged the UNHCR official, "Have you ever lived under a communist regime? They are liars, you cannot trust them." His or her final sentence brought home an even more grim precedent: "Look at the T.A.M. [Tiananmen Square massacre]"[43]

In another example, Vietnamese at the Chi Ma Wan camp made explicit comparisons between the changes in Eastern Europe and their own campaign for freedom in Hong Kong. Just days after the forced repatriations in December 1989, hundreds of Vietnamese signed an English-language petition to the UNHCR. They pointed to those "fighting for change in communist countries like East Germany, Czechoslovakia, Poland and Hungary . . . aren't they fighting for Human Rights and freedom."[44] The Chi Ma Wan petitioners connected their own escape from communist Vietnam to the nonviolent anti-Soviet revolutions in Czechoslovakia, Bulgaria, and Poland. In this rendition, they were all standing up to communist oppression. What these petitioners could not have anticipated was that the transformation of the former Soviet bloc into nominally liberal states would ultimately limit the resonance of their own anti-communist credentials.

For those who were "screened out," their inability to leave the tight confines of the camps intensified as Hong Kong moved toward implementing its plans for repatriation. Vietnamese within the camps often led protests and campaigns against the CSD, the Hong Kong police, and the Hong Kong government. They opposed their prolonged detention, forced repatriations, and the use of tear gas and excessive violence, which could easily engulf the young children within the camps. The subculture within the camp was also rife for abuse and exploitation at multiple levels. A Vietnamese woman who arrived in Hong Kong in 1988 when she was ten years old remembered her own fear of tear gas and raids against protesters. She witnessed the political contest that was raging within the camps, including lengthy hunger strikes that even resulted in individual deaths. She explained how the Hong Kong press regularly wrote of "riots," but she rejected this delegitimizing language, saying ruefully, "They called our demonstrations or protests 'riots.'" Still, the ongoing resistance and unending detention took a daily psychological toll. There were loudspeakers distributed throughout the camp: "Wherever you go, you hear things like, you should go back, if not you will be forced to go back. . . . There were announcements almost every day, so you go around the camp, it's very small and crowded, and you're mentally stressed due to the prolonged detention, and you hear this all the time, and then you see people being carried onto big lorries or transferred to another camp for forced repatriation."[45] This young woman spoke of the protests with some pride, but she also observed these hunger strikes and self-mutilations, which she admitted were scary and unsettling to witness.

Reading Hong Kong legal decisions and NGO reports, one is also struck by the level of physical violence and the regular threat of sexual violence Vietnamese women faced in the camps. Many young girls were subjected to sexual assault and rape. In 1993, Community and Family Services International concluded that detention multiplied the trauma Vietnamese women faced. While the report danced around sexual assault, it stated, "In general, women in the camps believed they could never feel safe in the camps."[46] A former NGO social worker was more direct. An Austrian woman, she worked within the Hong Kong camps for two years in 1989 and 1990. She documented how young women were particularly vulnerable, and how they often entered unequal and undesired relationships with men in the hope of warding off other assailants. She cited evidence first published by Refugee Concern Hong Kong: "Young women are being forced into relationships against their will and forced to have protectors so they don't have to have sex with ten different men, and only have to have one, even though they don't want to have sex with that one."[47] She also wrote of Hong Kong CSD guards sexually harassing Vietnamese women and even coercing "sexual favours" and prostitution. The author admitted that there was very little hard data because women were reluctant to openly testify or report any sexual abuse they may have suffered regardless of whether the attacker was a Hong Kong Chinese CSD officer or a Vietnamese man within the camp. She wrote, "The number of reports on sexual abuse that have been confided to me by Vietnamese women when I worked with them are unlimited and often gruesome, but most women would not permit me to make any official reports nor could they be convinced to speak out themselves. In the given state of affairs I was not persuaded either that this would have been to their advantage."[48] Although difficult to document, the echo of sexual violence further attested to the traumatic conditions of the Hong Kong camps.

There were also regular reports about crime and violence, which made the camps physically as well as psychologically dangerous. The Hong Kong CSD reported that in 1989 and 1990, gang violence and crime plagued the Whitehead Detention Centre. The acting superintendent documented 42 demonstrations, 7 incidents of "mass fighting," 355 reported crimes, 114 convictions, and 6,649 homemade weapons confiscated during those years.[49] CSD officers seized knives and makeshift defensive masks and shields (to protect against tear gas) which Vietnamese had made.[50] There were fights between southern and northern Vietnamese, personal disputes between individuals, and organized political campaigns against the UNHCR and Hong Kong's policies of repatriation.

Behind barbed wire, Vietnamese collective protest and violence were ways to demonstrate control over their physical selves and gain attention from allies and the media. Hunger strikes were regular occurrences. Using English-language signage, Vietnamese would engage in public hunger strikes, declaring "We are victims of the Hong Kong's screening."[51] Other Vietnamese resorted to self-mutilation and suicide attempts. In January 1990, just weeks after the first forced repatriation, two men held in the Whitehead Detention Centre learned that the RSRB had rejected their petitions. Their response was swift and violent, and they "stabbed themselves in the stomach . . . in an attempt to disembowel themselves" with twenty-centimeter homemade knives.[52] They committed these acts in the UNHCR office—an intentional decision to delegitimize the UNHCR. Like prisoners worldwide, the Vietnamese used their own bodies in protest, forcing the Hong Kong corrections officers and UNHCR to confront their claims to refugee status.[53] Hong Kong hospitals cited that the men had drawn lots and faced pressure from within the camp to act, leading to the desperate, yet coordinated, acts of self-harm.[54]

Hong Kong officials recognized that the suicide attempts were not only acts of despair, but political protests meant to draw international attention to repatriation. In Hong Kong, there was little sympathy toward these tactics. In one particularly crass analysis in the English-language *Hong Kong Standard Post*, columnist Kevin Sinclair wrote, "What a pageant. What a charade. What a bunch of phony actors these Vietnamese are, they threaten self-destruction and a posse of self-indulgent foreign fakers lament over their stage managed affairs.... The Vietnamese take pictures of each other lying sprawled in imaginary agony or unconsciousness. The film is then smuggled out of the camp by do-gooders employed as social workers in the camps who distribute this tawdry propaganda as 'proof' of their 'desperation.'"[55]

While particularly harsh and nasty, Sinclair was not wrong that the Vietnamese within the camp were doing their best to telegraph to the outside world, be it international human rights organizations, Vietnamese diasporic groups, or U.S. and British media, about their indefinite detention and looming repatriation. Reading between the lines of his contempt, one can see the organization, activism, and international networks Vietnamese within the camps needed to mobilize. The "do-gooder" social workers and the staged demonstrations were key pieces in their strategy. As a later group of Vietnamese camp leaders would retort, "To state that we could not organize our own demonstration, could not come up with the idea of yellow and red t-shirts (the color of the South Vietnamese flag) and could not lobby for media attention on our own, exposes the editor's prejudicial attitude towards the Vietnamese people."[56] Through these measures, Vietnamese succeeded in gaining allies within Hong Kong, especially among select expatriates, with Vietnamese American communities overseas, and through these networks, in the U.S. Congress.

U.S. and U.K.-based human rights lawyers kept up international pressure on Hong Kong, and numerous delegations visited the camps and issued reports.[57] For example, the Women's Commission for Refugee Children sent monitors into the camps to assess with a feminist eye the living conditions of

Vietnamese women in the camps. They argued that poorly trained immigration officers presumed that women and minors did not have independent asylum claims apart from those of their male spouses or family members. The committee also railed against the indefinite detention of young people, which led to malnutrition and nightmares: "No justifiable excuse exists for so imprisoning people—especially young children—who have committed no crime but rather have exercised their right to seek asylum."[58] Screened-out young children often spent years behind barbed wire, and one woman who had been a child in the camp remembered leaving the camp only twice in eight years, once for an outing and once for a hospital visit. She added she never saw trees, as the camp was fully concrete. Older children would even tease younger ones by pointing at CSD vehicles when they entered the camp and calling them "buffaloes." "The children innocently believed what we said, because they never saw anything outside the camp."[59] The American-based Lawyers Committee for Human Rights argued Hong Kong broadly practiced "arbitrary detention." With celebrities like Sigourney Weaver and legal heavyweights like Lani Guinier and Floyd Abrams on its board of directors, the Lawyers Committee insisted, "Without these guarantees, refugees may be returned to face persecution in violation of the most basic tenets of human rights law."[60]

Vietnamese in the camps and in the diaspora wrote to the UNHCR, the U.S., and the British governments with regularity, calling on the UNHCR to fulfill its mandate of protection. They critiqued the asylum hearing process, flagged the possibility of corruption in the process, and used the language of human rights.[61] This language was passionate, emotional, at times strident, and at other times heartbreaking, and it remained remarkably consistent from the outset of the CPA through its end in the late 1990s. For example, a translation of a Vietnamese-language petition to the UNHCR proclaimed, "Before leaving the country, we took this vow, Freedom or Death. Forced Repatriation is an inhuman act which has been condemned by all nations." The authors of the petition imagined themselves as a part of an international community and noted "all the human rights organizations in the world, the Amnesty Internationals, and the religious leaders" were behind them.[62]

Human rights resonated on multiple levels. First, Vietnamese within the camps identified anti-communism with human rights and made their claims based on what they saw as violations of human rights in Vietnam. Second, the grim conditions, risks of abuse, and indefinite detention set up the camps

FIGURE 11. Illustration of life in a closed camp during the Tet new year celebration. Vu Van Minh, *The Dinner of Traditional Tet in Closed Camp*. Courtesy of UC Irvine Libraries, Southeast Asian Archive, Project Ngoc Records.

themselves as constraining human rights. Amnesty International and Human Rights Watch had monitored prison conditions for years, and to many, the detention camps seemed like nothing more or less than prisons. Activists repeatedly claimed that the camps violated human rights because they detained individuals indefinitely in horrific conditions. Finally, the interview and asylum hearing process was rife with abuses, and the legalistic and individualistic methodology of human rights reporting found ample problems within the screening system itself. At times, advocates pointed to human rights abuses in Vietnam, but they were just as likely to wield charges of human rights violations at the camps.

Hong Kong government officials and the general population could not have disagreed more. From their perspective, the camps were unsafe, the Vietnamese were violent, and Hong Kong personnel and CSD officers were risking their own lives guarding them.[63] It was not that Hong Kong people were ignorant or dismissive of human rights language. Instead, like most, they were attuned to their own rights, and in this case, the risks of 1997. Hong Kong people claimed the goal was the lower bar of humanitarian protection, a promise on which most believed they had more than delivered.

Rather than shying away from the history of the camps, Hong Kong officials spoke of their experiences with pride, and many wanted Hong Kong's record of humanitarianism to be set straight.[64] Between 1975 and 1997, hundreds, if not thousands, of Hong Kong men and women worked in the camps as aid workers, guards, teachers, administrators, and social workers. This included the resources of the Hong Kong Civil Aid Service, the Corrections Services Department, Hong Kong civil servants, and nonprofit social service agencies such as Caritas and Save the Children. As Peter Lai, the first and last Hong Kong Chinese head of security under British rule, told researcher Carina Hoang, "We did a good thing. It was difficult and sometimes bloody annoying, especially when they turned nasty. But it was a good thing because over the years . . . I am a Catholic and whatever the rights and wrongs of the politics of it, I don't see a conscionable problem of saving people from the risk of death by drowning. So, there you go."[65] In poring through the archives at the Hong Kong Public Records Office, I found numerous letters from Amnesty International members from around the world supporting Vietnamese within the camps in a coordinated, targeted campaign, alongside testimonies from local Hong Kong municipalities about the burdens the camps placed on their communities. Hong Kong civil servants received and had to respond to both sets of petitions. My own interviews substantiated this. Eddy Chan, another career civil servant, echoed that Hong Kong did its best to provide humane conditions and act in a humanitarian way. He told me he faced constant criticism in the security branch, even as he ensured that Save the Children, Médecins Sans Frontières, Community Family Services International, and International Social Services provided educational and social services within the camps. "We [Hong Kong civil servants] felt unfairly treated, because we were at the forefront of the whole thing and we had very little international sympathy. We had a lot of international criticism, but very little international sympathy."[66]

Hong Kong and international NGOs often found themselves in a somewhat compromised position. They provided mental health services, vocational training, and language classes to Vietnamese, even as many recognized the horrendous, overcrowded conditions. There was a division among nonprofits, with direct service providers attempting to alleviate boredom and depression through child care, education, mental health counseling, and recreational activities, and with advocacy groups monitoring the camp conditions and the implementation of the CPA.[67] Expatriate and Hong Kong social workers, teachers, and later, advocates worked daily with Vietnamese in the camps. Hong Kong Chinese social workers explained how they were able to develop human connections with the Vietnamese, since they were not involved in the screening process. Even the CSD, which provided security, recruited new hires specifically to work in the Vietnamese camps, rather than the territory's prisons. At least some of these guards signed up because they were motivated to help the Vietnamese.

Hong Kong Chinese who worked in the camps often expressed ambivalence about their responsibilities. Their work could be a difficult balancing act. Like many of the Filipina social workers in Bataan, Caritas worker Brenda Ku recalled with pride the professionalism of her staff, who faced their work with "a lot of courage, love, and stamina."[68] CSD officers also articulated their experiences in terms of service and duty. For example, CSD officer Gordon Leung remembered his experiences with pride, but also emphasized the pressure he felt from local Hong Kong Chinese who blamed the British for the camps and later attacks by human rights organizations. "We tried to uphold in whatever way we could to deal with it in a most humane manner. I think at the end of the day, it's a humanitarian consideration that prevails. That I believe is right. It's not easy. We had to undergo such a lot of pressure, both within the legislature and local community."[69] Other Hong Kong professionals who worked in the camps expressed ambivalence about their roles. Joyce T'ang worked as a doctor with Médecins Sans Frontières and later the UNHCR. Her memories were colored by doubt. Identifying with the Vietnamese, she asked herself: "This is not what people had expected when they left everything behind in their home country. Why did they stay? . . . I still don't know what I would have done in their place. Which is worse: forcing them to repatriate or letting them stay indefinitely in detention? Were their years spent in Hong Kong entirely wasted? I have asked myself these questions many times but still can find no answer."[70]

Hong Kong Chinese people were also preoccupied about what the post-1997 future would look like. The Chinese government promised to implement its "one country, two systems" vision. This would allow Hong Kong to retain certain freedoms of speech and trade policies, but all under Chinese sovereignty.[71] However, many Hong Kong Chinese who had the economic wherewithal to do so began to emigrate. Securing an additional passport could act as an insurance policy, even if one planned to remain in Hong Kong. This became even more acute after the Tiananmen Square massacre in 1989.[72] In July 1989, a group of journalists and professionals wrote to British

MP Bernie Grant, asking him to support Hong Kong residents' full British citizenship with the right to live in the U.K.[73] Another Hong Kong Chinese expressed his anger and anxieties over Tiananmen Square (and the lack of a British response): "Should Britain still honor the Joint-Declaration and hand the six million people of Hong Kong over to a Communist government that has shown itself to be no better than the murderous regime of Pol Pot? If Britain decides to betray the people of Hong Kong by doing so, then it will have to live the moral responsibility of stage-managing one of the great tragedies of this tragic century."[74]

Several Hong Kong students drew astute parallels between the British negotiations with China and the British government's push for Vietnamese repatriation. "Hong Kong people have had their future and their nationality negotiated away for them by Britain." They believed this was similar to Britain's decision to "negotiate the lives and future of the Vietnamese refugees in their care." In both instances, the Hong Kong Chinese and the Vietnamese had little control over their ultimate fates and were resigned to lives under communist governments. The students concluded that Britain planned to "send the refugees away from this territory back to the notorious communist regime in Vietnam!"[75] These students were sympathetic, and they ultimately believed Hong Kong and the U.K. should do more for the Vietnamese. Far more Hong Kong Chinese, however, simply resented that Hong Kong provided asylum to Vietnamese, when they feared for their own future.[76]

While there was no causal link between the 1989 CPA, the Hong Kong policy of Vietnamese repatriation, and Tiananmen Square, these events collectively made the conflict between human rights and humanitarian protection even more acute. Tiananmen Square made Hong Kong people contemplate the fragility of the territory's future and their own potential status as refugees. A UNHCR desk officer wrote to Geneva headquarters and explained that Hong Kong's popular animosity against the Vietnamese had been exacerbated by the "dramatic rise in feelings of domestic insecurity in the territory resulting from June 4 events and subsequent developments in China."[77] He believed the Vietnamese were a veritable "scapegoat" for local anxieties that emanated from Hong Kong's uncertain future and the Chinese authoritarianism demonstrated by the Tiananmen crackdown.

In 1989, a Hong Kong poll reported that 95 percent of Hong Kong people believed that the Vietnamese camps were a "serious" or "very serious" problem, and 84 percent wanted to end the policy of first asylum. Only 2 percent of respondents reported that the camps were a "minor nuisance."[78] Hong

Kong district offices also protested the creation of camps in their communities. Letters to the government included passages such as "The Government has made the decision [to build a camp] regardless of public views. We cannot remain silent any longer."[79] In another example that encapsulates the local pressure on Hong Kong government officials, a 1990 television special followed the stories of pregnant Vietnamese women in the Whitehead Detention Centre, located in the New Territories. The local nurses spoke plainly. They believed pregnant Vietnamese women drained their community's resources. "If we didn't have the Vietnamese, we could spend time with the [Hong Kong] mothers in labor and comfort them; now we spend less time on each patient." In the episode's conclusion, the journalist implied that Vietnamese women and children received care first, placing the care of Hong Kong infants at risk.[80] The message was alarmist—Hong Kong babies were being sacrificed for Vietnamese families.

Hong Kong civil servants constantly felt crushed between two extremes. On the one hand, they faced hostility and pressure from Hong Kong Chinese who had little sympathy for the Vietnamese on their shores. On the other hand, they were under attack from western NGOs, U.S. politicians, and Vietnamese American activists, who kept up a steady stream of attacks against the camps and the screening process. Many Hong Kong immigration and security officers felt besieged for implementing a thankless policy. They believed repatriation would enable Vietnamese to restart their lives instead of lingering in detention centers for years on end. In this formulation, screening and repatriation *were* humanitarian actions.

REPATRIATION: VOLUNTARY, FORCED, OR "ORDERLY"

Given the disastrous international publicity following the December 1989 forced repatriations, Hong Kong agreed to halt them in the short term. Yet UNHCR, Hong Kong, U.K., U.S., and Vietnamese government officials all knew that the CPA would only be successful if Vietnamese started returning to Vietnam in substantial numbers. Approximately 10,000 had returned between 1990 and 1991, a not insignificant number, but tens of thousands of the "screened out" refused to "volunteer."[81]

Initially, the U.S. and Vietnamese governments found unusual common ground in that both opposed "forced repatriation." One of the reasons

Vietnam agreed to the repatriations at all was to improve its international standing with the UN and Great Britain. However, it did not appreciate the public relations black eye of its citizens being dragged onto and off of airplanes, and it demanded repatriates return with "dignity." Likewise, in 1989 and the early 1990s, the United States kept the CPA at arm's length. It publicly supported the principle of voluntary repatriation, but it balked at forced repatriation or anything that approached it. This frustrated Hong Kong officials to no end. The U.S. government did not oppose repatriation, or deportation, when it came to Haitians and Mexicans.[82] As one Hong Kong letter writer vented: "Enough of this idiotic hypocrisy. It is time we looked after ourselves. Let us borrow a leaf from the official policy of the American government, form our own coastguard and force anyone out of our territorial waters who are not legally entitled to enter as the Americans do with the Haitian boat people."[83] In an interview with Carina Hoang, Eddy Chan emphasized his frustration with American hypocrisy: "They [the Americans] disliked everything that we did. When they were trying to repatriate their illegal immigrants from Mexico, they didn't even bother telling the press! But what we did in Hong Kong, we involved everybody else. We tried to tell them we had nothing to hide; we tried to do it as humanely as possible and without unnecessary force."[84] All this was true—the U.S. government deported Mexicans without any qualms and increasingly detained and deported Haitians with substantive asylum claims—but it still could not stomach forced repatriations back to Vietnam. It contradicted decades of U.S. anti-communist rhetoric, policy, and practice.

Much was made of whether the repatriations were "voluntary," and thus sanctioned by the UNHCR, Vietnam, and the United States, or forced. The entire goal of the screening process was to pressure Vietnamese to "volunteer" to repatriate. The UNHCR and Hong Kong government "counseled" this choice and provided no alternative other than more time in the bare and violent conditions of the camps. Consequently, for many Vietnamese in the camps, the voluntary repatriations did not feel voluntary. In order to de-escalate the tensions and implement the CPA, many proponents wanted to move away from the binary language. In 1990, Oxfam Director Chris Bale argued for jettisoning all language such as "forced, "mandatory," and "non-objectors." According to the *South China Morning Post,* he urged that repatriation become the norm, and that the government excise unhelpful adjectives. "When we blur distinctions between voluntary and mandatory we get away from unhelpful terminology. Nobody wants forced repatriation. It is not something Hong Kong wants to do and it is not something that Margaret Thatcher wants to do because it leads to embarrassing questions in parliament, but we do want to get Vietnamese boat people back."[85]

Perhaps ironically, the Vietnamese government was more willing to compromise on this point than the United States was. Here too we see the conscious evasion of undesirable categories. Vietnamese government official Nguyen Dinh Bin played with the somewhat false distinction between "forced" and "voluntary" repatriation. "When you say this shirt is not white, it does not mean it is black. . . . I mention this because black and white are extremes—like forced and voluntary."[86] He, for one, seemed willing to live with the contorted language and shades of gray, or at least "not black." Although the Vietnamese government insisted on voluntary repatriation, it did not necessarily see all repatriations that fell short of a full-fledge public desire to return as "forced." This linguistic dance demonstrated how the Vietnamese were more willing than the Americans to accept the murkiness between voluntary and forced repatriations. Their goal was to work cooperatively with the UNHCR and the U.K. in return for improved standing in the international community. Hong Kong security officer Clinton Leeks stated bluntly that the Americans, "because of their hang-up about Vietnam," were more difficult to negotiate with than the Vietnamese.[87]

In October 1990, the UNHCR, the U.K., and Hong Kong negotiated a new agreement to restart voluntary repatriations. Vietnamese within the camps protested. They recognized that if Hong Kong and Vietnam had come to an agreement on "voluntary" repatriations, non-voluntary ones would be close behind. More than two thousand marched in the Whitehead Detention Centre. Waving flags and chanting slogans against repatriation, these Vietnamese "lashed out" and expressed their "loss of faith" in the UNHCR.[88] Other Vietnamese engaged in days-long hunger strikes, with more than fifty individuals hunger-striking to protest the UNHCR's agreement to counsel "non-volunteers."[89] UN officials maintained that Vietnamese had to choose between "dignity," that is, voluntary repatriation, and "deportation."[90] The UNHCR also promised cash incentives to entice Vietnamese to return.

The Hong Kong government did not blink. After an almost two-year pause in forced repatriations due to the legal challenges, Hong Kong instituted the euphemistically named Orderly Repatriation Program in 1991. As one Hong Kong editorial commented, "We now have to bite the bullet and accept the fact these forced departures will be marked by some harrowing scenes," namely CSD officers dragging Vietnamese onto planes under

FIGURE 12. Vietnamese take to the roofs of the camp buildings in protest, Hong Kong, 1990. Courtesy of UC Irvine Libraries, Southeast Asian Archive, Project Ngoc Records.

duress.[91] Hong Kong officials began the "orderly repatriations" with a group of "double-backers," Vietnamese who had received UNHCR funds and returned to Vietnam once, only to come back to Hong Kong and try for asylum and resettlement a second time. This was a less sympathetic group than those who had been waiting in the camps, and Hong Kong initiated the "orderly repatriation" of these double-backers to make a point and disincentivize return escapes. Still, the scene was stark. One reporter described a young woman "half-dragged, half-lifted, sobbing with the finality of lost hope." She could not hear the woman's screams over the airplane's engine, but "no words were needed. Her twisting body, her cheap red jacket dragged half-off as woman camp officers grabbed both arms, the dragging feet, the tousled hair, and the head thrown back in open-mouthed despair, all told their own story."[92] Hong Kong insisted that "force" was not used, that is, individuals were not physically harmed or attacked in the repatriation process. While technically perhaps true, the Hong Kong government continued both with "voluntary" repatriations that many Vietnamese did not see as voluntary and with "orderly repatriations," or forced repatriations.

Scholar W. Courtland Robinson reported that Hong Kong removed only 2,100 people through the Orderly Repatriation Program before 1995; however, the sense of fear and anger in the camps was real.[93] The program was used to compel people into volunteering, and documentary evidence of the "orderly repatriations" attests to extremely physical encounters, with Hong Kong CSD guards carrying prone individuals onto airplanes.[94] Vietnamese within the camps and the diasporic community rejected the careful distinction between voluntary, "orderly" and "forced." In their eyes, there was no way in which detention and repatriation could be seen as humanitarian actions.

DIASPORIC ACTIVISM AND POST–COLD WAR HUMAN RIGHTS

From the United States, Vietnamese American activists looked at the Hong Kong camps and saw Vietnamese being ill treated, disrespected, and worse yet, in their eyes, sacrificed on a global stage. The vast majority of Vietnamese Americans had fled themselves, either in 1975, the late 1970s, or after the 1979 Geneva conference, and they too had waited in camps. By the late 1980s, Vietnamese American activists had gained a modicum of political and economic security, thousands of Vietnamese Americans donated money and signed petitions, and smaller numbers volunteered (in both Hong Kong and the Philippines) and lobbied Congress against repatriation. A commitment to anti-communism and an antipathy to the Socialist Republic of Vietnam often mobilized their public rhetoric, and community leaders remained staunch foes of Hanoi.[95] They also envisioned themselves as championing human rights, and given the United States' track record of privileging anti-communist refugees, there was reason to believe this language would gain traction.

Vietnamese American activists often invoked a language of gratitude and obligation when making their case against the CPA. They appealed to first-asylum countries, the UNHCR, and in particular, the United States, which they thanked for "accepting us and giving us a new chance on rebuilding our lives."[96] As scholar Mimi Thi Nguyen has demonstrated, this rhetoric worked ideologically to cement the Vietnamese American community to resettlement countries, often erasing the histories of military and neoliberal violence, war, and betrayal that predated them.[97] In this case, the language of gratitude also served to frame these diasporic activists' calls on the U.S. government to accept more Vietnamese as refugees and to use its political power to pressure the UNHCR and first-asylum countries to reject repatriation.

College students at the University of California, Irvine, organized Project Ngoc, a volunteer, student-based advocacy group, which punched above its weight. Inspired by African American and Chicano activism on American college campuses, Vietnamese American students looked at the conditions in Hong Kong with outrage and mobilized. Led by young Vietnamese Americans, Project Ngoc created transnational networks between California and Hong Kong and sought to aid the Vietnamese in the camps and impact U.S. policy. Students headed out to the Asian Gardens Mall in Westminster, California, and set up information tables to talk to Vietnamese Americans and other Californians about Hong Kong's camps. Their educational efforts were effective, and they ultimately raised thousands of dollars from the community. Mai-Phuong Nguyen was one of the lead organizers, and she remembered Project Ngoc did "crazy stuff," like placing an advertisement in the *New York Times* "ratting on" the UNHCR. They demanded to know "How can you [the UNHCR] let this happen? These people deserve refugee status. They are modified refugees so what if they do not have the paper work?"[98] Mai-Phuong Nguyen recognized that it was becoming increasingly difficult for Vietnamese to "prove" their refugee claims, and she dedicated countless hours to advocacy.

Project Ngoc enabled young people to develop leadership skills and make connections between Vietnamese Americans in the United States and Vietnamese in the camps. For many, there was a sense of personal recognition, as well as anger and anxiety about how much harder it was for Vietnamese families to gain refugee status and resettlement after 1989 compared to their own experiences from the late 1970s and early 1980s. For example, Nicole Nguyen's family fled Vietnam in the early 1980s and landed in Malaysia. Because she was a young child at the time, her memories of the camp in Malaysia were foggy. She added, "To me as a child growing up in that environment. I didn't find it harsh because I didn't see all the things that were happening." Her parents sheltered her from their anxiety about the future, and she remembered being able to be outside, where she could "hang out and play in the dirt." However, in college at UC Irvine, she felt moved to join Project Ngoc.[99] She remembered her first meeting. There was a video about the camps, which emphasized the unsanitary conditions, crowding, and detention-like facilities. This sparked her interest and a politics of recognition. "Ohh, that's about the boat people. I was a part of that." She went to her parents and asked if they had suffered like the Vietnamese in the video, and her parents confirmed that they had experienced similar traumas, but that they preferred not to share these experiences with their young children. She reflected on her personal journey into activism. "I didn't know that these camps still existed. I just thought it was my family that went through that process, but it was thousands and thousands of people some camps were really bad conditions that people were in. That sort of channeled, start[ed] my passion . . . to help others who were less fortunate than I am. I end[ed] up being very active in the community raising awareness."[100]

Project Ngoc even sponsored volunteers to go to Hong Kong and see the camps for themselves firsthand. Volunteers taught English and art to Vietnamese in Hong Kong camps. Other organizations, like the Philippine-based Center for Assistance to Displaced Persons, also recruited young college students to volunteer in Palawan and Bataan. The result was often transformative for the young Vietnamese Americans involved. Tu-Uyen Nguyen had to convince her father to let her travel to Southeast Asia as one of the Project Ngoc volunteers. At first he resisted, but ultimately he agreed she could go. "[I] had very little idea of what I was getting myself into, but I think that experience really changed my life because it opened up, again, just this whole new world to me of how, in a sense, lucky I was and how other people in the world don't have the same kinds of privileges that I have, right? And to be able to see that, it really, I think, helped to solidify for me, what it meant to be in America . . . it was a really life changing experience."[101]

One of Project Ngoc's most innovative initiatives promoted arts education and exchange. In 1990, Project Ngoc had members assist an artist-driven project in Hong Kong, after which the volunteers returned to Orange County with artwork produced within the camps. They then mounted an exhibition in California to display the powerful images Vietnamese created in detention. The paintings included images asking the UNHCR or U.S. to save the Vietnamese from the camps, canvases which attested to the mendacity of the Vietnamese government, and more abstract images of confinement and rejection. They were not alone in being moved by the power of Vietnamese artwork produced within the camps. Other Vietnamese Americans, like journalist and community activist Paul Tran, also ensured these paintings and drawings were preserved. These public events and artistic collaborations resonated as transnational acts of solidarity, and Vietnamese Americans sought to make the despair within the camps legible thousands of miles outside Hong Kong.[102]

Not only college students, but Vietnamese American professionals turned their attention to advocacy. In the 1980s, Boat People SOS was based in San

FIGURE 13. Vietnamese artist's representation of a protest within a Hong Kong closed camp. Quan Ha, *Rebel*. Courtesy of UC Irvine Libraries, Southeast Asian Archive, Paul Tran Files on Southeast Asian Refugees.

Diego, and it had supported rescues at sea; however, in 1989, it relocated to northern Virginia and gained new leadership under Nguyen Dinh Thang. Boat People SOS kept its eyes on human rights violations in Vietnam and advocated for the Vietnamese in the camps. It became a fierce critic of the screening process and the CPA. One petition sent to the U.S. State Department read, "Vietnam has not ended its abuses of human rights against its own citizenry. . . . Many former political prisoners, religious leaders, intellectuals, dissidents, human rights activists, and citizens of Vietnam who had been cruelly persecuted by their government have been erroneously screened out as non-refugees."[103] Throughout the early 1990s, Boat People SOS developed into a transnational organization that was effective in Hong Kong and in Washington, D.C.

Like Project Ngoc, Boat People SOS dedicated significant financial resources to aiding Vietnamese within the camps, and most importantly, it launched a legal wing, Legal Assistance to Vietnamese Asylum Seekers, to provide direct representation in screenings. Its lawyers enabled hundreds of Vietnamese to have better legal representation in Hong Kong and the

Philippines, and therefore a better chance at being "screened in." In principle, Boat People SOS accepted the logic of screenings and repatriation, but in most of its literature and public testimony, the organization presented all Vietnamese as refugees at all times. In this way, it was similar to Hong Kong–based Refugee Concern, and both organizations fought for their clients to be "screened in" and to escape repatriation. Boat People SOS also refused to accept the distinction between "voluntary" and "forced" repatriation, and it argued that repatriation simply could not be voluntary given the pressure within the camp. "Those who return only do so out of despair, frustration and fear for their family's safety in the camps, not because they have confidence in the system. They know that screening is unfair and unjust, designed and implemented only as a means of deterrence."[104] Their newsletter regularly asked, "What is a refugee?" and would profile the stories of those "screened out." The goal was to convince readers that the CPA regularly denied "real" refugees asylum in Hong Kong and Southeast Asia.

Boat People SOS also succeeded in finding friends and allies in the U.S. Congress, and Nguyen Dinh Thang became a familiar presence on the hill. In 1990, he testified before the House Subcommittee on Asian and Pacific Affairs on the implementation of the Comprehensive Plan of Action. Representatives from Refugees International and Catholic Charities testified about Hong Kong's arbitrary screening mechanisms, and they advocated for a new "holding center" for the screened-out on American territory to prevent involuntary repatriations. Nguyen Dinh Thang was the only Vietnamese American who testified at this hearing. When pressed by Representative Stephen Solarz on whether there was unanimity in the Vietnamese American community, he replied, "I would say, Mr. Chairman, that there is a unanimous consensus among the Vietnamese community against forced repatriation. On the question of a holding center, there are some differences of opinion, seeing that there might be some difficulties in the area."[105] While the United States ultimately did not establish a holding center, this was only one of Nguyen Dinh Thang's many visits to Capitol Hill. Throughout the 1990s he gained more congressional allies, and as one of the few Vietnamese Americans in the room he claimed legitimacy and authority as a national spokesperson.

With the 1992 election of Bill Clinton and the U.S. government's movement toward normalization with Vietnam, the stakes for the Vietnamese within the camps became even more acute. In 1994, the United States lifted the embargo, which had been in place since 1975, and in 1995, the U.S. renewed diplomatic relations with Vietnam. For those Americans who opposed normalization, many did so because of their long-standing belief that Vietnam secretly harbored remaining POWs, despite all evidence to the contrary. Few Americans were cognizant that thousands of Vietnamese actually remained behind barbed wire in places like Hong Kong. In contrast, Vietnamese American advocacy groups like Boat People SOS made it their mission to draw the attention of the American public and U.S. elected officials to the Vietnamese still in camps and cast repatriation as a betrayal of U.S. values in the Cold War:

> Dear President [Clinton], Do not betray Human Rights; Do not abandon the principles of American Humanitarianism and Values! Your government is supporting and financing for a program through which victims of persecution are being forcibly repatriated to the communist of Vietnam.... These victims include many thousands of Vietnamese veterans, once being American allies and severely persecuted for having fought against communism; many hundreds of religious leaders, human rights supporters, reactionary soldiers, anti-government elements, and former political prisoners.... Your government is not only supporting but also actively asking these people to return to the Vietnamese communists.[106]

Using the language of human rights, Boat People SOS emphasized the suffering of Vietnamese who would be sent back to Vietnam. It also hit on the symbolic role Vietnam veterans occupied in American popular culture; however, in this case, it emphasized the role of South Vietnamese veterans, a population few Americans acknowledged. It asked politicians to shift their perspective and recognize the ongoing fears and suffering of South Vietnamese veterans, many of whom remained in camps in Hong Kong and Southeast Asia.

Project Ngoc, Boat People SOS, and Refugee Concern, along with other voluntary agencies, succeeded in providing large numbers of Vietnamese within the camps better legal representation and a greater chance of resettlement. However, none of these organizations was ultimately able to stem the tide against repatriation, forced or voluntary. In 1992, Hong Kong accelerated the pace of voluntary repatriations. Under pressure, and despairing in the closed camps, thousands of Vietnamese did begin to return to Vietnam. Others chose to remain in the camps. Despite cash incentives, prison-like conditions, and no political promises, approximately 16,000 people hoped to evade repatriation and hold out for resettlement.[107] Global events, however, were moving rapidly, and these individuals soon found themselves caught between the U.S.-Vietnam move toward normalization and Hong Kong's eye on 1997.

Vietnamese within the camps were well aware of the rapidly approaching dead-lines. By 1994, all of these individuals had been "screened out," and despite the UNHCR's and Hong Kong's best efforts, they had refused repatriation. The intensity of their demonstrations escalated. For example, hunger striker Nguyen Van Hoa used the strongest language possible to protest his confinement and his willingness to hold out for refugee status in face of the CPA, UNHCR, and "orderly repatriation." After being hospitalized, he proclaimed, "I am not afraid of death and I already to die for freedom, but my death, if it happens in such a situation I am afraid will certainly be covered up and it will be insignificant because the reason or motive for my death may be [distorted]."[108]

In April 1994, the stress, volatility, and potential violence in the Whitehead Detention Centre hit a peak. With the quickening pace of repa-triations, a group of 1,500 Vietnamese organized a protest, which included public hunger strikes and collective actions. Many wore all white and mourn-ing headbands. Labeling the leaders of these protests "troublemakers," the CSD coordinated a plan to remove them from Whitehead and relocate them to another center. The result was a dramatic assault, complete with tear gas, Vietnamese climbing to the rooftops, and a direct confrontation between the CSD and the Vietnamese. In all, 587 CSD officers and 762 Hong Kong police entered the camp to try to maintain control. Vietnamese shouted, "Protest against forced repatriation! Protest against the violation of human rights! The people of Hong Kong, please help the boat people!"[109] CSD offic-ers fired dozens of cartridges of mace and tear gas, particularly targeting the Vietnamese who had sought refuge on the roofs.

Because of the violence and immediate publicity, the Hong Kong govern-ment ordered a formal inquiry led by a judge and a medical professor. These appointees interviewed Vietnamese, security personnel, CSD officers, and the police, and they investigated whether the show of force had been neces-sary. Over a hundred pages in length, the inquiry concluded that the use of coordinated force had been appropriate. It admitted that CSD officers had assaulted Vietnamese, but it concluded that the Vietnamese had also exag-gerated their injuries. It also noted that CSD officers had been too quick to turn to tear gas rather than negotiate with camp leaders.[110] However, for the purposes of the Hong Kong government, the matter had been investigated, the wrongdoings acknowledged, and the repatriations were to continue.

Refugee Concern and Vietnamese advocates were unconvinced, and they hit back with their own "inquiry," concluding that Hong Kong government officials had violated Vietnamese human rights in the camps. Refugee Concern utilized the tactics of other international human rights organizations by issuing its own fact-finding report. Unlike the government inquiry, Refugee Concern's inquiry legitimized the Vietnamese protests, deeming them well organized and an expression of free speech. Through separate interviews with Vietnamese in the camps, the Refugee Concern inquiry concluded that the CSD officers' fears that Vietnamese would throw Molotov cocktails or take the camp staff hostage were unfounded and exaggerated. It criticized the CSD for using tear gas and mace "outside the guidelines and law regarding minimal force," and it believed there was a deliberate cover-up of injuries and assaults on Vietnamese. Although the Refugee Concern report acknowledged that Vietnamese took to the roofs, it justified these actions as a form of protest. The government had the right to move people from one camp to the next, but it had been required to provide more advance notice for such an operation. To do otherwise was "grossly negligent." "We find that the 7 April operation was calculated to intimidate all asylum seekers to cease their peaceful hunger strikes and demonstrations."[111]

The Refugee Concern report condemned the 1994 Whitehead raid on three grounds. First, it chastised the UNHCR for abdicating its humanitarian role of protection. If Hong Kong and the UNHCR believed that the camps and repatriation were humanitarian, how could it justify the violence, assault, and tear gas sprayed at the Vietnamese? "We find that the UNHCR failed in a variety of respects to fulfill its mandated monitoring role. We find that had strong UNHCR monitors been at Whitehead when the operation began and been permitted to enter, there is a strong likelihood that their presence would have tempered the actions of the riot officers and senior CSD and police officers." Second, it utilized the language of human rights to support the Vietnamese right to protest—"that people's human right to freedom of expression be respected and that intimidation not be used against people conducting genuinely peace demonstrations." Finally, regarding the crux of the matter, it called for many of the Vietnamese to be resettled either in France or the United States. Refugee Concern believed the screening process had failed. The report pointed to former soldiers (and their families) who had fought with the French and South Vietnamese armies, individuals who faced religious discrimination, and "those whose decisions on refugee status are so bad that the substantive issue as to whether they are in fact refugees has been obscured."[112] In both its form and its claims, Refugee Concern used the language and methods of human rights advocates to defend the Vietnamese against repatriation.

In Hong Kong, the years between 1994 and 1997 remained extremely tense, and Hong Kong CSD officers remember a high degree of stress. They were tasked with maintaining order in the camps, and at times, physically implementing "orderly repatriations." The number of repatriations grew in 1996 and reached more than 9,000 by 1997.[113] The CSD even memorialized these years by archiving and displaying the Vietnamese camp protesters' homemade weapons and gas masks in the Hong Kong Correctional Services museum. The exhibit also includes looped video footage of CSD officers hauling prone Vietnamese individuals onto airplanes. The sanitized language of "orderly" and "repatriation" stood in opposition to the loud, visually chaotic, and emotionally traumatic videos. The CSD's decision to display these videos in a museum, rather than conceal them, provides insight into the government's perspective. It wanted to demonstrate the physical threats facing Hong Kong CSD officers (not the Vietnamese), and it viewed the Vietnamese camp experience as a testament to the CSD's humanitarian capabilities and professionalism.

With this, Vietnamese American activists turned to the U.S. Congress to try and stave off the repatriations. New Jersey Republican Chris Smith became the most vocal congressional representative against repatriation, and Boat People SOS's staunchest ally. He also led the charge against what he saw as U.S. acquiescence to the CPA and Hong Kong's policy.[114] Smith's language exuded an old-fashioned Cold War anti-communism, which remained powerful even as the U.S. was establishing diplomatic relations with Vietnam. He dismissed the CPA as a "scheme," and railed against the screening process.[115] He became a vocal irritant to the UNHCR, Hong Kong officials, and even the State Department as he sought to block repatriation. In 1995, Smith attempted to pass legislation to relaunch INS interviews directly within the camps. The Hong Kong RSRB and the UNHCR mandate review did the "screening," so the "screened out" had never been interviewed by U.S. INS officers. Smith wanted to change this, and he thought the INS would be more open to the Vietnamese refugee claims. If passed, his proposed legislation would undermine almost a decade of U.S. cooperation with the UNHCR and Hong Kong, so the U.S. State Department opposed Smith's efforts. UNHCR officials said the legislation, and its promise of new American interviews, was akin to "playing with fire," and they feared it would lead to even more violence in the camps.[116] With seeming amnesia as to the low INS acceptance rates in the mid-1980s, Smith and his congressional allies hoped to save these Vietnamese from a return to Vietnam.[117] With the collapse of the Soviet Union, anti-communism was no longer a dominant diplomatic imperative, but it did retain a stickiness. This meant that the U.S. government was sometimes willing to develop preferential programs for Vietnamese and take a stand against repatriation, even as it passed punitive laws like the 1996 Illegal Immigration Reform and Responsibility Act, which increasingly criminalized immigration through detention and deportation.

With Congress pressing for new legislation to undermine the CPA, the State Department offered an ingenious compromise—the ROVR program (Resettlement Opportunity for Vietnamese Returnees). Again, Vietnamese Americans were part of this political compromise and proposal. In this instance, Le Xuan Khoa of IRAC worked with Refugees International to advocate for what he termed the "gray-area people." He believed that there was a cohort of "real refugees" who had been unjustly screened out and needed to be rescreened, but he also recognized the need to follow through with the CPA.[118] He believed these new interviews by U.S. officials could be conducted in Vietnam. The ROVR program would encourage Vietnamese in the Hong Kong and other Southeast Asian camps to return to Vietnam. It then committed to offering new INS-directed interviews for these returnees, but only *back* in Vietnam. Dubbing it the ROVR program underscored its double-edged nature, seeming to invoke the childhood game "red rover, red rover," where someone on one team tries to break through a human chain on the other team, and the human chain tries to push them back. Unlike most bureaucratic acronyms it resonated on multiple levels, raising questions about refugees' desire to break through the chain and camp authorities' desire to push them back.

For Vietnamese within the Hong Kong camps, ROVR was a tough sell. Not surprisingly, they worried that if they returned to Vietnam, the urgency would diminish, and they would not qualify for resettlement in the United States. They were skeptical that the U.S. would make good on its promise. This was essentially an American end game and an attempt to provide some solace and hope for its former allies. Many feared that this was yet another "trap," and they were uncertain whether they should hold their ground in Hong Kong or return to Vietnam with just a promise of another interview. Initially, the State Department officials who went to Hong Kong in the summer of 1996 found few takers. For example, they applauded 100 former RVN officers' decision to return to Vietnam as a "major triumph of ROVR in

Hong Kong," even though, "the major disappointment" was that there were several thousand Vietnamese in the camps, and only this small number had volunteered for ROVR.[119] Most Vietnamese in Hong Kong rightly judged that they would not qualify for ROVR interviews if they returned, since many were from northern Vietnam.

Eventually, close to six thousand Vietnamese voluntarily repatriated from Hong Kong to Vietnam in 1996 in order to apply through the ROVR program, and in this way, the U.S. was seen as helping to facilitate the closure of the Hong Kong camps before 1997 without completely reneging on its sense of obligation to former allies.[120] The ROVR program provided for new immigration interviews for Vietnamese who had "close association with the United States in the past," were religious leaders, or were persons of concern for the United States.[121] However, the ROVR program only applied to a subset of Vietnamese within the camps. The nonprofit Migration and Refugee Services cautioned, "Implementation of this new program will not be easy. Returning to Vietnam for many refugees may be a difficult undertaking especially if they are uncertain as to whether or not they meet the criteria for resettlement in the U.S. However, with the end of CPA and the imminent closure of most Southeast Asian camps already a reality, refugees may have little choice but to try to take advantage of this last opportunity for resettlement in the United States."[122]

Migration and Refugee Services was genuinely positive about the ROVR program because it got the categories "right." It believed the U.S. interviewers in Vietnam would be sympathetic and provide a generous definition of refugee status. It concluded: "Several thousand persons who would have had little or no chance are now likely to be resettled."[123] In this situation, the U.S. was trying to balance its efforts to satisfy three separate constituencies: Congress and Vietnamese American advocates who saw the Hong Kong Vietnamese as refugees, its allies in Hong Kong and Southeast Asia who sought to close the camps, and its own immigration officials.

Following through with the ROVR program, the INS sent interviewers to Vietnam in the late 1990s. By the end of the program, close to 20,000 Vietnamese had qualified (it expanded its parameters and included family members and individuals who might have missed earlier cutoff dates). Le Xuan Khoa expressed a degree of pride in the ROVR program, as it had provided new interviews for thousands of Vietnamese.

As of August 1996, Southeast Asian first-asylum countries and Hong Kong had repatriated close to 100,000 Vietnamese through the CPA. Hong

Kong repatriated 66,696, Thailand, 16,815, Indonesia 12,672, and Malaysia 9,130.[124] Because the stakes were high for the UNHCR's reputation and for the future lives of the Vietnamese, the UNHCR placed eight full-time monitors in Vietnam to ensure that the repatriates were not persecuted. Vietnam gave the UNHCR a wide berth and agreed to in-country monitors for the duration of the program. Over the course of the 1990s, UNHCR staff visited approximately one-third of the repatriates.[125] Most repatriates received cash on return. Those who left voluntarily received more as an incentive, and the amount changed over the course of the CPA implementation, with individuals generally receiving between US$240 and $360. The UNHCR and the European Union invested significant sums, more than $35 million in cash grants and $45 million in reintegration programs and complementary development projects for the broader communities.[126] This included local infrastructure projects and small business loans. Aid workers learned that they needed to support both the repatriates and the Vietnamese who had stayed, otherwise there was the risk of jealousy (and possible incentive for others to leave) if the repatriates gained undue advantages. One of the European directors cited a "50% rule," whereby 50 percent of the loans were made to repatriates and 50 percent to locals who had never left.[127]

Human rights organizations remained skeptical of the UNHCR's and Hong Kong government's positive spin on the repatriation program, and they sent their own monitors to write counter-reports. Refugee Concern published numerous accounts of individuals returned to Vietnam who then spoke of their lack of freedom. Its newsletter ran headlines like "Forced Returnee Faces Death Sentence in Vietnam: UNHCR and HK Government Powerless," and "UNHCR Monitoring Flawed: Returnees Not Provided Reintegration Assistance."[128] Refugee Concern charged that the UNHCR provided limited help and only accepted a very narrow definition of "persecution."[129] Human Rights Watch also monitored the CPA's closure in Hong Kong. It repeated reports of individuals who had been active anticommunists within Hong Kong camps and who were arrested on return, a man who was rearrested for a 1990 "illegal departure," and a recent convert to Christianity who faced harassment back in Vietnam.[130] Anthropologist James Freeman highlighted repatriation's consequences on unaccompanied minors, a particularly vulnerable group, when they were not reunited with immediate family. While he too saw "no evidence of political persecution," young people sometimes faced neglect and abandonment on return. He emphasized that Vietnamese communities often stigmatized repatriates and treated them as "outsiders."[131] These stories continued to linger as warnings and cautions.

The UNHCR remained firm that the CPA had been a success. UNHCR officials admitted repatriates faced economic hardships and discrimination, but "anything amounting to persecution in a Convention [1951] sense was rare."[132] Officers explained that some repatriates were able to improve their economic position because of their newfound English-language skills, which made them competitive in a market just opening for tourism, while the majority picked up where they had left off. Others started small businesses and took an entrepreneurial turn.[133] According to most reports, the majority of repatriates were able to reintegrate into family and economic networks, even if it was with a level of resignation.[134]

Hong Kong observers concurred. Cheung-Ang Siew Mei, the executive director for Action, a Hong Kong–based NGO that provided services in the camps, visited Vietnam to see for herself how the repatriates were faring.

> I went to Vietnam in 1993 to see the people who had been repatriated. . . . We drove from Hanoi to Mong Kai, and it was relatively safe. They had used the money to buy a bike or set up a hairdressing shop, and I saw that they were doing well, it was pretty okay. There weren't police everywhere, and I was a passenger in a private car, all by myself, and came back in one piece. The UNHCR had a representative there, and so did the Hong Kong immigration department through the British Embassy in Hanoi. I have a clear conscience, life was not so bad in Vietnam. They were back with their relatives, and the ones I visited were fine.[135]

The UNHCR believed only a minority remained unemployed and vulnerable in Vietnam. In this rendition, the contentious program had been worth it.[136] The camps had closed, and people had moved on with their lives.

WITNESS, CLOSURE, AND CONTINUED CAMPAIGNS

In 1997, Britain relinquished sovereignty over Hong Kong after more than 150 years of rule. With great pomp and circumstance, British Governor Chris Patten lowered the Union Jack on July 1, 1997. For years, Hong Kong officials had worried about the "residue" of Vietnamese in the camps, and it was true that there were approximately 1,200 still in Hong Kong after 1997. Many of these individuals remained in Pillar Point, an open camp, until 2000, after which most stayed in Hong Kong, in often marginalized and precarious economic situations. For many Hong Kong Chinese, the main legacy was the unpaid UNHCR bill of over a billion Hong Kong dollars.[137]

In my interviews, many of the Hong Kong Chinese who worked in the camps reflected on their experiences positively, not unlike the Filipina English teachers and social workers in Bataan. They pushed aside the barrage of criticism they faced and focused on the first-asylum policy and personal relationships they had developed. They expressed pride in their work and the role Hong Kong had played in the crisis. Most of the Hong Kong social workers, government workers, and CSD officers I met had come to terms with the repatriations and remained committed that this had been the correct course of action. They reflected on the repatriations as a necessary element of the bureaucratic process. Others noted, unemotionally, that the government developed the policy and they were following it. Given the practice of returning the Chinese along the border, Hong Kong simply could not keep the camps open indefinitely. It had been untenable.

Cheung-Ang Siew Mei remembered her participation in the repatriations as an act of witness. She explained that she had watched the removal of non-refugees from the camps because some parties were needed to monitor the government operation and ensure it was carried out in a humane way. She did not try to minimize the experience. As part of the independent monitoring team, she and her organization had to watch them "yank people" onto trucks. She shared that she had worked with some people in the camps knowing that they were not refugees. "I don't have any judgment about this, as they just wanted a better life, the war had finished, they were not ethnic Chinese, they were not RVN soldiers." For her, it wasn't right to have them live in camps or remain indefinitely in limbo.

Christian Action's agreement to observe the repatriations was controversial. Many agencies initially did not want to do it, but Cheung-Ang Siew Mei felt it was necessary. Her job was to ensure that no unnecessary violence and overuse of tear gas would occur. Still, she admitted that it was like watching a little war: "People were being repatriated—it was going to happen—and so we thought we should monitor it and watch to make sure they're not abused. They're going to go home anyway, so we should at least make sure they're not abused. We have to trust the status determination policy. . . . We witnessed it to make sure it was a fair process. We wanted to make sure there could be some dignity."[138]

Even though the repatriations were upsetting to watch, she was committed to the policy. She reiterated that the Vietnamese who were returning to Vietnam had not been persecuted, but wanted a better life in the west. "The [repatriation] policy was pragmatic." It was not a pleasant experience, but Cheung-Ang Siew Mei believed her position as an NGO observer ensured minimal levels of force and protected the principle of asylum for refugees. Today, she remains with Christian Action and provides direct services for refugees, asylum seekers, migrant domestic workers, ethnic minorities, new arrivals from mainland China, and low-income families in Hong Kong.[139]

The UNHCR looked back on the CPA as a success. It had managed to broker a regional agreement, end the overwhelming numbers of people leaving Vietnam by boat, and close the camps. Hong Kong had forced its hand, but the UNHCR came around to embracing the CPA as an effective end game. A former American NGO worker reflected that she had been a harsh critic of the CPA at the time, but in retrospect, the policy succeeded in resettling people and closing the camps—a goal that had seemed unattainable in the 1980s. "I don't know, it's not as black and white, at least for me, as it was back then." She added that whenever there's a cutoff date, there's a sense of arbitrariness and injustice. She also saw the CPA's regional approach as a strength.[140] UNHCR officials emphasized that they had preserved the right to first asylum and ultimately saved lives that would otherwise have been lost at sea. UNHCR official Jean Noel-Wetterwald explained, "We should not forget the situation we were faced with six or seven years ago, with asylum crumbling in the region, people dying at sea, and being raped, and with a seemingly impossible situation to solve."[141]

A career UNHCR officer was animated as he looked back on the UNHCR's work with the Vietnamese. In our lengthy conversation, he said much of CPA's success was due to Sergio Vieira de Mello's "flair," and that through his leadership, the UNHCR had been able to solve an intractable problem.[142] "The CPA, well that was a brave moment of political courage." He noted that Vieira de Mello initially had misgivings about the CPA but decided it was worth a try. In his estimation, the risk had paid dividends and was a major accomplishment.[143] The CPA put an end to Vietnamese risking attacks by pirates and death at sea, and the international community invested significant resources into first-asylum countries and asylum determination processes. However, he cautioned, the CPA was not a model that could be easily replicated. It was expensive and required extensive international cooperation. The convergence of the end of the Cold War, Vietnam's desire to rejoin the international community, and normalization with the United States meant that Vietnam was willing to play by UNHCR rules. It allowed the UNHCR monitors free reign in Vietnam, and Vietnam did not have a policy of retaliation against the repatriates. For many UNHCR officials, the CPA succeeded in saving lives and closing the camps. Despite all the criticism from human rights activists, they affirmed their success in humanitarian protection.

Somewhat tragically and unexpectedly, human rights and humanitarianism came into direct conflict in late-colonial Hong Kong. Not only were humanitarianism and human rights not synonymous, they articulated competing visions of the post–Cold War era. Hong Kong officials, both British and Chinese, maintained that they had fulfilled their humanitarian obligations with care and aplomb. In Hong Kong, anxieties over human rights focused on 1997 and the transition to Chinese sovereignty, and not on legal protections at the Refugee Status Review Board. For Vietnamese Americans, Hong Kong was a call to arms, and there was a multi-generational movement to recognize the lives and stories of the men and women held behind barbed wire. Shocking images of CSD shooting tear gas into the camps or dragging individuals onto planes showcased human rights violations. For the thousands who returned to Vietnam, their stories ranged from reintegration in communities to eventual preferential resettlement in the United States through the ROVR program. Others even returned to Hong Kong through arranged marriages in the early twenty-first century.[144] These individuals' lives had become entangled with international and local geopolitics, and their routes led in unanticipated directions far outside the well-known narrative of Vietnamese migration or the Cold War.

For the UNHCR, the United States government, and diasporic activists, Hong Kong was ground zero for the debate over the CPA throughout the 1990s. Hong Kong's proactive initiation of screening and repatriations had set in motion new regional policies, international outrage, and ultimately, camp closures. However, while Hong Kong increased the number of repatriate flights throughout the 1990s, the Philippines resisted the CPA's end game and commitment to repatriation. The "screened out" in Palawan would face very different choices and possibilities after 1996. Diasporic activists, many of whom had cut their teeth in Hong Kong, moved their efforts from Hong Kong to the Philippines. Vietnamese American activists and Catholic clergy found themselves negotiating with Filipino politicians in Palawan and Manila about the status and living conditions of several thousand Vietnamese men and women well into the twenty-first century.

SIX

Palawan and Diasporic Imaginaries,
1996–2005

WHEN THE CPA CAME TO A CLOSE IN 1996, the Philippines stood alone. Unlike Hong Kong, with violent showdowns and multiple "orderly repatriation" flights between 1989 and 1996, the Philippine government orchestrated a single forced repatriation flight in February 1996. If Malaysia and Hong Kong asserted their independence by pushing Vietnamese off or by pressuring the UNHCR to accept repatriation, the Philippines asserted its independence by allowing the Vietnamese to stay. What followed was a demonstration of the Philippines' sovereign approach to the CPA, the long hand of the U.S. government, and the ambitious visions of the diasporic Vietnamese community.

The Philippine government's self-styled generosity was a legacy of its identification with humanitarian action. It was a surprisingly easy ideological path from the Marcos regime's Philippine Refugee Processing Center in Bataan to President Fidel Ramos's decision to halt repatriation flights from Palawan in 1996.[1] In allowing "screened-out" Vietnamese to stay, the Philippine government demonstrated its independence from the UNHCR and the CPA's regional requirements. The Philippines repeatedly invoked its Catholic faith, and Catholic bishops and nuns played leading roles as protectors of the remaining Vietnamese. This combined a long-standing rhetoric of compassion and humanitarianism with a tenacious Cold War anticommunist Catholic politics that survived the fall of the Berlin Wall and the collapse of the Soviet Union. The Philippines also did not face any serious risks in taking this stand. The United States did not encourage the Philippines to follow through with the CPA and repatriate the remaining screened-out Vietnamese in Palawan. After 1996, the CPA formally ended, and so the UNHCR was no longer a dominant player. This led to more intensive bilateral negotiations between the United States and the Philippines over the final Vietnamese population, and within a few years, the U.S. would even permit new interviews and facilitate the migration for a significant number of the "screened-out" Vietnamese.

By the 1990s, diasporic Vietnamese directly influenced U.S. policy toward the Vietnamese in the Philippines through activist networks. Vietnamese Americans' ability to shift political opinions and policies was substantially stronger than the letter-writing campaigns and petitions they had circulated twenty years prior. At this stage, there were also numerous organizations working to support the Vietnamese in Palawan, and while they shared a common objective, resettlement, they drew on different strengths and networks. Based in the Philippines, the Center for Assistance to Displaced Persons (CADP) relied on its strong ties to the Catholic hierarchy and politicians within the Philippines, and its volunteers and leadership lobbied for permanent resettlement there. CADP inspired Vietnamese Americans to donate money, and even more impressively, to travel to Palawan and volunteer directly in the camps. For many young Vietnamese Americans, CADP, like Project Ngoc, offered formative experiences connecting their American and Vietnamese identities to the precarious lives of those left behind in the camps. Importantly, CADP's institutional ties were in the Philippines. In contrast, Boat People SOS lobbied U.S. Congress members and held out for nothing short of resettlement in the United States. It too raised money and called on volunteers in the United States and Southeast Asia, but it found much of its strength in relationships on Capitol Hill. Finally, Hoi Trinh, a Vietnamese Australian, launched a dynamic advocacy program in which he embraced the cause of the remaining Vietnamese in the Philippines. He set up a makeshift office in Manila and aggressively advocated for resettlement in the United States, Australia, and Canada. He managed individual cases and pressured these countries to reopen their doors to Vietnamese who had repeatedly been denied refugee status.

For the Vietnamese, Palawan was the unlikely stage for debates over whether Vietnamese would be forcibly repatriated, remain in the Philippines in a self-sustaining model village named Viet Ville, or leave for futures in the United States or other Anglophone resettlement countries. Documentary filmmakers and photographers profiled them in a series of films and publications, including *The Forgotten Ones, In Limbo,* and *Stateless.* [2] Yet they were not forgotten. Their stories, and the question of whether or not they were refugees, resonated and provoked political debates within the Philippines, the United States, and the Vietnamese diasporic population itself.

PALAWAN: THE "PRISON WITHOUT WALLS"
AND THE OPEN CAMP

In 1979, the Philippine government opened the Philippine First Asylum Center in Puerto Princesa, Palawan. Initially prepared to house 2,000 individuals, it soon held between 5,000 and 7,000 people. In the hierarchy of camps, Palawan was a step below the Philippine Refugee Processing Center (PRPC) in Bataan and its promise of resettlement, but definitely several steps preferable to Hong Kong's harsh closed camps after 1982 and its subsequent repatriation campaign in the 1990s.

Within the Philippines, Palawan stands apart from central Luzon, the Visayas, and Mindanao, as an island on the periphery. Tourist boosters and environmental activists alike have referred to it as the Philippines' "last frontier," a place whose biodiversity and indigenous populations must be "rescued" from development and modern influence.[3] This sense of exceptionalism also informed early-twentieth-century American colonial ideas of the island. U.S. prison reformers in the Philippines reimagined Palawan as a place where Manila's overcrowded urban prisons could be emptied and where Filipino prisoners could rebuild their lives through physical labor. Unlike a traditional prison with cells and armed guards, American colonial administrators built the Iwahig penal colony on Palawan as an experiment, "a prison without walls." There were no guards, prisoners were paid for their work, and there was ample contact between convicts and the local community. America's paternalistic colonial policies created disciplinary structures between Manila and Palawan and demonstrated the importance of seemingly peripheral regions.[4] Iwahig's "prison without walls" still exists only forty kilometers from Palawan's capital, Puerto Princesa.[5]

Given this history, it is perhaps not surprising that Palawan represented the most open of the Southeast Asian camps. Established on the margins of Puerto Princesa, the camp abutted the island's major airstrip, and the Philippine Western Command kept guard. However, Vietnamese could generally leave the camp at will, shopping in town and setting up small noodle stands for Filipino customers. Hien Trong Nguyen, a teenager who fled Vietnam by himself in 1984, remembered being lonely in the camp, but he also remarked on the freedom he had to go into town whenever he liked, as long as he returned by curfew.[6] Tri C. Tran concurred that life was better in Palawan than it was in Malaysia or Hong Kong, adding, "We had a certain degree of freedom."[7] The camp offered a broad range of social services, including mental

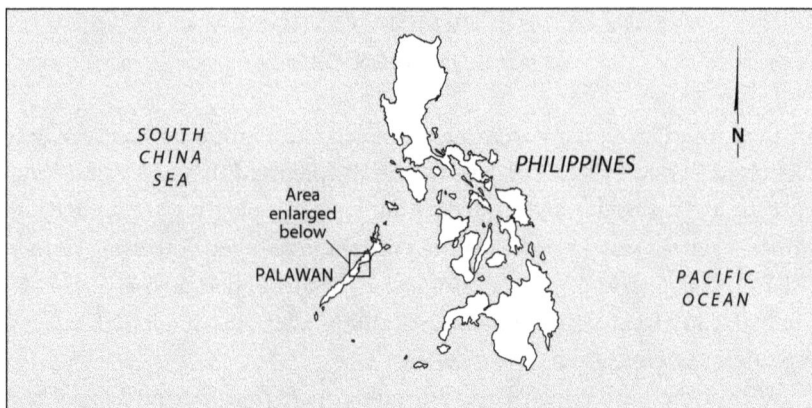

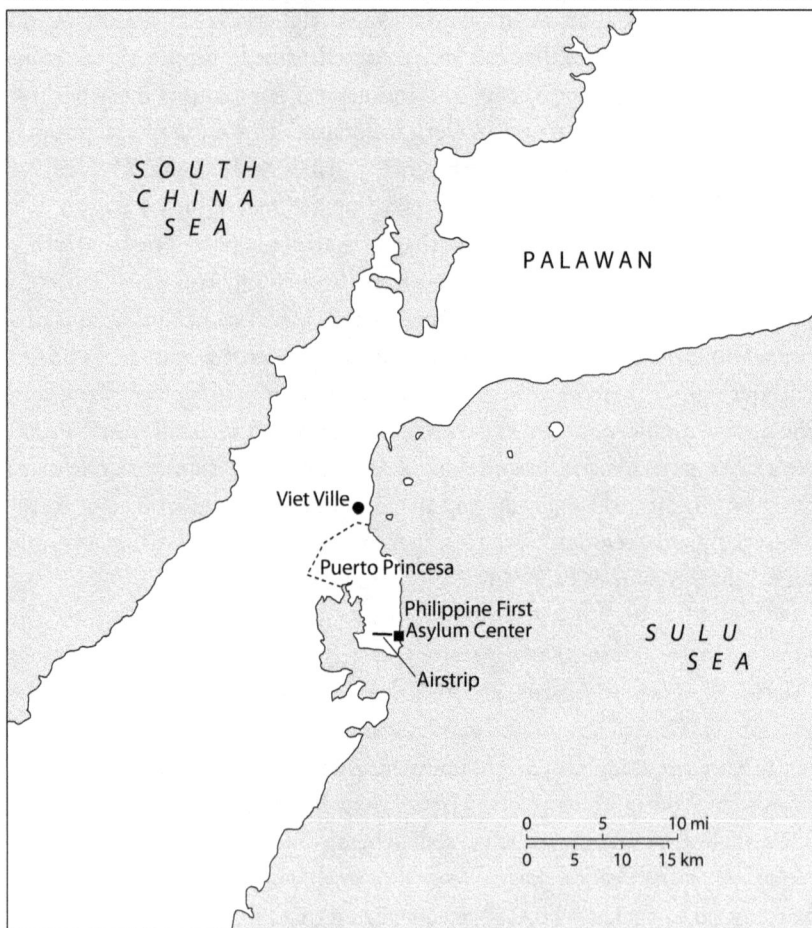

MAP 4. Palawan, site of the Philippine First Asylum Center.

health counseling, medical care, material assistance, English classes, childcare, youth programming, scouting, and an athletic program. Vietnamese ran the internal affairs of the camp, which included a 100-person Vietnamese security detail, a Vietnamese representative committee, and even a camp judicial committee, which policed internal infractions.[8]

However, despite Palawan's relative autonomy, it was still a camp. Between 1979 and 1989, close to 40,000 Vietnamese passed through Palawan. The majority remained for a few months to a few years and then resettled in a third country.[9] Palawan was more than 800 miles from southern Vietnam (almost triple the distance to Malaysia), and although the risk of encountering pirates was lower, the journey remained risky and lengthy. As a result, Palawan generally had a lower population, rarely getting above 10,000 inhabitants, than other first-asylum camps in Southeast Asia and Hong Kong. Once Vietnamese received a resettlement placement, they would then travel to the PRPC in Bataan for the standard six-month English-language and cultural orientation classes. Then in 1989, the Philippines signed the Comprehensive Plan of Action. After March 14, 1989, all incoming Vietnamese would be subject to screening. At that point, only those who were "screened in" would go on to Bataan, and the "screened out" would remain in the camp in Palawan.

Thus, the camp in Palawan and the PRPC worked in tandem, and English teachers and social workers often served in both camps. However, while Bataan signaled a move onward toward resettlement, Palawan was identified with uncertainty and possible repatriation. As a result, some Vietnamese sought clandestine refuge in the PRPC after 1989. One Filipina social worker remembered that Vietnamese men and women would enter the PRPC illegally from Palawan, something that I found nowhere else in the written record. She explained that these individuals were supposed to wait in Palawan for their asylum hearings and appeals, but sometimes they had extended family already at the PRPC. The Vietnamese who had been "screened out" would then sneak into the PRPC. The former social worker did not comment on how Vietnamese surreptitiously traveled from Palawan to Bataan. Presumably, these men and women hoped that they would be able to blend in and leave for the United States with their families. The social worker's job was to investigate families who tried to smuggle in their relatives. She remembered, "We call[ed] them illegal entries." Other people in the camp would make complaints, and she would search the bunks, and sometimes find individuals hiding. Once caught, the PRPC officials would hold them in the Monkey House, or the camp jail, and then send them back to Palawan.

When I asked how frequently this occurred, she responded, "Several times, many of them came. . . . I was able to escort one time also, around six refugees returning back to Palawan."[10] Her story attested to individuals' ingenuity and the contradictory proximity between the PRPC and Palawan. For Vietnamese seeking resettlement in the United States, the distance between the PRPC and Palawan could be great indeed.

At the same time, the Vietnamese in Palawan, with an almost 50 percent acceptance rate, faced much better odds of being "screened in" as refugees than did their counterparts in Hong Kong. By 1992, the Philippines had screened 7,952 Vietnamese for refugee status, with 3,245 "screened in."[11] Most commentators attributed these positive rates to the Philippines' more generous reading of screening guidelines and the lack of local hostility. However, there were still several thousand "screened out" who waited in limbo as they exhausted their legal appeals. UNHCR and Philippine officials hoped they would eventually opt for voluntary repatriation. Scholars noted that Vietnamese men and women stuck in Palawan exhibited similar stress levels, anxiety, and depression as those who waited under far harsher physical conditions in Thailand and Hong Kong.[12]

After 1989, many Vietnamese described Palawan as a prison, despite its relative openness. Critiques came from Vietnamese already settled abroad and from within the camp. For example, in 1993, well into the CPA, Thu-Oanh Nguyen wrote to the UNHCR high commissioner, Sadako Ogata, on behalf of her sister, whose asylum claim had been rejected in Palawan: "The conditions in these camps are abysmal, and the screening process is a joke. The camps are dirty, poorly run and little better than prisons, where everything is for sale by the Camp Officials." Thu-Oanh Nguyen rejected the idea of Palawan's comparative advantage, and instead equated it to the far harsher camps in Southeast Asia. "Even safety reportedly has a price. And this is Palawan, which is considered a benign camp. We have heard that conditions are much worse in Malaysia, Thailand, and Indonesia. . . . Is it any wonder that suicide rates and self-immolations are rising (especially amongst women) in the camps? The list of the atrocities being committed in the camps could go on for several pages."[13] The UNHCR denied her claims, insisting that "the camp in Palawan is not a prison." However, the UNHCR also confirmed that it did not recognize her sister as a refugee: "As the Vietnamese are considered to be illegal immigrants by the Government of the Philippines, unless they are determined to be refugees, it is clear that they are not free to travel around the country or to settle outside of Palawan camp."[14] The UNHCR pointed to the Philippines' sovereignty. According to the UNHCR, the Philippine government was acting in accordance with the internationally agreed-upon CPA and holding asylum hearings, which screened some in and some out.

Far more disruptive than written complaints from abroad were increasingly volatile protests from within the camp. For example, Cuc, a young girl who arrived in Palawan after the CPA, was initially screened out with her family. Her father, a high-ranking RVN officer, took a leading role against repatriation in the early 1990s. While her memories of the camp were generally nostalgic, she also recalled regular protests, strikes, and violent confrontations between the Vietnamese and Filipino authorities:

> There were a lot of strikes. I remember my dad said we're going on strike, so people like America would know about us and would like, help us to come here. So we had really a big strike, like one week or so. They just came out there; they just sat there. They would sometimes yell out . . . the camp authorities were not nice about this, actually. The strike went for seven days or so, and then the police, the Filipino [police] came with firefighters and they would, like, spray water on us and beat up some of the people and rocks were thrown. So it was getting violent.[15]

The Vietnamese who had been "screened out" had lost all faith in the UNHCR, an entity they now blamed for their precarious position and potential repatriation. Although the conditions in Palawan never reached the same level of violence, overcrowding, or hostility as in Hong Kong, the screened-out community was increasingly desperate. The Vietnamese no longer perceived the UNHCR to be a protector, but rather saw it as a prison guard.

To respond to the unrest, the UNHCR devised a training guide so its personnel could know how to react to "critical incidents." The graphic details of the handbook upend the idea that the openness of the camp led to consent or gratitude. The handbook also reveals the instability and fear present, even in an open camp like Palawan. For example, the training manual provided instructions for how UNHCR personnel should respond to mass suicides, self-inflicted wounds, hostage taking (of UNHCR personnel), violent demonstrations and riots, attacks on UNHCR property, hunger strikes, stoning (of UNHCR personnel), and verbal and physical harassment of UNHCR staff. The manual explained that "the asylum seekers perceived that the UNHCR Office and its staff are directly/indirectly involve [sic] in the result of their [negative] decisions, thus, they blame UNHCR and its staff because of this."[16] Even though the worst-case scenario, mass suicides and physical attacks, did not materialize, UNHCR personnel feared violence could erupt at any moment.

Like in Hong Kong, diasporic Vietnamese who had immigrated and resettled in English-speaking countries before the CPA saw the Vietnamese "stuck" in Palawan as a population needing their aid. And unlike in Hong Kong, they developed key alliances and relationships with local Philippine leaders. Without a doubt, the most forceful and persistent advocate for the Vietnamese in Palawan was Sister Pascale Le Thi Triu, a Vietnamese nun who made her home in the Philippines for more than twenty years.

SISTER PASCALE AND REIMAGINING
VIETNAMESE-FILIPINO SOLIDARITIES

By all accounts, Sister Pascale was a charismatic personality. A member of the Daughters of Charity, Sister Pascale received a scholarship to pursue a degree in social work in 1972. She chose the Philippines over India and the United States because of its Catholic identity, its poverty, and its cultural similarities to Vietnam. When Saigon fell in 1975, she remained in the Philippines, and her role shifted from student to refugee resettlement worker and advocate.[17] In 1975, the Daughters of Charity and the Catholic Bishops' Conference of the Philippines founded the Center for Assistance to Displaced Persons (CADP), which over time became synonymous with Sister Pascale's leadership. At first, Sister Pascale aided Vietnamese women who had relationships with Filipino military personnel and overseas workers during the war. On arrival in the Philippines, many Vietnamese women discovered that their Filipino "husbands" had Filipina wives. The Philippines prohibited divorce, and so the women also learned that their children were illegitimate. With no legal recourse and often abandoned by their "husbands," the women remained in the Philippines as "displaced persons." Sister Pascale assisted these women, provided many with basic social services, and even hired them to work with her in CADP.[18] Soon the center expanded its scope and initiated social service projects at the PRPC in Bataan and in Palawan. In Bataan, there were more than two dozen NGOs, each providing a specific niche service, but in Palawan, CADP became the most powerful NGO. It mobilized camp volunteers, professional Filipinos, Catholic clergy, and overseas Vietnamese volunteers to run its many programs. These included English classes, basic job training, self-help classes, and after 1989, help for the screened out in mounting their appeals.

In written accounts and conversations, Sister Pascale emerges as the dominant figure advocating for the Vietnamese in Palawan. She was repeatedly described as a force of nature, her diminutive size contrasting with her steel will. As a nun and a Vietnamese national, she claimed legitimacy in the camps, and she could be a cultural translator to a Filipino and international audience. Filipino social workers and teachers spoke of her commitment and overwhelming influence within the camp. A man whose Vietnamese mother had been abandoned by her Filipino spouse in the 1970s pointed to Sister Pascale with love, loyalty, and reverence. A UNHCR officer reported, "The impact of individuals such as Sister Pascale of CADP and Cardinal Sin touches all residents [in Palawan]."[19]

These repeated testaments to Sister Pascale reframe analyses by scholars Mimi Thi Nguyen and Yến Lê Espiritu of Vietnamese "gratitude." Both critique how the U.S. framed itself as "saving" Vietnamese and incorporating them into a multicultural nation, which seemingly then absolved the United States of imperial violence abroad and structural racism at home. However, in this case, CADP displaced stories of American rescue in favor of rescue by a Vietnamese nun in the Philippines. The language of gratitude and "saving refugees" remained, but Sister Pascale positioned herself and CADP, a definitively Catholic entity which elevated diasporic Vietnamese and Filipino leadership, over the United States.

CADP reached out to young people in the United States to travel to and serve in Palawan. The first Vietnamese American volunteer was Father Vien Nguyen (who would later lead the Vietnamese American community in New Orleans after Hurricane Katrina).[20] Father Vien escaped Vietnam with his family in 1975, and as an adolescent he became aware that those who fled after 1978 were often terrorized by Thai pirates. The stories of rape and violence left a strong impression on him, invoking both feelings of vengeance and anger. When he learned of Sister Pascale's work in the Philippines, he decided to act and help those in the camps. He was already training for the priesthood, but he took an untraditional path and left the seminary for the Philippines for nine months in 1984–85. During this initial stint, Father Vien became an English teacher, and he mentored unaccompanied minors. He believed that his relative youth allowed him to develop close connections with the young Vietnamese in the camps, and they trusted him. The camp and the Philippines became a defining presence in his life. Father Vien returned every year between 1987 and 1994, ultimately reaching out to other college-aged students to volunteer with him.

He believed Sister Pascale strategically recruited Vietnamese Americans so Vietnamese in the camps could learn from them. "I was very much influenced by Sister Pascale," he reflected. He believed she intentionally emphasized overseas volunteers to "show the Vietnamese refugees what they could be." "The only difference between us and them was opportunity, that if they had the opportunity, they would be exactly like us. I think that was very, very much at the core of why she used the overseas volunteers." Father Vien adopted Sister Pascale's commitment to the Philippines, and he believed she did not receive enough credit for her mission. She created a framework for Vietnamese self-government within the camp, and she consistently pressed the Filipino military personnel to respect the Vietnamese, and she intervened quickly if problems arose. "It was more preventive than cure," he explained. Sister Pascale fostered a culture of autonomy and self-reliance within the camp, and she insisted that the Filipino guards were there to protect the perimeter but not to interfere with daily life. She had good relationships with the Philippine military officers, and when there was a problem, she went straight to the top. Father Vien remembered that in one instance, when she was refused entry to a military commander's headquarters, Sister Pascale walked along the shore from the camp to the military compound and knocked on the commander's door. In other words, she made things happen. "I appreciated that, the overseas volunteers appreciated that, because we knew the story of the other refugee camps. . . . When there's no problems, you don't realize that advocacy is there."[21]

Another Vietnamese American volunteer also remarked on the strong impression Palawan made on him. He was a college student and motivated to help because of the explicit images coming out of Hong Kong. He identified with the people waiting in the camp, and he hoped to make a difference. "I've always thought it was by sheer luck I was here [in the United States]. I didn't do anything special. I was just able to be in the right place at the right time. I had all these opportunities, and so I wanted to give back and work at the grassroots. So, I just did it."[22] He taught English and was a liaison within the camp. He believed having Vietnamese Americans in the camp placed pressure on the Filipino authorities. American volunteers were also American observers. "By design I think, Sister Pascale thought one of the roles of CADP and the volunteers was to advocate for the boat people's rights.

Though not common, in isolated instances of mistreatment, we would be tasked . . . [with] going and talking to the Western Command [Philippines] and also the UNCHR and try to help resolve certain conflicts. We were a presence, and we could speak up for the boat people when they couldn't speak up for themselves."[23] Like Father Vien, he too returned several times and assisted in recruiting more Vietnamese Americans to volunteer in Palawan. These connections created networks between the Philippines and the United States and carved out a role for Vietnamese Americans.

Although the UNHCR and CADP had worked cooperatively with each other throughout the 1980s, the two often came to loggerheads over the implementation of the CPA. The UNHCR repeatedly complained that CADP administered the camp as if the CPA did not exist, and as if repatriation, voluntary or otherwise, would be kept at bay indefinitely. UNHCR officer Christine Mougne toured Palawan in 1992, and her meeting with a group of Vietnamese women ended abruptly when she mentioned repatriation. Mougne lamented Palawan's "almost endemic" "repatriation blindness." She concluded that everything in Palawan seemed to "conspire *against*" repatriation, and CADP and Catholic leadership "perpetuate[d] the illusion" that all the Vietnamese were refugees.[24] By the mid-1990s, Vietnamese waiting in Palawan also received thousands of dollars in remittances from abroad, boosting their quality of life and contributing to the island's economy. With little incentive to leave, Vietnamese hoped that if they held out, they would ultimately receive refugee status and circumvent the CPA.

By the mid-1990s, the UNHCR had amped up the pressure on screened-out Vietnamese by limiting the social services offered within the camp. This included cutting back on electricity and drinking water, withdrawing funds for language and vocational programs, prohibiting businesses within the camp, and regulating remittances.[25] CADP balked at what it saw as inhumane measures which deprived camp members of, among other things, educational opportunities. In defiance, CADP maintained a full menu of classes throughout the mid-1990s, supplementing what were otherwise "inadequate" programs funded by the UNHCR.[26] The UNHCR's reduction of social services (e.g., English classes, basic literacy programs, and medical services) left the door open for CADP to position itself as the primary advocate for the Vietnamese in Palawan.

If Hong Kong moved too quickly and too harshly for the UNHCR, the Philippines did not seem to move at all. For the UNHCR, the Philippines was a surprising headache given its years of cooperation. Hong Kong,

Malaysia, Indonesia, and Thailand had collectively repatriated tens of thousands of Vietnamese by 1996 and were clearly working to close up the camps, but the Philippines had yet to send anyone back who was not a real volunteer. In January 1996, approximately 2,700 screened-out Vietnamese remained in Palawan with the international deadline, June 30, just months away. The UNHCR would not fund any camps after that date. For the regional solution to work, all the partners had to be on board with screening and, ultimately, repatriation. The UNHCR blamed the Philippine government for not fully implementing the CPA and organizing repatriation flights. It chalked up the low rates of voluntary repatriation from Palawan to "the absence of a firm government/political will to take clear steps regarding the screened-out asylum seekers."[27] It urged the Philippine government to stand with the CPA and not be a regional outlier.

The Philippines vacillated. On the one hand, the Catholic Church possessed a great deal of power, and the Philippine government was proud of its international reputation and identification with humanitarianism. The Palawan camp also generated a fair number of jobs in an under-resourced region, and Vietnamese remittances enhanced the local economy as well.[28] There was no local pressure to close the camps— in fact, quite the opposite. On the other hand, Philippine officials had made an international commitment to the CPA. Undersecretary for Foreign Affairs Rodolfo Severino explained, "They (Vietnamese) really have to go. . . . We want the camp to be empty by June. . . . If they were led to believe they could stay here indefinitely, this was not by the Philippine government."[29] The *Philippine Star* reiterated that repatriation or deportation had become an international norm, and it pointed to the new U.S. policy of detaining Cubans in Guantánamo Bay, stating, "Even the land of liberty ceases to be a beacon for the tired, the poor, the huddled masses yearning to breathe free when it comes to dealing with 20th century refugees." The Philippines "must have the gumption to show them the door."[30] In February 1996, the Philippine government decided to bite the proverbial bullet and began preparations for the first forced repatriation flight out of Palawan.

Rumors began to circulate, and roughly 600 to 700 Vietnamese simply left the camp and hid outside of its borders, effectively thwarting any ability to repatriate them.[31] However, hundreds of Vietnamese remained. Bishop Pedro Arigo arrived at his new pulpit in Puerto Princesa at this very moment. He remembered that repatriation was the "burning" issue of the day. To demonstrate his support for the Vietnamese, he celebrated a mass within the camp, and he spoke out against repatriation as a violation of human rights.[32] The camp was tense and on alert. Everyone knew the government was preparing to make a move.

On February 14, 1996, the Philippine military entered the camp and seized individuals for repatriation. The camp erupted in protests. Because the camp bordered the airstrip, more than one thousand Vietnamese defied the perimeter and flooded the runway, attempting to physically block the plane, which was poised to take off for Vietnam. One woman lay face down on the tarmac, and others "wailed" that they were being separated from their families.[33] Women and children encircled the men, hoping that they could protect them from forced removal.[34] Philippine soldiers responded with water cannons and tear gas to ensure the planes could leave with the repatriates aboard. The Philippine government claimed that all the Vietnamese on the plane were there voluntarily, but given the heavy military presence, tear gas, and physical attempts to halt the flights, their claims rang false. The plane took off with eighty-plus Vietnamese "volunteers" on board.[35]

Quite the reverse from the response to repatriations in Hong Kong, the Filipino press did not look kindly at the forced repatriation flight. Despite earlier calls for repatriation, many editorials characterized it as a black eye on the Philippines: "Whether they are political refugees or simply people seeking a better life at this point does not make a difference. The archipelago can surely accommodate 2000 more human beings. . . . To those who have decided to permanently stay, let's extend our welcome."[36] In this configuration, the elaborate screening process, which determined who was and who was not a refugee, diminished in importance in one rhetorical swoop. Leading Filipino journalist Max Solvien concurred that the repatriation flight made a travesty of the Philippines' claims to Catholic principles: "What sort of 'civilized' and 'Christian' people are we? . . . The hollow phrase, 'there is a limit to our hospitality,' probably translate[s] into 'there's a limit to our budget.' It's a combination of lack of cash aside from lack of compassion." Solvien concluded that the forced repatriations were an anathema and challenged the Philippines' pride in being the "only Catholic nation" in Asia. "If we were the 'only Muslim nation' in Asia, our shame would be no less."[37] Solvien also stressed that Filipino politicians were well-versed in the country's support for the former South Vietnam, and he essentially chided that they should know better. President Fidel Ramos had served in the Philippine Civic Action Group during the war, and Solvien argued for a continuity of the Philippines' long-term humanitarian commitment and sympathy for the Vietnamese. He recognized that the economic lure of 1990s Vietnam was real; however, he argued this did not erase the history of Vietnam's human rights abuses or the re-education camps.[38]

In the face of this negative publicity, Sister Pascale and the Catholic bishops seized the moment and brokered a deal with the Ramos government. The CADP promised to be financially responsible for the roughly 2,500 remaining "screened-out" Vietnamese. The Philippine government agreed the Vietnamese could stay indefinitely, even after the UNHCR withdrew its funding in June 1996. There would be no additional forced repatriations from the Philippines.

The Philippine government and the CADP formalized this understanding with the 1996 Memorandum of Understanding (MOU). The agreement stipulated that the CADP would buy property, build a new settlement, and support the remaining Vietnamese in Palawan. Employing somewhat paternalistic language, the MOU characterized the Vietnamese as needing help in reaching economic independence. "During their stay in this new site, all efforts must be employed to make them more productive and self-reliant in consonance with their individual and collective values and aspirations."[39] CADP promised to lead this new community and adhere to a principle of "self-reliance" and "self-management" without any additional dollars from the Philippine government. The mayor of Puerto Princesa, Edward Hagedorn, endorsed the MOU, and other signatories included the commanding general of the Philippines Western Command, Bishop Ramon Arguelles, Bishop Pedro Arigo, Palawan governor Salvador Socrates, and the secretary of the Department of Foreign Affairs, Domingo Siazon. The religious leadership, the provincial and municipal elected officials, the military, and the federal government all signed on to the settlement.

Local Catholic and political officials heralded the MOU as a concrete sign of Filipino humanitarianism and Catholic charity. President Ramos emphasized the cooperation between the government and the church in finding a solution and creating a refuge for the remaining Vietnamese in Palawan: "A compassionate society, as we regard ours to be, is measured by the willingness of its members to accept the duty of caring for their neighbors. . . . We can no more refuse to lend them the assistance that we can give them than deny our tradition of hospitality and caring. With this MOU, we have proven once again that the church and the government can harmoniously work together towards the realization of a common objective."[40] The Catholic bishops echoed these sentiments and identified themselves as saving and protecting the

FIGURE 14. Sister Pascale Le Thi Triu signs the Memorandum of Understanding with the Philippine government allowing the remaining "screened-out" Vietnamese to stay in the Philippines, July 17, 1996. President Fidel Ramos is in the center. AP photo / Fernando Sepe Jr.

Vietnamese. "To our Vietnamese brothers and sisters . . . we will not let you down! Be sure about that."[41] The remaining screened out would not be cast back to communist Vietnam, and they could thank the Catholic Church.

Interestingly, in Bishop Arguelles's speech, he called on more than Catholic charity to explain the Philippines' distinct course of action. He also pointed to the anti-Marcos EDSA, or People Power, Revolution. "EDSA taught us that peace is possible when men and women of goodwill are in solidarity with one another. We did that as one people. We can do that together with other peoples." Bishop Arguelles not only claimed the MOU's legitimacy through his clerical position, but through the precedent of People Power from 1986. Almost ironically, Marcos himself had welcomed the Vietnamese in the 1980s using the language of Catholic humanitarianism, and now Bishop Arguelles connected the need to support Vietnamese refugees with the political lessons learned through the EDSA revolution. He concluded that the Church "believes in the Filipinos' innate generosity of spirit and of hospitality."[42]

While the MOU addressed immediate financial questions, it left key political ones unanswered, including the fact that the Vietnamese would have a nebulous legal status in the Philippines. The MOU called them "Vietnamese nationals." The Vietnamese were supposed to register in what would be dubbed Viet Ville, and then they could travel within the Philippines. However, they did not receive Filipino nationality or permanent residency. While the Vietnamese and the CADP celebrated the opening of Viet Ville, this legal question would simmer, revealing vastly different strategies of diasporic activism.

VIET VILLE

First, CADP had to build a new Vietnamese village outside the former refugee camp. The idea was a settlement that could house and support more than 2,000 Vietnamese. CADP pitched the project as a community effort, funded with overseas dollars from the diaspora and made concrete through the volunteer labor of the Vietnamese in Palawan. In just a matter of months, CADP raised somewhere between $1.2 and $1.3 million.[43] Overseas Vietnamese, enjoying greater economic stability after having spent fifteen to twenty years in the United States, Canada, and Australia, willingly donated to the project, which protected the Vietnamese in the Philippines from forced repatriations.

From late summer 1996 through 1997, the CADP mobilized the volunteer labor of the Vietnamese in Palawan.[44] The result was Viet Ville, a new communal village complete with single-family houses, temples, churches, community centers, administrative offices, and small restaurants, located roughly twenty-five kilometers outside Puerto Princesa. Initially there were approximately 150 houses, and the village hosted lively activities for religious celebrations, Tet, and the Autumn Moon festival. CADP presented Viet Ville as a place where Vietnamese who had languished in the camps could relearn skills needed for economic independence, self-reliance, and professionalism.[45] It documented the construction of Viet Ville, which, remarkably, was built in a matter of months. Che Nhat Giao, a representative of the remaining Vietnamese nationals, wrote to the *Palawan Times* that staying in the Philippines was like "a miracle."[46] The Vietnamese promised they would obey local laws and "succeed in becoming self-reliant economic heroes."[47] The sign planted firmly at the entrance to Viet Ville (and still standing as of 2015) read, "The Viet Village is a symbol of eternal friendship between Filipinos and Vietnamese and the beginning of a new era of co-existence and cooperation."[48] To Sister Pascale and CADP, the Philippines, and not the United States, was the benevolent state that had provided sanctuary.

With the threat of repatriation gone, CADP focused on making Viet Ville a viable community. The most obvious way to do that was to cultivate small businesses and market Viet Ville as a tourist destination, complete with *pho* restaurants and the kind of fresh French bread typical of Vietnamese *banh mi* sandwiches. CADP promoted Viet Ville as a special ethnic enclave where one could experience Vietnamese "authenticity."[49] However, Viet Ville could not employ all its residents, and so others found work in Puerto Princesa.[50] Young people went to local Philippine schools and learned Tagalog, and over time, dozens of families moved into the broader community in Palawan, and then also to the Visayas, Mindanao, and Manila.

In 1998, just over a year after Viet Ville's inaugural mass, Sister Pascale began her campaign for permanent residency for Vietnamese in the Philippines. This was a bold move which embraced a Filipino future for this Vietnamese community. Sister Pascale imagined Vietnamese remaining in the Philippines with the full protection of legal residency and the possibility of Filipino citizenship. The best chance for this outcome was if President Ramos issued an executive order.[51] Legal status would be the final act of Philippine humanitarian assistance. She was not alone in calling for permanent residency. The *Philippine Free Press* opined that Viet Ville was a "living testament to human rights and Filipino hospitality ... We offered them refuge and they rewarded us with their honest toil; let us reward their responsibility with more freedom. They deserve it [permanent residency], and as the only country that stood by human rights in this case, we deserve it as well."[52] The *Free Press* matched this sweeping language with an editorial cartoon depicting three people in traditional conical hats labeled "Vietnamese refugees" saluting the Philippine flag.

CADP also mobilized its overseas supporters to lobby the Philippine government. Drafting a form letter, Vietnamese American volunteers circulated the template, calling on their peers to write to the Philippines' Department of Foreign Affairs and key elected officials. The letters applauded Viet Ville and heralded it as a model for Vietnamese integration in the Philippines: "The world continues to marvel at the success of the Vietnamese Village established in Palawan. We read glowing reports about the Village and about the great progress its residents have made toward self-sufficiency and harmonious relations with their Filipino neighbors."[53] Vietnamese American organizations called on the Philippines to grant the Vietnamese permanent

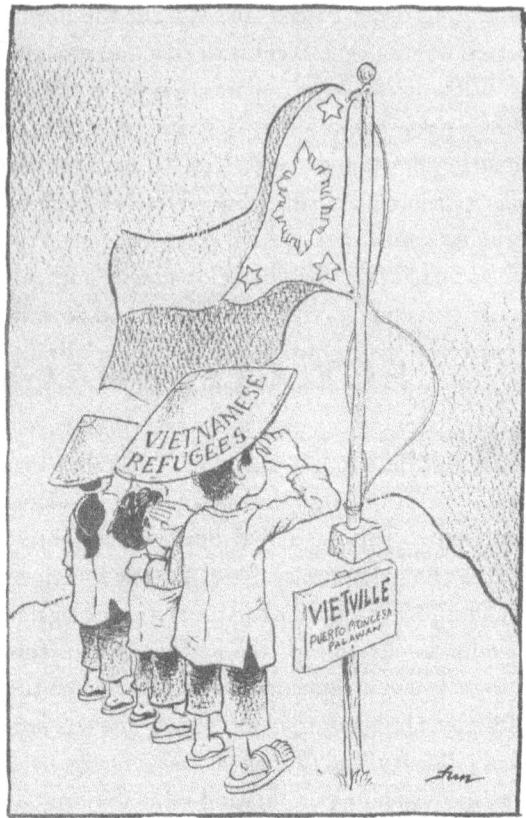

FIGURE 15. Editorial cartoon supporting the Vietnamese right to stay in the Philippines, showing Vietnamese pledging loyalty to the Philippine flag. Illustration by Jun Aquino, *Philippine Free Press,* February 21, 1998, Ateneo de Manila University, Rizal Library.

resident status as a way for them "to rebuild their new lives in freedom and liberty." The Washington Area League of Vietnamese Associations added that the Vietnamese would be loyal to the Philippines.[54] CADP's allies and supporters hoped that these missives, circulated through the first generation of email networks, could persuade Philippine lawmakers.

In lobbying Filipino politicians, Sister Pascale made an explicit link between granting the Vietnamese Philippine residency and the vulnerable status of overseas Filipino workers. By the late 1990s, overseas workers became the central driver of the Philippine economy, but these workers often faced precarious legal protections, discrimination, and exploitation in the Middle East, Asia, Europe, and North America. Sister Pascale argued that granting permanent residency to the Vietnamese would demonstrate how a country should protect migrant minority populations and serve as a model for how host countries could respect overseas workers.[55] This pitch held particular sway with its Philippine audience, given that by the 1990s, there were hundreds of thousands of overseas Filipino workers at any one time.[56] Unlike the call to anti-communist solidarity or refugee rescue within the Vietnamese American community, here was a call that might resonate in the Philippines. Sister Pascale imagined overseas Filipino workers and Vietnamese in Palawan as being on a continuum of vulnerable migrants, all of whom needed protection and depended on foreign countries to respect their rights and well-being. This was not just an appeal to paternalism, but instead it emphasized self-interest and nationalism.

Bishop Ramon Arguelles echoed this line of reasoning, emphasizing the massive numbers of Filipinos who worked abroad as guest workers:

> Six million of you Filipinos ARE ALIENS in the land of Taiwan, Japan, Malaysia, in America, Europe, Australia, and so many other places in the world. I am sure that this gesture of assisting the remnants of refugees and asylum seekers will bring blessings to the inhabitants of this land and the Filipinos whom circumstances have forced to go to other lands. The pleas of millions of undocumented Filipinos, I hope will be given a favorable response by those concerned because we publicly proclaim that we do not do to others what we do not want others to do to us.[57]

Senator Leticia Ramos Shahani agreed that the Philippines had an obligation to protect foreigners because of its reliance on remittances from overseas workers. She explained, "Our nation deplored and denounced the mistreatment of our migrants working abroad. While we know abuses are being committed against our OCSs [sic], still, a majority of them are treated with respect and dignity by citizens of their host countries. In return, basic human morality obliges us to provide the same respect and humane treatment to our Vietnamese brothers and sisters in Palawan. Mr. President I assume that much like our Filipino migrant workers, asylum seekers too are victims, victims of injustice, victims of tyranny of poverty, political discrimination and general indifference."[58] Pairing overseas workers and the Vietnamese, these advocates spoke to the precariousness of the Philippine economy and migratory networks in the late twentieth century. Here one can see a solidarity with migrants' itinerant, vulnerable lives, regardless of whether their journeys began because of economic insecurity or political persecution.

Yet despite Sister Pascale's lobbying and political supporters, President Ramos did not sign an executive order before he left office in 1998. The Vietnamese in the Philippines did not gain Filipino residency, and so they could not travel abroad and lacked formal status for employment and educational opportunities.

Sister Pascale, a Vietnamese woman who lived decades of her adult life in the Philippines, imagined the Philippines as a place where Vietnamese could resettle and thrive. Although she supported resettlement in the United States, Canada, or Australia, she believed that pragmatically, the Philippines was the best shot for the remaining Vietnamese to move on with their lives. She was able to communicate this vision to Vietnamese in the diaspora, and she lobbied for their dollars and for volunteers. When the only other option on the table was forced repatriation, Vietnamese Americans lined up to help. Sister Pascale also called on solidarity with the Philippines through the language of Catholic compassion and labor protection. Filipinos also migrated around the world, and she made connections between the need to protect foreigners in the Philippines with the need to protect Filipinos abroad. Sister Pascale's diasporic plans clearly imagined and embraced the Philippines as a partner.

Yet when given a choice, resettlement in the Philippines or resettlement in the United States, Australia, or Canada, the majority of Vietnamese in the Philippines opted to leave. Although it seemed like a lost cause at the time, activist Vietnamese Australian lawyer Hoi Trinh and Boat People SOS succeeded in lobbying the United States, Australia, and Canada to reopen immigration interviews for the "stateless" Vietnamese in the Philippines.

STATELESS

Vietnamese diasporic activists not affiliated with CADP, particularly Hoi Trinh's VOICE (Vietnamese Overseas Initiative for Conscience Empowerment) and Boat People SOS, never embraced a Filipino future for this remaining Vietnamese population. With the threat of repatriation removed, they remained focused on resettlement in wealthier, more developed countries with large diasporic Vietnamese communities. In their eyes, the Vietnamese in Palawan were "stateless," and Filipino residency would at best complicate and at worst stymie any possibility of resettlement in the west.[59] In this configuration, the Vietnamese in the Philippines were a population to be saved by diasporic Vietnamese activists who had learned to navigate new political landscapes. Nothing short of reuniting with families and resettlement in the United States, Canada, and Australia would be acceptable or just. These newly minted U.S. and Australian citizens could save their compatriots from endless limbo in the Philippines. Le Xuan Khoa, the former director of one of the first Vietnamese American organizations, IRAC (later SEARAC), reflected some years later that at the time he would not have put money on these overseas activists, but ultimately they succeeded.[60]

In the United States, Boat People SOS had made its mark advocating against repatriation and for the refugee claims of Vietnamese in Hong Kong after the 1989 CPA. During these years, it also established programs in Palawan and worked alongside CADP. While CADP provided direct services and education within the camps, Boat People SOS took up the legal docket. Boat People SOS funded LAVAS (Legal Assistance for Vietnamese Asylum Seekers), which also operated in Hong Kong, funding lawyers to defend Vietnamese asylum claims in Palawan. LAVAS hired both Filipino lawyers and overseas Vietnamese, and they worked in the camps to help Vietnamese navigate the Philippine and UNHCR screening and appeals procedures.

After the dramatic 1996 confrontation on the tarmac in Palawan, Nguyen Dinh Thang, the executive director of Boat People SOS, applauded the Philippines' decision to halt repatriation flights. However, he did not join Sister Pascale and CADP's celebrated MOU and the plan to relocate the Vietnamese in Viet Ville. Instead, he insisted the U.S. government should unilaterally reopen the Vietnamese cases in Palawan. He argued that since only the Philippines immigration officers and the UNHCR had evaluated the "screened out," U.S. officials had never interviewed them. Waving aside the reasons behind the CPA, namely that the United States had stopped accepting the Vietnamese in the mid-1980s, which in turn had led to growing "long-stayer" populations, Nguyen Dinh Thang believed this group had strong asylum claims that the U.S. government would recognize.

On February 16, 1996, just two days after the controversial repatriate flight, Nguyen Dinh Thang wrote to Filipina LAVAS lawyer Corazon Gaite, asking for advice in contacting Filipino legislators. Unlike Sister Pascale, his network was in the United States, and he was unfamiliar with the Philippine political landscape. "I know the U.S. Congress pretty well but am totally ignorant about its Philippines counterpart." He understood that Philippine politicians were empathetic toward the Vietnamese because many saw similarities between the Vietnamese fleeing political persecution and their own experiences under the Marcos regime. However, he believed the United States would be willing to resettle the majority of the Vietnamese population remaining in the Philippines, and he wanted to act toward that end.[61] He also alerted Vietnamese in Palawan to the risk of mercury contamination on the proposed site for Viet Ville. There was extensive mining on Palawan, leading to mercury deposits and environmental hazards throughout the island. Sister Pascale and the Palawan politicians minimized the risks as standard for the region at large. Sister Pascale also charged that this was only a campaign intent on creating fear and "destroying the credibility" of the Catholic Church, CADP, and Viet Ville.[62] Palawan Governor Salvador Socrates downplayed the critiques and environmental analysis, writing to Sister Pascale, "We are fully aware of the mercury contamination issue: it is not really as bad as described in the notice." He stated that the area had been certified by the government to be "free from any contamination." He advised Sister Pascale to move forward with construction of the village in the initial site.[63]

CADP's Filipino allies were frustrated by these charges against Viet Ville. Bishop Arguelles spoke out against "certain well-meaning supporters" who have sent reports "belittle[ing] the importance or need of the planned project."[64] He resented the rumors circulating against Viet Ville. To Bishop Arguelles, these U.S.-based activists were simply stirring up trouble and making promises they could not keep. He suggested this campaign did not appreciate the Philippines' generosity and sovereignty. In his eyes, this outside American group was acting superior and trying to tell the Philippine government what to do. Vietnamese Americans were still Americans. The bishop came down hard against this pressure, applauding the Philippine government's sovereign independence. "We will not be dictated to by outsiders. . . . We Filipinos are very sensitive about our sovereignty."[65] He asked all of his parishioners to help make "the Vietnamese Village in the Philippines" succeed. Having dedicated time, energy, and political capital to protecting the Vietnamese and establishing Viet Ville, he had little patience for an overseas Vietnamese activist group trying to interfere in Philippine politics.

While the fears of mercury poisoning remained, in many ways, Viet Ville served only to intensify the distinction between CADP and Boat People SOS. The real battle was not over environmental concerns, but over whether the Vietnamese in Palawan should resettle permanently in the Philippines, or if they should hold out for the possibility of resettlement in the United States. Sister Pascale always supported resettlement in the west, but she believed that door had closed. To protect the Vietnamese in the Philippines, she advocated that the Philippines should grant the Vietnamese permanent resident status, and she remained committed to that idea. She pointed to a

Vietnamese woman who had started a *nuoc mam* (Vietnamese fish sauce) business in Palawan and whose son had had a chance to study in Japan. Because they did not have legal residency, he could not travel legally outside the Philippines and was unable to take advantage of this opportunity abroad.[66] If the mother and son had Filipino residency, then he would have been able to travel to Japan and advance his career. Sister Pascale's objectives were pragmatic, and she believed the Vietnamese should move on with their lives in the Philippines.

In 1997, Vietnamese Australian Hoi Trinh also entered the scene. He became the single most prominent legal advocate for Vietnamese in the Philippines and later the founder of VOICE. The forced repatriations in Hong Kong motivated Hoi Trinh, like thousands of other Vietnamese in the diaspora, to become politically active and champion the Vietnamese in the camps.[67] Underwhelmed by his career in corporate law in Australia and seeking a radical change, he moved to the Philippines to dedicate himself to the remaining Vietnamese asylum cases. Two documentary films, *In Limbo* and *Stateless,* have profiled Hoi Trinh and his campaign to convince Australia and the United States to recognize his clients' asylum claims and resettle them. The films showcase his passion and the shoestring nature of his project, complete with volunteer lawyers and limited material resources. They follow Hoi Trinh as he compiles asylum claims, files, and personal histories, readying his clients for the all-important interviews with immigration officials.[68] In the films, Hoi Trinh takes on the role of rescuing the remaining Vietnamese, without any acknowledgment of CADP, Viet Ville, the Philippine Catholic Church, or the possibility of permanent residency in the Philippines.[69] Instead, the Vietnamese are stateless, without papers, and in need of the political and economic support of the Vietnamese diasporic community.

Setting up shop in Manila, Hoi Trinh began seeing Vietnamese clients who wanted to resettle outside of the Philippines. Staffed with volunteers from the United States and Australia, his team worked with individual Vietnamese on navigating the immigration bureaucracy. In their first group of forty-five applicants, they prepared careful case files with detailed stories and biographies for Australian immigration interviews. Of these forty-five, the Australian government agreed to resettle nine. While only a small percentage, this opening represented a huge victory for Hoi Trinh and propelled the campaign. With renewed energy and optimism, Hoi Trinh continued to pressure Australia, and ultimately the United States and Canada, to interview the Vietnamese still in the Philippines.

In the films, the economic picture and opportunities for the Vietnamese appear grim. For example, one of the Vietnamese women worked with Hoi Trinh's team somewhat surreptitiously. She did not want her friends and neighbors to know she was interviewing with the Australian embassy, because if they thought she was leaving the Philippines, they would not repay the money they owed her. Others worked in the informal economy, peddling on the streets of Manila on bicycle. One woman pointed to an existential vulnerability, stating, "We live in a foreign country. It feels very lonely. Even though the Philippines is a democratic nation, we still don't have any civil rights. We live here illegally. We feel very isolated and lost. When the native people raise their voices, we must stay quiet and not argue."[70] To some extent, she romanticized the west and minimized the work of Filipino allies, for of course she would still be in a foreign country if she resettled in Australia or the United States. However, these Vietnamese men and women wanted economic and political stability, and this woman clearly was not satisfied with staying in the Philippines.

The volunteers working with Hoi Trinh also found sustenance in assisting the Vietnamese, like the earlier students who had volunteered with Project Ngoc and CADP. Here was a way to support a marginal population that was still "stuck" between Vietnam and the United States, and who many Vietnamese Americans and Vietnamese Australians realized could easily have been themselves or their relatives. With financial support from the Vietnamese diaspora, Hoi Trinh was able to provide basic living expenses for himself and a small cadre of volunteers. A white Australian woman, Linda Philipps, also joined the team, and for her it was a revelation that there were still Vietnamese in the Philippines. "I thought the Vietnamese boat people thing was over, and finished, and everyone was resettled and everyone was happy . . . [then] I heard Hoi Trinh on the radio." Inspired, she contacted him and up and moved to Manila. Quan Nguyen was a Vietnamese American who resettled in the United States when he was nine years-old. When he traveled to the Philippines to assist the remaining Vietnamese, he believed everything in his life was coming full circle. "I don't know who took care of my papers. . . . Now I see the big picture . . . how much paper goes into the process, and how long people have to wait for the final day" in the Philippines.[71] He worked with Hoi Trinh meticulously organizing files, preparing individuals for their interviews, and trying to create paper trails that would convince state bureaucracies of his clients' refugee claims. What struck him most was the arbitrariness of the process.

American-based Le Xuan Khoa spoke generously of both Sister Pascale and Hoi Trinh, but he acknowledged that the two sometimes butted heads. "There was a time that Hoi Trinh and Sister Pascale, CADP Director, differed with each other so strongly that the asylum seekers often felt caught between these two dedicated benefactors. Honestly, I did not think that Hoi Trinh's effort would be successful."[72] Yet Hoi Trinh and his volunteers were not discouraged and persevered. In 2002, they successfully lobbied the Australian government to accept over two hundred Vietnamese, again fueling optimism that all the Vietnamese in the Philippines could be resettled in the west.

At this point, Sister Pascale and the Catholic bishops redoubled their efforts to pass legislation in the Philippine Congress granting the remaining Vietnamese permanent residency. Having failed to achieve this goal through an executive action, they hoped their political connections would push them past the post in the legislative branch. Sister Pascale's influence only extended within the Philippines, where she knew the ins and outs. She had no such pull with American and Canadian politicians. She believed the Philippines was the best opportunity for Vietnamese resettlement and security, and the time was now. Sister Pascale and the bishops worried that the other diasporic Vietnamese organizations would not be able to deliver on their promises, and the Vietnamese would be left in the Philippines forever without status and rights. Congressman Abraham Kahlil Mitra, representing Palawan, sponsored "The Social Integration Act of 2003 for the Remaining Vietnamese Nations," and it had substantial support, with fourteen co-sponsors.[73] The Philippine House voted for the bill; however, Hoi Trinh and Boat People SOS lobbied Philippine legislators *not* to pass the bill.

Hoi Trinh and Boat People SOS knew that if Vietnamese had legal status in the Philippines, then they would not be eligible for resettlement in the United States or a third country.[74] Once an individual gained asylum in one country, he or she could not apply for it in another.[75] The United States would only contemplate new interviews and potential resettlement placements if the Vietnamese had *no* legal status in the Philippines. In other words, their identity as "stateless" individuals was politically valuable if they wanted the chance, albeit not a guarantee, of relocating to a wealthier resettlement country and of reuniting with other overseas family members. Hoi Trinh's success gave new hope to many Vietnamese in the Philippines, who then turned against Filipino residency. Without unified support from the Vietnamese community, the bill lost momentum. Senate president pro tem Juan M. Flavier agreed to delay the bill, and it died in the Senate.[76]

The majority of the Vietnamese in Palawan and Manila chose to throw their lot in with Hoi Trinh's campaign.[77] If given the chance, they would leave the Philippines. These men and women thanked the Philippines and Filipino lawmakers for their ongoing support, but they did not want to stay in the Philippines or have Filipino residency. They wanted to be reunited with family, and they wanted to be in the western resettlement countries. Not only did they write letters, but they organized their files, went to Manila, and prepared for interviews. After his initial success with the Australian government, Hoi Trinh turned to the United States.

In the early 2000s, the United States was contemplating expanding trade opportunities with Vietnam. Vietnamese American groups strategically linked the fate of the remaining Vietnamese in Palawan to Vietnam's internal human rights record and these economic changes. Diplomatic relations between the U.S. and Vietnam were opened during the Clinton years, and trade between the two former enemies was modest at first; however, in 2000, the United States signed a bilateral trade agreement with Vietnam, granting it conditional most-favored-nation status and accelerating economic ties.[78] For Vietnamese American organizations, which wanted to keep U.S. attention on Vietnam's human rights violations, the Vietnamese in Palawan remained a visible population they could help, even if the United States exerted only limited pressure on Vietnam's domestic politics. In a 2004 Senate hearing on the future of U.S.-Vietnam relations, Senator Sam Brownback (R-KS) applauded the robust trade and travel between the United States and Vietnam, but he also emphasized unresolved and ongoing human rights abuses. Yet even before Senator Brownback reiterated the examples of persecution against Vietnamese Catholics and democracy advocates, he cited the Vietnamese in Palawan. Their primacy in his litany of "lingering" problems was notable.[79] Brownback ignored the United States' careful and restricted immigration criteria in the 1980s and its acquiescence to the 1989 CPA. Instead, he urged the State Department to admit the remaining 1,400-plus Vietnamese in the Philippines, confident they would meet the U.S. refugee standard.

Not only did Brownback couple abuses in Vietnam and trade relations with the fates of the Vietnamese in Palawan, so did Viet D. Dinh, the most prominent Vietnamese American in President George W. Bush's administration. By 2004, the 9/11 attacks, the war on terror, and the wars in Iraq and Afghanistan had clearly displaced the U.S. war in Vietnam as the dominant paradigm for understanding U.S. foreign policy. Viet D. Dinh was an assistant attorney general from 2001 to 2003, and he became the most visible author of the 2001 Patriot Act. His identification with the Patriot Act merged his refugee story and the restriction on civil liberties in the name of "security" after 9/11. Scholar Mimi Thi Nguyen has argued that Viet D. Dinh's prominence in the Bush administration served the ideological purpose of merging American liberalism and stories of multicultural inclusion with the disciplining power of the state and the violence of neoliberalism.[80] In his Senate testimony, Viet D. Dinh opened with a plea for the Vietnamese in Palawan and their eligibility for refugee status in the United States even before he delved into Vietnam's human rights abuses and trade relations.[81] This twinning of the legal status of the Vietnamese in Palawan and human rights abuses in Vietnam demonstrated the symbolic weight Vietnamese Americans attributed to this population. While the U.S. might not have been able to pressure Vietnam's government to uphold religious or political freedom, it still could bring this final population to the United States. Viet D. Dinh's testimony underscored his personal story as a Vietnamese refugee who succeeded in America and his authority as a leading legal voice in the war on terror. As the most prominent Vietnamese American in the George W. Bush administration, he served as the embodiment of a bridge between the Cold War and the post-9/11 era.

Vietnam's bid for full membership in the World Trade Organization meant that there were multiple hearings on U.S.-Vietnam relations in the early twenty-first century. Nguyen Dinh Thang from Boat People SOS continued to use his proximity to Congress to keep up the pressure on Vietnam's human rights abuses. He reminded members of Vietnam's human rights abuses, corruption, and human trafficking, and punctuated his testimony with individual stories of political and religious persecution. However, he turned away from Vietnam in his concluding remarks and urged his listeners to remember the Vietnamese in the Philippines. He ended with a pitch for granting asylum to the Vietnamese in Palawan as an "expeditious" and "generous" final "closure" to the thirty-year saga of the Vietnamese refugees.[82] With the U.S. military and war-making apparatus fully entrenched in the war on terror, the Vietnamese in Palawan could be viewed as a sympathetic, limited population which could be graciously admitted into the United States and viewed as "closure" to an anachronistically imagined simpler time.

By 2004, Democratic and Republican elected officials spoke positively about the Vietnamese community in the Philippines and their chances to resettle in the United States. Characterizing the Vietnamese in the Philippines as "stateless," politicians believed that it was time to end the war in Vietnam for these men and women.[83] Representative Chris Smith (R-NJ), the longtime ally of Boat People SOS, and Senator Sam Brownback (R-KS) carried the water for the Vietnamese in Palawan in Congress and remained staunch advocates for U.S. interviews. With tens of thousands of Vietnamese repatriated, Brownback noted the small size of the population in Palawan: "There is a group of Vietnamese refugees in the Philippines that are left over from the Vietnamese boat people. I think it's about 1,200 to 1,800 . . . this is fifteen years old now, and it's a limited population pool and I think they need to be allowed into the United States."[84] Representative Zoe Lofgren (D-CA), representing the city of San Jose and its large Asian American population, also voiced support for the Vietnamese in Palawan. Unlike Brownback, she emphasized the Philippines' generosity, but she added she had a "soft spot" for this cause.[85] The bipartisan support framed the issue of the Vietnamese in Palawan as somehow outside of politics, and as something that could be solved with a humanitarian gesture, and a small one at that. While activists like Hoi Trinh and Nguyen Dinh Thang spoke of human rights and legal appeals, Congress members responded to a human relations story, one with ideological value for some and direct consequences for constituents' family members for others. With less than 2,000 people eligible, both Democrats and Republicans could support the Vietnamese as "refugees" in a moment when the U.S. was engaged in new, and seemingly unending, wars in the Middle East.

The U.S. State Department agreed to interview the remaining Vietnamese in the Philippines.[86] In 2004, the U.S. government opened the Vietnamese cases in Palawan and sent immigration officers to Manila. These interviews were still fraught, and Vietnamese spent substantial time and resources preparing their cases with Hoi Trinh and his team. The United States did not accept everyone. It would not welcome any Vietnamese who had previously committed fraud or had a history of criminal activity. It would not interview or accept any Vietnamese who had married a Filipino or Filipina. These individuals could apply for Filipino residency.[87] By placing those with Filipina or Filipino spouses outside its mandate, the U.S. government rewarded those who held out for U.S. resettlement and had not integrated themselves in the Philippines. Eventually the majority of Vietnamese were successful in their interviews and claims and resettled in the United States, with others relocating to Canada, Australia, and Europe. In October 2005, 229 Vietnamese from Palawan landed in California. The *Orange County Register* reported, in somewhat over-the-top prose, that the Vietnamese were eating their first bowl of *pho* in more than a dozen years. Given the robust sales of *pho* in Palawan, this seems unlikely. However, the American journalist also emphasized their lack of rights in the Philippines, including their inability to buy property or hold "normal jobs." Hoi Trinh emerged as a dedicated superman: "Almost single-handedly, he took up their cause—before anyone would listen—and persuaded the United States to accept them. For that, he is their hero." The story treated Sister Pascale somewhat dismissively, singling her out only for giving the Vietnamese "false hope." Representative Loretta Sanchez (D-CA) attributed the success to more than Hoi Trinh, pointing to the activist nature, network, and lobbying of the Vietnamese American community in Orange County. She commented, "If the Vietnamese community wasn't as strong as it was in advocating for these refugees, . . . we would've forgotten about them over there."[88]

Longtime advocate and Vietnamese American leader Le Xuan Khoa was honestly shocked at Hoi Trinh's success in reopening the doors to the United States and taking on a "mission impossible," stating that "Hoi swam against the current." He believed Hoi Trinh's advocacy and the U.S. turnaround was "amazing."[89] Father Vien echoed this sentiment. After supporting the CPA and denying the "screened out" any chance at refugee status, the United States did an about-face. "I have to tell you, I was totally shocked. I thought the U.S. was being nuts." The U.S. had fought Vietnamese advocates "tooth and nail," but ten years later, it agreed to accept hundreds of Vietnamese it had previously denied. "I have no idea what the U.S. was doing."[90] Perhaps it was a combination of Hoi Trinh's passion and Vietnamese American lobbying. Perhaps it was the relatively small numbers and political value for U.S. Congress members with Vietnamese American constituencies or ideological commitments. Regardless, CADP's and Hoi Trinh's activism demonstrated the unanticipated and multi-vocal politics of Vietnamese in camps and in resettlement countries. More than thirty years after the fall of Saigon, the U.S. government, the Philippines, Vietnamese in the Philippines, and Vietnamese in the diaspora were still negotiating over who was a refugee and who would be resettled.

· · ·

Palawan itself remains a place seemingly peripheral and yet in many ways on the front lines of growing international disputes. Today it is most notable for being in close proximity to the Southeast Asian battles with China over the Spratly Islands. On this count, the Philippines and Vietnam are in a tacit alliance against China's growing military ambitions. Palawan also touts its environmental beauty and "the best beaches in the world," even as mining and environmental degradation persist. In the twenty-first century, journalists have also been murdered in the streets of Puerto Princesa, as they have in much of the Philippines.[91] In other words, Palawan has not been immune to the problems and controversies of recent Philippine politics. A small number of Vietnamese remain. Most have married Filipinos or have backgrounds that excluded them from resettlement in the United States. The *chao long* restaurants (serving the Vietnamese rendition of *pho* in the Philippines) are marketed as one of the aspects that make Palawan unique and add to local "color."

When I visited Palawan in 2015, Viet Ville was overgrown, largely empty, and emitted a ghost town-like atmosphere. The remaining Vietnamese and Filipinos living and working in the camp were friendly, proud of the community's former stature, and generous to me on all counts. The majority of Vietnamese who remain in Palawan now live outside of Viet Ville, either in Puerto Princesa or closer to town. The single remaining business is a Vietnamese restaurant serving *pho, canh chua, bun,* and other Vietnamese specialties. The men and women I spoke with asked me to be sure and tell people about the restaurant, and I can attest to the food's deliciousness. There are far fewer tourists to Viet Ville than there used to be, although Palawan's overall rise in eco-tourism and backpackers over the past decade has kept Viet Ville on the tourist itinerary. Most guidebooks and city flyers recommend that visitors enjoy the Vietnamese restaurants and even take a motorized tricycle to Viet Ville for lunch. There are also a number of *chao long* restaurants lining the streets of Puerto Princesa. Yet despite these restaurants and the small Vietnamese-Filipino community, the robust Vietnamese community that Sister Pascale, the Palawan Catholic bishops, and CADP imagined would thrive is no longer there.

Throughout the 1990s, the Philippines positioned itself as more humanitarian, more generous, and more Catholic than other Southeast Asian nations. Both the Marcos regime and the post-EDSA governments envisioned the Philippines as a place welcoming to Vietnamese. In addition, the modest numbers of Vietnamese in the archipelago, and most importantly the tacit, and often financial, support of the United States allowed the Philippines to stake out this ground. Halting the repatriation flights enabled the Philippines to celebrate an independent sovereign stand while not disrupting or threatening its relationship with the United States.

For the Vietnamese in Palawan, the two dominant diasporic visions put forward by Sister Pascale and Hoi Trinh presented a stark contrast in justice, humanitarianism, and resettlement. As someone who has traveled to Palawan and met with the Filipino bishops, lawyers, and politicians who advocated for the Vietnamese in Palawan, I feel great sympathy for their campaign. CADP and many Filipinos organized to make their legal resettlement in the Philippines a possibility. Sister Pascale and CADP provided social services to Vietnamese in Palawan for almost two decades, and over time, she reenvisioned this role as a political protector. Against the odds, the UNHCR, and the CPA's regional agreement, she fought repatriation and won. Faced with several thousand unsettled Vietnamese in the Philippines, Sister Pascale followed what she saw as a pragmatic course championing economic self-sufficiency and legal status in the Philippines. She had mobilized, nurtured, sometimes antagonized, and sometimes mentored a generation of Vietnamese and Filipino volunteers who built bridges and created meaning for the diaspora and Southeast Asian communities in the peripheral locale of Palawan. The United States could be an ally, but it was not the be-all and end-all of her political vision.

And while I would have shared Sister Pascale and Le Xuan Khoa's initial doubts in Hoi Trinh's campaign, the Vietnamese in Palawan did not. In the end, they wanted to move to America, Canada, and Australia. Driven by combined desires to reunite with family and loved ones and a recognition of the material improvements for their lives, they took their chances with the organizations that promised a future outside the Philippines. Not afraid to stick to Cold War language and anti-communist rhetoric that had served them in the past, diasporic Vietnamese activists found this consistency paid dividends. They also were able to tie the futures of the Vietnamese in Palawan to larger campaigns for human rights in Vietnam as the U.S. normalized its relationship with its former enemy. These diasporic networks found strong backers across partisan divides. No longer asking for humanitarian refuge, shelter, food, and temporary relief, diasporic Vietnamese stayed true to human rights language and learned to crank the gears of U.S. bureaucracy.

Of course, most refugees and people stranded in between around the globe would not be so lucky at the turn of the twenty-first century. The Haitians at the U.S. naval base in Guantánamo Bay would be just one example, as would the many Iraqi translators who found it near impossible to secure visas after the U.S. military no longer needed their services. But the

Vietnamese in Palawan, with the help of Hoi Trinh and VOICE, gathered their papers and got in line to tell their stories to U.S., Australian, and Canadian immigration officers in Manila. Vietnamese Americans and Vietnamese Australians stood beside them and promised a future outside the Philippines. For most Vietnamese in Palawan, this is the future they chose.

Epilogue

BY 2019, ONE WOULD IMAGINE THAT THE STORY of Vietnamese camps, repatriation, and struggles over refugee status had finally been resolved, for better or for worse. However, with the election of President Donald Trump, it was not.

The denial of refugee status, "the wall," the "Muslim ban," and deportation became his presidency's signature issues. In 2018, the U.S. government under Trump lowered the number of refugees admitted into the United States to under 30,000 for the first time since the 1980 Refugee Act.[1] Caught in this xenophobic and overtly racist political battle, a vulnerable group of Vietnamese who entered the United States between 1975 and 1995 unexpectedly found themselves targets for deportation.

It's hard to wrap one's head around the ironies. The U.S. had resisted repatriation, sparred with first-asylum countries, and admitted thousands of Vietnamese through specialized programs from the 1970s through the twenty-first century. Then, in 2017, the United States began moving on deportation proceedings for some of the very same Vietnamese who were in Southeast Asian camps or transited through the Orderly Departure Program.

Of the almost one million Vietnamese who entered the United States, several thousand committed crimes or came in contact with the law before they had applied for or gained citizenship. With this blemish on their record, they were unable to become naturalized U.S. citizens. Many of these individuals served time and on release faced deportation orders; however, because of a special understanding between Vietnam and the United States, the government did not act on these orders. Vietnam did not want to admit these convicted nationals, and the United States viewed them as refugees still needing protection. The U.S. and Vietnamese governments signed a memorandum of understanding in 2008 which protected this cohort from deportation. In 2017, Donald Trump's Department of Homeland Security changed course. It reinterpreted the policy and argued that deporting these Vietnamese, all of whom had lived in the United States for more than twenty years, was a priority.[2]

Individuals who had established full lives in the United States and who had never contemplated deportation now faced imminent risks to their status.[3] Pham Chi Cuong was a teenager when he came to the United States in 1990. He is an Amerasian who entered through the Orderly Departure Program. Once in America, he had initial run-ins with the law. He served eighteen months in prison in 2000 on assault and battery charges and then was arrested for drunk driving in 2007. Despite these problems, he also became a sushi chef, married, and had three children in Florida. He even earned enough money to visit Vietnam several times over the years. Although he had regular check-ins with Immigration and Customs Enforcement (ICE), he believed he was secure and was looking toward the future. Then in 2017, ICE began to target Vietnamese like Pham Chi Cuong. He was deported in December 2018 along with seventeen other Vietnamese. Uprooted from his family and community, he now lives in Ho Chi Minh City. He explained his Vietnamese family was not willing to help him, and he faces job discrimination and residual hostility due to his identity as an Amerasian. He worries about his family's economic stability back in Florida as well. "My life is over, everything is disconnected. . . . I call my family on Viber and try to keep in touch every day. The only thing we can do is pray to God."[4]

Mirroring earlier moments of activism, Vietnamese Americans mobilized in New Orleans, Houston, and California, and the Southeast Asian Resource Action Center (SEARAC) made advocating against deportations one of its central campaigns.[5] In New Orleans, Minh Nguyen, a community organizer, argued, "These folks already did their time. It's not fair for something like this to come back and bite them . . . They have every right to be here. They were protected. . . . They never had to worry about being deported and now all of a sudden they are at risk."[6] The Vietnamese American community has found allies at high levels in the government. The U.S. ambassador to Vietnam, Ted Osius, resigned in protest over the deportations.[7] Republican elected officials responded in bafflement and outrage that Vietnamese stories no longer had any special pull on American humanitarianism. Representative Ed Royce (R-CA) and Representative Mike McCall (R-TX) wrote to Secretary of State Mike Pompeo about their concerns and enlisted language heavy with Cold War history, pointing to America's "special responsibility" to Vietnamese who fought with the United States and faced persecution and re-education camps "because of their association with us." On a pragmatic level, the aggressive move also potentially alienated Vietnamese American voters, one of the few non-white minority blocs that regularly voted for Republican politicians.[8] Yet it's not clear if any of these allies or actions stopped the Department of Homeland's decision to move faster on these deportation cases.

As I was completing this book and writing about Hong Kong and Malaysia, I felt almost nostalgic for the time when Malaysian, Hong Kong, Philippine, British, and U.S. government officials worried about international opinion. Hundreds if not thousands of documents attest to their fears about sullying their reputation by "pushing off" Vietnamese boats and by the dire conditions of the camps. Even if it was strategic or superficial, they felt compelled that the camps and asylum hearings appear "humanitarian," at least on their own terms. In today's anti-refugee landscape, this language of concern, even if it was driven by pragmatic politics, seems old-fashioned and oddly admirable. The idea that shame or liberal values might influence international refugee policy seems a remote artifact of the Cold War. Instead, the United States government has reinvented itself as a new kind of leader in refugee policy—one that detains, deports, separates families, and cages children without apology. In 2019, U.S. government lawyers claimed that migrant children in camps along the southern border were not entitled to toothbrushes or soap.[9] Given the Trump administration's animosity toward non-white immigrants and refugees, regardless of whether they are documented or undocumented, it seems almost quaint to think that Cold War platitudes or calls to humanitarianism or human rights might compel changes in U.S. policy.

In Camps argues that we need to pay closer attention to camps in host countries. In recent years, the United States has accepted fewer and fewer people, and resettlement has affected less than one percent of refugees worldwide. Given these numbers, regional and local perspectives will likely continue to shape who is and who is not a refugee. As of this writing, Lebanon and Turkey are both pressuring Syrians within their borders to return to Syria. Turkey's hostility toward Kurdish minorities, the divisions between secular and religious-identified political parties, and its relationships with the United States and Russia all affect its policies toward the more than three million Syrians inside its borders. Mexico is also emerging as a pivotal player. The United States aims to convince Mexico to host Central Americans in

Mexico, rather than proceeding with asylum hearings in the United States. Mexico's specific history with the United States, the border, and its own crisis of violence will invariably influence how it responds to this demand. In all cases, host countries shape the contours of how refugee policies are conceived, managed, and implemented.

Activism will also continue to percolate within camps and on their perimeters. Vietnamese in the camps and in the diaspora practiced legal, political, and direct activism. It was not always clear which tactics and coalitions would succeed and which would not. What was clear was that refugee status was in flux, and the stakes were high. The Vietnamese in the camps waited, they told their stories, they maneuvered, they waited more, and sometimes they protested. Many, but not all, reached a third country for resettlement. Vietnamese relied on a range of strategies: letter writing, lawsuits, and direct action. They also found allies and developed transnational networks to make the camps visible and their situation urgent. Although they are not well publicized, there have been numerous hunger strikes in U.S. detention centers holding people from Central America. In an ICE detention center in Louisiana, where I live, more than a hundred people staged a hunger strike in August 2019.[10] Creatively and tenaciously placing pressures on the system, Vietnamese activists too shaped the contours of refugee policy, and they occasionally succeeded in gaining status when others might have given up hope. Moving forward, activism and coalition building inside and outside of camps should not be surprising, although state repression often seems more likely than release and liberation.

Finally, combinations of wars, political persecution, structural poverty, and climate change suggest that the numbers of those forced to flee their homes will only grow, even if we cannot predict when and where. Future U.S. administrations may move the pendulum back toward earlier norms, accepting select, ideologically aligned populations, or move U.S. refugee policy into a more generous register. Or the United States might stand behind its more punitive policies, and other countries may replace the United States as desirable resettlement destinations. One can imagine governments hewing to older standards of humanitarianism, refashioning and protecting human rights to new ends, or jettisoning both principles altogether. However, the trajectory for Vietnamese, from refugees to asylum seekers to repatriates, demonstrates just how contingent time- and place-specific refugee status can be.

I began this book with two sets of images and protests, one for repatriation from Vietnamese on Guam, the other against repatriation, led by

Vietnamese in Palawan. I conclude with a third. In December 2018 in Little Saigon in Westminster, California, Vietnamese Americans took to the streets carrying homemade signs. Once again, in English and in Vietnamese, the placards spoke to the long shadow of the U.S. war and emphasized the politics of family and reunification. One woman's sign reminded American observers of the U.S. war, "We Are Here Because You Were There." "*Pho*-get Trump," proclaimed a second. An elderly man wore a placard stating, "Deporting Vietnam War Refugees Is Shameless, Immoral, Inhuman."[11] These protesters' demands resonate with the longer tradition of diasporic activism and the Vietnamese protests in the camps.

ACKNOWLEDGMENTS

Like many projects, this book took much longer to write and took me to far more places than I ever anticipated. At one point, I had to promise my daughter that I would not leave again until after I had written one hundred pages. Fortunately for everyone in my family, I have completed both my long trips and many pages of writing.

I would like to begin by thanking my colleagues and interlocutors in the Philippines, Malaysia, and Hong Kong, without whom this book would not have been possible. I cannot begin to adequately express my gratitude to the dozens of people who spoke with me, pointed me in the right direction for documents, and took their time to help me in ways big and small. In the Philippines, I would like to thank colleagues at Ateneo de Manila University, especially Charlie Veric, Ann Lan Candelaria, and colleagues with *Kritika Kultura*. I will single out Oscar Campomanes, who provided both intellectual engagement with my project and regular assistance finding documentary images to the very end. Jun Tolentino was an intrepid guide and research assistant in Bataan province, and Daisy Fernandes generously welcomed me in the Bataan Technology Park (on the grounds of the former Philippine Refugee Processing Center). My conversations with Connie Acosta, George Chiu, Bernard Kerblat, Nina Ermita Magallanes, Steven Muncy, and Susan Quimpo were critical to my understanding of the camps in the Philippines. Benjamin D. Weber helped me navigate Manila and Palawan. When I first met Father Vien in New Orleans, I did not know I would become so dependent on, and grateful for, his connections in Palawan. I thank him for his remarkable generosity and vision, and for introducing me to his friends and colleagues in the Philippines. I'd also like to thank Vicente Rafael and Noah Theriault for introducing me to their colleagues and helping me prepare for my trip. For my research in Hong Kong, I thank Carina Hoang, who generously put me in touch with her colleagues there. Peter Lai organized an impressive itinerary for my trip. Thanks also to Bonnie Wong, Joyce Ho, Mark Daly, John Carroll, Yuk Wah Chan, and Jodie Cheng. In Malaysia, I would like to thank Ngu Ik Tien, Danny Wong, Marek Rutkowski, the staff of the Malaysian Red Crescent Society, and Choong Pui Yee. Special shout-outs to Carlson Chew Yee Herng, my research assistant, who went above and beyond, and Anuar Ngah, who was my guide to Pulau Bidong and a fount of knowledge about the Vietnamese in Terengganu. In Singapore, I had the great pleasure of meeting Wen-Qing Ngoei, S. R. Joey Long, Gerard Sasges, Michael Montesano, and Lyle Fearnley.

At the UNHCR archives in Geneva I valued the assistance of Heather Faulkner, Karunakaran Kanthasamy, and Mederic Droz-Dit-Busset in the archives, and conversations with Larry Bottinick and Julian Herrera raised new questions. I also appreciate the International Catholic Migration Commission's generosity and interest in my project. In Geneva, Sarha Simpson was a marvelous host. In the U.K., Paul Gilroy and Vron Ware welcomed me into their home and provided needed insights at a key juncture. In the United States, Thuy Vo Dang and the Southeast Asian Archive at the University of California, Irvine, were particularly helpful throughout. In addition, I appreciate the professional help of archivists at Radcliffe's Arthur and Elizabeth Schlesinger Library and the U.S. Army War College's Military History Institute in Carlisle, PA. In Washington, D.C., I benefited from early conversations with Nguyen Dinh Thang and Elisabeth Ferris. Harriet McGuire regularly offered me a bed in Washington, and I still hope that one day Lionel Rosenblatt and I will be able to meet in person. I want to thank Pipo Bui and Sarah Chilgren, friends I met in Vietnam more than two decades ago, who I was lucky to reconnect with over the course of this research.

Tulane University has been my intellectual home for more than a decade, and I am grateful to my community within the History Department and throughout the university. This book is better because of Rosanne Adderley, Mohan Ambikaiper, Carl Bankston, Kathy Carlin, Emily Clark, Sarah Cramsey, Clare Daniel, Subah Dayal, Brian Demare, Kathryn Edwards, Lupe García, Blake Gilpin, Karissa Haugeberg, Andy Horowitz, Walter Isaacson, Patty Kissinger, Michelle Lacey, Anna Mahoney, Elisabeth McMahon, Cheryl Naruse, Marline Otte, Linda Pollock, Cam Tran, Allison Truitt, Aidan Smith, Randy Sparks, Mark Vail, Mark Van Landingham, Carola Wenk, and Justin Wolfe. I would also like to thank Donna Deneen, Patrice Downes, and Susan McCann for their administrative support, and my undergraduate research assistants, Courtney Liss and Venu Reddy, who assisted me with microfilm and bibliographic work. I am also lucky to have had a wonderful group of graduate students to keep me current and on the ball: Jesse Chanin, Sarah Fouts, Josh Goodman, Michael Guitérrez, Mira Kohl, Christina LeBlanc, Karla Rosas, and Caleb Smith.

I have also had the good fortune of having many engaged readers along the way. In particular, Yến Lê Espiritu provided timely insights and suggested valuable strategies for bringing this sometimes unwieldy narrative together, and I'm grateful for the Tulane Provost Office's Faculty Networking Grant for sponsoring her visit to Tulane. Many others also read drafts and provided valuable feedback: Dan E. Bender, Mark Bradley, John Carroll, Clare Corbould, Brian Demare, Eli Feinstein, Madeline Hsu, Ken Lipman, Michael McGandy, Rebecca McKenna, Marguerite Nguyen, Sarah Snyder, Steve Striffler, Allison Truitt, and Colleen Woods.

I have learned to embrace conferences as places for intellectual exchange and friendship. To that end, I would like to thank the following colleagues: Julio Capó, Christopher Capozzola, Vernadette Vicuña Gonzalez, Andrew Friedman, Carina Hoang, Julia Irwin, Paul Kramer, Julian Lim, Simeon Mann, Ana Minian, Naomi Paik, James Pangilinan, Crystal Parikh, Sam Vong, Julie Weiss, and Elliott Young. I also had the opportunity to present my research at the University of Chicago Pozen Family Center for Human Rights, the Northeastern University Graduate Conference in International History, the Scope of Slavery Conference at Harvard University, the New York University Refugee Studies Symposium, and Macquarie University's Vietnam War in the Pacific conference. I would also like to thank the Organization of American Historians—Japanese Association for American Studies, which enabled me to spend two weeks in Japan, hosted by Kotaro Nakano and Osaka University. I also learned a great deal from Kawashima Masaki, Taihei Okada, and Masaki Sho. Gunter Bischoff has been a remarkable friend and colleague, and I value our regular lunchtime conversations over *pho*. Finally, I must thank two colleagues I first met while studying the U.S. naval base in Guantánamo Bay and who inspire me in their commitment to scholarship and public engagement: Liz Ševčenko and David Vine.

This project began with my interest in the repatriates in Guam, and to that end, I was honored to work with Trần Đình Trụ and co-translate *Ship of Fate: A Memoir of a Vietnamese Repatriate*. Bac Hoai Tran continues to be a remarkable colleague, and Masako Ikeda had confidence in this translation project from the get-go.

Research projects also need funding. I would like to thank the U.S. Army Military History Institute's General and Mrs. Matthew B. Ridgway Research Grant for the initial grant that jump-started this project. In addition, I received much-needed financial support in the form of a Tulane University Lavin Bernick Faculty Research Grant and from Tulane University's School of Liberal Arts and its Lurcy Fund.

At the University of California Press, I would like to thank Niels Hooper for sticking with this project and continuing to publish innovative work; the external reviewers for their insightful comments; and Robin Manley for his ability to get this book across the finish line. I also would like to thank Jan Spauschus for her careful reading and copyediting, and Bill Nelson for designing the maps. For the cover art, I am grateful to Molly Nutt and Tyler Rollins Fine Art Gallery, and most importantly, Tiffany Chung for allowing me to include her beautiful, evocative artwork on the cover.

Finally, my close friends and family have been amazingly patient. Sarah Allison, Mirna Adjami, Deborah Evans, Heather Ikemire, Jeanne Jaubert, Danielle Kleinman Pizzolatto, Katy Patterson, Wendy Pearlman, Eileen Stevens, and

Suzanne Travers have listened to me talk about refugees and camps for more hours than I care to count, and through it all, they have offered friendship, tough questions, and time to think about other things. My mother-in-law, Miriam Weinstein, herself a writer, came whenever we asked to help with childcare and keeping everyone on track. Especially when my daughters were younger, her help was invaluable and allowed me to develop the "three week" research dive. My father-in-law, Peter Feinstein, was always ready to talk about the newest scholarship in U.S. history. My mother, Evelyn J. Baum, did not live to see the completion of this book, but we did have the chance to eat croissants together in Paris. I hope her commitment to immigrants' rights and her sense of justice live on. My father, Ken Lipman, has been a constant source of support, telling me to work less and watch more television. He also read the whole manuscript right as I was finishing, and gave me the confidence to feel it was complete. Thank you.

Liza and Ruthie can't remember a time before I was writing this book. You are both the most wonderful girls. Maybe someday you will read this—or maybe you won't. Either way, I am thankful every day for the love, laughter, and delight you bring to our lives. I don't promise there won't be another book, but for now, no more long research trips. And to my husband Eli, thank you for believing in me, loving me, and tolerating the hours when I'm at the computer even though I should turn it off. I love you, and I'm ready to be your girlfriend again.

NOTES

INTRODUCTION

1. Stephen Vines, "Philippines Forces People back to Vietnam," *Independent*, February 15, 1996, www.independent.co.uk/news/world/philippines-forces-boat-people-back-to-vietnam-1319072.html (accessed August 4, 2018).

2. W. Courtland Robinson, *Terms of Refuge: The Indochinese Exodus and the International Response* (London: Zed Books, 1998), p. 294. Japan, Singapore, and Macau also hosted Vietnamese during these years. Using UNHCR statistics, Robinson records that of 839,228 Vietnamese who survived their escape and landed in a first-asylum site, 42,913 traveled by land, while the vast majority fled by sea. In addition, approximately 240,000 people from Cambodia and approximately 360,000 people from Laos sought refuge during this era, the vast majority of whom entered camps in Thailand. Robinson, *Terms of Refuge*, p. 294.

3. A simple word search for "Vietnamese refugees" in the *New York Times* database generates 885 articles from 1975. This would not necessarily include reporting on Laotian, Cambodian, or Hmong populations.

4. Gil Loescher, *The UNHCR and World Politics: A Perilous Path* (New York: Oxford University Press, 2001), pp. 204–9.

5. Laura Madokoro, *Elusive Refuge: Chinese Migrants in the Cold War* (Cambridge, MA: Harvard University Press, 2016), pp. 17, 188; Mimi Thi Nguyen, *The Gift of Freedom* (Durham, NC: Duke University Press, 2012).

6. Yuk Wah Chan, ed., *The Chinese/Vietnamese Diaspora: Revisiting the Boat People* (New York: Routledge, 2011).

7. For theorizing on the centrality of camps in liberal democracies, see Jenna M. Loyd and Alison Mountz, *Boats, Borders, and Bases: Race, the Cold War, and the Rise of Migration Detention in the United States* (Oakland: University of California Press, 2018); Jordanna Bailkin, *Unsettled: Refugee Camps and the Making of Multicultural Britain* (New York: Oxford University Press, 2018); A. Naomi Paik, *Rightlessness: Testimony and Redress in U.S. Prison Camps since World War II* (Chapel Hill: University of North Carolina Press, 2016); Laleh Khalili, *Time in the Shadows:*

Confinement in Counterinsurgency (Stanford, CA: Stanford University Press, 2013); Susan Carruthers, *Cold War Captives: Imprisonment, Escape, and Brainwashing* (Berkeley: University of California Press, 2009). For the classic work on camps, rights, and refugees, see Hannah Arendt, *The Origins of Totalitarianism* (Cleveland, OH: Meridian Books, 1951).

8. Robinson, *Terms of Refuge*, pp. 294–95. Also, notably, China accepted over 200,000 Chinese Vietnamese who were ejected from Vietnam during the 1979 war. See Yuk Wah Chan, *Chinese/Vietnamese Diaspora* and "Vietnamese or Chinese: Viet-Kieu in the Vietnam-China Borderlands," *Journal of Chinese Overseas* 1, no. 1 (November 2005): 217–32.

9. David FitzGerald, *Refuge beyond Reach: How Rich Democracies Repel Asylum Seekers* (New York: Oxford University Press, 2019); Aristide R. Zolberg, "Managing a World on the Move," *Population and Development Review* 32 (2006): 223–25; Aristide R. Zolberg, *A Nation by Design: Immigration Policy in the Fashioning of America* (Cambridge, MA: Harvard University Press, 2008).

10. Samuel Moyn, *The Last Utopia: Human Rights and History* (Cambridge, MA: Harvard University Press, 2010), pp. 216–21; Samuel Moyn, "Theses on Humanitarianism and Human Rights," *Humanity Journal* 9 (2016), http://humanityjournal.org/blog/theses-on-humanitarianism-and-human-rights/ (accessed March 3, 2017); Jan Eckel and Samuel Moyn, eds., *The Breakthrough* (Philadelphia: University of Pennsylvania Press, 2014). Also see William I. Hitchcock, "Human Rights and the Laws of War: The Geneva Conventions of 1949," in *The Human Rights Revolution*, ed. Akira Iriye, Petra Goedde, and William I. Hitchcock (New York: Oxford University Press, 2012). I also argue that the creation of the Office of Human Rights and Humanitarian Affairs merged "human rights" and "humanitarianism" within the State Department bureaucracy; Jana K. Lipman, "'A Precedent Worth Setting': Military Humanitarianism and the U.S. Military and the 1975 Evacuation," *Journal of Military History* 79, no. 1 (January 2015): 151–79. For other approaches to human rights and humanitarianism, see Samuel Vong, "Compassionate Politics: The History of Indochinese Refugee Migration and the Transnational Politics of Care, 1975–1994" (PhD diss., Yale University, 2013); Bronwyn Leebaw, "The Politics of Impartial Activism: Humanitarianism and Human Rights," *Perspectives on Politics* 5, no. 2 (June 2007): 223–39.

11. Michael Barnett, *Empire of Humanity: A History of Humanitarianism* (Ithaca, NY: Cornell University Press, 2011); David Forsythe, *The Humanitarians: The International Committee of the Red Cross* (Cambridge: Cambridge University Press, 2005); Julia Irwin, *Making the World Safe: The American Red Cross and a Nation's Humanitarian Awakening* (New York: Oxford University Press, 2013); Stephen Porter, *Benevolent Empire: U.S. Power, Humanitarianism, and the World's Dispossessed* (Philadelphia: University of Pennsylvania Press, 2017).

12. Brendan Simms and D. J. B. Trim, eds., *Humanitarian Intervention: A History* (Cambridge: Cambridge University Press, 2011).

13. For works that include analyses of Asian governments, humanitarianism, and Vietnamese refugees, see Madokoro, *Elusive Refuge;* Ayako Sahara, "Globalized

Humanitarianism: U.S. Imperial Formation in Asia and the Pacific through the Indochinese Refugee Problem" (PhD diss., University of California, San Diego, 2012); Sara E. Davies, *Legitimising Rejection: International Refugee Law in Southeast Asia* (Leiden: Martinus Nijhoff Publishers, 2008); Sara E. Davies, "Saving Refugees or Saving Borders? Southeast Asian States and the Indochinese Refugee Crisis," *Global Change, Peace & Security* 18, no. 1 (February 2006): 3–24. On Vietnamese Americans and the use of humanitarianism, see Samuel Vong, "'Compassion Gave Us a Special Superpower': Vietnamese Women Leaders, Reeducation Camps, and the Politics of Family Reunification, 1977–1991," *Journal of Women's History* 30, no. 3 (Fall 2018): 107–37. On how the Philippines developed its own vein of humanitarianism, see James Pangilinan, "Screening Subjects: Humanitarian Government and the Politics of Asylum at Palawan" (master's thesis, University of Washington, 2014).

14. There is an extensive literature on human rights and foreign relations. See Stefan-Ludwig Hoffman's historiographical essay for a broad interpretation of the field, "Human Rights and History," *Past and Present* 232 (August 2016): 279–310; see also Kenneth Cmiel, "The Emergence of Human Rights Politics in the United States," *Journal of American History* 86, no. 3 (December 1999): 1231–50; Lynn Hunt, *Inventing Human Rights: A History* (New York: W. W. Norton, 2008); Moyn, *The Last Utopia;* Sarah Snyder, *Human Rights Activists and the End of the Cold War* (Cambridge: Cambridge University Press, 2011); Akira Iriye, Petra Goedde, and William I. Hitchcock, eds., *The Human Rights Revolution* (New York: Oxford University Press, 2012); Barbara Keys, *Reclaiming American Virtue: The Human Rights Revolution of the 1970s* (Cambridge, MA: Harvard University Press, 2014); Mark Bradley, *The World Reimagined: Americans and Human Rights in the Twentieth Century* (Cambridge: Cambridge University Press 2016).

15. W. Courtland Robinson, "The Comprehensive Plan of Action for Indochinese Refugees, 1989–1997: Sharing the Burden and Passing the Buck," *Journal of Refugee Studies* 17, no. 3 (2004): 319–33. For another perspective on the Comprehensive Plan of Action, see Alexander Betts, "Comprehensive Plan of Action: Insights from CIREFCA and the Indochinese CPA," UNHCR Working Paper No. 120, January 2006, www.unhcr.org/en-us/research/working/43eb6a152/comprehensive-plans-action-insights-cirefca-indochinese-cpa-alexander-betts.html (accessed August 26, 2019).

16. Heonik Kwon, *The Other Cold War* (New York: Columbia University Press, 2010). On the trauma and afterlives of war, also see Heonik Kwon, *Ghosts of War in Vietnam* (Cambridge: Cambridge University Press, 2013).

17. While this book emphasizes Vietnamese American activism, these networks included Vietnamese Canadians, Vietnamese Australians, and Vietnamese who had resettled in Europe.

18. Yến Lê Espiritu, *Body Counts: The Vietnam War and Militarized Refugees* (Berkeley: University of California Press, 2014); Yến Lê Espiritu, "The 'We-Win-Even-When-We-Lose' Syndrome: U.S. Press Coverage of the Twenty-Fifth Anniversary of the 'Fall of Saigon,'" *American Quarterly* 58, no. 2 (2006): 329–52; Yến Lê Espiritu, "Toward a Critical Refugee Study: The Vietnamese Refugee Subject in

U.S. Scholarship," *Journal of Vietnamese Studies* 1, no. 1–2 (2006): 410–32. Scholars at the University of California then spearheaded the Critical Refugees Collective, http://criticalrefugeestudies.com/ (accessed September 4, 2018).

19. Mimi Thi Nguyen, *The Gift of Freedom;* Viet Thanh Nguyen, "Refugee Memories and Asian American Critique," *positions: asia critique* 20, no. 3 (2012): 911–42; Viet Thanh Nguyen, *Nothing Ever Dies: Vietnam and the Memory of War* (Cambridge, MA: Harvard University Press, 2016); Eric Tang, *Unsettled: Cambodian Refugees in the NYC Hyperghetto* (Philadelphia: Temple University Press, 2015).

20. For foundational works in the field, see Liisa Malkki, "Speechless Emissaries: Refugees, Humanitarianism, and Dehistoricization," *Cultural Anthropology* 11, no. 3 (August 1996): 377–404; Liisa Malkki, "Refugees and Exile: From 'Refugee Studies' to the National Order of Things," *Annual Review of Anthropology* 24 (October 1995): 495–523. Her more recent work includes *The Need to Help: The Domestic Arts of International Humanitarianism* (Durham, NC: Duke University Press, 2015). For Vietnamese experiences in camps in particular, also see Peter Gatrell, *The Making of the Modern Refugee* (New York: Oxford University Press, 2015), chapter 7, "'Village of Discipline': Revolutionary Change and Refugees in Southeast Asia," pp. 203–22; Yến Lê Espiritu, *Body Counts,* pp. 24–80; Mimi Thi Nguyen, *The Gift of Freedom,* pp. 33–82.

21. For works that recognize the distinctions between different cohorts of Vietnamese migrants, see Sucheng Chan, ed., *The Vietnamese American 1.5 Generation: Stories of War, Revolution, Flight, and New Beginnings* (Philadelphia: Temple University Press, 2006); John Chr. Knudsen, *Chicken Wings: Refugee Stories from a Concrete Hell* (Bergen: Magnat Folag, 1992); John Chr. Knudsen, *Capricious Worlds: Vietnamese Life Journeys* (Münster: LIT Verlag, 2005). In addition, almost all scholarship examines Vietnamese migration after the war. For an exception, see Sam Vong's work, which analyzes internal displacement within South Vietnam during the war: "'Assets of War': Military Displacements, Deterritorialization, and the Strategic Uses of Refugees during the Vietnam War, 1965–1975," *Journal of American Ethnic History* (forthcoming, 2020).

22. For just a few popular literary examples that feature 1975 migrants, see Viet Thanh Nguyen, *The Sympathizer* (New York: Grove Press, 2016); Lan Cao, *Monkey Bridge* (New York: Penguin, 1998); and G. B. Tran, *Vietnamerica* (New York: Villard, 2011).

23. Previous scholarship on U.S.-Vietnam relations has not recognized the prominent role played by Vietnamese Americans. For example, Edwin Martini's *Invisible Enemies* analyzes U.S.-Vietnam relations after 1975 but does not include an analysis of immigration or refugee politics. The scholarship of Amanda Demmer and of Sam Vong promises to be an important corrective to this lacuna. Edwin Martini, *Invisible Enemies: The American War on Vietnam* (Amherst: University of Massachusetts, 2007); Vong, "'Compassion Gave Us a Special Superpower'"; Amanda Demmer, "The Last Chapter of the Vietnam War: Normalization, Non-Governmental Actors, and the Politics of Human Rights, 1975–1995" (PhD diss., University of New Hampshire, 2017). Demmer's forthcoming book will be published by Cam-

bridge University Press. On imperial suburban geographies, see Andrew Friedman, *Covert Capital: Landscapes of Denial and the Making of U.S. Empire in the Suburbs of Northern Virginia* (Berkeley: University of California Press, 2013).

24. For the growing literature that investigates Vietnamese American politics, see Phuong Tran Nguyen, *Becoming Refugee American: The Politics of Rescue in Little Saigon* (Urbana: University of Illinois Press, 2017); Tuan Hoang, "From Reeducation Camps to Little Saigons: Historicizing Vietnamese Diasporic Anticommunism," *Journal of Vietnamese Studies* 11, no. 2 (2016): 43–95; Thanh Thuy Vo Dang, "Anti-Communism as Cultural Praxis: South Vietnam, War, and Refugee Memories in the Vietnamese American Community" (PhD diss., University of California, San Diego 2008).

25. Judith Kumin, "Orderly Departure from Vietnam: Cold War Anomaly or Humanitarian Innovation?" *Refugee Survey Quarterly,* vol. 27, no. 1 (2008): 104–17. For more analysis of the ODP and normalization between the United States and Vietnam, see Demmer, "Last Chapter."

26. W. Courtland Robinson's *Terms of Refuge* is the most comprehensive book that includes all three populations and extensive information about the Thai camps. For the growing scholarship on Hmong, Cambodian, and Laotian refugees, see Melissa Borja, "The Government Alone Cannot Do the Total Job: The Possibilities and Perils of Religious Organizations in Public-Private Refugee Care," in *Shaped by the State: Toward a New Political History of the Twentieth Century,* ed. Brent Cebul, Lily Geismer, and Mason B. Williams (Chicago: University of Chicago Press, 2018); Melissa Borja, "Speaking of Spirits: Oral History, Religious Change, and the Seen and Unseen Worlds of Hmong Americans," *Oral History Review* 44, no. 1 (2017): 1–18; Tang, *Unsettled;* Chia Youyee Vang, *Hmong America: Reconstructing Community in Diaspora* (Urbana: University of Illinois Press, 2010); Ma Vang, "The Refugee Soldier: A Critique of Recognition and Citizenship in the Hmong Veterans' Naturalization of Act of 1997," *positions: asia critique* 20, no. 3 (2012): 685–712; Aihwa Ong, *Buddha Is Hiding: Refugees, Citizenship, and the New America* (Berkeley: University of California Press, 2003).

27. I had translators in Kuala Lumpur, Malaysia, to help with Malay- and Chinese-language periodicals. In addition, I also had assistance with some Vietnamese-language documents. When I rely on a translator, it is documented in the notes.

28. Scholars already conducting this work include Quan Tran, "Remembering the Vietnamese Boat People Exodus: A Tale of Two Memorials," *Journal of Vietnamese Studies* 7, no. 3 (Fall 2012): 80–121.

29. Steven DeBonis, *Children of the Enemy: Oral Histories of Vietnamese Amerasians and their Mothers* (Jefferson, NC: McFarland, 1994); James M. Freeman and Nguyen Dinh Huu, *Voices from the Camps: Vietnamese Children Seeking Asylum* (Seattle: University of Washington Press, 2003); James Freeman, *Hearts of Sorrow: Vietnamese-American Lives* (Stanford, CA: Stanford University Press, 1991); Carina Hoang, ed., *Boat People: Personal Stories from the Vietnamese Exodus, 1976–1996* (Western Australia: Carina Hoang Communications, 2011); Carina Hoang, "From Both Sides of the Fence: Vietnamese Boat People in Hong Kong, 1975–2000" (PhD

diss., Curtin University, 2018) and http://vietnameseboatpeople.hk/oral-history/ (accessed, March 1, 2019); Mary Terrell Cargill and Jade Quang Huynh, eds., *Voices of Vietnamese Boat People: Nineteen Narratives of Escape and Survival* (Jefferson, NC: McFarland, 2001); Nathalie Nguyen, *South Vietnamese Soldiers: Memories of the War and After* (Santa Barbara, CA: Praeger Press, 2016); Nathalie Nguyen, *Memory Is Another Country: Women of the Vietnamese Diaspora* (Santa Barbara, CA: Praeger Press, 2009); and Viet Stories: Vietnamese American Oral History Project, Southeast Asian Archive, UC Irvine Libraries, http://sites.uci.edu/vaohp/ (accessed August 18, 2017).

Vietnamese naming practices are different from English naming practices. Most Vietnamese names have three parts: the surname comes first, followed by a middle name, followed by the individual's given name. When using someone's given (first) name, it is almost always preceded by a relational pronoun/honorific indicating the relationship between the two people. Throughout my research, I consulted many documents, accounts, and oral histories that used the traditional Vietnamese format (surname, middle name, first name) and others that followed the English format (first name, surname). In this book, I chose to follow the convention that was used in the original document or account.

30. "Convention and Protocol Relating to the Status of Refugees," text of 1951 convention, www.unhcr.org/protect/PROTECTION/3b66c2aa10.pdf (accessed July 11, 2017).

31. Madeline Hsu, *The Good Immigrants: How the Yellow Peril Became the Model Minority* (Princeton, NJ: Princeton University Press, 2015), pp. 130–97; Meredith Oyen, *The Diplomacy of Migration: Transnational Lives and the Making of U.S.-China Relations in the Cold War* (Ithaca, NY: Cornell University Press, 2016).

32. The U.S. also signed the 1967 UNHCR Protocol on Refugees in 1968. On U.S. refugee history, see, Gil Loescher and John A. Scanlan, *Calculated Kindness: Refugees and America's Half-Open Door, 1945 to the Present* (New York: Free Press, 1986); Carl Bon Tempo, *Americans at the Gate* (Princeton, NJ: Princeton University Press, 2008); Porter, *Benevolent Empire;* Maria Cristina García, *Havana, U.S.A.: Cuban Exiles and Cuban Americans in South Florida, 1959–1994* (Berkeley: University of California Press, 1996); Maria Cristina García, *Seeking Refuge: Central American Migration to Mexico, the United States, and Canada* (Berkeley: University of California Press, 2006).

33. Robinson, *Terms of Refuge,* pp. 187–230; Knudsen, *Capricious Worlds,* pp. 16–20, 39–59; Gatrell, *Making of the Modern Refugee,* pp. 203–22.

34. Howard Adelman and Elazar Barkan, *No Return, No Refuge: Rites and Rights of Minority Repatriation* (New York: Columbia University Press, 2011). Also see UNHCR, www.unhcr.org/en-us/solutions.html (accessed March 3, 2017).

35. Clinton Leeks to U.S. Consulate, Re: Voice of America, February 8, 1991, Hong Kong Public Records Series 770-4-1, Publications Relating to Refugees.

36. Knudsen, *Chicken Wings,* and Yến Lê Espiritu, *Body Counts.*

37. UNHCR figures, June 2018, www.unhcr.org/figures-at-a-glance.html (accessed March 14, 2019).

CHAPTER 1. "GIVE US A SHIP"

A portion of chapter 1 first appeared as " 'Give Us a Ship': The Vietnamese Repatriate Movement on Guam, 1975" in *American Quarterly*, Vol. 54, Issue 1, March 2012, pp. 1–31. © 2012 The American Studies Association.

1. Tran Dinh Tru, *Ship of Fate: Memoir of a Vietnamese Repatriate,* trans. Bac Hoai Tran and Jana K. Lipman (Honolulu: University of Hawai'i Press, 2017), pp. 46, 58.

2. U.S. Department of Health, Education, and Welfare, Vital Statistics of the United States, 1975, www.cdc.gov/nchs/data/statab/mort75_2a_ta.pdf (accessed July 21, 2010).

3. Leanne McLaughlin, "Legislature Nixes Funds," *Pacific Daily News* (hereafter *PDN*), April 24, 1975.

4. Recent scholarship on Guam includes Alfred Peredo Flores, "'No Walk in the Park': U.S. Empire and the Racialization of Civilian Military Labor in Guam, 1944–1962," *American Quarterly* 67, no. 3 (2015): 813–35; Christine Taitano DeLisle, "Destination Chanorro Culture: Notes on Realignment, Rebranding, and Post-9/11 Militourism in Guam," *American Quarterly* 68, no. 3 (2016): 563–72; Tiara R. Na'puti and Michael Lujan Bevacqua, "Militarization and Resistance from Guahan: Protecting and Defending Pagat," *American Quarterly* 67, no. 3 (2015): 837–58; Michael Lujan Bevacqua, "The Exceptional Life and Death of a Chamorro Soldier: Tracing the Militarization of Desire in Guam, ~~USA~~," in *Militarized Currents: Towards a Decolonized Future in Asia and the Pacific,* ed. Shetsu Shigematsu and Keith Camacho (Honolulu: University of Hawai'i Press, 2010), pp. 33–62; Keith Camacho, *Cultures of Commemoration: The Politics of War, Memory, and History in the Mariana Islands* (Honolulu: University of Hawai'i Press, 2011); *The Insular Empire: America in the Marianas,* dir. Vanessa Warheit, 2010.

5. Robert F. Rogers, *Destiny's Landfall: A History of Guam* (Honolulu: University of Hawai'i Press, 1995), p. 230.

6. In contrast, the United States permitted direct elections for governor of Puerto Rico beginning in 1948. Guam also gained a non-voting delegate to Congress in 1972.

7. Ann Laura Stoler, "Tense and Tender Ties: The Politics of Comparison in North American History and (Post) Colonial Studies," *Journal of American History* 88, no. 3 (December 2001): 829–65; Ann Laura Stoler, "Intimidations of Empire: Predicaments of the Tactile and Unseen," in *Haunted by Empire: Geographies of Intimacy in North American History,* ed. Ann Laura Stoler (Durham, NC: Duke University Press, 2006), pp. 1, 4, 9–10; also see Benedict Anderson, *Specters of Comparison: Nationalism, Southeast Asia, and the World* (New York: Verso, 1998), pp. 3, 21–22.

8. Yến Lê Espiritu, "The 'We-Win-Even-When-We-Lose' Syndrome"; Yến Lê Espiritu, *Body Counts;* Jana K. Lipman, "'Give Us a Ship': The Vietnamese Repatriate Movement in Guam, 1975," *American Quarterly* 64, no. 1 (2012): 1–31; Heather Stur, "'Hiding behind the Humanitarian Label': Refugees, Repatriates, and the

Rebuilding of America's Benevolent Image after the Vietnam War," *Diplomatic History* 39, no. 2 (January 2014): 223–44; Larry Clinton Thompson, *Refugee Workers in the Indochina Exodus, 1975–82* (Jefferson, NC: McFarland, 2010), pp. 62–74.

9. Martini, *Invisible Enemies,* pp. 14–24.

10. Demmer, "Last Chapter." On MIA/POW issues, see H. Bruce Franklin, *MIA or Mythmaking in America* (Brooklyn, NY: Lawrence Hill,1992); Michael Allen, *Until the Last Man Comes Home: POWs, MIAs, and the Unending Vietnam War* (Chapel Hill: University of North Carolina Press, 2012); Natasha Zaretsky, *No Direction Home: The American Family and the Fear of National Decline, 1968–1980* (Chapel Hill: University of North Carolina Press, 2007). On Amerasians, see Jana K. Lipman, "'The Face Is the Roadmap': Vietnamese Amerasians in Political and Popular Culture, 1980–1988," *Journal of Asian American Studies* 14, no. 1 (2011): 33–68; Allison Varzally, *Children of Reunion: Vietnamese Adoptions and the Politics of Family Migrations* (Chapel Hill: University of North Carolina Press, 2017).

11. Vietnamese Humanitarian Assistance and Evacuation Act of 1975, Committee on International Relations, April 18, 1975, 94th Congress, 1st session, Elizabeth Holtzman Papers, Arthur and Elizabeth Schlesinger Library (hereafter Holtzman Papers), Folder 242.3 [Refugees: Indochina], bills, revisions, reports, etc., 1975.

12. James Wieghart, "Ford Requests 507M to Settle Viets in U.S.," *Daily News,* May 6, 1975, and Mary McGrory, "Hearts of Stone," *New York Post,* May 6, 1975, Holtzman Papers, Folder 242.4 [Refugees: Indochina], clippings, 1975.

13. Letter to Elizabeth Holtzman, n.d., Holtzman Papers, Folder 242.20 [Refugees: Indochina], Vietnamese, Cambodian, 1975.

14. Lipman, "'A Precedent Worth Setting'"; Sahara, "Globalized Humanitarianism'; Stur, "Hiding behind the Humanitarian Label."

15. Bill Summary H.R. 6096, Vietnam Humanitarian Assistance and Evacuation Act (94th Congress, 1975–76), https://beta.congress.gov/bill/94th-congress/house-bill/6096 (accessed July 23, 2014); and John W. Finney, "Emergency Funds: Action on New Arms Assistance Is Viewed as Improbable," *New York Times,* April 24, 1975.

16. "Three More Carriers Put to Sea for Possible Use in Evacuation," *New York Times,* April 20, 1975; John W. Finney, "Fear in Pentagon," *New York Times,* April 22, 1975; and David E. Rosenbaum, "U.S. Plans Waiver to Admit up to 130,000 Indochinese," *New York Times,* April 23, 1975.

17. Senator Kennedy Releases Report on President's Program to Resettle Refugees from Cambodia and South Vietnam, June 9, 1975, p. 17, Vietnamese Refugee Project Papers, U.S. Army Military History Institute, Box 14. For the military's account of the operation, see Frank Pew, *The Role of the U.S. Army Forces Command in Project New Arrivals: Reception and Care of Refugees from Vietnam* (Ft. McPherson, GA: Historical Office of the Chief of Staff of the U.S. Army Command, 1981). Report located at the Military History Institute, Carlisle, PA.

18. Also see Ayako Sahara, "Operations New Life/Arrivals: The U.S. National Project to Forget the Vietnam War" (master's thesis, University of California, San Diego, 2009), and Stur, "Hiding behind the Humanitarian Label."

19. K.J. Carroll, *Operation New Life: After Action Report* (Guam, 1975); Larry Clinton Thompson, *Refugee Workers,* pp. 64–66.

20. "Where They Are," *PDN,* April 28, 1975.

21. Rogers, *Destiny's Landfall,* pp. 252; Benedict Anderson, *Under Three Flags: Anarchism and the Anti-Colonial Imagination* (London: Verso, 2005), pp. 205, 224.

22. K.J. Carroll, *Operation New Life,* pp. 30–33, 40–43.

23. George Gonsalves, "Operation New Life: Camp Orote—A Study in Refugee Control and Administration, Doctrine and Practice" (master's thesis, Ft. Leavenworth Defense Technical Information Center, 1976), p. 51.

24. K.J. Carroll, *Operation New Life,* p. iii.

25. Oral history of Bruce Lam by Tram Vo, Viet Stories: Vietnamese American Oral History Project, Southeast Asian Archive, UC Irvine Libraries (hereafter VAOHP), 2012, http://ucispace.lib.uci.edu/bitstream/handle/10575/11947 /vaohp0050_f01_eng.pdf?sequence=2 (accessed September 24, 2018).

26. Oral history of Annie Thuy Tran by Suzanne Thu Nguyen, VAOHP, 2013, http://ucispace.lib.uci.edu/bitstream/handle/10575/8406/vaohp0120_f01 .pdf?sequence=2 (accessed September 24, 2018).

27. Oral history of Tom Phan by Thuy Vo Dang, VAOHP, 2013, http://ucispace .lib.uci.edu/handle/10575/14145 (accessed September 24, 2018).

28. Oral history of Chau Nguyen by Thuy Vo Dang, VAOHP, 2013, http://ucispace .lib.uci.edu/bitstream/handle/10575/11973/vaohp0054_f01_eng.pdf?sequence=4 (accessed September 24, 2018).

29. Oral history of Minh Hau Nguyen by Rachel Mock, VAOHP, 2012, http:// ucispace.lib.uci.edu/bitstream/handle/10575/5223/vaohp0042_f01.pdf?sequenc =31 (accessed September 24, 2018).

30. Oral history of Cathy Lam by Lotusa Chan, VAOHP, 2012, http://ucispace .lib.uci.edu/bitstream/handle/10575/9871/vaohp0112_f01.pdf?sequence=3 (accessed September 24, 2018).

31. Oral history of Thu Huyen by Michelle Lee Pham, VAOHP, 2012, http:// ucispace.lib.uci.edu/bitstream/handle/10575/11309/vaohp0057_f01_eng.pdf? sequence=3 (accessed September 24, 2018).

32. Tran Dinh Tru, *Ship of Fate,* pp. 61–62.

33. Review of U.S. Policy on Repatriates, July 23, 1975, U.S. National Archives and Records Administration (hereafter NARA), Record Group 220, Records of Temporary Committees, Commissions, and Boards, Interagency Task Force on Indochina Refugees, 1975–1976, Box 4, Folder 9/6 Repatriation.

34. K.J. Carroll, *Operation New Life,* p. 17.

35. Ronn Ronck, "Some Are Waiting to Return," *PDN,* May 14, 1975.

36. David Binder, "U.S. Wary of Refugees on Guam Who Seek Repatriation," *New York Times,* September 4, 1975.

37. Susan Guffey, "'I Didn't Plan to Come Here,' S. Viet Who Stole Airplane," *PDN,* May 2, 1975; "Refugees Eager to Leave," *PDN,* July 7, 1975; Dave Hendrick, "Refugees Waiting to Return Number More than 1000 Here," *PDN,* June 2, 1975.

38. "Some Viets Want to Go Back Even under Threat of Death," *PDN*, June 25, 1975.

39. Testimony of Thirteen Repatriates, July 28, 1975, NARA, Record Group 59, Central Foreign Policy Files, 1973–1976, 1975STATE177651. (All Record Group 59 records accessed electronically through NARA Access to Archival Databases [AAD] September 25, 2018.)

40. "'Criminal Act' Possible in Drugging," *PDN*, August 16, 1975; Jack Anderson, "Guam Refugee Drugging," *PDN*, August 27, 1975.

41. *Washington Post* Story on Repatriation, September 13, 1975, NARA, Record Group 59, 1975STATE21891; "Refugees on Guam Await UN Help," *Washington Post*, September 11, 1975.

42. Testimony of Thirteen Repatriates, July 28, 1975, NARA, Record Group 59, 1975STATE177651.

43. Message, June 25, 1975, Military History Institute, Vietnamese Refugee Project Papers, Box 4; Interviews with Repatriates on Eglin Air Force Base, June 10, 1975, NARA, Record Group 220, Box 4, Folder 9/6 Repatriation.

44. Tran Dinh Tru, *Ship of Fate*, pp. 149–51.

45. Ronn Ronck, "He Wants to 'Go Home to Die,'" *PDN*, May 28, 1975.

46. Kissinger, Review of U.S. Policy on Repatriates, July 23, 1975, NARA, Record Group 220, Box 4, Folder 9/6 Repatriation.

47. Kissinger, Review of U.S. Policy on Repatriates, July 23, 1975, NARA, Record Group 220, Box 4, Folder 9/6 Repatriation; Martha Alcott, "Viets Stage Demonstration," *Southwest Times Record*, June 21, 1975.

48. "80 Refugees Want Repatriation 'Now,'" *PDN*, June 22, 1975.

49. Chips Quinn, "'Not Giving Up' until They're Home," *PDN*, July 6, 1975.

50. " ... At Ft. Chaffee, a Protest March against Repatriates' Protest March," *PDN*, June 23, 1975; "Viets Show Gratitude," *Southwest Times Record*, June 23, 1975.

51. Pham Kim Vinh, *The Politics of Selfishness: Vietnam, the Past as Prologue* (San Diego: Pham Kim Vinh, 1977), pp. 128–33.

52. "80 Refugees Want Repatriation 'Now,'" *PDN*, June 22, 1975.

53. Press Guidelines for Senior Civil Coordinators and Press Officers, July 4, 1975, NARA, Record Group 220, Box 4, Folder 9/6 Repatriation.

54. Dave Hendrick, "Refugees Waiting to Return Number More than 1000 Here," *PDN*, June 2, 1975.

55. Untitled Image, September 20, 1975, NARA, Record Group 319, Records of the Army Staff, Records Regarding Operation New Life and New Arrivals, 1975–76, Box 19. Translation by Marguerite Nguyen.

56. Tran Dinh Tru, *Ship of Fate*, pp. 95–96.

57. "Repatriates Plan Strike for Today," *PDN*, July 11, 1975.

58. "Refugee Hunger Strike Falls Short of Mark," *PDN*, July 12, 1975.

59. "We Are on Hunger Strike," *PDN*, July 12, 1975.

60. Chips Quinn, "Repatriates Walk Out, Get Less than Mile," *PDN*, July 25, 1975.

61. Susan Guffey, "Repatriate Shows Continue; Group Moved to Apra," *PDN*, July 26, 1975.

62. K.J. Carroll, *Operation New Life,* p. 17.

63. Photo, "Hunger Strike until Die," *PDN,* September 6, 1975; "A Group Divided," *PDN,* September 7, 1975.

64. Secretary of State to U.S. Mission Geneva, July 19, 1975, NARA, Record Group 59, 1975STATE170890; and Secretary of State to U.S. Mission, July 22, 1975, 1975STATE171829.

65. "80 Refugees Want Repatriation 'Now,'" *PDN,* June 22, 1975; Chips Quinn, "Repatriates Plan for Strike Today," *PDN,* July 11, 1975; Susan Guffey, "Repatriate Shows Continue: Group Moved to Apra," *PDN,* July 26, 1975.

66. Secretary of State to U.S. Mission, Re: Vietnamese Repatriates, July 22, 1975, NARA, Record Group 59, 1975State171829; and Secretary of State to U.S. Embassy Bangkok, Repatriates, July 23, 1975, 1975STATE170895.

67. Action Memorandum, September 4, 1975, NARA, Record Group 59, 1975STATE 208902.

68. Susan Guffey, "'They'd Be the Last to Deny Compassion,'" *PDN,* May 1, 1975.

69. John L. Anderson, Letter to the Editor, *PDN,* May 3, 1975.

70. Leanne McLaughlin, "In Special Meet, Senators Ok Aid," *PDN,* May 3, 1975; "Events Are Making SRF Decision Obsolete," *PDN,* May 4, 1975. For a first-person account by a U.S. civilian on Guam, see Richard Mackie, *Operation New Life: The Untold Story* (Concord, CA: Solution Publishing, 1998).

71. Leanne McLaughlin, "How Big a Welcome Mat?" *PDN,* May 4, 1975.

72. Ricardo Bordallo, "The Governor's Report," *PDN,* May 4, 1975.

73. Leanne McLaughlin, "How Big a Welcome Mat?" *PDN,* May 4, 1975.

74. U.S. Secretary of State to U.S. Mission Geneva, July 19, 1975, NARA, Record Group 59, 1975STATE170890.

75. Secretary of State to RUMTBK/AmEmbassy Bangkok, Re: Repatriates, July 23, 1975, NARA, Record Group 59, 1975STATE170895.

76. Leann McLaughlin, "Ada Resolution Passes Senators," *PDN,* September 6, 1975.

77. "Task Force Replies 'No' to Wake, Ship Ideas," *PDN,* September 8, 1975.

78. "Give Repatriates a Ship: Bordallo," *PDN,* July 20, 1975; "The Ship Solution . . . ," *PDN,* August 25, 1975.

79. Tran Dinh Tru, *Ship of Fate,* pp. 83–84.

80. "Give Repatriates a Ship: Bordallo," *PDN,* July 20, 1975.

81. Situation Summary, September 5, 1975, NARA, Record Group 319, Box 1, Folder Situation Summaries June 12–July 31, 1975.

82. Exiled Camp Asan, Guam, "The Bitter Cry of a Vietnamese Old Man Living in Exile by the American Policy," September 6, 1975, Holtzman Papers, Folder 242.20 [Refugees: Indochina], Vietnamese, Cambodian, 1975.

83. To Whom It May Concern, September 9, 1975, Holtzman Papers, Folder 242.20 [Refugees: Indochina], Vietnamese, Cambodian, 1975.

84. "What Do We Want from Washington," n.d., Holtzman Papers, Folder 242.20 [Refugees: Indochina], Vietnamese, Cambodian, 1975.

85. Civil Disturbance Plan—Garden Plot, December 13, 1975, NARA, Record Group 319, Box 2, Folder Situation Summaries December 13–30, 1975; and Briefing Outline for U.S. of A., October 15, 1975, Record Group 319, Box 16, Folder Message Traffic for Repatriate Situation on Guam.

86. Civil Disturbance Plan—Garden Plot, December 13, 1975, NARA, Record Group 319, Box 2, Folder Situation Summaries December 13–30, 1975.

87. "Repatriates Will Get a Ship to Sail Home," *PDN,* October 1, 1975.

88. David L. Teibel, "Viet Vessel Resounds with Work," *PDN,* October 10, 1975.

89. George R. Blake, "'Sinister Scheme' How PRG Views Ship Plan," *PDN,* October 5, 1975; "Ship, Repatriates Can Enter Vietnam, Agency Reports," *PDN,* October 27, 1975.

90. "Repatriation 'Irresponsible,' North Vietnam," *PDN,* October 18, 1975.

91. Secretary of State to AmEmbassy Helsinki, Re: Action Memorandum: Repatriation of Vietnamese Refugees, September 4, 1975, NARA, Record Group 59, 1975STATE208902.

92. Secretary of State to JCS, Repatriate Ship, October 17, 1975; Secretary of State to RUHNSAA/CINCPACREP, Re: Plan for Public Affairs Handling of Vietnamese Repatriates on Guam, October 12, 1975. Both documents in NARA, Record Group 319, Box 16, Folder Message Traffic for Repatriate Situation on Guam.

93. Secretary of State to U.S. Mission Geneva, Re: Vietnamese Repatriates, October 6, 1975, NARA, Record Group 59, 1975STATE237422; Tran Dinh Tru, *Ship of Fate,* p. 103.

94. Ed Kelleher, "Ship's Port Undetermined," *PDN,* October 15, 1975.

95. Secretary of State to CINCPAC, Re: Meeting with Repatriate Leadership Committee, October 9, 1975, NARA, Record Group 59, 1975STATE241102; Secretary of State to CG Fort Chaffee, et Al., Re: Guidance on Counseling Repatriates, October 2, 1975, Record Group 59, 1975STATE235686; Julia Taft to Admiral Carroll, Re: Guidance on Out-Processing and Departure of Repatriate Ship, October 13, 1975, Record Group 319, Box 16, Folder Message Traffic for Repatriate Situation on Guam.

96. Secretary of State to CINCPACREP GUAM, Re: Final Out-Processing Procedures for Camp Asan Repatriates, Preliminary Scenario, October 10, 1975, NARA, Record Group 59, 1975STATE242815.

97. Secretary of State to CINCPCREP Guam, Re: Repatriates, October 21, 1975, NARA, Record Group 59, 1975STATE249847.

98. Jim Eggensperger, "Repatriate Ship Leaves to an Uncertain Future," *PDN,* October 17, 1975.

99. Tran Dinh Tru, *Ship of Fate,* pp. 159–64.

100. Larry Clinton Thompson, *Refugee Workers,* pp. 72–73; Sucheng Chan, *Vietnamese American 1.5 Generation,* pp. 64–65.

101. Subj: Vietnamese Repatriates in Nha Trang, December 13, 1975, NARA, Record Group 319, Box 2, Folder Situation Summaries December 13–30, 1975. Larry Clinton Thompson, *Refugee Workers,* pp. 66–73. For more detail and first-person accounts related to the re-education camps, see James Freeman, *Hearts of Sorrow;*

Doan Van Toai and David Chanoff, *The Vietnamese Gulag* (New York: Simon and Schuster, 1986); Nghia M. Vo, *The Bamboo Gulag: Political Imprisonment in Communist Vietnam* (Jefferson, NC: McFarland, 2004); and Andrew Pham, *The Eaves of Heaven: A Life in Three Wars* (New York: Random House, 2008).

102. Tran Dinh Tru, *Ship of Fate*, p. 192.

103. Tran Dinh Tru, *Ship of Fate*, p. 195.

104. Sucheng Chan, *Vietnamese American 1.5 Generation*, pp. 66–68, 74–75.

CHAPTER 2. TO "SHOOT" OR TO "SHOO"

1. U.S. Comptroller General, *The Indochinese Exodus: A Humanitarian Dilemma*, April 24, 1979, p. 5, Holtzman Papers, Folder 155.16 [Refugee bill: hearing], June 27, 1979. Sucheng Chan, *Vietnamese American 1.5 Generation*, p. 75–76; Yến Lê Espiritu, *Body Counts*, p. 52. In the 1970s, Trengganu was the common romanized spelling for the region, while as of this writing, the standard romanization is Terengganu. To allow for consistency and clarity, I use the contemporary spelling Terengganu throughout.

2. "What Do We Get for Being Nice?" *New Straits Times* (hereafter *NST*), June 5, 1979.

3. "Malaysia to Put 75,000 Refugees Back Out to Sea," *New York Times,* June 16, 1979; M. G. G. Pillai and Patrick Keatley, "Malaysia Threatens to Shoot Refugees," *Guardian,* June 16, 1979; Henry Kamm, "Malaysia Is Said to Drop Plan to Fire on Refugees," *New York Times,* June 17, 1979; "'Shoot on Sight': Malaysia Will Evict 76,000 Boat People," *Los Angeles Times,* June 15, 1979; John Sharkey, "Malaysia Announces Plan to Expel All Vietnamese Refugees," *Washington Post,* June 16, 1979; William Chapman, "Malaysia, in Clarification, Says It Will Not Shoot Refugees," *Washington Post,* June 19, 1979.

4. "Refugees: What Now?" *Sabah Times,* June 18, 1979.

5. "How Tough?" *NST,* June 6, 1979.

6. "What Mahathir Didn't Really Say," *Asia Week,* June 29, 1979 (*NST* archive, Kuala Lumpur). *Asia Week* also added that it was unclear if Mahathir actually made the blunt statement, citing a lack of international reporters or direct recordings, but noted he did not backtrack or directly refute the claim.

7. K. Das, "Malaysia Shocks the World into Action," *Far Eastern Economic Review* (hereafter *FEER*), June 29, 1979; William Chapman, "Malaysia, in Clarification, Says It Will Not Shoot Refugees," *Washington Post,* June 19, 1979. The UNHCR confirmed this; see Sampatkumar, UNHCR Cable, June 18, 1979, Fonds UNHCR 11 Records of the Central Registry (hereafter UNHCR Fonds 11), Series 2 Classified Subject Files, 1971–1984, 391.46 International Conference on Indochina 1979, Box 599.

8. Sara Davies analyzes why Southeast Asian countries did not recognize international refugee law or human rights law. She focuses much of her attention on Malaysia's refusal to sign the 1951 convention; however, she also notes that Malaysia

cannot simply be cast out as a "racist state." Malaysia sheltered more incoming Vietnamese than any other Southeast Asian country, and was second only to Thailand as far as overall numbers. (Thailand faced tens of thousands of people from Laos and Cambodia as well as Vietnam.) Davies, *Legitimising Rejection,* pp. 9–19, 106–113, 142–50. China also resettled more than 200,000 Chinese Vietnamese in southern China. Robinson, *Terms of Refuge,* p. 50.

9. For an analysis of Pulau Bidong, see Quan Tue Tran, "Remembering the Boat People Exodus: A Tale of Two Memorials," *Journal of Vietnamese Studies* 7, no. 3 (2012): 80–121. For statistics, Yến Lê Espiritu, *Body Counts,* p. 52.

10. Robinson, *Terms of Refuge,* pp. 42–3.

11. Bon Tempo, *Americans at the Gate,* p. 148.

12. Madokoro, *Elusive Refuge;* Sahara, "Global Humanitarianism," pp. 170–71.

13. Bradley, *The World Reimagined,* pp. 128–55; Keys, *Reclaiming American Virtue.*

14. Danny Wong Tze Ken, "The Cham Arrivals in Malaysia: Distant Memories and Rekindled Links," *Archipel* 85 (2013): 151–65.

15. Sucheng Chan, *Vietnamese American 1.5 Generation,* pp. 65–68, 71–73.

16. Nguyen Minh Quang, "The Bitter Legacy of the 1979 China-Vietnam War," *The Diplomat,* February 23, 2017, https://thediplomat.com/2017/02/the-bitter-legacy-of-the-1979-china-vietnam-war/ (accessed July 12, 2019).

17. Yuk Wah Chan, "Hybrid Diaspora and Identity Laundering: A Study of the Return Overseas Chinese Vietnamese in Vietnam," *Asian Ethnicity* 14, no. 4 (2013): 525–41, DOI:10.1080/14631369.2013.803802. The removal of close to 250,000 Vietnamese is a relatively undocumented story, particularly given the size and scope of the population. Also see Rewi Alley, *Refugees from China* (Beijing: New World Press, 1980); Xiaorong Han, "Exiled to the Ancestral Land: The Resettlement, Stratification and Assimilation of the Refugees from Vietnam in China," *International Journal of Asian Studies* 10, no. 1 (2013): 25–46; Xiaorong Han, "From Resettlement to Rights Protection: The Collective Actions of the Refugees from Vietnam in China since the Late 1970s," *Journal of Chinese Overseas* 10 (2014): 197–219.

18. Robinson, *Terms of Refuge,* pp. 23–28; Sucheng Chan, *Vietnamese American 1.5 Generation,* pp. 66–68.

19. Cheah Boon Kheng, *Red Star over Malaya: Resistance and Social Conflict during and after the Japanese Occupation, 1941–1946* (Singapore: Singapore University Press, 2003); T. N. Harper, *The End of Empire and the Making of Malaya* (Cambridge: Cambridge University Press, 1999); Danny Wong Tze Ken, "View from the Other Side: The Early Cold War in Malaysia from the Memoirs of Former MCP members," in *Southeast Asia and the Cold War,* ed. Albert Lau (London: Routledge, 2012), pp. 85–101; Joseph M. Fernando, "The Cold War, Malayan Decolonization, and the Making of the Federation of Malaysia," in *Southeast Asia and the Cold War,* ed. Albert Lau (London: Routledge, 2012), pp. 67–84.

20. As quoted in Barry Wain, *Malaysian Maverick: Mahathir Mohamad in Turbulent Times* (Basingstoke: Palgrave Macmillan, 2009), pp. 22–33. There is an extensive literature on racial identities and politics in Malaysia. For a sampling, see

Rachel Leow, *Taming Babel: Language in the Making of Malaysia* (Cambridge: Cambridge University Press, 2016); David C. L. Lin, ed., *Overcoming Passion for Race in Malaysia Cultural Studies* (Leiden: Brill, 2008); Joel S. Kahn, *Other Malays: Nationalism and Cosmopolitanism in the Modern Malay World* (Honolulu: University of Hawai'i Press, 2006).

21. Also see Mohamad Mahathir, *The Malay Dilemma* (Singapore: Asia Pacific Press, 1970). Mahathir was prime minister from 1981 to 2003 and was re-elected prime minister in 2018, this time under the banner of the opposition party.

22. The *Far Eastern Economic Review* estimated that anywhere from 66 to 80 percent of the Vietnamese leaving by boat were Chinese Vietnamese. Michael Richardson, "Singapore Slams the Door," *FEER*, November 10, 1978.

23. Guy Sacerdoti, "How Hanoi Cashes In," *FEER*, June 15, 1979.

24. Robinson, *Terms of Refuge*, pp. 29–33; Sucheng Chan, *Vietnamese American 1.5 Generation*, pp. 71–77.

25. Guy Sacerdoti, "Plight of the 'Ship of Gold,'" *FEER*, November 24, 1978.

26. Guy Sacerdoti, "Plight of the 'Ship of Gold,'" *FEER*, November 24, 1978.

27. Robinson, *Terms of Refuge*, pp. 39–45; K. Das, "Answer to a Desperate Plea," *FEER*, December 8, 1978.

28. For a more in-depth analysis of Southeast Asian–U.S. diplomacy, see Wen-Qing Ngoei, "'A Wide Anticommunist Arc': Britain, ASEAN, and Nixon's Triangular Diplomacy," *Diplomatic History* 41, no. 5 (November 2017): 903–32. Also see Zakaria Haji Ahmad, "Vietnamese Refugees and ASEAN," *Contemporary Southeast Asia* 1 no. 1 (May 1979); Wen-Qing Ngoei, *Arc of Containment: Britain, the United States, and Anti-Communism in Southeast Asia* (Ithaca, NY: Cornell University Press, 2019).

29. "Borderline Security," *FEER*, June 1, 1979.

30. K. Das, "Refugees: Rocking ASEAN's Boat," *FEER*, June 15, 1979.

31. Alias Jawawi, Letter to the Editor, *FEER*, January 19, 1979.

32. "Ghazali: Emergency Rules Needed to Prevent Red Threat," *NST*, June 30, 1979.

33. Letter translated from the Chinese. Letter from Mr. Lau Kim Huat for Tran Thanh Du to "Those Responsible for Broadcasts," September 5, 1977, UNHCR Fonds 11, Series 2, 100.MLS.SRV Vietnamese Refugees to Malaysia 1976–78, Vol. 2, Box 128.

34. Yahaya Ismail, "Dari Vietnam Tanpa Cinta: Masalah Pendatang Haram" (From Vietnam without love: The problems of illegal immigrants), *Mastika,* January 1979, trans. Carlson Chew Yee Herng. Also see Yahaya Ismail, *Masalah Pendatang Haram Vietnam* (Vietnam: Illegal immigrant problems), trans. Carlson Chew Yee Herng (Kuala Lumpur: Dinamika Kreatif, 1979).

35. "How Tough?" *NST*, June 6, 1979.

36. Halinah Bamadhaj, "Unwanted Guests in a Once Tranquil Society," *NST,* May 17, 1979; "Missing Viets Left Malaysia for Good," *NST,* May 23, 1979.

37. *Lari Dari Naraka Komunis* (Running from the communist hell), Malaysian Information Department, Za'ba Memorial Library, University of Malaya, May 1979, trans. Choong Pui Yee.

38. Khalid Mohd, "Pelarian Vietnam: Pemindahan, Terlalu Lembab" (Vietnamese refugees: Slow evacuation), *Mastika,* August, 1979, trans. Carlson Chew Yee Herng.

39. Ismail, "Dari Vietnam Tanpa Cinta: Masalah Pendatang Haram," and *Masalah Pendatang Haram Vietnam,* pp. 84–85.

40. "Xuezhou mahua lianweihui tongguo yijuean qianglie qianze yuenan zhengquan kongbu zhongzu miejue xingjing" (MCA condemns ethnic cleansing), *China Press,* June 21, 1979, trans. Carlson Chew Yee Herng; "The Source of the Problem: Refugees," *Sin Chew Jit Poh,* June 18, 1979, trans. Choong Pui Yee.

41. Ismail, *Masalah Pendatang Haram Vietnam,* pp. 84–85.

42. "Lim Kit Siang Calls on UN to Host Debate on How Vietnamese Are Causing Insecurities in Southeast Asia," *China Press,* June 12, 1979, trans. Carlson Chew Yee Herng.

43. "Lilintai xiwang zhengfu yanjiu yuenan minjian wenti genyuan niding chu youxiao duice" (Lee Lam Thye wishes the government could research the root cause of the Vietnamese refugee problem and work out countermeasures), *China Press,* June 19, 1979, trans. Carlson Chew Yee Herng.

44. "Lim Kit Siang Requests the Government Stop Pushing Away Refugee Boats," *Sin Chew Jit Poh,* August 3, 1979, trans. Choong Pui Yee.

45. Don Thu Nguyen, "Reminiscences," in Carina Hoang, *Boat People,* pp. 38–39.

46. Hai Au, "Goodbye An Min," in Carina Hoang, *Boat People,* pp. 90–91.

47. Jean Luc, "Fire," in Carina Hoang, *Boat People,* p. 112.

48. Miss Yee, "Unforgettable Voyage," in Lesleyanne Hawthorne, ed., *Refugee: The Vietnamese Experience* (Melbourne: Oxford University Press, 1982), pp. 243–45.

49. For more on compassion and refugee politics, see Vong, "'Compassion Gave Us a Special Superpower,'" and Pangilinan, "Screening Subjects."

50. Tran T. D., in Hawthorne, *Refuge,* pp. 263–69.

51. Robinson, *Terms of Refuge,* p. 54.

52. "$45m for Refugees," *NST,* April 8, 1979.

53. Julie Forsythe and Tom Hoskins, "Visit to Pulau Bidong Refugee Camp," May 1979, American Friends Service Committee pamphlet; Kamaruddin Abdul Rahman, "Trengganu to Produce 30,000 Barrels of Crude Oil a Day," *NST,* December 28, 1977; "1.5 Billion Oil Project," *NST,* May 25, 1979; "Five Oil Projects for Trengganu," *NST,* March 5, 1979.

54. K. Das, "An Accidental Deterrent," *FEER,* April 27, 1979.

55. Forsythe and Hoskins, "Visit to Pulau Bidong."

56. U.S. Office of Refugees, Kuala Lumpur, to Secretary of State, Health Factors in Malaysian Boat Refugee Camps, October 23, 1979, document requested under Freedom of Information Act (hereafter FOIA); U.S. Embassy, Kuala Lumpur, to Secretary of State, Indochinese Boat Refugees in Malaysia, Pulau Bidong Camp, November 24, 1978, FOIA documents. All FOIA documents are in the author's possession.

57. "Refugees Are Reluctant to Help Themselves," *Sabah Times,* May 29, 1979.

58. "'Ratman' of Pulau Bidong," *Malaysian Red Crescent Society Newsletter,* 1980–1981, National Archives of Malaysia, No. 2007/0020104.

59. K. Das and Guy Sacerdoti, "Digging In for a Long Stay," *FEER,* December, 22, 1978.

60. Thuy Trang Lai, "To See My Mother Again," in Carina Hoang, *Boat People,* pp. 42–43.

61. Oral history of Thai Quoc Ha by Thuy Vo Dang, VAOHP, 2012, http://ucispace.lib.uci.edu/handle/10575/13300 (accessed March 6, 2018). Also see oral history of Huy Bui by Khang Ngueyn, VAOHP, 2012, http://ucispace.lib.uci.edu/bitstream/handle/10575/5886/vaohp0092_f01.pdf?sequence=2 (accessed March 6, 2018).

62. New Year Greeting from the Vietnamese Refugee Committee on Pulau Bidong to Malaysian Red Crescent Society, December 1981, National Archives of Malaysia, No. 2013/0017451.

63. Hunt Janin, "The Few Helping the Many: A Case Study of the Malaysian Red Crescent Society and the Vietnamese Boat People," unpublished paper, June 12, 1991, National Archives of Malaysia, 1997/0001893W; Karen Martha Low, "The Vietnamese Boat People: An Academic Study" (law thesis, University of Malaya, 1983–84).

64. "Plan to Curb Local Purchase for the Viets," *NST,* June 2, 1979; "Viets Blamed for Rise in Beef Price," *NST,* June 1, 1979.

65. "Lure of Black Market Trade with Viets at Pulau Bidong," *NST,* March 7, 1979.

66. "Boat People May Disrupt Trengganu Umno Position," *NST,* July 6, 1979.

67. Halinah Bamadhaj, "Unwanted Guests in a Once Tranquil Society," *NST,* May 17, 1979.

68. Freeman, *Hearts of Sorrow,* pp. 317–19.

69. Hawthorne, *Refugee,* pp. 263–69.

70. Loescher, *The UNHCR and World Politics,* p. 194.

71. This period also saw several private initiatives, particularly "mercy ships," which went to sea to rescue Vietnamese in the waters between Thailand, Malaysia, and Singapore. The most famous were the *Cap Anamur* and the *Ile de Lumière.* See Robinson, *Terms of Refuge,* p. 167.

72. 1979 Report on UNHCR Activities, Regional Office for Eastern South Asia, UNHCR Fonds 11, Series 2, 110.MLS Programming Malaysia 1976–80, Vol. 1, Box 289.

73. High Commissioner Opening Statement, November 12, 1978, UNHCR Fonds 11, Series 2, 391.39 Consultation with Governments on Indochinese Refugees 1978, Vol. 3, Box 595. Also see Note for the File, P. Von Gunten, Head Kuala Trengganu Sub Office, October 16, 1978, UNHCR Fonds 11, Series 2, 100.MLS.SRV Refugees from SRV to Malaysia 1978–79, Vol. 3, Box 128.

74. From Secretary of State, Subject: Demarche to GOM on Conditions at Pulau Bidong, December 1, 1978, FOIA documents.

75. U.S. Embassy, Subject: UNHCR Operations on Malaysian Coast, October 16, 1978, FOIA documents. For another example of the UNHCR's thinness on the ground, see U.S. Embassy, Subject: Situation on Pulau Bidong, December 29, 1978, FOIA documents.

76. Han Hai Van, in Hawthorne, *Refugee,* pp. 270–71.

77. Malaysian Red Crescent Society, Annual Report, 1981, No. 2007/0020008; Appreciation Letter from Vietnamese Refugee to Mr. Lim Meng Ah (MRCS Staff), No. 2013/0017489; Letter of Gratitude from Vietnamese Refugee to MRCS, No. 2013/0017465, all in the National Archives of Malaysia. In the intervening years, Vietnamese Americans, Australians, and Canadians have returned to Malaysia and erected monuments and memorials thanking Malaysia and the MRCS. Also see Quan Tue Tran, "Remembering the Boat People Exodus."

78. Ahmad, "Vietnamese Refugees and ASEAN," p. 69.

79. Edward C. Burks, "Hamilton Fish Sees No End to Vietnamese Refugees," *New York Times,* March 11, 1979; on congressional engagement with Vietnamese refugees and resettlement, see Demmer, "Last Chapter."

80. Bon Tempo, *Americans at the Gate,* pp. 160–62.

81. Cable, Kelly, UNHCR, March 19, 1979, UNHCR Fonds 11, Series 2, 100. MLS.SRV Refugees from SRV to Malaysia 1978–79, Vol. 3, Box 128; Holtzman, A Report on My Trip to Southeast Asia, Holtzman Papers, Folder 10.97.

82. Cable, UNHCR, March 19, 1979, UNHCR Fonds 11, Series 2, 100.MLS. SRV Refugees from SRV to Malaysia 1978–79, Vol. 3, Box 128; Holtzman, A Report on My Trip to Southeast Asia, Holtzman Papers, Folder 10.97; Holtzman, Talking points for the American Friends Service Committee, May 11, 1979, Holtzman Papers, Folder 10.35 [Speech re: refugee policy].

83. Statement by the Hon. Elizabeth Holtzman at the UNHCR Consultation on Indochinese Refugees, December 11–12, 1978, Holtzman Papers, Folder 9.92.

84. U.S. Embassy in Kuala Lumpur, Subject: Pulau Bidong, December 22, 1978, FOIA documents.

85. Sucheng Chan, *Vietnamese American 1.5 Generation,* pp. 68–69; U.S. Comptroller General, The Indochinese Exodus: A Humanitarian Dilemma, April 24, 1979, p. 49, Holtzman Papers, Folder 155.16 [Refugee bill: hearings], June 27, 1979.

86. Sucheng Chan, *Vietnamese American 1.5 Generation,* pp. 68–69.

87. U.S. Comptroller General, The Indochinese Exodus: A Humanitarian Dilemma, April 24, 1979, p. 55–56, Holtzman Papers, Folder 155.16 [Refugee bill: hearings], June 27, 1979. Also see Larry Clinton Thompson, *Refugee Workers,* pp. 158–59.

88. U.S. Comptroller General, The Indochinese Exodus: A Humanitarian Dilemma, April 24, 1979, pp. 50–51, Holtzman Papers, Folder 155.16 [Refugee bill: hearings], June 27, 1979.

89. U.S. Embassy, Kuala Lumpur, Subject: Indochinese Boat Refugees Malaysia, November 15, 1978, FOIA documents.

90. "Illegal Immigrants: Tolerance Wearing Thin," *Daily Express* (Sabah), June 13, 1979.

91. "UN Conference on Indo-Chinese 'Refugees,'" *Sabah Times,* December 9, 1978.

92. UNHCR Report, June 12, 1979, UNHCR Fonds 11, Series 2, 100.MLS.SRV Refugees from SRV to Malaysia 1978–79, Vol. 3, Box 128.

93. "The Exodus and the Agony," *FEER,* December 22, 1978.

94. "All Viet Boats Checked," *Sabah Times,* March 20, 1979.

95. "Ghaz: Still More than 50,000 Vietnamese Here," *Sabah Times,* April 6, 1979.

96. Davies, *Legitimising Rejection,* pp. 143–47.

97. Thomas McKenna, *Muslim Rulers and Rebels: Everyday Politics and Armed Separatism in the Southern Philippines* (Berkeley: University of California Press, 1998), pp. 156, 182–86; I. K. Khan, *Islam in Modern Asia* (New Delhi: MD Publications, 2006). For analysis of Philippine regional politics and state-building, see Patricio N. Abinales, *Making Mindanao: Cotabato and Davao in the Formation of the Philippine Nation-State* (Manila: Ateneo de Manila University Press, 2000).

98. "$3.6 Million in Aid for Filipino Refugees in Sabah," *NST,* September 19, 1977; Report on UNHCR Activities in 1979, Malaysia, UNHCR Fonds 11, Series 2, 110.MLS Programming Malaysia 1976–80, Vol. 1, Box 289.

99. S. Sothi Rachagan, "Refugees and Illegal Immigrants: The Malaysian Experience with Filipino and Vietnamese Refugees," in *Refugees: A Third World Dilemma,* ed. John R. Rogge (Totowa, NJ: Rowman & Littlefield, 1987), pp. 253–68. Also see Azizah Kassim, "Filipino Responses in Sabah: State Responses, Public Stereotypes, and the Dilemma over their Future," *Southeast Asian Studies* 47, no. 1 (June 2009). This led to far more controversial polices in the twenty-first century, as opposition leaders challenged that Filipinos illegally gained Malaysian identity cards and voting rights. See Andrew Carruthers, "Sabah ICs for Sabahans: Will It Help?" ISEAS Yusof Ishak Institute *Perspective,* no. 11 (March 2016), www.iseas .edu.sg/images/pdf/ISEAS_Perspective_2016_11.pdf (accessed January 24, 2019).

100. Consultative Meeting with Interested Governments on Refugees and Displaced Persons in Southeast Asia, Geneva, 11–12 December 1978, Draft Summary Report, Issued December 19, 1979, UNHCR Fonds 11, Series 2, 391.39 Consultations with Governments on Indochinese Refugees, 1979, Vol. 4, Box 596.

101. News and Views by Malaysian Embassy in Bangkok, January 16, 1979, UNHCR Fonds 11, Series 2, 100.MLS.SRV Refugees from SRV to Malaysia 1978–79, Vol. 3, Box 128.

102. Margaret Thatcher, June 17, 1979, UNHCR Fonds 11, Series 2, 391.46 International Conference on Indochina, 1979, ICE-JAP, Box 599.

103. Robinson, *Terms of Refuge,* pp. 50–54; Sucheng Chan, *Vietnamese American 1.5 Generation,* pp. 81–82.

104. Cheong Mei Sui, "Let's Have Deal First—Ghazali," *NST,* July 11, 1979.

105. "Why Refugee Camps Are Packed: Ghaz," *NST,* July 15, 1979.

106. "They'll Do Anything to Gain Sympathy: Ghaz," *NST,* July 16, 1979.

107. "Geneva Gains," *NST,* July 23, 1979.

108. Kumin, "Orderly Departure from Vietnam." For more analysis of the Orderly Departure Program and normalization between the United States and Vietnam, see Demmer, "Last Chapter."

109. All told, resettlement countries offered 260,000 spaces for 372,000 people waiting in camps throughout Southeast Asia. Sucheng Chan, *Vietnamese American Generation 1.5,* p. 81.

110. Robinson, *Terms of Refuge,* pp. 52–58.

111. Demmer, "Last Chapter"; Bradley, *The World Reimagined,* pp. 163–64. Bradley points to the 1970s as a watershed for "holocaust memory" being used to inform American conceptions of human rights.

112. Quoted in Robinson, *Terms of Refuge,* p. 53.

113. Menachem Begin, June 19, 1979, UNHCR Fonds 11, Series 2, 391.46 International Conference on Indochina, 1979, Vol. 1, Box 597.

114. Relations with the Palestine Liberation Organization, July 19, 1979, UNHCR Fonds 11, Series 2, 391.46 International Conference on Indochina, 1979, Vol. 4, Box 597.

115. For a more in-depth critique of Vietnamese resettlement and Israeli-Palestinian politics and refugees, see Evyn Le Espiritu, "Archipelago of Resettlement: Vietnamese Refugee Settlers in Guam and Israel-Palestine" (PhD diss., University of California, Berkeley, 2018); "Vexed Solidarities: Vietnamese Israelis and the Question of Palestine," *LIT: Literature Interpretation Theory* 29, no. 1 (2018): 8–28.

116. Alex Oon, Singapore, "Letter to the Editor: An Island of Hope," *FEER,* July 6, 1979.

117. Letter from Free Vietnamese Community in Hawaii, December 10, 1978, UNHCR Fonds 11, Series 2, 391.39 Consultations with Governments on Indochinese Refugees 1978, Vol. 3, Box 595.

118. Letter, January 25, 1979, UNHCR Fonds 11, Series 2, 391.39 Consultations with Governments on Indochinese Refugees 1978, Vol. 4, Box 596. Translation by author.

119. Letter from Vietnamese Groups of Orange County to UNHCR, July 20, 1979, UNHCR Fonds 11, Series 2, 391.46 International Conference on Indochina, 1979, Vol. 4, Box 597.

120. Open Letter to the Socialist Republic of Vietnam, UNHCR Fonds 11, Series 2, 391.46 International Conference on Indochina, 1979, Vol. 2, Box 597. Also see Larry Clinton Thompson, *Refugee Workers,* pp. 146–48. Thompson describes the debate among anti-war activists about whether or not to condemn the new socialist Vietnamese government, but he does not note the hundreds of unpublished Vietnamese American signatures added to the letter in an appeal to the UNHCR.

121. Open Letter to the International Conference on Indochinese Refugees, July 12, 1979 (Portland), UNHCR Fonds 11, Series 2, 391.46 International Conference on Indochina, 1979, Vol. 2.

122. IRAC's name would change multiple times, from Indochina Refugee Action Center to Indochina Resource Action Center and finally to Southeast Asia Resource Action Center (SEARAC).

123. Le Xuan Khoa, "The Voice of Refugees: The Story of a Refugee Organization," presented at the Library of Congress, May 2, 2009; telephone interview with Le Xuan Khoa, September 7, 2018.

124. Le Xuan Khoa interview, September 7, 2018.

125. Ralph Frammolino, "Vietnamese Contributions: $40,000 Is Donated to Help Boat People," *Los Angeles Times,* April 2, 1986.

126. Sulochini Nair, "Question of First Asylum Does Not Arise for Malaysia," *NST,* July 10, 1979.

127. Notably, Japan became the largest financial donor to the UNHCR for this program. Ayako Sahara argues that through these donations Japan became an "honorary white member in the international community." Sahara, "Globalized Humanitarianism," pp. 201–61.

128. Sucheng Chan, *Vietnamese American 1.5 Generation,* pp. 82–84; Hataipreuk Rkasnuam and Jeanne Batalova, "Vietnamese Immigrants in the United States," Migration Policy Institute, August 25, 2014, www.migrationpolicy.org/article /vietnamese-immigrants-united-states-2 (accessed August 24, 2019).

129. Bon Tempo, *Americans at the Gate,* pp. 173–79.

130. "Geneva Gains," *NST,* July 23, 1979.

CHAPTER 3. A MODEL CAMP

1. Mario A. Hernando, "Refugees in Bataan: New Breed, New Problems, New Prospects," *Malaya,* June 9, 1991.

2. Of the close to 400,000 Southeast Asians who transited through the PRPC over fifteen years, only a few hundred became "long-stayers." This was generally due to violent crimes committed within the camp, medical holds, or charges of communist affiliation. A small cohort of these unsettled Vietnamese were then transferred to the Palawan First Asylum Camp. For examples, see U.S. Embassy Manila to State Department, "Long-Staying Refugees in the PRPC: Statistical Analyses and Summaries," September 22, 1986, FOIA documents.

3. The majority of Southeast Asians at the PRPC were Vietnamese; however, there were sizeable populations of Laotians and Cambodians. The camp generally referred to all of them as "Indochinese," but I have opted for Southeast Asian, which is the more contemporary usage. In 1988, Adelaida Reyes placed the population at approximately 75 percent Vietnamese and 25 percent Laotian, Cambodian, and other Southeast Asian identities (Adelaida Reyes, *Songs of the Caged, Songs of the Free: Music and the Vietnamese Refugee Experience* [Philadelphia: Temple University Press, 1999], pp. 41–44). By 1991, the total numbers more or less matched Reyes's earlier assessments, with 194,000 Vietnamese, 70,000 Cambodians, and 40,000 Laotians (Hernando, "Refugees in Bataan"). After 1991, the Vietnamese were disproportionately Vietnamese Amerasians. This chapter focuses only on the Vietnamese experiences in the camps, and there is significant work to be done on the experiences of other Southeast Asian communities at the PRPC.

4. A large number of studies were conducted about the PRPC during the 1980s. The strongest works are John Chr. Knudsen, *Boat People in Transit: Vietnamese in Refugee Camps in the Philippines, Hongkong, and Japan* (Bergen: University of

Bergen, 1983); John Chr. Knudsen, *Vietnamese Survivors: Processing Involved in Refugee Coping and Adaptation* (Bergen: University of Bergen, 1988); James W. Tollefson, *Alien Winds: The Reeducation of America's Indochinese Refugees* (New York: Praeger, 1989); Reyes, *Songs of the Caged,* pp. 41–75; Yến Lê Espiritu, *Body Counts,* pp. 58–60. Also see Carol A. Mortland, "Transforming Refugees in Refugee Camps," *Urban Anthropology and Studies of Cultural Systems and World Economic Development* 16, no. 3/4 (1987): 375–404; Vance Geiger, "Southeast Asian Refugees in the Philippine Refugee Processing Center" (PhD diss., University of Florida, 1994); Emmanuel N. Santos, "Cultural Transformation in a Total Institution: The Philippine Refugee Processing Center (PRPC) Refugees" (master's thesis, University of Ateneo de Manila, 1990). On Vietnamese Amerasians at the PRPC, see DeBonis, *Children of the Enemy.*

5. Roughly 90 percent of Vietnamese at the PRPC resettled in the United States, with the remaining 10 percent resettling in Norway, Canada, Great Britain, Germany, Australia, or another country. For the best works on Vietnamese resettlement in Norway, see the work of John Christian Knudsen.

6. Mortland, "Transforming Refugees"; Santos, "Cultural Transformation."

7. Demmer, "Last Chapter," pp. 152–53.

8. "The Philippine Refugee Processing Center," pamphlet, 1980, p. 1 (Cornell University Library holding).

9. Simeon Man, *Soldiering through Empire* (Oakland: University of California Press, 2018), pp. 49–76.

10. Pangilinan, "Screening Subjects," p. 20.

11. "The Philippine Refugee Processing Center," pamphlet, 1980, p. 1.

12. Draft of Secretary General's Report on Geneva Southeast Asian Refugee Meeting, October 19, 1979, UNHCR Fonds 11, Series 2, 391.46, International Conference on Indochina, 1979, Vol. 5, Box 598; Deputy High Commissioner's Mission to South East Asia, April 9, 1979, UNHCR Fonds 11, Series 2, 391.39, International Conference on Indochina, 1979, Vol. 5, Box 596.

13. Robinson, *Terms of Refuge,* p. 294.

14. David F. Schmitz, *The United States and Right-Wing Dictatorships, 1965–1989* (Cambridge: Cambridge University Press, 2006), pp. 230–40.

15. Mark R. Thompson, *The Anti-Marcos Struggle: Personalistic Rule and Democratic Transition in the Philippines* (New Haven, CT: Yale University Press, 1995), pp. 35–37, 42.

16. James B. Goodno, *The Philippines: Land of Broken Promises* (London: Zed Books, 1991), pp. 50–65; Stanley Karnow, *In Our Image: America's Empire in the Philippines* (New York: Ballantine Books, 1989), pp. 356–88.

17. Karnow, *In Our Image,* p. 381; Goodno, *The Philippines,* p. 67.

18. Jose V. Fuentecilla, *Fighting from a Distance: How Filipino Exiles Helped Topple a Dictator* (Urbana: University of Illinois Press, 2013), pp. 51–53; Schmitz, *The United States and Right-Wing Dictatorships,* pp. 230–40.

19. Goodno, *The Philippines,* pp. 73, 76.

20. Also see Pangilinan, "Screening Subjects," pp. 37, 44.

21. Keys, *Reclaiming American Virtue,* p. 157. On the distinctions between human rights and humanitarianism, also see Lipman, "'A Precedent Worth Setting.'"

22. U.S. Embassy Manila to State Department, Second Anniversary of the PRPC, January 23, 1982, FOIA documents.

23. Report on UNHCR BO Manila Activities in 1982–83, Programme for 1983–84, UNHCR Fonds 11, Series 2, 110.PHI Programming, Philippines, 1982–83, Vol. 5, Box 300.

24. Also see Imelda Marcos's 2017 website listing the PRPC among her accomplishments: http://imelda.mybcnet.net/?p=3339 (accessed July 21, 2017).

25. Man, *Soldiering through Empire.*

26. For an analysis of Tobias's service in Vietnam, see Matthew Jagel, "'Showing Its Flag': The United States, the Philippines, and the Vietnam War," University of Toronto Department of History, *Past Tense: Graduate Review of History* 2 (2013): 18–41, https://pasttensejournal.files.wordpress.com/2016/05/jagel-showing-its-flag .pdf (accessed July 21, 2017).

27. Karnow, *In Our Image,* pp. 376–77.

28. Miguel A. Bernad, "The First Year of the PhilCag in Vietnam," *Philippines Studies* 16, no. 1 (1968): 131–54.

29. Pope John Paul II Memorial, PRPC, Bataan, March 2015, personal photograph. After 1995, the PRPC was transformed into the Bataan Technology Park, and a large memorial was built to honor Pope John Paul's visit.

30. World Refugee Report to the U.S. Congress, Fiscal Year 1984, Cable from Manila, May 25, 1984, FOIA documents.

31. J. K. Fasick, "Construction and Operation of the Refugee Processing Center in Bataan, the Philippines," GAO Office, February 6, 1981, www.gao.gov/products /ID-81-27 (accessed June 9, 2015).

32. Scholar Ayako Sahara argues that the United States essentially outsourced a portion of the burden of its resettlement program onto the Philippines. Sahara, "Globalized Humanitarianism," pp. 154–200.

33. "Reports on Refugee Aid: U.N. High Commissioner for Refugees, Refugees in Somalia, Refugees in Pakistan, Bataan Refugee Processing Center—Reports of Staff Study Missions to the Committee on Foreign Affairs," U.S. House of Representatives, March 1981; Fasick, "Construction and Operation of the Refugee Processing Center in Bataan, the Philippines," GAO Office, February 6, 1981, www.gao.gov /products/ID-81-27 (accessed June 9, 2015).

34. UNHCR Manila, August 31, 1979, Cable, UNHCR Fonds 11, Series 2, 100. PHI.SRV Refugees from SRV to PHI, 1976–84, Vol. 4, Box 159.

35. G. V. Tobias to UNHCR, October 23, 1980, UNHCR Fonds 11, Series 3, 010. PHI, Folder A—External Relations with Governments, Philippines.

36. Visit of California State Joint Legislative Committee on Refugees, December 5, 1983, FOIA documents.

37. Draft Report of Secretary General's Report on Geneva Southeast Asian Refugee Meeting, October 19, 1979, UNHCR Fonds 11, Series 2, 391.46 International Conference on Indochina, 1979, Vol. 5, Box 598.

38. Report on Branch Office Manila Activities in 1982–83 and Programme for 1983–84, UNHCR Fonds 11, Series 2, 110.PHI Programming, Philippines, 1982–83, Vol. 5.

39. UNHCR Activities during 1981 in the Philippines Report on Protection, UNHCR Fonds 11, Series 2, 110.PHI Programming, Philippines, 1981–82, Vol. 3, Box 300.

40. Report on UNHCR, Branch Office Manila Activities in 1982–83 and Programme for 1983–84, UNHCR Fonds 11, Series 2, 110.PHI Programming, Philippines, 1982–83, Vol. 5.

41. Steve Lohr, "At Camp 'Hilton,' Vietnamese Learn Ways of U.S.," *New York Times,* September 22, 1984.

42. UNHCR Background and Briefing on PRPC, Morong, Bataan, June 10, 1986, UNHCR Fonds 11, Series 3, 010.PHI, Folder A—External Relations with Governments, Philippines.

43. UNHCR Background and Briefing on PRPC, Morong, Bataan, June 10, 1986, UNHCR Fonds 11, Series 3, 010.PHI, Folder A—External Relations with Governments, Philippines.

44. UNHCR Background and Briefing on PRPC, Morong, Bataan, June 10, 1986, UNHCR Fonds 11, Series 3, 010.PHI, Folder A—External Relations with Governments, Philippines.

45. Vance Geiger's 1994 dissertation recounts a "riot" in 1989 due to a market fight between a Vietnamese Amerasian man and a Filipino, but this seems to be more of an exception than the rule. In addition, the increased number of unaccompanied young Amerasians after 1988 led to greater instability and violence within the PRPC, but this rarely manifested itself as explicitly political protest, as it would in Hong Kong and other first-asylum camps after 1989.

46. Chandler Burr, "Where Asian Refugees Learn the Basics of Daily Life in the U.S.," *Christian Science Monitor,* October 28, 1987.

47. 1980 PRPC Planning Manual, Community Family Services International files, Manila, Philippines.

48. Tollefson, *Alien Winds;* Mortland, "Transforming Refugees"; Geiger, "Southeast Asian Refugees"; and Santos, "Cultural Transformation."

49. This, however, was not the case for Vietnamese Amerasians who came directly from Vietnam and often had traumatic experiences at the PRPC; see DeBonis, *Children of the Enemy.* Most Amerasians arrived at the PRPC after 1988.

50. Oral history of Paul Chi Hoang by Daisy Herrera Duran, VAOHP, 2012, http://ucispace.lib.uci.edu/handle/10575/5910 (accessed July 24, 2017).

51. Cargill and Huynh, *Voices of Vietnamese Boat People,* p. 97.

52. Cargill and Huynh, *Voices of Vietnamese Boat People,* p. 141.

53. Personal photograph, PRPC, Philippines, 2015.

54. Oral history of Hoang Dai Hai by Thuy Vo Dang, VAOHP, 2013, http://ucispace.lib.uci.edu/handle/10575/11410 (accessed July 24, 2017).

55. Knudsen, *Boat People in Transit,* pp. 165, 174.

56. For a creative short film on the PRPC and memory, see Evyn Le Espiritu, dir., *Where Is the Spirit of the Vietnamese People?* https://vimeo.com/131453166 (accessed October 13, 2017).

57. Joanna C. Scott, *Indochina's Refugees: Oral Histories from Laos, Cambodia, and Vietnam* (Jefferson, NC: McFarland, 1989), p. 72.

58. Scott, *Indochinese Refugees,* pp. 93–94.

59. Fasick, "Construction and Operation of the Refugee Processing Center in Bataan, the Philippines," GAO Office, February 6, 1981, www.gao.gov/products /ID-81-27 (accessed June 9, 2015).

60. Tollefson, *Alien Winds,* p. 3.

61. Interview with Gene Boggs, March 5, 2015, Manila; Tollefson, *Alien Winds,* p. 95.

62. Tollefson, *Alien Winds,* p. 89.

63. There is an extensive popular literature on the Battle of Bataan and the Bataan Death March. For a brief overview, see Karnow, *In Our Image,* pp. 291–305. For a critique of American memorialization and the erasure of U.S. colonial history in the Philippines, see Vernadette Vicuña Gonzalez, *Securing Paradise: Tourism and Militarism in Hawai'i and the Philippines* (Durham, NC: Duke University Press, 2013), pp. 83–114.

64. Karnow, *In Our Image,* pp. 330–32.

65. Gonzalez, *Securing Paradise,* p. 84.

66. Folder Bataan 1970 Census of Population and Housing, Republic of the Philippines, Department of Commerce and Industry, Local History (Vertical Files), Region III Bataan, Filipianas Collection, University of the Philippines.

67. Simeon Man, "The GI Movement in the Third World," in *The Rising Tide of Color: Race, State Violence, and Radical Movements across the Pacific,* ed. Moon-Ho Jung (Seattle: University of Washington Press, 2015), pp. 281–88; Man, *Soldiering through Empire.*

68. Boggs interview, March 5, 2015.

69. The Philippine government would later convert Subic Bay into a free-trade zone as part of the 1992 Bases Conversion Act, demonstrating the somewhat unnerving interchangeability of militarized zones and free-trade zones. On the similar conversion of Clark Air Force Base, see Vernadette Vicuña Gonzalez, "Military Bases, 'Royalty Trips,' and Imperial Modernities: Gendered and Racialized Labor in the Postcolonial Philippines," *Frontiers: A Journal of Women's Studies* 28 (2007).

70. Peter C. Warr, "Export Processing Zones: The Economics of Enclave Manufacturing," *Research Observer* 4 (January 1989): 70–71.

71. "Tax Collection in BEPZ—P1.5 M," *Bataan Zone Newsletter,* September 1, 1975, University of the Philippines Library.

72. Karnow, *In Our Image,* p. 383.

73. "Explosive Nuke Report out Monday—Saguisag," *Malaya,* June 28, 1986; "Losses from Nuke Plant," *Philippine Daily Express,* May 9, 1985. In this article, the

cost of $355,000 per day covers the daily operation, not just the interest rate. Both articles located in City Library of Balanga, News Clippings, File "Power Resources" and "BNPP."

74. National Organization against Nuclear Power and Weapons, "'No Nukes' Refutes Westinghouse, Plant Safety Issues Skirted," *Malaya,* July 14, 1986, City Library of Balanga, News Clippings, File "Power Resources."

75. Karnow, *In Our Image,* p. 383. In addition, see "Westinghouse Burns Nuke Plant Papers," *Manila Times,* June 29, 1986, City Library of Balanga, News Clippings, File "BNPP": "Westinghouse, the contractor of the controversial Bataan Nuclear Plant, allegedly destroyed important documents to hide the possible involvement of deposed President Marcos in the shady transaction, foreign reports reaching the *Manila Times* said yesterday.... Earlier reports said Marcos had earned no less than $80 million in payoff from the Westinghouse sale."

76. Zeny Morato, "Anti-Nuke Rally Held," *Bataan Star,* August 1–7, 1984. Issues of the *Bataan Star* are housed at the University of the Philippines Library.

77. Zeny Morato, "Anti-Nuke Rally Held," *Bataan Star,* August 1–7, 1984.

78. "Stop Nuclear Power Plant, FM Asked," *Bataan Star,* October 31–November 6, 1984.

79. After much searching in Balanga, Morong, and Manila, I was able to find only eight weeks of the *Bataan Star* on microfilm at the University of the Philippines. In these issues there were numerous articles about the nuclear power plant and only one about the PRPC. Moreover, in none of the UNHCR or U.S. government documents was the nuclear power plant ever mentioned.

80. The NPA was just one faction of the anti-Marcos left and represented a Maoist-inspired armed guerilla unit. Anti-Marcos activists also included a large urban movement, both communist-affiliated and socially democratic. In addition, there were ongoing conflicts between the Marcos government and Muslim separatists in the south; see Goodno, *The Philippines,* pp. 83–104. For diasporic anti-Marcos activism, see Fuentecilla, *Fighting from a Distance.*

81. Cable, February 16, 1987, UNHCR Fonds 11, Series 3, 010.PHI, Folder A—External Relations with Governments, Philippines.

82. Interview with Luwalhati (Lulu) Pablo, Manila, February 18, 2015.

83. There is a large literature on overseas Filipino workers and guest labor programs. For a sampling, see Catherine Ceniza Choy, *Empire of Care: Nursing and Migration in Filipino American History* (Durham, NC: Duke University Press, 2003); Rhacel Parrenas, *Servants of Globalization: Migration and Domestic Work* (Stanford, CA: Stanford University Press, 2015); Nicole Constable, *Maid to Order: An Ethnography of Filipina Workers* (Ithaca, NY: Cornell University Press, 1997); Ruri Ito, "Negotiating Partial Citizenship under Neoliberalism: Regularization Struggles among Filipino Domestic Workers in France (2008–2012)," *International Journal of Japanese Sociology* 25, no.1 (2016): 69–84.

84. Maruja M. B. Asis, "The Philippines' Culture of Migration," Migration Policy Institute, January 1, 2006, www.migrationpolicy.org/article/philippines-culture-migration (accessed October 11, 2017).

85. Interview with Nida Magallanes, Manila, February 21, 2015.

86. Pablo interview, February 18, 2015.

87. Interview with Connie Acosta, Manila, February 21, 2015.

88. Interview with George Chiu, Manila, February 19, 2015.

89. Interview with Susan Quimpo, Manila, February 19, 2015. Also see Susan Quimpo and Nathan Quimpo, eds., *Subversive Lives: A Family Memoir of the Marcos Years* (Athens: Ohio University Press, 2016).

90. Quimpo interview, February 19, 2015.

91. Quimpo interview, February 19, 2015.

92. Toffelson, *Alien Winds;* also see *Passages: A Journal of Refugee Education,* produced by the Overseas Refugee Training Program and funded by the U.S. Department of State's Bureau of Refugee Services.

93. I found a treasure trove of former readers located in the Milwaukee Public Library, presumably placed there by a former PRPC English teacher, and in dusty boxes at the former PRPC itself. All the readers below were published by the International Catholic Migration Commission at the PRPC in Morong, Philippines.

94. For example, Linda Dumo, *The Star Apple Tree,* and Allan Blackstock, *Luu Binh and Duong Le.* All ICMC readers available at the Milwaukee Public Library in Wisconsin.

95. Sharon Snyder (author), Al Medilo (illustrator), *The Fourth of July.*

96. Srisuda Walsh (author), Bobbie M. Maralg III (illustrator), *Pocket Money.*

97. Alan Blackstock (author), Jonie Arroyo (illustrator), *Thao Gets a Haircut.*

98. Isabel Garcia with Cycle 119 Team (authors), Mario C. Hernandez (illustrator), *Who Is My Friend?*

99. Also see Murray Dubin, "Taking Action against Bigotry: Teen to Be Honored for Intervening in Attack," *Philadelphia Inquirer,* June 8, 1988.

100. Alan Blackstock (author), Bing Reynoso (illustrator), *Too Much Freedom.* Also see Mimi Thi Nguyen, *The Gift of Freedom.*

101. Tracy Wood, "Officer's Killer Gets Life without Parole," *Los Angeles Times,* April 5, 1988.

102. Quimpo interview, February 19, 2015.

103. G. V. Tobias to UNHCR, Philippine Position Paper Submitted to Minister Jose D. Ingles of the Philippine Ministry of Foreign Affairs, October 23, 1980, UNHCR Fonds 11, Series 3, 010.PHI, Folder A—External Relations with Governments, Philippines.

104. Letter from General Tobias to Gregg Beyer, UNHCR—July 15, 1985, UNHCR Fonds 11, Series 3, 010.PHI, Folder A—External Relations with Governments, Philippines.

105. Interview with Maria Teresa Alagón, Morong, February 23, 2015.

106. Quimpo, *Subversive Lives.* In this family memoir, Quimpo does not mention her time at the PRPC even once. The only discussions of refugees involve the struggles of Filipino radicals to gain asylum abroad.

107. Chiu interview, February 19, 2015.

108. Magallanes interview, February 21, 2015.

109. G. V. Tobias to Gregg Beyer, May 9, 1986, UNHCR Fonds 11, Series 3, 010. PHI, Folder A—External Relations with Governments, Philippines.

110. José G. Burgos Jr., "Tobias and the Refugees," *Malaya,* May 11, 1986.

111. Alagón interview, February 23, 2015.

112. Fuentecilla, *Fighting from a Distance,* pp. 9–10.

113. Raul Manglapus, "Refugees Need to Be Men and Women of Vision," *Manila Chronicle,* March 2, 1988, UNHCR Fonds 11, Series 3, 841.PHI Press Extracts and Clippings, Philippines.

114. Article on Refugees by Secretary for Foreign Affairs Raul S. Manglapus, from Pierce Gerety, Representative in the Philippines, March 2, 1988, UNHCR Fonds 11, Series 3, 841.PHI Press Extracts and Clippings, Philippines.

115. DeBonis, *Children of the Enemy;* Lipman, "'The Face is the Roadmap'"; Varzally, *Children of Reunion;* Sabrina Thomas, "The Value of Dust: Policy, Citizenship, and Vietnam's Amerasian Children" (PhD diss., Arizona State University, 2015); Kieu-Linh Caroline Valverde, "From Dust to Gold: The Vietnamese Amerasian Experience," in *Racially Mixed People in America,* ed. Maria P. P. Root (Newbury Park, CA: Sage, 1992), pp. 144–62; Demmer, "Last Chapter."

116. DeBonis, *Children of the Enemy.*

117. Interview with Y. Esguerra, Morong, February 23, 2015. Adelaida Reyes also analyzes the divisions between the ODP arrivals, who were generally more adept at navigating bureaucracies, and those who suffered in boat escapes and first-asylum camps, who were often more traumatized. Reyes, *Songs of the Caged,* pp. 52–55.

118. Reyes, *Songs of the Caged,* pp. 52–55.

119. Demmer, "Last Chapter."

120. Center for Applied Linguistics, Survey of the Pre-Arrival Training Needs of Former Political Prisoners from Vietnam, February 15, 1992, Item No. 1849138021000, Box 138, Folder 021, Families of Vietnamese Political Prisoners Association Collection, Vietnam Center and Archive, Texas Tech University (hereafter FVPPA Collection, Texas Tech) (accessed November 14, 2018). The Texas Tech Vietnam Center and Sam Johnson Vietnam Archive has an extensive online digital database that includes the records of the FVPPA and many other valuable collections. For this book, all citations for the FVPPA were located using the Virtual Vietnam Archive, https://vva.vietnam.ttu.edu.

121. FVPPA, Agenda for Meeting with Ann Morgan, Director of Training, Department of State, September 15, 1992, Item No. 1849138006000, Box 138, Folder 006, FVPPA Collection, Texas Tech (accessed November 14, 2018).

122. Khuc Minh Tho (FVPPA) to Sister Pascale (CADP), April 8, 1993, Item No. 1849138021000, Box 138, Folder 021, FVPPA Collection, Texas Tech (accessed November 14, 2018).

123. Sister Margarita Tran Binh (CADP) to Mrs. Khuc Minh Tho (FVPPA), September 16, 1992, Item No. 1849118036000, Box 118, Folder 036, FVPPA Collection, Texas Tech (accessed November 14, 2018).

124. "Behold Bataan," https://bataan.gov.ph/tourism/travel/bataan-technology-park (accessed November 13, 2018).

CHAPTER 4. HONG KONG

1. Barbara Basler, "Boat People Find Fewer and Fewer Safe Harbors," *New York Times,* June 19, 1988; Chan Kwok Bun, "Hong Kong's Response to the Vietnamese Refugees: A Study in Humanitarianism, Ambivalence, and Hostility," *Southeast Asian Journal of Social Science* 18, no. 1 (1990): 95.

2. Andrew McEwen, "UN Fears New Curb on Boat People Will Sink Vietnam Deal," *Times* (London), June 16, 1988, Press and TV/Radio Reports, Hong Kong Record Series (hereafter HKRS) 770–4-5. HKRS 770 is the Record Series for Files Relating to Vietnamese Refugees. All HKRS records are from the Public Records Office, Government Record Services, Government of Hong Kong Special Administrative Region.

3. Claudia Mo, "Bemused Boat People Miss Deadline of New Hong Kong Refugee Policy," ASI/AFP, June 16, 1988, Press and TV/Radio Reports, HKRS 770–4-5.

4. Up until the 1997 handover, white British officials filled high-level government positions within the Hong Kong government, while Hong Kong Chinese occupied many of the civil service positions. This was particularly true for the Security Branch, which oversaw the Vietnamese camps. Security was the last branch to appoint a Hong Kong Chinese, Peter Lai, to be its chief officer. The Hong Kong census only began enumerating "ethnic minorities," those with a non-Chinese ethnicity, in 2001. Minorities made up 5.1 percent of Hong Kong's population, with Filipinos and Indonesians (typically domestic guest workers) making up the bulk of this population. White British residents made up 5.5 percent (18,909) of this population, and white Americans and Canadians were 2.7 percent (9,334). All people of African descent (British, American, Canadian, etc.) were designated in a general "other" category. See 2001 Hong Kong census, Frederick W. H. Ho, Thematic Report, Ethnic Minorities, www.statistics.gov.hk/pub/B11200332001XXXXB0200 .pdf (accessed May 22, 2018).

5. Hong Kiu Yuen, "Proxy Humanitarianism: Hong Kong's Vietnamese Refugee Crisis" (master's thesis, University of Hong Kong, 2014). Also see Madokoro, *Elusive Refuge.*

6. Loyd and Mountz, *Boats, Borders, and Bases;* Jana K. Lipman, "'The Fish Trusts the Water, and It Is in the Water that It Is Cooked': The Caribbean Origins of the Krome Detention Center," *Radical History Review* 115 (2013): 115–41; Carl Lindskoog, *Detain and Punish: Haitian Refugees and the Rise of the World's Largest Immigration Detention System* (Gainesville: University of Florida Press, 2018).

7. IRAC changed its name from Indochina Refugee Action Center to Indochina Resource Action Center in 1983.

8. Yuk Wah Chan, "Revisiting the Vietnamese Refugee Era: An Asian Perspective from Hong Kong," in Yuk Wah Chan, ed., *The Chinese/Vietnamese Diaspora,* p. 10.

9. World Bank Data, Hong Kong and Singapore populations, Google, www .google.com/publicdata/explore?ds=d5bncppjof8f9_&met_y=sp_pop_totl&idim =country:HKG:SGP&hl=en&dl=en (accessed November 1, 2016).

10. Laura Madokoro's *Elusive Refuge* is the most comprehensive work on how refugee and humanitarian politics and discourses shaped Hong Kong from 1949 to 1975.

11. Yuk Wah Chan, "Revisiting the Vietnamese Refugee Era," pp. 3–19.

12. Chi-Kwan Mark, "The 'Problem of People': British Colonials, Cold War Powers, and Chinese Refugees in Hong Kong, 1949–1962," *Modern Asian Studies* 41, no. 6(2007): 1145–81; Glen Peterson, "To Be or Not to Be a Refugee: The International Politics of the Hong Kong Refugee Crisis, 1949–1955," *Journal of Imperial and Commonwealth History* 36, no. 2 (2008): 171–95; Chan Kwok Bun, "Hong Kong's Response," pp. 97–100. The U.S. also agreed to accept several thousand Chinese as refugees for the first time as part of the 1953 Refugee Relief Act, most of whom came through Hong Kong. This acted to ideologically "save" Chinese from the communist world. See Hsu, *The Good Immigrants;* Madokoro, *Elusive Refuge;* Oyen, *The Diplomacy of Migration,* pp. 154–84.

13. "Leaving Vietnam," 2010 Hong Kong Stories, Radio Television Hong Kong, Hong Kong University Library Media Services; Yuk Wah Chan, "Hybrid Diaspora and Identity-Laundering," pp. 525–41.

14. John M. Carroll, *A Concise History of Hong Kong* (Lanham, MD: Rowman & Littlefield, 2007), pp. 150–60.

15. Agnes Ku, "Immigration Policies, Discourses, and the Politics of Belonging in Hong Kong, 1950–1980," *Modern China* 30, no. 3 (July 2004): 326–60, 348.

16. Hong Kong, December 10, 1974, Foreign and Commonwealth Office (hereafter FCO) 21/1274, Illegal Immigration from China to Hong Kong. All FCO documents are from the British National Archives in London.

17. Control of Illegal Immigration from China, November 15, 1974, FCO 21/1273, Illegal Immigration from China to Hong Kong. Emphasis in original.

18. Hong Kong and Indian Ocean Department, Hong Kong: Parliamentary Questions by Robin Cook, MP, December 8, 1975, FCO 21/1420, Illegal Immigration from China to Hong Kong.

19. Record of Conversation between the Lord Goronwy-Roberts and the Governor of Hong Kong, July 29, 1974, FCO 21/1273, Illegal Immigration from China to Hong Kong.

20. Yến Lê Espiritu, *Body Counts;* Knudsen, *Chicken Wings.*

21. A Statement on Hong Kong's New Refugee Policy, January 20, 1975, FCO 21/1418, Illegal Immigration from China to Hong Kong; Hong Kong and Indian Ocean Department, Chinese Immigrants, June 23, 1975, FCO 21/1419, Illegal Immigration from China to Hong Kong.

22. British Red Cross Society, December 18, 1974, FCO 21/1274, Illegal Immigration from China to Hong Kong.

23. Record of Conversation between the Lord Goronwy-Roberts and the Governor of Hong Kong, July 29, 1974, FCO 21/1273, Illegal Immigration from China to Hong Kong.

24. Far Eastern Department, Overt Intelligence Reports: Punishment of Repatriates, October 8, 1975, FCO 21/1420, Illegal Immigration from China to Hong Kong.

25. Association of the National Assembly of ROC, 1974, FCO 21/1274, Illegal Immigration from China to Hong Kong. Laura Madokoro, Meredith Oyen, and Madeline Hsu have also written about the political actions of anti-communist Chinese organizations, which fought for refugee status for Chinese in Hong Kong and for humanitarian resettlement. These Republic of China (Taiwan)–based organizations included Aid Refugee Chinese Intellectuals (ARCI) and Free China Relief Association (FCRA). Although technically non-governmental organizations, they had very close ties to the ROC.

26. Free China Relief Association, December 10, 1974, FCO 21/1274, Illegal Immigration from China to Hong Kong.

27. Illegal Immigrants to Hong Kong from China, December 23, 1974, FCO 21/1274, Illegal Immigration from China to Hong Kong.

28. Hong Kong Government, Immigration Hong Kong's Perennial Problem, 1980, FCO 40/1203, Immigration from China to Hong Kong.

29. R. D. Clift to Mr. Murray, May 14, 1980, FCO 40/1201, Immigration from China to Hong Kong.

30. Ku, "Immigration Policies," pp. 354–55.

31. Peter Blaker MP to Michael Grylls MP, April 23, 1980, FCO 40/1200, Immigration from China to Hong Kong.

32. Carina Hoang, "From Both Sides of the Fence."

33. Oral history of Lam Tuyet Mai by Thuy Vo Dang, VAOHP, 2012, http://ucispace .lib.uci.edu/bitstream/handle/10575/3279/vaohp0087_f01_eng.pdf?sequence=5 (accessed April 26, 2018); oral history of Hung Luu by Vivian Luu, VAOHP, 2014, http://ucispace.lib.uci.edu/bitstream/handle/10575/11468/vaohp0189_f01.pdf? sequence=13, (accessed April 26, 2018); and Woo Chan Chan in Hawthorne, *Refugee,* pp. 285–90.

34. Knudsen, *Boat People in Transit,* pp. 67–72.

35. Oral history of Hung Luu by Vivan Luu, VAOHP, 2014, http://ucispace.lib .uci.edu/bitstream/handle/10575/11468/vaohp0189_f01.pdf?sequence=13 (accessed April 26, 2018).

36. "The Refugee Influx," September 13, 1983, article translated from the Chinese press by Jane Lo, Commissioner for Chinese Language, Publications Relating to Refugees, HKRS 770-2-9.

37. Revised 1982 Project Report, UNHCR Fonds 11, Series 2, 110.HKG Programming, Hong Kong, 1982, Vol. 3, Box 271.

38. Woo Chan Chan, in Hawthorne, *Refugee,* pp. 285–90.

39. Knudsen, *Boat People in Transit,* pp. 66–67, and Yuk Wah Chan, "Revisiting the Vietnamese Refugee Era," p. 7.

40. 1983 Project Report, UNHCR Fonds 11, Series 2, 110.HKG Programming, Hong Kong, 1982, Vol. 3, Box 271. Knudsen states the numbers of Chinese Vietnamese after 1980 were even lower, clocking in at less than 2 percent each year between 1980 and 1982 (Knudsen, *Boat People in Transit,* p. 67).

41. Madokoro, *Elusive Refuge,* pp. 187–213.

42. Martin Thomas, Vietnamese Boat People in Hong Kong: Report for the Parliamentary Liberal Party, January 15, 1988, UNHCR Fonds 11, Series 3, 100. HKG.SRV Refugee Situations, Folder A.

43. Madokoro, *Elusive Refuge,* pp. 187–213.

44. Yuk Wah Chan, "Revisiting the Vietnamese Refugee Era," p. 6.

45. Hong Kong Annual Report 1981, UNHCR Fonds 11, Series 2, 110.HKG Programming, Hong Kong, 1982, Vol. 3, Box 271.

46. Assessment on the Conditions at Kai Tak North Refugee Camp, May 8, 1982, Statistics on Refugees, 1982, HKRS 770-2-4. Also see Knudsen, *Boat People in Transit,* pp. 75–76.

47. Hong Kong, Note for the File, UNHCR Fonds 11, Series 2, 110.HKG Programming, Hong Kong, 1982–83, Vol. 4, Box 271.

48. Vietnamese Refugees, Closed Camp Option: Operation Devise, August 18, 1982, Statistics on Vietnamese Prepared by RCC, HKRS 770–2-4.

49. Hong Kong, 1983–1984 Report, UNHCR Fonds 11, Series 2, 110.HKG Programming, Hong Kong, 1984, Vol. 9, Box 272.

50. *A Camp at Lantau* (n.d.), UNHCR film archives.

51. "Vietnamese Refugees 1983," Radio Television Hong Kong, April 9, 1983, Hong Kong University Library Media Services.

52. For just a few examples, see British Refugee Council, *Behind Barbed Wire: Vietnamese Refugees in the Closed Camps of Hong Kong* (London: British Refugee Council, 1984); Refugee Action, "Refugees from Vietnam in Hong Kong," 1986; Oxfam, "How Hong Kong Cares for Vietnamese Refugees," 1986. All reports found at Oxford University in the Refugee Studies Centre Collections, Box EV-DH Vietnamese in Hong Kong, 40–67. See also Knudsen, *Boat People in Transit;* Linda Hitchcox, *Vietnamese Refugees in Southeast Asia Camps* (New York: Palgrave Macmillan, 1991); Leonard Davis, *Hong Kong and the Asylum-Seekers from Vietnam* (New York: Palgrave Macmillan, 1991).

53. British Refugee Council, *Behind Barbed Wire.*

54. Oxfam, "How Hong Kong Cares."

55. Oxfam, "Vietnamese Refugees in Hong Kong: The Way Forward,"1987, UNHCR Fonds 11, Series 3, 100.HKG.SRV Refugee Situations, Folder A; BBC Radio Four, December 24, 1987, Transcript of Interview with Chris Bale of Oxfam, Press and TV/Radio Reports, HKRS 770-4-5.

56. Knudsen, *Capricious Worlds,* p. 39.

57. M.4, Baily Chan, May 5, 1983, Publications Relating to Refugees, HKRS 770-2-9.

58. M.10, C. E. Leeks, July 12, 1983, Publications Relating to Refugees, HKRS 770-2-9.

59. M.9, C. H. K. Lau, July 11, 1983, Publications Relating to Refugees, HKRS 770-2-9.

60. M.10, P.J. Williamson, July 13, 1983, Publications Relating to Refugees, HKRS 770-2-9.

61. D. G. Jeafferson, Secretary of Security to Oxfam, Re: Oxfam Report, February 11, 1988, UNHCR Fonds 11, Series 3, 100.HKG.SRV Refugee Situations, Folder B.

62. Hong Kong Secretary of Security to Oxfam, February 11, 1988, UNHCR Fonds 11, Series 3, 100.HKG.SRV Refugee Situations, Folder B.

63. Interview with Mak Pak Lam by Carina Hoang, http://vietnameseboatpeople .hk/oral-history/mak-pak-lam/ (accessed January 18, 2019).

64. William Branigan, "Surge of Boat People Hits SE Asia; U.S. Row Delays Resettlement," *Washington Post,* May 19, 1981.

65. Comments from Correctional Services Department, C. K. Lau, November 2, 1982, Vietnamese Refugees Resettlement from Refugee Closed Camps, HKRS 770–3-1.

66. Telegram to UK Mission in Geneva, July 13, 1983, FCO 58/3437, Refugees in Hong Kong; Vietnamese Refugees in Hong Kong, February 23, 1983, FCO 58/3436, Refugees in Hong Kong.

67. Vietnamese Refugees: U.S. Views, May 20, 1983, FCO 58/3437, Refugees in Hong Kong.

68. MP's Comment Sparks Reaction, extract from the GIST dated January 9, 1987, Chinese Press and TV Summaries, HKRS 770–4-3.

69. C. M. J. Segar, South East Asian Department, Lord Belstead's Meeting with the Governor of Hong Kong, January 25, 1983, FCO 40/1630, Repatriation.

70. Repatriation Seen as Long-Term Solution, extract from the GIST dated September 23, 1986, Chinese Press and TV Summaries, HKRS 770–4-3.

71. Economic Migrants Face Repatriation, extract from the GIST dated March 31, 1987; extract from the GIST dated September 23, 1987; and extract from the GIST dated November 12, 1987; transcript of an item on Vietnamese refugees on Radio-3's *Hong Kong Today,* April 3, 1987. All in Chinese Press and TV Summaries, HKRS 770–4-3.

72. BBC Radio Four, April 14, 1987, and BBC Radio Four *Today* program, April 15, 1988, Press and TV/Radio Reports, HKRS 770–4-5.

73. Brief for Lord Belstead's Visit, December 6, 1982, and R. D. Clift, HK Department, Vietnamese Refugees in Hong Kong, May 31, 1983, FCO 40/1623, Vietnamese Refugees and Hong Kong.

74. Security Branch, Brief for Lord Belstead's Visit to Hong Kong, 6th December 1982, November 27, 1982, FCO 40/1623, Vietnamese Refugees and Hong Kong.

75. A special thank you here to Paul Gilroy for teaching me about this particular linguistic formulation and history of "voluntary repatriation."

76. "'Help Immigrants to Return,'" *Times* (London), January 25, 1965; Donley T. Studlar, "British Public Opinion, Color Issues, and Enoch Powell: A Longitudinal Study," *British Journal of Political Science* 4, no. 3 (July 1974): 376–78.

77. "Race Relations," *Times* (London), December 31, 1968.

78. Studlar, "British Public Opinion," pp. 376–78.

79. Sundar Katwala, "The Enoch Myth," *Guardian,* April 23, 2008, www .theguardian.com/commentisfree/2008/apr/23/theenochmyth (accessed May 30,

2018); Enoch Powell's "River of Blood" speech, www.telegraph.co.uk/comment /3643823/Enoch-Powells-Rivers-of-Blood-speech.html (accessed May 30, 2018); Camilla Schofield, *Enoch Powell and the Making of Postcolonial Britain* (Cambridge: Cambridge University Press, 2015).

80. Vietnamese Refugees, July 1983, FCO 58/3437, Refugees in Hong Kong.

81. Repatriation of Vietnamese, February 23, 1983, FCO 58/3436, Refugees in Hong Kong.

82. Lord Belstead, Vietnamese Refugees in Hong Kong, March 21, 1983, FCO 40/1630, Repatriation of Vietnamese Refugees from Hong Kong.

83. C.M.J. Segar, South East Asian Department, Lord Belstead's Meeting with the Governor of Hong Kong, January 25, 1983, FCO 40/1630, Repatriation of Vietnamese Refugees from Hong Kong.

84. C.M.J. Segar, South East Asian Department, Vietnamese Refugees in Hong Kong, March 8, 1983, FCO 40/1630, Repatriation of Vietnamese Refugees from Hong Kong.

85. J.E. Holmes, Vietnamese Refugees in Hong Kong, March 28, 1983, FCO 40/1630, Repatriation of Vietnamese Refugees from Hong Kong.

86. Mr. Clift's Visit to Hong Kong, May 22–28, 1983, FCO 40/1623, Vietnamese Refugees and Hong Kong.

87. Vietnamese Refugees, May 10, 1983, FCO 58/3437, Refugees in Hong Kong.

88. Executive Committee Meeting of UNHCR in Geneva, 1983, October 21, 1983, FCO 40/1624, Vietnamese Refugees and Hong Kong.

89. John Carroll, *A Concise History of Hong Kong*, pp. 178–79; C.K. Lau, *Hong Kong's Colonial Legacy* (Hong Kong: Chinese University Press, 1997), pp. xi–xvi; Wong Yiu-Chung, "'One Country' and 'Two Systems': Where Is the Line?" in *"One Country, Two Systems" in Crisis: Hong Kong's Transformation since the Handover,* ed. Wong Yiu-Chung (Lanham, MD: Lexington Books, 2004), p. 1.

90. John Carroll, *A Concise History of Hong Kong,* p. 182.

91. John Carroll, *A Concise History of Hong Kong,* pp. 182–217; Lau, *Hong Kong's Colonial Legacy,* pp. 23–35.

92. John Carroll, *A Concise History of Hong Kong,* pp. 177–78.

93. Lau, *Hong Kong's Colonial Legacy,* pp. 1–22.

94. Note for File, Hong Kong, UNHCR Fonds 11, Series 2, 110.HKG Programming Hong Kong, 1982–83, Vol. 4, Box 271.

95. BBC Radio Four *Today* program, April 15, 1988, Press and TV/Radio Reports, HKRS 770-4-5.

96. Fazul Karim, Re: LegCo and Ad Hoc Group on Refugees, December 16, 1986, UNHCR Fonds 11, Series 3, 100.HKG.SRV Refugee Situations, Folder A.

97. Rita Fan, "Hong Kong and the Vietnamese Boat People: A Hong Kong Perspective," *International Journal of Refugee Law,* special issue (1990): 144–71.

98. Yuk Wah Chan, "Revisiting the Vietnamese Refugee Era," p. 6.

99. Leonard Davis argued it received more press than almost any other issue in the Hong Kong press, and his book went on to republish numerous articles, op-eds, and letters to the editor from the English-language *South China Morning Post* and

Hong Kong Standard. Davis, *Hong Kong and the Asylum-Seekers,* pp. 78–79. Chris Pomery, "Colony Plea to Britain on Refugees," *Times* (London), May 25, 1988.

100. Solve VR Problem before 1997: Fan, Extract from the GIST dated November 18, 1987, Chinese Press and TV Summaries, HKRS 770-4-3; Hong Kong Legislative Council, Official Report of Proceedings, January 7, 1987, www.legco.gov.hk /yr86–87/english/lc_sitg/hansard/h870107.pdf (accessed June 5, 2018); Hong Kong Legislative Council, Official Report of Proceedings, December 2, 1987, www.legco .gov.hk/yr87–88/english/lc_sitg/hansard/h871202.pdf (accessed June 5, 2018).

101. BBC Radio Four, Jim Buddulph's Report on Vietnamese Refugee Problem, September 22, 1987, and BBC Radio Four *Today* program, April 15, 1988, Press and TV/Radio Reports, HKRS 770-4-5.

102. Hong Kong Legislators Threaten Action on Vietnamese Refugees, September 9, 1988, AFP, and BBC Radio Four *Today* program, April 15, 1988, Press and TV /Radio Reports, 70-4-5.

103. Fan, "Hong Kong and the Vietnamese Boat People."

104. Views on VR Issue, Extract from the GIST dated December 4, 1987, Chinese Press and TV Summaries, HKRS 770-4-3.

105. Andrew McEwen, "Princess Faced by Camps Storm," *Times* (London), March 22, 1988.

106. BBC Radio Four *Today* program, April 15, 1988, Press and TV/Radio Reports, HKRS 770-4-5.

107. "Why the Refugee Issue Stirs Up Emotions," *Hong Kong Standard,* April 20, 1989, UNHCR Fonds 11, Series 3, 100.HKG.SRV Refugee Situations, Folder C.

108. BBC Radio Four, April 14, 1987, and BBC Radio Four *Today* program, April 15, 1988, Press and TV/Radio Reports, HKRS 770-4-5.

109. Chris Pomery, "Howe Finesse Leaves Hong Kong Divided," *Times* (London), June 1, 1988; Andrew McEwen, "UN Fears New Curb on Boat People Will Sink Vietnam Deal," *Times* (London), June 16, 1988.

110. Hon. Chief Secretary David Ford, LegCo, June 15, 1988, UNHCR Fonds 11, Series 3, 100.HKG.SRV Refugee Situations, Folder B.

111. Hei Ling Chau July 1988 Incident, Independent Inquiry, UNHCR Fonds 11, Series 3, 100.HKG.SRV Refugee Situations, Folder C; UNHCR Hong Kong to Geneva, August 5, 1988, UNHCR Fonds 11, Series 3, 100.HKG.SRV Refugee Situations, Folder B.

112. International Society for Human Rights, March 22, 1989, UNHCR Fonds 11, Series 3, 610.HKG.SRV Special Protection Problems, Repatriation and Vietnamese Refugees, Folder D; IRAC, Preliminary Observations and Recommendations for UNHCR on Status of Vietnamese Asylum Seekers in Hong Kong, September 30, 1988, UNHCR Fonds 11, Series 3, 100.HKG.SRV Refugee Situations, Folder C.

113. Hong Kong UNHCR to Vieira de Mello, June 9, 1988, UNHCR Fonds 11, Series 3, 100.HKG.SRV Refugee Situations, Folder B.

114. Hong Kong UNHCR Memo June 16, 1988, UNHCR Fonds 11, Series 3, 100.HKG.SRV Refugee Situations, Folder B; HK UNHCR to Vieira de

Mello, June 9, 1988, UNHCR Fonds 11, Series 3, 100.HKG.SRV Refugee Situations, Folder B.

115. Immediate for HICOM, Pursuant Fax Dated June 15, Ref UK/HK Reaction to UNHCR Note, June 16, 1988, UNHCR Fonds 11, Series 3, 100.HKG.SRV Refugee Situations, Folder B; G. Arnaout to Vieira de Mello, Re: Vietnamese Asylum Seekers in HK—UNHCR Participation in Screening, August 1, 1988, UNHCR Fonds 11, Series 3, 010.HKG External Relations, Folder B; Arnaout, Division of Refugee Law and Doctrine, to Vieira de Mello, UNHCR Participation in Screening, August 1, 1988, UNHCR Fonds 11, Series 3, 100.HKG.SRV Refugee Situations, Folder B.

116. Simon Riley, "No Escaping Persecution," *Times* (London), March 2, 1989, UNHCR Fonds 11, Series 3, 100.HKG.SRV Refugee Situations, Folder C.

117. Robinson, "The Comprehensive Plan of Action"; Robinson, *Terms of Refuge,* pp. 187–230.

118. Samantha Power, *Chasing the Flame: Sergio Vieira de Mello and the Fight to Save the World* (New York: Penguin, 2008). For the commentary on the Comprehensive Plan of Action, see pp. 66–69. Also see Betts, "Comprehensive Plan of Action."

119. Power, *Chasing the Flame,* pp. 65–69. On Vieira de Mello's role in the CPA and his pragmatism, see Robinson, "The Comprehensive Plan of Action."

120. Reporting on UNHCR Activities 1982–1983, March 30, 1983, UNHCR Fonds 11, Series 2, 110.HKG Programming, Vol. 5, Box 272.

121. Statement of Understanding between the HKG and UNHCR, September 23, 1988, UNHCR Fonds 11, Series 3, 100.HKG.SRV Refugee Situations, Folder B; Memo for Vieira de Mello, September 12, 1988, UNHCR Fonds 11, Series 3, 100. HKG.SRV Refugee Situations, Folder B.

122. There had also been an earlier repatriation program for Laotians waiting in Thailand, although on a much smaller scale; the UNHCR facilitated voluntary repatriation for approximately 2,000 people in the early 1980s. Thank you to Bernard Kerblat for alerting me to this precedent. Also see "The Lao Returnees in the Voluntary Repatriation Programme from Thailand," Indochinese Refugee Information Center Institute of Asian Studies, Chulalongkorn University, Occasional Paper Series No. 003, 1992 (ISEAS Library, Singapore); and Refugee Policy Group, Second International Conference on Indochinese Refugees: A New Humanitarian Consensus? May 1989 (ISEAS Library). In addition, W. Courtland Robinson, who went on to write the first major synthetic work on the Southeast Asian refugee crisis, testified about the Comprehensive Plan of Action in Congress in 1990. In his testimony, he too pointed to the Laotian screening and repatriation program as a model for success. See Courtland Robinson, *Hearing on Refugee Protection and Resettlement Issues Relating to Southeast Asia and Hong Kong, House Subcommittee on Asian and Pacific Affairs,* 101st Congress, 2nd Session, June 21, 1990.

123. Refugee Policy Group, Second International Conference on Indochinese Refugees: A New Humanitarian Consensus? May 1989 (ISEAS Library); Robinson, *Terms of Refuge,* pp. 194–98.

124. Dennis McNamara to Mr. Ghassan Arnaout, UNHCR, Re: Eligibility in SEAsia, April 11, 1989, UNHCR Fonds 11, Series 3, 391.89 International Conference on Indochinese Refugees, Folder C.

125. UN General Assembly, *Declaration and Comprehensive Plan of Action of the International Conference on Indo-Chinese Refugees, Report of the Secretary-General (A/44/523),* September 22, 1989, A/44/523, available at www.refworld.org/docid /3dda17d84.html (accessed June 11, 2018).

126. Robinson, *Terms of Refuge,* pp. 187–89.

127. Foreign Minister Nguyen Co Thach on ABC TV Australia, March 8, 1989, Press Cuttings, March 13, 1989, UNHCR Fonds 11, Series 3, 610.HKG.SRV Repatriation, Folder D.

128. On the Orderly Departure Program and "humanitarian issues," see Demmer, "Last Chapter," pp. 189–239; Lipman, "'The Face Is the Roadmap'"; Kumin, "Orderly Departure from Vietnam"; and U.S. General Accounting Office, "The Orderly Departure Program from Vietnam," 1990, http://archive.gao.gov/t2pbat10 /141353.pdf (accessed March 3, 2010).

129. Loyd and Mountz, *Boats, Borders, and Bases;* García, *Seeking Refuge.*

130. Benjamin Ziff, "Solarz Outlines Magnitude of Refugee Crisis," U.S. Information Service News Release, June 8, 1988, Press and TV/Radio Reports, HKRS 770-4-5.

131. Congressional Record H10825–28 (June 6, 1989).

132. Robinson, *Terms of Refuge,* pp. 175–77.

133. "Britain Demands Return to Vietnam of Boat People," *New York Times,* June 14, 1989.

134. Rone Tempest, "70 Nations Act to Stem Flow of 'Boat People,'" *Los Angeles Times,* June 15, 1989; Henry Kamm, "Britain and Vietnam Still at Odds on Refugees," *New York Times,* June 15, 1989.

135. This statistic is from 1990. Jie Zong and Jeanne Batalova, "Vietnamese Immigrants in the United States," Migration Policy Institute, June 8, 2016, www.migration policy.org/article/vietnamese-immigrants-united-states (accessed June 12, 2018).

136. Telephone interview with Le Xuan Khoa, September 7, 2018.

137. IRAC, Recommendations for Implementation of CPA for June 1989, April 3, 1989, UNHCR Fonds 11, Series 3, 391.89 International Conference on Indochinese Refugees, Folder C.

138. IRAC to UNHCR, May 17, 1989, UNHCR Fonds 11, Series 3, 391.89 International Conference on Indochinese Refugees, Folder E.

139. Le Xuan Khoa interview, September 7, 2018.

140. Thuy Vo Dang, "Project Ngoc at UCI, Vietnamese American Student Activism," diaCRITICS, June 4, 2012, http://diacritics.org/2012/06/project-ngoc-at-uci-vietnamese-american-student-activism/ (accessed January 15, 2019).

141. Richard Beene, "Leaders Seek Vietnamese Holding Centers to Stall Repatriations," *Los Angeles Times,* June 18, 1989, UC Irvine Libraries, Special Collections and Archives (hereafter UCI), Project Ngoc Records, MS-SEA016, Box 2, File 28, Refugee International 1990–1991.

142. Letter from Vietnamese Buddhist Association of Sacramento, May 26, 1989, UNHCR Fonds 11, Series 3, 391.89 International Conference on Indochinese Refugees, Folder E; Letter from Comité d'aide aux réfugiés, May 17, 1989, UNHCR Fonds 11, Series 3, 391.89 International Conference on Indochinese Refugees, Folder E (translation by author).

143. Indochinese Community's Response to the Refugee Crisis in Southeast Asia, 1989, UCI, Paul Tran Files on Southeast Asian Refugees, MS-SEA002, Box 4, Folder 9, Correspondence from Vietnamese Associations, 1989–1990.

144. Statement of Vietnamese American Community in the United States to President George Bush, June 12, 1990, UCI, Paul Tran Files on Southeast Asian Refugees, MS-SEA002, Box 4, Folder 9, Correspondence from Vietnamese Associations, 1989–1990.

145. Hong Kong University Students, May 17, 1989, UNHCR Fonds 11, Series 3, 100.HKG.SRV Refugee Situations, Folder C.

146. Law Students, Hong Kong, The Immigration Amendment Bill No. 2 Must Be Scrapped, June 2, 1989, UNHCR Fonds 11, Series 3, 391.89 International Conference on Indochinese Refugees, Folder E.

147. Letter by Sandra Yeung, n.d., UNHCR Fonds 11, Series 3, 391.89 International Conference on Indochinese Refugees, Folder E.

148. Letter by Fong Chi Man, Mandatory Repatriation Is Deplorable, May 15, 1989, UNHCR Fonds 11, Series 3, 391.89 International Conference on Indochinese Refugees, Folder E.

149. BBC, *Twenty-Four Hours,* May 23, 1988, Press and TV/Radio Reports, HKRS 770-4-5.

CHAPTER 5. "PROTEST AGAINST FORCED
REPATRIATION!"

1. UNHCR Hong Kong, For Immediate Attention, December 12, 1989, UNHCR Fonds 11, Series 3, 391.89 International Conference on Indochinese Refugees, Folder I. Also see Michael Bociurkiw, "No Hong Kong Haven for Vietnam's Boat People," *Los Angeles Times,* December 24, 1989; "There Is a Better Way," *Financial Times,* December 13, 1989, Views Expressed by the Public on the Vietnamese Refugee Issue, HKRS 770-4-8.

2. Senator Mark Hatfield to Governor David Wilson, December 22, 1989, Views Expressed by the Public on the Vietnamese Refugee Issue, HKRS 770-4-8.

3. "U.S. Aides Critical of Britain's Move," *New York Times,* December 13, 1989; Senator Mark Hatfield to Governor David Wilson, December 22, 1989, Views Expressed by the Public on the Vietnamese Refugee Issue, HKRS 770-4-8.

4. Advertisement, Open Letter to Prime Minister Thatcher, December 21, 1989, *South China Morning Post* (hereafter *SCMP*), Newspaper Cuttings, HKRS 766-1-1.

5. Letter to Cathay Pacific Airways, Interfaith Committee for Refugee Concerns, December 18, 1989, Views Expressed by the Public on the Vietnamese Refugee Issue, HKRS 770-4-8.

6. Clyde Haberman, "Pope Criticizes Hong Kong on Vietnamese," *New York Times,* December 18, 1989. Also see Position Paper of the Justice and Peace Commission of Hong Kong Catholic Diocese on Vietnamese Refugees, March 15, 1990, UCI, Project Ngoc Records, MS-SEA016, Box 1, Folder 2.

7. Steven Prokesch, "Thatcher Defends Refugee Policy," *New York Times,* December 13, 1989; Barbara Basler, "Hong Kong Opinion against Refugees," *New York Times,* December 15, 1989.

8. David Wilson to Senator Hatfield, December 29, 1989, Views Expressed by the Public on the Vietnamese Refugee Issue, HKRS 770-4-8.

9. Robinson, *Terms of Refuge,* p. 201; Carina Hoang, "From Both Sides of the Fence," p. 82.

10. Anthropologist Heonik Kwon cautions that the Cold War did not end instantaneously or create a clean break, but rather was experienced unevenly by everyday people, depending on local and national politics. Kwon, *The Other Cold War.*

11. For one example, see Anita Chan and Jonathan Unger, "Voices from the Protest Movement, Chongqing, Sichuan," *Australian Journal of Chinese Affairs* 24 (July 1990): 259–79.

12. Adi Ignatius, "For Hong Kong, All Bets on China Are Off," *Wall Street Journal,* June 8, 1989.

13. Archbishop of Canterbury to Governor David Wilson, December 14, 1989, Views Expressed by the Public on the Vietnamese Refugee Issue, HKRS 770-4-8.

14. Knudsen, *Chicken Wings;* Knudsen, *Capricious Worlds;* Freeman and Nguyen, *Voices from the Camps.* Also see Yến Lê Espiritu, *Body Counts,* for more on the flattening of Vietnamese stories due to the screening process.

15. Knudsen, *Chicken Wings,* pp. 20–24.

16. Amnesty International, Hong Kong: Protection of Vietnamese Asylum-Seekers: Developments since December 1989, July 11, 1990, p. 7, Oxford University, Refugee Studies Centre Collection (hereafter Oxford).

17. Amnesty International, "Hong Kong: Protection of Vietnamese Asylum-Seekers: Developments since December 1989," July 11, 1990, p. 7, Oxford.

18. "Screening under Scrutiny," *SCMP,* November 19, 1990, Newspaper Cuttings, HKRS 766-1-1.

19. Anonymous, "Qualifications in Question on Review Board," *SCMP,* October 24, 1989, Newspaper Cuttings, 766-1-1; "The Lottery," *Executive,* May 1994, Newspaper Cuttings, HKRS 766-2-1.

20. Knudsen, *Chicken Wings,* pp. 20–24.

21. Robert Van Leeuwan, UNHCR, to Hong Secretary of Security, December 29, 1989, UNHCR Fonds 11, Series 3, 391.89 International Conference on Indochinese Refugees, Folder I.

22. "Court Orders Re-Screening of Viet Man," *Hong Kong Standard* (hereafter *HKS*), February 19, 1991, Newspaper Cuttings, HKRS 766-1-1.

23. "Refugee Board's Decision Quashed," *HKS,* February 19, 1990, Newspaper Cuttings, HKRS 766–1-1; Press Release, February 18, 1991, UNHCR Fonds 11, Series 3, 840.HKG Press—HK, 1987–93, Folder D.

24. Rita Gomez, "'Incompetent' Interpreters Blamed for Screening Decision," *SCMP,* September 22, 1990, Newspaper Cuttings, HKRS 766–1-1.

25. Amnesty International, Memorandum to the Governments of Hong Kong and the UK Regarding the Protection of Vietnamese Asylum Seekers in Hong Kong, January 1990, Oxford.

26. UNHCR, Judicial Review of RSRB in Supreme High Court, February 18, 1991, UNHCR Fonds 11, Series 3, 840.HKG Press—HK, 1987–93, Folder D; "Ruling Upholds Right to a Fair Hearing," *SCMP,* February 19, 1991, and "Refugee Board's Decision Quashed," *HKS,* February 19, 1991, both Newspaper Cuttings, HKRS 766–1-1.

27. "Refugee Board's Decision Quashed," *HKS,* February 19, 1991, Newspaper Cuttings, HKRS 766–1-1.

28. Barbara Basler, "Hong Kong Court Rules on a Refugee," *New York Times,* February 19, 1991. Also see "Screening Rules to Stand Despite Court Decision," *HKS,* February 19, 1991, Newspaper Cuttings, HKRS 766–1-1.

29. Fiona MacMahon, "Screening System a Success: Leeks," *SCMP,* December 14, 1990, Newspaper Cuttings, HKRS 766–1-1.

30. Fiona MacMahon, "Board to Give Reasons for Viet Refusals," *SCMP,* April 27, 1990, Newspaper Cuttings, HKRS 766–1-1.

31. Amnesty International, Hong Kong: Protection of Vietnamese Asylum Seekers, Developments since December 1989, July 11, 1990, Oxford.

32. Lawyers Committee for Human Rights, Hong Kong's Refugee Status Determination Board: Problems in Status Determination for Vietnamese Asylum Seekers, March 1992, UNHCR Fonds 11, Series 3, 391.89 International Conference on Indochinese Refugees, Folder O.

33. "A Slow Boat to Freedom: Human Rights Lawyer Pam Baker Discusses Dedication to Human Rights," n.d., Newspaper Cuttings, HKRS 766–2-2.

34. Refugee Concern Hong Kong, UNHCR Memo, June 12, 1991, UNHCR Fonds 11, Series 3, 391.89 International Conference on Indochinese Refugees, Folder M; "Courting Publicity," *SCMP,* March 20, 1994, Newspaper Cuttings, HKRS 766–2-1.

35. One U.S. telegram speaks forthrightly of the UNHCR representative's dislike for Baker; Removal of Unaccompanied Minor Sparks Camp Protests, January 10, 1994, FOIA documents.

36. Marnie O'Neil, "Refugees Hit Out at 'Unfair Screening,'" *HKS,* November 2, 1993, Newspaper Cuttings, HKRS 766–1-1.

37. Yến Lê Espiritu, *Body Counts,* and Knudsen, *Chicken Wings.*

38. Amnesty International, Memorandum to the Governments of Hong Kong and the UK Regarding the Protection of Vietnamese Asylum Seekers in Hong Kong, January 1990, Oxford.

39. H.V.H. Testimony, UCI, Paul Tran Files on Southeast Asian Refugees, MS-SEA002, Box 4, Folder 27.

40. In Indonesia, 43 percent of Vietnamese were "screened in"; in Malaysia, 39 percent; in the Philippines, 53 percent; and in Thailand, 22 percent. See Robinson, *Terms of Refuge*, p. 206.

41. Refugee Concern Hong Kong, *Asylum,* June 1991, UCI, Project Ngoc Records, MS-SEA016, Box 1, Folder 7, Asylum 1990–1991.

42. Steven Muncy, Summary of the Mental Health Situation in the Detention Centers for Vietnamese Asylum Seekers in Hong Kong, Community and Family Services International, n.d., UCI, Project Ngoc Records, MS-SEA016, Box 1, Folder 2, 1990.

43. Questions and Statements by Vietnamese Asylum Seekers in Hong Kong, July 1989, UNHCR Fonds 11, Series 3, 840.HKG Press—HK, 1987–93, Folder D.

44. Petition Addressed to the Geneva Conference, December 19, 1989, UNHCR Fonds 11, Series 3, 100.HKG.SRV Refugee Situations, Folder E.

45. Interview with Carol Tong Thi Xuan, Hong Kong, June 22, 2016.

46. Community and Family Services International, "The Vietnamese in Hong Kong: A Women's Perspective on Detention, 1993," Oxford.

47. Elisabeth Mayer-Rieckh, "'Beyond Concrete and Steel,' Power Relations and Gender: The Case of Vietnamese Women in the Detention Centres in Hong Kong" (master's thesis, Institute of Social Studies, The Hague, 1992), p. 44, Oxford.

48. Mayer-Rieckh, "'Beyond Concrete and Steel,'" p. 58.

49. 1990, Supreme Court of Hong Kong, No. 1506, Judicial Review in the Matter of a Decision of the Secretary of Security, May 8, 1991 Judgment, HCMP001506/1990, Hong Kong University legal catalogue.

50. Hong Kong Correctional Services Department Museum, June 15, 2016. Ip Yu-chung, "Riots and Disturbances Related to Vietnamese Asylum Seekers in Hong Kong" (master's thesis, University of Hong Kong, 1994). This study traces accounts of violence in Hong Kong newspapers, and so these numbers are inexact, but they do give a sense of the constancy of violence in the camps. It also distinguishes between "riots" and "protests." According to the study, there were at least twenty-five "riots" and eighteen "protests" with five hundred or more participants.

51. Photo, September 1, 1990, Newspaper Cuttings, HKRS 766-1-1. There are dozens of accounts of hunger strikes in the Hong Kong media, U.S. documents, and UNHCR archives.

52. Fiona MacMahon and Shirley Yam, "Rejected Viets' Suicide Bid," *SCMP,* January 20, 1990, Newspaper Cuttings, HKRS 766-1-1.

53. Paik, *Rightlessness.*

54. Shirley Yam, "Boat People 'Forced into Suicide Bids,'" *SCMP,* February 2, 1990, Newspaper Cuttings, HKRS 766-1-1.

55. Kevin Sinclair, "Boat People's Suicide Sham Has No Thrust," *HKS,* March 1, 1990, Newspaper Cuttings, HKRS 766-1-1.

56. Letter to the Editor, Community Leaders, Tai A Chau Detention Centre, *HKS,* October 3, 1994, Newspaper Cuttings, HKRS 766-2-1.

57. Amnesty International, Memorandum to the Governments of Hong Kong and the UK Regarding the Protection of Vietnamese Asylum Seekers in Hong Kong, January 1990, Oxford.

58. Delegation of the Women's Commission for Refugee Children to Hong Kong, January 5–12, 1990, Oxford.

59. Carol Tong Thi Xuan interview, June 22, 2016.

60. Appeal for Lawyers Committee for Human Rights, n.d., UCI, Paul Tran Files on Southeast Asian Refugees, MS-SEA002, Box 4, Folder 10, Correspondence Related to Forced Repatriation; Lawyers Committee for Human Rights to Governor of Hong Kong, October 5, 1989, UNHCR Fonds 11, Series 3, 100.HKG.SRV Refugee Situations, Folder D.

61. For examples, see Ky Ngo to Vice President Dan Quayle, March 18, 1992, UNHCR Fonds 11, Series 3, 391.89 International Conference on Indochinese Refugees, Folder O.

62. Refugee Task Force USA, Protesting against the Unjust "Screening" Policy, Unofficial Translation, UNHCR Fonds 11, Series 3, 391.89 International Conference on Indochinese Refugees, Folder M.

63. May Fung, "I Feared for My Life: CSD Officer," *SCMP*, May 12, 1996, Newspaper Cuttings, HKRS 766-2-2.

64. I thank Carina Hoang for assisting me with my research contacts in Hong Kong. Hoang has also conducted and published a series of valuable oral histories with more than two dozen people in Hong Kong; see http://vietnamesediaspora .com/hongkong/about-us/ (accessed March 6, 2017). Also see her oral history collection, *Boat People;* and Carina Hoang, "From Both Sides of the Fence."

65. Oral history of Peter Lai by Carina Hoang, http://vietnamesediaspora.com /hongkong/oral-history/peter-lai/ (accessed February 3, 2017).

66. Interview with Eddy Chan, Hong Kong, June 22, 2016. Also see oral history of Eddy Chan by Carina Hoang, http://vietnamesediaspora.com/hongkong /oral-history/eddy-chan/ (accessed March 6, 2017).

67. See two contemporary master's theses written by Hong Kong students: Stella Ho Siu Ying, "A Study of the Social Work Students' Attitude towards the Vietnamese Refugee Problem in Hong Kong: Reflection of Social Work Values and Ethics" (Hong Kong University, 1990); and Alice Lee Pui Ling, "The Role of Non-Governmental Organizations in Detention Centres for Vietnamese Boat People" (Hong Kong University, 1992).

68. Brenda Ku, "The Vietnamese Refugee Program," in *They Sojourned in Our Land: The Vietnamese in Hong Kong, 1975–2000,* ed. Joyce Chang, Brenda Ku, Lum Bik, and Betty Ann Maheu (Hong Kong: Caritas Printing, 2003).

69. Gordon Leung, interview with Carina Hoang, http://vietnamesediaspora .com/hongkong/oral-history/gordon-leung/ (accessed March 10, 2017).

70. Joyce T'ang, "'Is It Cholera?'" in Chang et al., *They Sojourned in Our Land,* p. 28.

71. John Carroll, *A Concise History of Hong Kong,* pp. 180–83.

72. John Carroll, *A Concise History of Hong Kong,* 184–85, 195–98.

73. Teresa Ma et al., To Member of Parliament, July 11, 1989, Bernie Grant Archive, Hong Kong Correspondence, 1988–1992, BG P 18/2/148. It's notable that one of the signatories was Emily Lau, a journalist for the *Far Eastern Economic Review* and later a pro-democracy politician in Hong Kong.

74. Lee Yee, "Fear and Loathing in Hong Kong," *Wall Street Journal,* June 28, 1989.

75. Hong Kong University Students Sze Pui Yan, Cheung Chi Ho, Lam Yan Yin, and Wong King Kin, Hong Kong University Student Letter, May 17, 1989, UNHCR Fonds 11, Series 3, 100.HKG.SRV Refugee Situations, Folder C.

76. See "Is Screening Legal Mr. Lee?" *SCMP,* July 31, 1988, UNHCR Fonds 11, Series 3, 840.HKG Press—HK, 1987–93, Folder D; Chris Yeung and Daphne Cheng, "Demand to Scrap Policy on Refugees," *SCMP,* April 18, 1989, UNHCR Fonds 11, Series 3, 100.HKG.SRV Refugee Situations, Folder C; Chan Kwok Bun, "Hong Kong's Response," pp. 107–9.

77. UNHCR HK to Geneva, Vieira de Mello, August 16, 1989, UNHCR Fonds 11, Series 3, 100.HKG.SRV Refugee Situations, Folder D.

78. U.S. Consulate Hong Kong, Disturbances in Refugee Camps Continue as Poll Reveals Majority in Hong Kong Favor End to First Asylum, August 29, 1989, U.S. State Department, FOIA documents.

79. Letter to All Citizens of Hong Kong, Translation, July 11, 1989, Views Expressed by the Public on the Vietnamese Refugee Issue, HKRS 770–4-6.

80. "Prognosis Poor," April 11, 1990, Radio Television Hong Kong, Hong Kong University Library Media Services.

81. Robinson, *Terms of Refuge,* pp. 216–17. In 1993, there were 31,475 screened out in the camps and several thousand still facing hearings. Beryl Cook, "UN Studies Detention of Refugees," *SCMP,* July 5, 1993, Newspaper Cuttings, HKRS 766–1-1.

82. There are multiple direct examples of this; see AG Foulkes, Letter to the Editor, *SCMP,* November 23, 1989, and Michael Chugani, "U.S. Accused of Hypocrisy over Viets," *SCMP,* September 14, 1989, both Newspaper Cuttings, HKRS 766–1-1.

83. AG Foulkes, Letter to the Editor, *SCMP,* November 23, 1989, Newspaper Cuttings, HKRS 766–1-1.

84. Oral history of Eddy Chan by Carina Hoang, http://vietnamesediaspora .com/hongkong/oral-history/eddy-chan/ (accessed March 6, 2017).

85. Fiona MacMahon, "Oxfam Welcomes New Deal on Boat People," *SCMP,* September 27, 1990, UNHCR Fonds 11, Series 3, 840.HKG Press—HK, 1987–93, Folder D.

86. "Returnees Fall into Grey Area," *HKS,* November 9, 1991, Newspaper Cuttings, HKRS 766–1-1.

87. "End of a Dream," n.d., Newspaper Cuttings, HKRS 766–1-1.

88. Anthony Flores, "Push to Make UNH Pay for Returnees," n.d., UNHCR Fonds 11, Series 3, 840.HKG Press—HK, 1987–93, Folder D.

89. Franz Leung and Anthony Flores, "UN Switch on Viets," *HKS,* September 27, 1990, UNHCR Fonds 11, Series 3, 840.HKG Press—HK, 1987–93, Folder D.

90. John Pomfret, "A Shift at UN: Refugees Told to Go Home," n.d., UNHCR Fonds 11, Series 3, 840.HKG Press—HK, 1987–93, Folder D.

91. Opinion, *HKS,* November 9, 1991, Newspaper Cuttings, HKRS 766-1-1.

92. Ann Leslie, "Tragic, but They Had No Choice" (n.d.). Also see Barbara Basler, "Hong Kong Begins to Transport Vietnam People Back Home," *New York Times,* November 9, 1991; Jon Swain, "Violence and Fury as Refugees Forced Out," *Times* (London), November 10, 1991. All in Newspaper Cuttings, HKRS 766-1-1.

93. Robinson, *Terms of Refuge,* p. 217.

94. Carina Hoang's oral histories include security officers discussing how they would carry people onto planes in Hong Kong and once in Vietnam, would turn off the air conditioning and otherwise compel people to leave the planes. Carina Hoang, http://vietnameseboatpeople.hk/ (accessed January 31, 2020).

95. Thanh Thuy Vo Dang, "Anti-Communism as Cultural Praxis"; Tuan Hoang, "From Reeducation Camps to Little Saigons," pp. 43–95.

96. Appeal of the Vietnamese Community on the East Coast of the United States to the UN, the US, Congress, and Southeast Asia First Asylum Countries, April 30, 1989, UCI, Paul Tran Files on Southeast Asian Refugees, MS-SEA002, Box 4, Folder 9, Correspondence from Vietnamese Associations, 1989–1990.

97. Mimi Thi Nguyen, *The Gift of Freedom.*

98. Oral history of Mai-Phuong Nguyen by Lotusa Chan, VAOHP, 2012, http://ucispace.lib.uci.edu/bitstream/handle/10575/2086/vaohp0020_f01.pdf?sequence=3 (accessed February 4, 2019).

99. Oral history of Nicole Nguyen by Malessa Tem, VAOHP, 2012, http://ucispace.lib.uci.edu/bitstream/handle/10575/1629/vaohp0002_f01.pdf?sequence=2 (accessed February 5, 2019).

100. Oral history of Nicole Nguyen by Malessa Tem, VAOHP, 2012, http://ucispace.lib.uci.edu/bitstream/handle/10575/1629/vaohp0002_f01.pdf?sequence=2 (accessed February 5, 2019).

101. Oral history of Tu-Uyen Nguyen by Kassandra Tong, VAOHP, 2012, http://ucispace.lib.uci.edu/bitstream/handle/10575/5239/vaohp0066_f01.pdf?sequence=27 (accessed February 5, 2019).

102. Boat People: The Cry for Freedom, July 1991, Century Art Gallery, UCI, Project Ngoc Records, MS-SEA016, Box 1, Folder 3, Artwork. Also see Sophia Suk-Mun Law, *The Invisible Citizens of Hong Kong: Art and Stories of Vietnamese Boat-people* (Hong Kong: Chinese University Press, 2014).

103. Petition, October 19, 1991, to U.S. State Department, UCI, Project Ngoc Records, MS-SEA016, Box 2, File 16, Petition Letters.

104. Boat People SOS News Bulletin, April 1991, UCI, Project Ngoc Records, MS-SEA016, Box 1, Folder 12, Boat People SOS Bulletins.

105. Statement of Thang Nguyen, Boat People SOS, *Hearing on Refugee Protection and Resettlement Issues Relating to Southeast Asia and Hong Kong, House Subcommittee on Asian and Pacific Affairs,* 101st Congress, 2nd Session, June 21, 1990.

106. Viet Media, Free Viet, Boat People SOS, June 1996, Letter to President Clinton, Newspaper Cuttings, HKRS 766-2-2. For other examples of Vietnamese

American organizations calling on human rights, see Vietnamese Community of Southern California, Ban Binh Ban to President Clinton, June 21, 1995, UCI, Paul Tran Files on Southeast Asian Refugees, MS-SEA002, Box 16, Folder 7; "How to Save and/or Help Our VN Refugees ... This Is Really against the Human Rights Principles of the United Nations and the Conscience of the Humanity," Vietnamese Physician Association of Southern California, January 5, 1994, UCI, Paul Tran Files on Southeast Asian Refugees, MS-SEA002, Box 16, Folder 12.

107. In 1994, the CSD managed 15,875 Vietnamese in the camps. Hong Kong Correctional Museum display.

108. Rachel Clarke, "Vietnamese Inmate Alleges Brutality," *Eastern Express,* March 28, 1994, Newspaper Cuttings, HKRS 766-2-1.

109. Report of Justices of the Peace of the Inquiry into the Events surrounding the Removal of Vietnamese Migrants from the Whitehead Detention Centre on April 7, 1994, Government Inquiry June 10, 1994, Hong Kong University Library.

110. Report of Justices of the Peace of the Inquiry into the Events surrounding the Removal of Vietnamese Migrants from the Whitehead Detention Centre on April 7, 1994, Government Inquiry June 10, 1994, Hong Kong University Library.

111. Report of Refugee Concern into the Events surrounding the Transfer of Vietnamese Asylum Seekers from the Whitehead Detention Centre on April 7, 1994, July 8, 1994, Hong Kong University Library.

112. Report of Refugee Concern into the Events surrounding the Transfer of Vietnamese Asylum Seekers from the Whitehead Detention Centre on April 7, 1994, July 8, 1994, Hong Kong University Library.

113. Adrielle M. Panares and Brenda Ku, "The Vietnamese Saga," in Chang et al., *They Sojourned in Our Land,* p. 9.

114. Also see Robinson, *Terms of Refuge,* pp. 220–21.

115. Congressional Record, House, 141st Congress, H14349–51 (May 24, 1995).

116. Philip Shenon, "In Asia, Fears U.S. Bill May Impede Boat People's Return," *New York Times,* May 21, 1995; Gilman's Refugee Proposals, Skewering the CPA, May 17, 1995, FOIA documents; Demmer, "Last Chapter," pp. 323–27. Demmer is one of the few scholars who has written about the congressional debates over the CPA and the ROVR, or Resettlement Opportunity for Vietnamese Returnees, program.

117. Nguyen Dinh Thang, "Vietnamese Boat People: The Last Chapter, Boat People SOS," February 16, 2009 (in author's possession); Boat People SOS, History of the CPA and ROVR Program by Grover Joseph Rees, https://bpsoshmhd.wordpress.com/2009/05/06/l%E1%BB%8Bch-s%E1%BB%AD-history-the-comprehensive-plan-of-action-and-the-rovr-program/ (accessed May 26, 2017).

118. Telephone interview with Le Xuan Khoa, September 7, 2018.

119. ROVR Statistics for Hong Kong for June 17–23, July 2, 1996, FOIA documents; ROVR Update: Visit to Tai A Chau, June 21, 1996, FOIA documents.

120. U.S. Committee for Refugees World Refugee Survey 1997—Viet Nam, January 1, 1997, www.refworld.org/docid/3ae6a8b728.html (accessed May 26, 2017); Demmer, "Last Chapter," pp. 339–42.

121. Migration and Refugee Services, *Flash,* December 4, 1995, Item Number 1849125041000, Box 125, Folder 041, FVPPA Collection, Texas Tech, www.vietnam. ttu.edu/virtualarchive/items.php?item=1849125041000 (accessed July 17, 2019).

122. Migration and Refugee Services, *Flash,* December 4, 1995, Item Number 1849125041000, Box 125, Folder 041, FVPPA Collection, Texas Tech, www.vietnam. ttu.edu/virtualarchive/items.php?item=1849125041000 (accessed July 17, 2019).

123. Migration and Refugee Services, *Flash,* December 4, 1995, Item Number 1849125041000, Box 125, Folder 041, FVPPA Collection, Texas Tech, www.vietnam. ttu.edu/virtualarchive/items.php?item=1849125041000 (accessed July 17, 2019).

124. Robinson, *Terms of Refuge,* p. 294.

125. Human Rights Watch/Asia, Hong Kong: Abuses against Vietnamese Asylum Seekers in the Final Days of the Comprehensive Plan of Action, March 1997, Oxford.

126. EU Projects with Vietnam, May 16, 2016, https://eeas.europa.eu/delegations /vietnam_en/1898/EU%20Projects%20with%20Vietnam (accessed August 27, 2019); Fernando del Mundo, "End of an Era as UNHCR Scales Down Its Operations," *Refugees Magazine,* January 1, 1999, www.unhcr.org/en-us/publications /refugeemag/3b811f6e4/refugees-magazine-issue-113-europe-debate-asylum-viet-nam-end-era.html (accessed August 27, 2019).

127. Immigration and Refugee Board, Ottawa, "Vietnam: Information on the Treatment of Returnees," September 12, 1997, Oxford; Robinson, *Terms of Refuge,* pp. 262–63.

128. *Refugee Concern News Magazine,* Hong Kong, June/July 1994, UCI, Paul Tran Files on Southeast Asian Refugees, MS-SEA002, Box 15, Folder 10.

129. Nguyen Van Tien, "UNHCR Claims No Persecution in Vietnam," *Refugee Concern News Magazine,* Hong Kong, September/October 1994, UCI, Paul Tran Files on Southeast Asian Refugees, MS-SEA002, Box 15, Folder 10.

130. Human Rights Watch/Asia, Hong Kong: Abuses against Vietnamese Asylum Seekers in the Final Days of the Comprehensive Plan of Action, March 1997. For a public health study that concluded repatriates' health metrics were weaker than those of Vietnamese who had never left, see Hongyun Fu and Mark Van Landingham, "Mental and Physical Health Consequences of Repatriation for Vietnamese Returnees: A Natural Experiment Approach," *Journal of Refugee Studies* 23 (June 2010).

131. Freeman and Nguyen, *Voices from the Camps,* pp. 107–37, 112.

132. Margaret Piper, Report on Visit to Hong Kong and Vietnam, Refugee Council of Australia, December 1996, p. 14, Oxford.

133. Robinson, *Terms of Refuge,* pp. 262–64.

134. Linda Hitchcox, "Returnees within Their Communities: A Pilot Study of Local Attitudes and Economy Related to Development Policy," May 1991, Oxford.

135. Interview with Cheung-Ang Siew Mei, Hong Kong, June 16, 2016.

136. Piper, Report on Visit to Hong Kong and Vietnam, December 1996, pp. 14–16, Oxford.

137. Audit Commission, Report 51 of the Director of Audit, Chapter Two: Recoverability of the Outstanding Advances to the UNHCR, Hong Kong, October 1998. (In 2019 U.S. dollars, this is close to $150 million.)

138. Cheung-Ang Siew Mei interview, June 16, 2016.

139. Cheung-Ang Siew Mei interview, June 16, 2016.

140. Interview with E. Ferris, Washington, D.C., February 5, 2015.

141. Greg Torode, "Vietnam Sticks to Migrant Deadline," *SCMP*, May 29, 1997, Newspaper Cuttings, HKRS 766-2-2.

142. Interview with Bernard Kerblat, Manila, February 25, 2015. Alexander Betts also emphasized the personal charisma of and pivotal role played by Sergio Vieira de Mello. Betts, "Comprehensive Plan of Action," pp. 35–36, 44–45.

143. Kerblat interview, February 25, 2015.

144. Boat People SOS, UNHCR's Failures in the Comprehensive Plan of Action: A Factual Presentation, May 1996.

CHAPTER 6. PALAWAN AND DIASPORIC IMAGINARIES, 1996–2005

1. For the most thorough analysis of Filipino humanitarianism and Palawan, see Pangilinan, "Screening Subjects." On Vietnamese Americans and the use of humanitarianism, also see Vong, "'Compassion Gave Us a Special Superpower.'"

2. See Brian Doan, *The Forgotten Ones: A Photographic Documentation of the Last Vietnamese Boat People in the Philippines* (Westminster, CA: Vietnamese American Arts and Letters Association, 2004); Dai Le's film *In Limbo: A Vietnamese-Australian's Struggle to Resettle 50 Refugee Families in Australia,* 2002; and Duc Nguyen's film *Stateless,* 2015.

3. For a critique of this marketing and political strategy, see Noah Theriault, "Agencies of the Environmental State: Difference and Regulation on the Philippines' 'Last Frontier'" (PhD diss., University of Wisconsin, Madison, 2013).

4. Michael Salman, "'The Prison That Makes Men Free': The Iwahig Penal Colony and the Simulacra of the American State in the Philippines," in *Colonial Crucible: Empire in the Making of the Modern American State,* ed. Alfred W. McCoy and Francisco A. Scarano (Madison: University of Wisconsin Press, 2009), pp. 116–28; Benjamin Weber, "America's Carceral Empire: Punishment, Work, and Criminality at Home and Abroad, 1865–1945" (PhD diss., Harvard University, 2017).

5. For recent accounts, see "Murderers Wander with Machetes at Idyllic Philippine Prison," Inquirer.Net, June 22, 2014, http://newsinfo.inquirer.net/613299 /murderers-wander-with-machetes-at-idyllic-philippine-prison (accessed September 27, 2014).

6. Cargill and Huynh, *Voices of Vietnamese Boat People,* pp. 151–57.

7. Oral history of Tri C. Tran by Jimmy Huynh, VAOHP, 2012, http://ucispace .lib.uci.edu/bitstream/handle/10575/1633/vaohp0017_f01.pdf?sequence=3 (accessed August 9, 2018).

8. Knudsen, *Boat People in Transit,* p. 36. Also see Freeman and Nguyen, *Voices from the Camps,* p. 40; Reyes, *Songs of the Caged,* pp. 24–33.

9. Yến Lê Espiritu, *Body Counts,* p. 52.

10. Interview with Y. Esguerra, Morong, Philippines, February 23, 2015.

11. Davies, *Legitimising Rejection,* pp. 212–13.

12. Freeman and Nguyen, *Voices from the Camps,* p. 41.

13. Thu-Oanh Nguyen to Madame Sadako Ogata, October 8, 1993, UNHCR Fonds 11, Series 3, 100.PHI.Gen, Folder A, Refugee Situations.

14. UNHCR Response to Thu-Oanh Nguyen, October 19, 1993, UNHCR Fonds 11, Series 3, 100.PHI.Gen, Folder A, Refugee Situations.

15. Freeman and Nguyen, *Voices from the Camps,* p. 51.

16. Draft Guidelines for Critical Incidents Received on 9.10.91, UNHCR Fonds 11, Series 3, 001.PHI, General—Philippines.

17. Joachim Pham, "Q and A with Sr. Le Thi Triu: Working with the Expatriates of Vietnam," *Global Sisters Report,* December 17, 2015, http://globalsistersreport.org /blog/q/ministry/q-sr-pascale-le-thi-triu-working-expatriates-vietnam-35421 (accessed August 13, 2018).

18. Philippine Reception of Asylum Seekers and the Mission of CADP, 1975–2000, Center for Assistance for Displaced Persons Archives, Viet Ville, Palawan (hereafter CADP Archives). Also see Anne Lan K. Candelaria, "The Philippine Response to the Vietnamese Boat People's Plight from 1975–1999: A Policy Review" (master's thesis, Ateneo de Manila University, 2001), pp. 57–60; Robinson, *Terms of Refuge,* p. 23.

19. Christine Mougne, Social Services Mission to the Philippines, October 19–28, 1992, December 3, 1992, UNHCR Fonds 11, Series 3, 610.PHI.SRV Protection and General Legal Matters/Repatriates, Vietnamese Refugees in Philippines.

20. S. Leo Chiang, dir., *A Village Called Versailles,* 2009.

21. Interview with Father Vien Nguyen, New Orleans, September 21, 2018.

22. Telephone interview with V.P., August, 28, 2018.

23. V.P. interview, August 28, 2018.

24. Christine Mougne, Social Services Mission to the Philippines, October 19–28, 1992, December 3, 1992, UNHCR Fonds 11, Series 3, 610.PHI.SRV Protection and General Legal Matters/Repatriates, Vietnamese Refugees in Philippines (emphasis in the original).

25. Candelaria, "The Philippine Response," pp. 76–77.

26. Sister Myrna Bas, "The Church on Refugees," *Malaya,* February 29, 1996; Sister Pascale, Correspondence, November 15, 1994, Item Number 1849118060000, Box 118, Folder 060, FVPPA Collection, Texas Tech (accessed June 21, 2018).

27. Note for the File, Mission of M. Morales-O'Donnell and L. Hansson, February 25, 1993, Field Office Palawan, UNHCR Fonds 11, Series 3, 022.PHI Branch Office Reports.

28. American Embassy, Manilla, to D.C. State Department, March 19, 1992, FOIA documents.

29. "Integration Not an Option for Viet Refugees," *Business World Manila,* February 28, 1996.

30. "Time to Go Home," *Philippine Star,* November 18, 1995.

31. "Integration Not an Option for Viet Refugees," *Business World Manila,* February 28, 1996. For other accounts of Vietnamese just leaving and resettling in Manila and Cebu, see "UNHCR Leaves Fate of Vietnamese Refugees to RP Government," *Philippine Star,* July 3, 1995.

32. Interview with Bishop Pedro Arigo, Puerto Princesa, Philippines, March 2, 2015.

33. Max V. Solvien, "A Civilized People Cannot Indulge in the Hypocrisy of Forcibly Expelling Vietnamese," *Philippine Star,* February 16, 1996.

34. Oscar Evangelista and Susan Evangelista, "The Vietnamese in Palawan Philippines: A Study of Local Integration," in *Exploring Transnational Communities in the Philippines,* ed. Virginia A. Miralao and Lorna P. Makil (Quezon City: Philippine Migration Research Network, 2007), p. 78.

35. The exact numbers of Vietnamese on the repatriate flight is not clear. In the written record, I have seen the number listed as 81, 84, and 89.

36. "The Ending of the Boat People's Saga," *Malaya,* February 16, 1996.

37. Solvien, "A Civilized People."

38. Solvien, "A Civilized People."

39. Evangelista and Evangelista, "The Vietnamese in Palawan," pp. 79–80, and Candelaria, "The Philippine Response," pp. 80–82. The MOU is available as an appendix in Candelaria's master's thesis and in the CADP archives in Viet Ville.

40. President Fidel V. Ramos, Statement: Concern for Vietnamese Asylum Seekers, July 17, 1996, CADP Archives.

41. Joel Lacsin, "Church Bucks Viets' Repatriation Anew," *Philippine Star,* March 3, 1996.

42. Lacsin, "Church Bucks Viets' Repatriation."

43. Evangelista and Evangelista, "The Vietnamese in Palawan," p. 79; Candelaria, "The Philippine Response," p. 82.

44. Philippine Reception of Asylum Seekers and the Mission of CADP, 1975–2000, p. 32.

45. Philippine Reception of Asylum Seekers and the Mission of CADP, 1975–2000.

46. Mr. Che Nhat Giao, Representative, Remaining Vietnamese Nationals, "A Thank You Letter to the Philippine Government and Its People," *Palawan Times,* April 1–15, 1997.

47. "Viet Village Welcomes Remaining Vietnamese Nationals in RP," *Palawan Times,* April 1–15, 1997.

48. Author's photograph, March 2015.

49. Evangelista and Evangelista, "The Vietnamese in Palawan." The emphasis on Vietnamese entrepreneurship also resonates in other sites. See Marguerite Nguyen, "Refugee Pastoralism: Vietnamese American Self-Representation in New Orleans," in *Remaking New Orleans: Beyond Exceptionalism and Authenticity,* ed. Thomas Jessen Adams and Matt Sakakeeny (Durham, NC: Duke University Press, 2019), pp. 219–40.

50. Evangelista and Evangelista, "The Vietnamese in Palawan."

51. Evangelista and Evangelista, "The Vietnamese in Palawan"; and Candelaria, "The Philippine Response."

52. "Make Them One of Us," *Philippine Free Press,* February 21, 1998.

53. Emails, Advocacy Letters 2, February 2, 1998, CADP Archives.

54. Le Van Ba, Washington Area League of Vietnamese Associations, to President Fidel Ramos, March 1, 1998, Item Number 1849121023000, Box 121, Folder 023, FVPPA Collection, Texas Tech (accessed June 21, 2018).

55. Sister Pascale, CADP, A Request for an Executive Order Granting Permanent Residence to the Remaining Vietnamese Nationals, December 31, 1997, CADP Archives.

56. Maruja A.B. Asis, "The Philippines: Beyond Labor Migration, toward Development (and Possibly) Return," Migration Policy Institute, July 12, 2017, www.migrationpolicy.org/article/philippines-beyond-labor-migration-toward-development-and-possibly-return (accessed August 14, 2018).

57. Opening Remarks of Bishop Ramon Arguelles, MOU Signing, July 17, 1996, CADP Archives.

58. Senator Leticia Ramos-Shahani, An Alternative to Forcible Repatriation, May 20, 1996, CADP Archives.

59. Duc Nguyen, dir., *Stateless,* 2015; Pangilinan, "Screening Subjects," pp. 141–43.

60. Le Xuan Khoa, "The Voice of Refugees, or the Story of a Refugee Organization," May 2, 2009, Library of Congress, Boat People Retrospective.

61. Nguyen Dinh Thang to Corazon Gaite, February 16, 1996, Item Number 1849118060000, Box 118, Folder 060, FVPPA Collection, Texas Tech (accessed June 21, 2018).

62. Claude Daquer Jr., "Viet Village Occupation Gets Go Signal from PCSD," *Palawan Sun,* February 11–17, 1997, CADP Archives.

63. Salvador Socrates to Sister Pascale, January 9, 1997, Item Number 1849121023000, Box 121, Folder 023, FVPPA Collection, Texas Tech (accessed February 22, 2019).

64. Bishop Ramon Arguelles, New Year's Message, February 7, 1997, Item Number 1849125030000, Box 125, Folder 030, FVPPA Collection, Texas Tech (accessed June 21, 2018).

65. Bishop Ramon Arguelles, New Year's Message, February 7, 1997, Item Number 1849125030000, Box 125, Folder 030, FVPPA Collection, Texas Tech (accessed June 21, 2018).

66. "Vietnamese in Palawan Build Lives on Fragile Hope," Radio Free Asia, January 23, 2004, www.rfa.org/english/news/126502-20040123.html (accessed July 16, 2018).

67. Hoi Trinh, "Detained, Pending Repatriation," *Alternative Law Journal* 21, no.2 (April 1996): 64–66.

68. Dai Le, dir., *In Limbo,* 2002; Duc Nguyen, dir., *Stateless,* 2015. Also see "Refugees' Ray of Hope," *The Age,* October 10, 2002, www.theage.com.au/articles/2002/10/10/1034061299900.html (accessed July 11, 2018).

69. James Pangilinan also makes this point in "Screening Subjects," pp. 141–43.

70. Duc Nguyen, dir., *Stateless*.

71. Dai Le, dir., *In Limbo*.

72. Khoa, "The Voice of Refugees," pp. 32–33.

73. Evangelista and Evangelista, "The Vietnamese in Palawan," pp. 83–84.

74. Evangelista and Evangelista, "The Vietnamese in Palawan," pp. 83–85; Khoa, "The Voice of Refugees," pp. 32–33.

75. Nguyen Dinh Thang to Senator Raul Roco, February 21, 1996, Item Number 1849118037000, Box 118, Folder 037, FVPPA Collection, Texas Tech (accessed June 21, 2018).

76. Evangelista and Evangelista, "The Vietnamese in Palawan," pp. 83–84; Khoa, "The Voice of Refugees," pp. 32–33; Tom Berg, "Stuck in Philippines for Fourteen Years, Vietnamese Refugees May Finally Make It to U.S.," *Orange County Register,* December 4, 2003, https://groups.google.com/forum/#!topic/soc.culture .vietnamese/QJMs6OTp2gk (accessed August 15, 2018).

77. Vietnamese Community in the Philippines Announcement, July 8, 2003, CADP Archives; Le Xuan Khoa, "The Voice of Refugees," pp. 32–33.

78. Michael F. Martin, "U.S.-Vietnam Economic Trade Relations: Issues for the 114th Congress," Congressional Research Service, May 20, 2016, https://fas.org/sgp /crs/row/R41550.pdf (accessed August 15, 2018).

79. *Trade and Human Rights: The Future of U.S.-Vietnamese Relations, Hearing before the Subcommittee on East Asian and Pacific Affairs, U.S. Senate,* 108th Congress, 2nd Session, February 12, 2004.

80. Mimi Thi Nguyen, *The Gift of Freedom,* pp. 155–62.

81. *Trade and Human Rights: The Future of U.S.-Vietnamese Relations, Hearing before the Subcommittee on East Asian and Pacific Affairs, U.S. Senate,* 108th Congress, 2nd session, February 12, 2004.

82. *Human Rights in Vietnam: Hearing before the Subcommittee on Africa, Global Human Rights and International Operations of the Committee on International Relations, House of Representatives,* 109th Congress, 1st Session, June 20, 2005, pp. 74–75.

83. Demmer also writes about the multiple "last chapters" of the war; Demmer, "Last Chapter."

84. *Foreign Assistance Oversight: Hearing before the Committee on Foreign Relations, United States Senate,* 108th Congress, 2nd Session, March 2, 2004, p. 45.

85. *Funding for Immigration in the President's 2005 Budget: Hearing before the Subcommittee on Immigration, Border Security, and Claims of the Committee on the Judiciary, House of Representatives,* 108th Congress, 2nd Session, February 25 and March 11, 2004, p. 40.

86. *Foreign Operations, Export Financing, and Related Programs Appropriations for Fiscal Year 2005: Hearings before a Subcommittee of the Committee on Appropriations, U.S. Senate,* 108th Congress, 2nd Session, September 16, 2004, on H.R. 4818/S. 2812, p. 55.

87. *Foreign Operations, Export Financing, and Related Programs Appropriations for Fiscal Year 2005: Hearings before a Subcommittee of the Committee on Appropriations, U.S. Senate,* 108th Congress, 2nd Session, September 16, 2004, on H.R. 4818/S. 2812, p. 56.

88. Leonard Ortiz, "Exiles No More," *Orange County Register,* October 2, 2005, www.ocregister.com/2005/10/02/exiles-no-more/ (accessed July 16, 2018).

89. Telephone interview with Le Xuan Khoa, September 7, 2018; Khoa, "The Voice of Refugees," p. 33.

90. Interview with Father Vien, New Orleans, September 21, 2018.

91. "Palawan Broadcaster Shot Dead, Gunman Caught," GMA Newsonline, January 24, 2011, www.gmanetwork.com/news/news/regions/211319/palawan-broadcaster-shot-dead-gunman-caught/story/ (accessed August 17, 2018).

EPILOGUE

1. Susan Martin, "FY 2019 Ceiling on U.S. Refugee Resettlement: Bad Policy, Faulty Logic," Center for Migration Studies, September 28, 2018, https://cmsny.org/publications/martin-fy2019-refugee-ceiling/ (accessed July 10, 2019).

2. Shannon Dooling, "40 Years after the Vietnam War, Some Refugees Face Deportation under Trump," NPR, March 4, 2019, www.npr.org/2019/03/04/699177071/40-years-after-the-vietnam-war-some-refugees-face-deportation-under-trump (accessed March 7, 2019); Charles Dunst and Krishnadev Calamur, "Trump Moves to Deport Vietnam War Refugees," *Atlantic Monthly,* December 12, 2018; Eric Tang and Viet Thanh Nguyen, "Victims of War and Now Victims of the Trump Administration," *New York Times,* December 3, 2018.

3. Cambodians and Laotians have also faced deportation with increasing intensity. Many of these individuals had been born in camps in Thailand and so faced deportation to a country in which they had never lived. See Soo Ah Kwon, "Deporting Cambodian Refugees: Youth Activism, State Reform, and Imperial Statecraft," in *Ethnographies of U.S. Empire,* ed. Carole McGranahan and John F. Collins (Durham, NC: Duke University Press, 2018), pp. 411–30.

4. Michael Tatarski, "Why Is the U.S. Deporting Protected Vietnamese Immigrants?" *The Diplomat,* June 5, 2018, https://thediplomat.com/2018/06/why-is-the-us-deporting-protected-vietnamese-immigrants/ (accessed March 16, 2019); James Pearson, "'No Job, No Money': Life in Vietnam for Immigrants Deported by U.S.," Reuters, April 19, 2018, www.reuters.com/article/us-usa-vietnam-deportees/no-job-no-money-life-in-vietnam-for-immigrants-deported-by-u-s-idUSKBN1HR08E (accessed March 16, 2019).

5. IRAC became SEARAC in 1991. Also see current campaigns, www.searac.org/movement-building/campaigns/ (accessed March 7, 2019).

6. Rebecca Santana, "Vietnamese Community Rallies against U.S. deportations," AP, December 20, 2018, www.apnews.com/86ef2c1ce81245998e7072cee645ofc7 (accessed March 16, 2019).

7. Mike Ives, "The U.S. Ambassador Who Crossed Trump on Immigration," *New York Times,* September 7, 2018.

8. Emily Cadei, "Leading Republicans Question Trump Plan to Deport Vietnamese Refugees, Some in U.S. over 20 Years," *Sacramento Bee,* December 21, 2018, www.sacbee.com/news/politics-government/capitol-alert/article223391190.html (accessed March 7, 2019).

9. Tim Dickinson, "Trump Administration Argues Migrant Children Don't Need Soap," *Rolling Stone,* June 20, 2019, www.rollingstone.com/politics/politics-news /safe-sanitary-no-soap-beds-court-migrants-trump-850744/ (accessed August 28, 2019).

10. Chantal Da Silva, "More than one hundred immigrants on hunger strike at ICE facility allegedly pepper sprayed," *Newsweek,* August 7, 2019, www.newsweek.com/ice-detainees-hunger-strike-pepper-sprayed-excessive-force-1452953 (accessed January 31, 2020).

11. Anh Do, "Vietnamese Americans Rally in Little Saigon against Trump Administration's Push to Deport Thousands of War Refugees," *Los Angeles Times,* December 15, 2018, www.latimes.com/local/lanow/la-me-ln-vietnamese-refugee-march-20181215-story.html (accessed March 16, 2019).

NOTES TO PAGES 234–237 • 295

SELECTED BIBLIOGRAPHY

ARCHIVES AND LIBRARIES

Hong Kong

Hong Kong Public Records Office
University of Hong Kong Main Library

Malaysia

National Archives of Malaysia, Kuala Lumpur
National Library of Malaysia, Kuala Lumpur
Terengganu State Library
University of Malaya Library
  Central Library
  Za'ba Memorial Library

Philippines

Ateneo de Manila University
  Rizal Library, Filipiniana Section
  Rizal Library, Microform and Digital Resources Center
Bataan Technology Park, PRPC Museum and Memorial, Morong
Center for Assistance for Displaced Persons (CADP) Archives, Viet Ville,
  Palawan
City Library of Balanga
Palawan State University Library
Palawan Times Headquarters, Puerto Princesa
Puerto Princesa City Library
University of the Philippines Diliman, Manila

Filipiniana Books and Serials
Filipiniana Special Collections

Switzerland

United Nations High Commissioner for Refugees (UNHCR) Archives, Geneva

United Kingdom

Bernie Grant Archive, Bishopsgate Library, London
National Archives, Kew, London
Refugee Studies Centre Collections, Bodleian Social Science Library, University of
Oxford

United States

Elizabeth Holtzman Papers, Arthur and Elizabeth Schlesinger Library on the History of Women in America, Radcliffe Institute for Advanced Study, Harvard
University
Families of Vietnamese Political Prisoners Association (FVPPA) Collection, Vietnam Center and Sam Johnson Vietnam Archive, Virtual Vietnam Archive, Texas
Tech University, vietnam.ttu.edu
University of California, Irvine Libraries, Southeast Asian Archive, Irvine, CA
Paul Tran Files on Southeast Asian Refugees
Project Ngoc Records
Viet Stories: Vietnamese American Oral History Project (VAOHP), https://
sites.uci.edu/vaohp/
U.S. Army Military History Institute, U.S. Army War College, Carlisle, PA
U.S. National Archives and Records Administration, College Park, MD

PERIODICALS

The Age (Australia)
Asiaweek (Hong Kong)
Bataan Star (Philippines)
Business World Manila (Philippines)
China Press (Malaysia)
Christian Science Monitor (USA)
Daily Express (UK)
Eastern Express (Hong Kong)
Far Eastern Economic Review (Hong Kong)

Financial Times (UK)
The Guardian (UK)
Hong Kong Standard (Hong Kong)
The Independent (UK)
London Times (UK)
Los Angeles Times (USA)
Malaya (Philippines)
Manila Chronicle (Philippines)
Manila Times (Philippines)
Mastika (Malaysia)
New Straits Times (Malaysia)
New York Post (USA)
New York Times (USA)
Orange County Register (USA)
Pacific Daily News (Guam, USA)
Palawan Times (Philippines)
Philippine Daily Express (Philippines)
Philippine Free Press (Philippines)
Philippine Star (Philippines)
Sabah Times (Malaysia)
Sin Jew Jit Poh (Malaysia)
South China Morning Post (Hong Kong)
Southwest Times Record (USA)
Times (UK)
Wall Street Journal (USA)
Washington Post (USA)

PUBLISHED SOURCES

Abinales, Patricio N. *Making Mindanao: Cotabato and Davao in the Formation of the Philippine Nation-State*. Manila: Ateneo de Manila University Press, 2000.

Adelman, Howard, and Elazar Barkan. *No Return, No Refuge: Rites and Rights of Minority Repatriation*. New York: Columbia University Press, 2011.

Ahmad, Zakaria Haji. "Vietnamese Refugees and ASEAN." *Contemporary Southeast Asia* 1, no. 1 (May 1979): 66–74.

Allen, Michael. *Until the Last Man Comes Home: POWs, MIAs, and the Unending Vietnam War*. Chapel Hill: University of North Carolina Press, 2012.

Alley, Rewi. *Refugees from China*. Beijing: New World Press, 1980.

Anderson, Benedict. *Specters of Comparison: Nationalism, Southeast Asia, and the World*. New York: Verso, 1998.

———. *Under Three Flags: Anarchism and the Anti-Colonial Imagination*. London: Verso, 2005.

Arendt, Hannah. *The Origins of Totalitarianism*. Cleveland, OH: Meridian Books, 1951.

Asis, Maruja M. B. "The Philippines' Culture of Migration." Migration Policy Institute, 2006, www.migrationpolicy.org/article/philoppines-culture-migration.

Bailkin, Jordanna. *Unsettled: Refugee Camps and the Making of Multicultural Britain*. New York: Oxford University Press, 2018.

Barnett, Michael. *Empire of Humanity: A History of Humanitarianism*. Ithaca, NY: Cornell University Press, 2011.

Bernad, Miguel A. "The First Year of the PhilCag in Vietnam." *Philippines Studies* 16, no. 1 (1968): 131–54.

Betts, Alexander. "Comprehensive Plan of Action: Insights from FIREFCA and the Indochinese CPA." UNHCR Working Paper No. 120, January 2006, www.unhcr.org/en-us/research/working/43eb6a152/comprehensive-plans-action-insights-cirefca-indochinese-cpa-alexander-betts.html.

Bevacqua, Michael Lujan. "The Exceptional Life and Death of a Chamorro Soldier: Tracing the Militarization of Desire in Guam, ~~USA~~." In *Militarized Currents: Towards a Decolonized Future in Asia and the Pacific,* ed. Shetsu Shigematsu and Keith Camacho. Honolulu: University of Hawai'i Press, 2010.

Bon Tempo, Carl. *Americans at the Gate*. Princeton, NJ: Princeton University Press, 2008.

Borja, Melissa. "The Government Alone Cannot Do the Total Job: The Possibilities and Perils of Religious Organizations in Public-Private Refugee Care." In *Shaped by the State: Toward a New Political History of the Twentieth Century,* ed. Brent Cebul, Lily Geismer, and Mason B. Williams. Chicago: University of Chicago Press, 2018.

———. "Speaking of Spirits: Oral History, Religious Change, and the Seen and Unseen Worlds of Hmong Americans." *Oral History Review* 44(1) 2017: 1–18.

Bradley, Mark. *The World Reimagined: Americans and Human Rights in the Twentieth Century*. Cambridge: Cambridge University Press, 2016.

British Refugee Council. *Behind Barbed Wire: Vietnamese Refugees in the Closed Camps of Hong Kong*. London: British Refugee Council, 1984.

Camacho, Keith. *Cultures of Commemoration: The Politics of War, Memory, and History in the Mariana Islands*. Honolulu: University of Hawai'i Press, 2011.

Candelaria, Anne Lan K. "The Philippine Response to the Vietnamese Boat People's Plight from 1975–1999: A Policy Review." Master's thesis, Ateneo de Manila University, 2001.

Cao, Lan. *Monkey Bridge*. New York: Penguin, 1998.

Cargill, Mary Terrell, and Jade Quang Huynh, eds. *Voices of Vietnamese Boat People: Nineteen Narratives of Escape and Survival*. Jefferson, NC: McFarland, 2001.

Carroll, John M. *A Concise History of Hong Kong*. Lanham, MD: Rowman & Littlefield, 2007.

Carroll, K. J. *Operation New Life: After Action Report.* Guam, 1975.

Carruthers, Andrew. "Sabah ICs for Sabahans: Will It Help?" ISEAS Yusof Ishak Institute *Perspective,* no. 11 (March 2016): 1–8.

Carruthers, Susan. *Cold War Captives: Imprisonment, Escape, and Brainwashing.* Berkeley: University of California Press, 2009.

Chan, Anita, and Jonathan Unger. "Voices from the Protest Movement, Chongqing, Sichuan." *Australian Journal of Chinese Affairs* 24 (July 1990): 259–79.

Chan Kwok Bun. "Hong Kong's Response to the Vietnamese Refugees: A Study in Humanitarianism, Ambivalence, and Hostility." *Southeast Asian Journal of Social Science* 18, no. 1 (1990): 94–110.

Chan, Sucheng. *The Vietnamese American 1.5 Generation: Stories of War, Revolution, Flight, and New Beginnings.* Philadelphia: Temple University Press, 2006.

Chan, Yuk Wah, ed. *The Chinese/Vietnamese Diaspora: Revisiting the Boat People.* New York: Routledge, 2011.

———. "Hybrid Diaspora and Identity Laundering: A Study of the Return Overseas Chinese Vietnamese in Vietnam." *Asian Ethnicity* 14, no. 4 (2013): 525–41.

———. "Vietnamese or Chinese: Viet-Kieu in the Vietnam-China Borderlands." *Journal of Chinese Overseas* 1, no.1 (November 2005): 217–32.

Chang, Joyce, Brenda Ku, Lum Bik, and Betty Ann Maheu, eds. *They Sojourned in Our Land: The Vietnamese in Hong Kong, 1975–2000.* Hong Kong: Caritas Printing, 2003.

Choy, Catherine Ceniza. *Empire of Care: Nursing and Migration in Filipino American History.* Durham, NC: Duke University Press, 2003.

Cmiel, Kenneth. "The Emergence of Human Rights Politics in the United States." *Journal of American History* 86, no. 3 (December 1999): 1231–50.

Constable, Nicole. *Maid to Order: An Ethnography of Filipina Workers.* Ithaca, NY: Cornell University Press, 1997.

Dang, Thanh Thuy Vo. "Anti-Communism as Cultural Praxis: South Vietnam, War, and Refugee Memories in the Vietnamese American Community." PhD diss., University of California, San Diego, 2008.

Davies, Sara E. *Legitimising Rejection: International Refugee Law in Southeast Asia.* Leiden: Martinus Nijhoff Publishers, 2008.

———. "Saving Refugees or Saving Borders? Southeast Asian States and the Indochinese Refugee Crisis." *Global Change, Peace & Security* 18, no. 1 (February 2006): 3–24.

Davis, Leonard. *Hong Kong and the Asylum-Seekers from Vietnam.* New York: Palgrave Macmillan, 1991.

DeBonis, Steven. *Children of the Enemy: Oral Histories of Vietnamese Amerasians and Their Mothers.* Jefferson, NC: McFarland, 1994.

DeLisle, Christine Taitano. "Destination Chanorro Culture: Notes on Realignment, Rebranding, and post-9/11 Militourism in Guam." *American Quarterly* 68, no. 3 (2016): 563–72.

Demmer, Amanda. "The Last Chapter of the Vietnam War: Normalization, Non-governmental Actors, and the Politics of Human Rights, 1975–1995." PhD diss., University of New Hampshire, 2017.

Doan, Brian. *The Forgotten Ones: A Photographic Documentation of the Last Vietnamese Boat People in the Philippines.* Westminster, CA: Vietnamese American Arts and Letters Association, 2004.

Doan Van Toai, and David Chanoff. *The Vietnamese Gulag.* New York: Simon and Schuster, 1986.

Eckel, Jan, and Samuel Moyn. *The Breakthrough.* Philadelphia: University of Pennsylvania Press, 2014.

Espiritu, Evyn Le. "Archipelago of Resettlement: Vietnamese Refugee Settlers in Guam and Israel-Palestine." PhD diss., University of California, Berkeley, 2018.

———. "Vexed Solidarities: Vietnamese Israelis and the Question of Palestine." *LIT: Literature Interpretation Theory* 29, no. 1 (2018): 8–28.

Espiritu, Yến Lê. *Body Counts: The Vietnam War and Militarized Refugees.* Berkeley: University of California Press, 2014.

———. "Toward a Critical Refugee Study: The Vietnamese Refugee Subject in U.S. Scholarship." *Journal of Vietnamese Studies* 1, no. 1–2 (2006): 410–32.

———. "The 'We-Win-Even-When-We-Lose' Syndrome: U.S. Press Coverage of the Twenty-Fifth Anniversary of the 'Fall of Saigon.'" *American Quarterly* 58, no. 2 (2006): 329–52.

Evangelista, Oscar, and Susan Evangelista. "The Vietnamese in Palawan Philippines: A Study of Local Integration." In *Exploring Transnational Communities in the Philippines,* ed. Virginia A. Miralao and Lorna P. Makil. Quezon City: Philippine Migration Research Network, 2007.

Fan, Rita. "Hong Kong and the Vietnamese Boat People: A Hong Kong Perspective." *International Journal of Refugee Law,* special issue (1990): 144–71.

Fernando, Joseph M. "The Cold War, Malayan Decolonization, and the Making of the Federation of Malaysia." In *Southeast Asia and the Cold War,* ed. Albert Lau. London: Routledge, 2012.

FitzGerald, David. *Refuge beyond Reach: How Rich Democracies Repel Asylum Seekers.* New York: Oxford University Press, 2019.

Flores, Alfredo Peredo. "'No Walk in the Park': U.S. Empire and the Racialization of Civilian Military Labor in Guam, 1944–1962." *American Quarterly* 67, no. 3 (2015): 813–35.

Forsythe, David. *The Humanitarians: The International Committee of the Red Cross.* Cambridge: Cambridge University Press, 2005.

Franklin, Bruce H. *MIA or Mythmaking in America.* Brooklyn, NY: Lawrence Hill Books,1992.

Freeman, James. *Hearts of Sorrow: Vietnamese-American Lives.* Stanford, CA: Stanford University Press, 1991.

Freeman, James M., and Nguyen Dinh Huu. *Voices from the Camps: Vietnamese Children Seeking Asylum.* Seattle: University of Washington Press, 2003.

Friedman, Andrew. *Covert Capital: Landscapes of Denial and the Making of U.S. Empire in the Suburbs of Northern Virginia.* Berkeley: University of California Press, 2013.

Fuentecilla, Jose V. *Fighting from a Distance: How Filipino Exiles Helped Topple a Dictator.* Urbana: University of Illinois Press, 2013.

García, Maria Cristina. *Havana, U.S.A.: Cuban Exiles and Cuban Americans in South Florida, 1959–1994.* Berkeley: University of California Press, 1996.

———. *Seeking Refuge: Central American Migration to Mexico, the United States, and Canada.* Berkeley: University of California Press, 2006.

Gatrell, Peter. *The Making of the Modern Refugee.* New York: Oxford University Press, 2015.

Geiger, Vance. "Southeast Asian Refugees in the Philippine Refugee Processing Center." PhD diss., University of Florida, 1994.

Gonsalves, George. "Operation New Life: Camp Orote—A Study in Refugee Control and Administration, Doctrine and Practice." Master's thesis, Ft. Leavenworth Defense Technical Information Center, 1976.

Gonzalez, Vernadette Vicuña. "Military Bases, 'Royalty Trips,' and Imperial Modernities: Gendered and Racialized Labor in the Postcolonial Philippines." *Frontiers: A Journal of Women's Studies* 28 (2007): 28–59.

———. *Securing Paradise: Tourism and Militarism in Hawai'i and the Philippines.* Durham, NC: Duke University Press, 2013.

Goodno, James B. *The Philippines: Land of Broken Promises.* London: Zed Books, 1991.

Han, Xiaorong. "Exiled to the Ancestral Land: The Resettlement, Stratification and Assimilation of the Refugees from Vietnam in China." *International Journal of Asian Studies* 10.1 (2013): 25–46.

———. "From Resettlement to Rights Protection: The Collective Actions of the Refugees from Vietnam in China since the Late 1970s." *Journal of Chinese Overseas* 10 (2014): 197–219.

Harper, T. N. *The End of Empire and the Making of Malaya.* Cambridge: Cambridge University Press, 1999.

Hawthorne, Lesleyanne, ed. *Refugee: The Vietnamese Experience.* Melbourne: Oxford University Press, 1982.

Hitchcock, William. "Human Rights and the Laws of War: The Geneva Conventions of 1949." In *The Human Rights Revolution,* ed. Akira Iriye, Petra Goedde, and William I. Hitchcock. New York: Oxford University Press, 2012.

Hitchcox, Linda. *Vietnamese Refugees in Southeast Asia Camps.* New York: Palgrave Macmillan, 1991.

Hoang, Carina, ed. *Boat People: Personal Stories from the Vietnamese Exodus, 1976–1996.* Western Australia: Carina Hoang Communications, 2011.

———. "From Both Sides of the Fence: Vietnamese Boat People in Hong Kong, 1975–2000." PhD diss., Curtin University, 2018.

Hoang, Tuan. "From Reeducation Camps to Little Saigons: Historicizing Vietnamese Diasporic Anticommunism." *Journal of Vietnamese Studies* 11, no. 2 (2016): 43–95.

Hoffman, Stefan-Ludwig. "Human Rights and History." *Past and Present* 232 (August 2016): 279–310.

Hsu, Madeline. *The Good Immigrants: How the Yellow Peril Became the Model Minority.* Princeton, NJ: Princeton University Press, 2015.

Hunt, Lynn. *Inventing Human Rights: A History.* New York: W.W. Norton, 2008.

Ip Yu-chung. "Riots and Disturbances Related to Vietnamese Asylum Seekers in Hong Kong." Master's thesis, University of Hong Kong, 1994.

Irwin, Julia. *Making the World Safe: The American Red Cross and a Nation's Humanitarian Awakening.* New York: Oxford University Press, 2013.

Ismail, Yahaya. *Masalah Pendatang Haram Vietnam* (Vietnam: Illegal immigrant problems). Trans. Carlson Chew Yee Herng. Kuala Lumpur: Dinamika Kreatif, 1979.

Ito, Ruri. "Negotiating Partial Citizenship under Neoliberalism: Regularization Struggles among Filipino Domestic Workers in France (2008–2012)." *International Journal of Japanese Sociology* 25, no.1 (2016): 69–84.

Jagel, Matthew. "'Showing Its Flag': The United States, the Philippines, and the Vietnam War." University of Toronto Department of History, *Past Tense: Graduate Review of History* 2 (2013): 18–41.

Kahn, Joel S. *Other Malays: Nationalism and Cosmopolitanism in the Modern Malay World.* Honolulu: University of Hawai'i Press, 2006.

Karnow, Stanley. *In Our Image: America's Empire in the Philippines.* New York: Ballantine Books, 1989.

Kassim, Azizah. "Filipino Responses in Sabah: State Responses, Public Stereotypes, and the Dilemma over Their Future." *Southeast Asian Studies* 47, no. 1 (June 2009): 52–88.

Keys, Barbara. *Reclaiming American Virtue: The Human Rights Revolution of the 1970s.* Cambridge, MA: Harvard University Press, 2014.

Khalili, Laleh. *Time in the Shadows: Confinement in Counterinsurgency.* Stanford, CA: Stanford University Press, 2013.

Khan, I.K. *Islam in Modern Asia.* New Delhi: MD Publications, 2006.

Kheng, Cheah Boon. *Red Star over Malaya: Resistance and Social Conflict during and after the Japanese Occupation, 1941–1946.* Singapore: Singapore University Press, 2003.

Knudsen, John Chr. *Boat People in Transit: Vietnamese in Refugee Camps in the Philippines, Hongkong, and Japan.* Bergen: University of Bergen, 1983.

———. *Capricious Worlds: Vietnamese Life Journeys.* Münster: LIT Verlag, 2005.

———. *Chicken Wings: Refugee Stories from a Concrete Hell.* Bergen: Magnat Folag, 1992.

———. *Vietnamese Survivors: Processing Involved in Refugee Coping and Adaptation.* Bergen: University of Bergen, 1988.

Ku, Agnes. "Immigration Policies, Discourses, and the Politics of Belonging in Hong Kong, 1950–1980." *Modern China* 30, no. 3 (July 2004): 326–60.

Kumin, Judith. "Orderly Departure from Vietnam: Cold War Anomaly or Humanitarian Innovation?" *Refugee Survey Quarterly* 27, no. 1 (2008): 104–17.

Kwon, Heonik. *Ghosts of War in Vietnam.* Cambridge: Cambridge University Press, 2013.

———. *The Other Cold War.* New York: Columbia University Press, 2010.

Kwon, Soo Ah. "Deporting Cambodian Refugees: Youth Activism, State Reform, and Imperial Statecraft." In *Ethnographies of U.S. Empire,* ed. Carole McGranahan and John F. Collins. Durham, NC: Duke University Press, 2018.

Lau, C. K. *Hong Kong's Colonial Legacy.* Hong Kong: Chinese University Press, 1997.

Law, Sophia Suk-Mun. *The Invisible Citizens of Hong Kong: Art and Stories of Vietnamese Boatpeople.* Hong Kong: Chinese University Press, 2014.

Leebaw, Bronwyn. "The Politics of Impartial Activism: Humanitarianism and Human Rights." *Perspectives on Politics* 5, no. 2 (June 2007): 223–39.

Leow, Rachel. *Taming Babel: Language in the Making of Malaysia.* Cambridge: Cambridge University Press, 2016.

Lin, David C. L., ed. *Overcoming Passion for Race in Malaysia Cultural Studies.* Leiden: Brill, 2008.

Lindskoog, Carl. *Detain and Punish: Haitian Refugees and the Rise of the World's Largest Immigration Detention System.* Gainesville: University of Florida Press, 2018.

Ling, Alice Lee Pui. "The Role of Non-Governmental Organizations in Detention Centres for Vietnamese Boat People." Master's thesis, Hong Kong University, 1992.

Lipman, Jana K. "'The Face Is the Roadmap': Vietnamese Amerasians in Political and Popular Culture, 1980–1988." *Journal of Asian American Studies* 14, no. 1 (2011): 33–68.

———. "'The Fish Trusts the Water, and It Is in the Water that It Is Cooked': The Caribbean Origins of the Krome Detention Center." *Radical History Review* 115 (2013): 115–41.

———. "'Give Us a Ship': The Vietnamese Repatriate Movement in Guam, 1975." *American Quarterly* 64, no. 1 (2012): 1–31.

———. "'A Precedent Worth Setting': Military Humanitarianism and the U.S. Military and the 1975 Evacuation." *Journal of Military History* 79, no. 1 (January 2015): 151–79.

Loescher, Gil. *The UNHCR and World Politics: A Perilous Path.* New York: Oxford University Press, 2001.

Loescher, Gil, and John A. Scanlan. *Calculated Kindness: Refugees and America's Half-Open Door, 1945 to the Present.* New York: Free Press, 1986.

Loyd, Jenna M., and Alison Mountz. *Boats, Borders, and Bases: Race, the Cold War, and the Rise of Migration Detention in the United States.* Oakland: University of California Press, 2018.

Mackie, Richard. *Operation New Life: The Untold Story.* Concord, CA: Solution Publishing, 1998.

Madokoro, Laura. *Elusive Refuge: Chinese Migrants in the Cold War.* Cambridge, MA: Harvard University Press, 2016.

Mahathir, Mohamad. *The Malay Dilemma.* Singapore: Asia Pacific Press, 1970.

Malkki, Liisa. *The Need to Help: The Domestic Arts of International Humanitarianism.* Durham, NC: Duke University Press, 2015.

———. "Refugees and Exile: From 'Refugee Studies' to the National Order of Things." *Annual Review of Anthropology* 24 (October 1995): 495–523.

———. "Speechless Emissaries: Refugees, Humanitarianism, and Dehistoricization." *Cultural Anthropology* 11, no. 3 (August 1996): 377–404.

Man, Simeon. "The GI Movement in the Third World." In *The Rising Tide of Color: Race, State Violence, and Radical Movements across the Pacific,* ed. Moon-Ho Jung. Seattle: University of Washington Press, 2015.

———. *Soldiering through Empire.* Oakland: University of California Press, 2018.

Mark, Chi-Kwan. "The 'Problem of People': British Colonials, Cold War Powers, and Chinese Refugees in Hong Kong, 1949–1962." *Modern Asian Studies* 41, no. 6 (2007): 1145–81.

Martini, Edwin. *Invisible Enemies: The American War on Vietnam.* Amherst: University of Massachusetts Press, 2007.

Mayer-Rieckh, Elisabeth. "'Beyond Concrete and Steel,' Power Relations and Gender: The Case of Vietnamese Women in the Detention Centres in Hong Kong." Master's thesis, Institute of Social Studies, The Hague, 1992.

McKenna, Thomas. *Muslim Rulers and Rebels: Everyday Politics and Armed Separatism in the Southern Philippines.* Berkeley: University of California Press, 1998.

Mortland, Carol A. "Transforming Refugees in Refugee Camps." *Urban Anthropology and Studies of Cultural Systems and World Economic Development* 16, no. 3/4 (1987): 375–404.

Moyn, Samuel. *The Last Utopia: Human Rights and History.* Cambridge, MA: Harvard University Press, 2010.

———. "Theses on Humanitarianism and Human Rights." *Humanity Journal* 9 (2016): 2–16.

Na'puti, Tiara R., and Michael Lujan Bevacqua. "Militarization and Resistance from Guahan: Protecting and Defending Pagat." *American Quarterly* 67, no. 3 (2015): 837–58.

Ngoei, Wen-Qing. *Arc of Containment: Britain, the United States, and Anti-Communism in Southeast Asia.* Ithaca, NY: Cornell University Press, 2019.

———. "'A Wide Anticommunist Arc': Britain, ASEAN, and Nixon's Triangular Diplomacy." *Diplomatic History* 41, no. 5 (November 2017): 903–32.

Nguyen, Marguerite. "Refugee Pastoralism: Vietnamese American Self-Representation in New Orleans." In *Remaking New Orleans: Beyond Exceptionalism and Authenticity,* ed. Thomas Jessen Adams and Matt Sakakeeny. Durham, NC: Duke University Press, 2019: 219–40.

Nguyen, Mimi Thi. *The Gift of Freedom.* Durham, NC: Duke University Press, 2012.

Nguyen, Nathalie Huynh Chau. *Memory Is Another Country: Women of the Vietnamese Diaspora.* Santa Barbara, CA: Praeger Press, 2009.

———. *South Vietnamese Soldiers: Memories of the War and After.* Santa Barbara, CA: Praeger Press, 2016.

Nguyen, Phuong Tran. *Becoming Refugee American: The Politics of Rescue in Little Saigon.* Urbana: University of Illinois Press, 2017.

Nguyen, Viet Thanh. *Nothing Ever Dies: Vietnam and the Memory of War.* Cambridge, MA: Harvard University Press, 2016.

———. "Refugee Memories and Asian American Critique." *positions*: asia critique 20, no. 3 (2012): 911–42.

———. *The Sympathizer.* New York: Grove Press, 2016.

Ong, Aiwha. *Buddha Is Hiding: Refugees, Citizenship, and the New America.* Berkeley: University of California Press, 2003.

Oyen, Meredith. *The Diplomacy of Migration: Transnational Lives and the Making of U.S.-China Relations in the Cold War.* Ithaca, NY: Cornell University Press, 2016.

Paik, A. Naomi. *Rightlessness: Testimony and Redress in U.S. Prison Camps since World War II.* Chapel Hill: University of North Carolina Press, 2016.

Pangilinan, James. "Screening Subjects: Humanitarian Government and the Politics of Asylum at Palawan." Master's thesis, University of Washington, 2014.

Parrenas, Rhacel. *Servants of Globalization: Migration and Domestic Work.* Stanford, CA: Stanford University Press, 2015.

Peterson, Glen. "To Be or Not to Be a Refugee: The International Politics of the Hong Kong Refugee Crisis, 1949–1955." *Journal of Imperial and Commonwealth History* 36, no. 2 (2008): 171–95.

Pew, Frank. *The Role of the U.S. Army Forces Command in Project New Arrivals: Reception and Care of Refugees from Vietnam.* Ft. McPherson, GA: Historical Office of the Chief of Staff of the U.S. Army Command, 1981.

Pham, Andrew. *The Eaves of Heaven: A Life in Three Wars.* New York: Random House, 2008.

Pham Kim Vinh. *The Politics of Selfishness: Vietnam, the Past as Prologue.* San Diego: Pham Kim Vinh, 1977.

Porter, Stephen. *Benevolent Empire: U.S. Power, Humanitarianism, and the World's Dispossessed.* Philadelphia: University of Pennsylvania Press, 2017.

Power, Samantha. *Chasing the Flame: Sergio Vieira de Mello and the Fight to Save the World.* New York: Penguin, 2008.

Quimpo, Susan, and Nathan Quimpo, eds. *Subversive Lives: A Family Memoir of the Marcos Years.* Athens: Ohio University Press, 2016.

Rachagan, S. Sothi. "Refugees and Illegal Immigrants: The Malaysian Experience with Filipino and Vietnamese Refugees." In *Refugees: A Third World Dilemma,* ed. John R. Rogge. Totowa, NJ: Rowman & Littlefield, 1987.

Redfield, Peter. *Space in the Tropics: From Convicts to Rockets in French Guiana.* Berkeley: University of California Press, 2000.

Reyes, Adelaida. *Songs of the Caged, Songs of the Free: Music and the Vietnamese Refugee Experience.* Philadelphia: Temple University Press, 1999.

Robinson, W. Courtland. "The Comprehensive Plan of Action for Indochinese Refugees, 1989–1997: Sharing the Burden and Passing the Buck." *Journal of Refugee Studies* 17, no. 3 (2004): 319–33.

———. *Terms of Refuge: The Indochinese Exodus and the International Response.* London: Zed Books, 1998.

Rogers, Robert F. *Destiny's Landfall: A History of Guam.* Honolulu: University of Hawai'i Press, 1995.

Sahara, Ayako. "Globalized Humanitarianism: U.S. Imperial Formation in Asia and the Pacific through the Indochinese Refugee Problem." PhD diss., University of California, San Diego, 2012.

———. "Operations New Life/Arrivals: The U.S. National Project to Forget the Vietnam War." Master's thesis, University of California, San Diego, 2009.

Salman, Michael. "'The Prison That Makes Men Free': The Iwahig Penal Colony and the Simulacra of the American State in the Philippines." In *Colonial Crucible: Empire in the Making of the Modern American State,* ed. Alfred W. McCoy and Francisco A. Scarano. Madison: University of Wisconsin Press, 2009.

Santos, Emmanuel N. "Cultural Transformation in a Total Institution: The Philippine Refugee Processing Center (PRPC) Refugees." Master's thesis, Ateneo de Manila University, 1990.

Schmitz, David. *The United States and Right-Wing Dictatorships, 1965–1989.* Cambridge: Cambridge University Press, 2006.

Schofield, Camilla. *Enoch Powell and the Making of Postcolonial Britain.* Cambridge: Cambridge University Press, 2015.

Scott, Joann C. *Indochina's Refugees: Oral Histories from Laos, Cambodia, and Vietnam.* Jefferson, NC: McFarland, 1989.

Simms, Brendan, and D. J. B. Trim. *Humanitarian Intervention: A History.* Cambridge: Cambridge University Press, 2011.

Snyder, Sarah. *Human Rights Activists and the End of the Cold War.* Cambridge: Cambridge University Press, 2011.

Stoler, Ann Laura. *Haunted by Empire: Geographies of Intimacy in North American History.* Durham, NC: Duke University Press, 2006.

———. "Tense and Tender Ties: The Politics of Comparison in North American History and (Post) Colonial Studies." *Journal of American History* 88, no. 3 (December 2001): 829–65.

Studlar, Donley T. "British Public Opinion, Color Issues, and Enoch Powell: A Longitudinal Study." *British Journal of Political Science* 4, no. 3 (July 1974): 376–78.

Stur, Heather. "'Hiding behind the Humanitarian Label': Refugees, Repatriates, and the Rebuilding of America's Benevolent Image after the Vietnam War." *Diplomatic History* 39, no. 2 (January 2014): 223–44.

Tang, Eric. *Unsettled: Cambodian Refugees in the NYC Hyperghetto.* Philadelphia: Temple University Press, 2015.

Theriault, Noah. "Agencies of the Environmental State: Difference and Regulation on the Philippines' 'Last Frontier.'" PhD diss., University of Wisconsin, Madison, 2013.

Thomas, Sabrina. "The Value of Dust: Policy, Citizenship, and Vietnam's Amerasian Children." PhD diss., Arizona State University, 2015.

Thompson, Larry Clinton. *Refugee Workers in the Indochina Exodus, 1975–82.* Jefferson, NC: McFarland, 2010.

Thompson, Mark R. *The Anti-Marcos Struggle: Personalistic Rule and Democratic Transition in the Philippines.* New Haven, CT: Yale University Press, 1995.

Tollefson, James W. *Alien Winds: The Reeducation of America's Indochinese Refugees.* New York: Praeger,1989.

Tran Dinh Tru. *Ship of Fate: Memoir of a Vietnamese Repatriate.* Trans. Bac Hoai Tran and Jana K. Lipman. Honolulu: University of Hawai'i Press, 2017.

Tran, G. B. *Vietnamerica.* New York: Villard, 2011.

Tran, Quan. "Remembering the Vietnamese Boat People Exodus: A Tale of Two Memorials." *Journal of Vietnamese Studies* 7, no. 3 (Fall 2012): 80–121.

Trinh, Hoi. "Detained, Pending Repatriation." *Alternative Law Journal* 21, no. 2 (April 1996): 64–66.

Valverde, Kieu-Linh Caroline. "From Dust to Gold: The Vietnamese Amerasian Experience." In *Racially Mixed People in America,* ed. Maria P. P. Root. Newbury Park, CA: Sage, 1992.

Vang, Chia Youyee. *Hmong America: Reconstructing Community in Diaspora.* Urbana: University of Illinois Press, 2010.

Vang, Ma. "The Refugee Soldier: A Critique of Recognition and Citizenship in the Hmong Veterans' Naturalization of Act of 1997." *positions: asia critique* 20, no. 3 (2012): 685–712.

Varzally, Allison. *Children of Reunion: Vietnamese Adoptions and the Politics of Family Migrations.* Chapel Hill: University of North Carolina Press, 2017.

Vo, Nghia M. *The Bamboo Gulag: Political Imprisonment in Communist Vietnam.* Jefferson, NC: McFarland, 2004.

Vong, Samuel. "'Assets of War': Military Displacements, Deterritorialization, and the Strategic Uses of Refugees during the Vietnam War, 1965–1975." *Journal of American Ethnic History* (forthcoming, 2020).

———. "'Compassion Gave Us a Special Superpower': Vietnamese Women Leaders, Reeducation Camps, and the Politics of Family Reunification, 1977–1991." *Journal of Women's History* 30, no. 3 (Fall 2018): 107–37.

———. "Compassionate Politics: The History of Indochinese Refugee Migration and the Transnational Politics of Care, 1975–1994." PhD diss., Yale University, 2013.

Wain, Barry. *Malaysian Maverick: Mahathir Mohamad in Turbulent Times.* Basingstoke: Palgrave Macmillan, 2009.

Warr, Peter C. "Export Processing Zones: The Economics of Enclave Manufacturing." *Research Observer* 4 (January 1989): 70–71.

Weber, Benjamin. "America's Carceral Empire: Punishment, Work, and Criminality at Home and Abroad, 1865–1945." PhD diss., Harvard University, 2017.

Wong Tze Ken, Danny. "The Cham Arrivals in Malaysia: Distant Memories and Rekindled Links." *Archipel* 85 (2013): 151–65.

———. "View from the Other Side: The Early Cold War in Malaysia from the Memoirs of Former MCP Members." In *Southeast Asia and the Cold War,* ed. Albert Lau. London: Routledge, 2012.

Wong Yiu-Chung. "'One Country' and 'Two Systems': Where Is the Line?" In *"One Country, Two Systems" in Crisis: Hong Kong's Transformation since the Handover,* ed. Wong Yiu-Chung. Lanham, MD: Lexington Books, 2004.

Ying, Stella Ho Siu. "A Study of the Social Work Students' Attitude towards the Vietnamese Refugee Problem in Hong Kong: Reflection of Social Work Values and Ethics." Master's thesis, University of Hong Kong, 1990.

Yuen, Hong Kiu. "Proxy Humanitarianism: Hong Kong's Vietnamese Refugee Crisis." Master's thesis, University of Hong Kong, 2014.

Zaretsky, Natasha. *No Direction Home: The American Family and the Fear of National Decline, 1968–1980.* Chapel Hill: University of North Carolina Press, 2007.

Zolberg, Aristide R. "Managing a World on the Move," *Population and Development Review* 32 (2006): 222–53.

———. *A Nation by Design: Immigration Policy in the Fashioning of America.* Cambridge, MA: Harvard University Press, 2008.

INDEX

Cham, 57, 77. *See also* Cambodia

Chan, Yuk Wah, 6

China: camps in, 5; exodus of "refugees" from, 130; interference of, 63; military ambitions of, 230; repatriation in, 129; resettlement in, 57, 256n8; reversion of sovereignty of Hong Kong to, 10, 127–29, 146–48, 160, 179, 180, 197; and the United States, 87; war of Vietnam with, 85, 87, 135, 136, 244n8. *See also* Chinese Revolution; Tiananmen Square

Chinese Exclusion Act, 15

Chinese Malaysians, 6, 53, 56–67. *See also* Malaysia

Chinese Revolution, 16, 129, 130, 146. *See also* China

Chinese Vietnamese, 12, 50, 56–66, 80, 87, 130; exodus of, 134, 136; in Hong Kong, 135–37. *See also* Vietnam

Christian Action, 197–99

Clark Air Force base, 106. *See also* Philippines

climate change, 236

Clinton, President Bill, 163, 189

Cold War: anti-communist politics of the, 7, 10, 24, 33, 92, 132, 163, 190, 193; authoritarian leadership in Southeast Asia in the, 7, 94; détente in the, 56; dynamics of the, 154, 160, 172; end of the, 8–11, 162, 199, 281n10; Malaysia in the, 56–66; refugee policy in the, 16, 20, 88, 129, 172, 235

communism: agents of, 53, 61–64; and anti-communism, 50, 60; critics of, 9; ideology of, 87; label of, 34; rescue from, 16, 24, 130; unification under, 33

Community and Family Services International, 101, 112, 173, 178

Comprehensive Plan of Action (CPA), 17, 18, 121, 125, 153–55, 161–67, 171, 172, 178–82, 188, 194–201, 205, 211, 221, 226; protest of Vietnamese in Palawan against the, 2–4, 3*fig.*, 220–32; protest of Vietnamese in the United States against the, 156–58, 185–90. *See also* Geneva conference (1989)

Correctional Services Department (CSD), 138, 141, 161, 173, 174, 179, 183, 185, 191;

officers of the, 193; violence of the, 200. *See also* Hong Kong

Cuba, 8, 81, 154

Cultural Revolution, 130, 131. *See also* China

Czechoslovakia, 170, 172

Daughters of Charity, 208. *See also* Le Thi Triu, Sister Pascale

Democratic Action Party, 63. *See also* Malaysia

Democratic Republic of Vietnam. *See* North Vietnam

Deng Xiaoping, 146

deportation, 17, 131, 136; forced, 41, 182, 183; from Thailand, 294n3; from the United States, 233, 234. *See also* repatriation

deterrence: in Hong Kong, 129, 138, 139, 143, 150, 166; in Malaysia, 52–54

diasporic activism, 5, 8–13, 55, 56, 82–84, 83*fig.*, 88, 122–24, 128, 129, 132, 156–58, 161, 185–90, 202, 208, 220–29, 231, 234, 236, 237. *See also* activism; protest; Vietnamese Americans; Vietnamese Australians

dictators: Filipino, 94, 120, 121; Latin American, 9, 55, 95

dissidents: anti-Soviet, 55; Vietnamese, 57

Do Giau, 167, 168

Eisenhower, President Dwight, 16

El Salvador, 21

empire: American, 6, 7, 11, 13, 113; British, 6, 7, 13; civilizing mission of, 8; politics of, 9; violence of, 11

English as a Second Language (ESL), 113–16, 115*fig.*, 116*fig.*, 119

Espiritu, Yến Lê, 11, 81, 209, 240, 209

Export Processing Zone (EPZ), 106, 107*map*, 108, 110. *See also* Bataan

Families of Vietnamese Political Prisoners Association (FVPPA), 122, 123

Fan, Rita, 148, 149

Far Eastern Economic Review, 60, 61, 160

Humanitarian Operation program, 49, 122
human rights: abuses of, 95, 98, 99; claims
    of, 5, 76, 84, 139; commitment to, 73, 76,
    88; critics on the basis of, 92, 93; dia-
    sporic activism and, 185–90; and foreign
    relations, 245n14; language of, 9, 13, 21,
    56, 73, 79, 82, 83, 86, 157, 164, 165, 172,
    177, 190, 192, 231; values of, 8–11; in
    Vietnam, 85, 226; violations of, 26, 84,
    150, 162, 164, 172, 176, 177, 192, 200, 213,
    226; visions of, 11, 82, 160. See also
    activism; non-governmental
    organizations
Human Rights Watch, 177, 196

Immigration Act (1965), 73
Immigration and Customs Enforcement
    (ICE), 234; detention centers of the,
    236
Immigration and Naturalization Services
    (INS), 75, 88, 141, 142, 145, 149, 154, 155,
    193, 194, 195. See also United States
Indochina Refugee Action Center (IRAC),
    55, 84, 85, 122, 128, 151, 156, 157, 201,
    262n122, 271n7. See also Le Xuan Khoa;
    Southeast Asian Resource Action
    Center
Indonesia, 4, 13, 50, 51, 80, 88, 91, 99; camps
    in, 5, 63, 85, 94, 99; Chinese population
    of, 62; first asylum for refugees in, 86,
    124, 125; government of, 17
In Limbo, 223. See also Hoi Trinh
International Catholic Migration Com-
    mission, 101, 114–16
International Monetary Fund, 94
International Rescue Committee, 131
International Social Services, 178
Islam: prohibitions of, 102. See also
    Muslims
Ismail, Yahaya, 61, 63
Israel, 81, 82

Japan, 13, 74, 98, 263n127; resettlement in,
    74; travel to, 223
John Paul II, Pope, 96, 97, 162
Johnson-Reed Act, 15
Joint Voluntary Agency, 75, 145. See also
    non-governmental organizations

Kennedy, Senator Edward, 88
Kissinger, Secretary of State Henry, 41
Knudsen, John Christian, 18, 102, 134, 139,
    165
Kuala Lumpur, 62, 66, 74. See also
    Malaysia

Laos, 13, 100. See also Laotians
Laotians, 13, 263n3, 278n122; deportation
    of, 294n3; repatriation of, 278n122;
    resettlement in the United States of, 84,
    91. See also Laos
Lau, Emily, 160
Laurel, Herman, 119, 120
Lawyers Committee for Human Rights, 9,
    168, 176
Lebanon, 235
Le Duan, 154
Leeks, Clinton, 18, 139, 168, 183
Legal Assistance to Vietnamese Asylum
    Seekers (LAVAS), 188, 221
Le Minh Tan, 34, 35, 37, 46
Lennox, George Gordon, 33, 34. See also
    United Nations High Commissioner
    for Refugees
Le Thi Triu, Sister Pascale, 111, 112, 123,
    208–23, 215fig., 225, 229, 231. See also
    Daughters of Charity
Le Xuan Khoa, 84, 85, 156, 157, 194, 195, 221,
    225, 229, 231
Lim Kit Siang, 63
Loescher, Gil, 71
Lofgren, Representative Zoe, 228
Los Angeles Times, 116
Lutheran Immigration and Refugee Ser-
    vices, 131

MacLehose, Governor Murray, 131
Madokoro, Laura, 5, 55, 137
Malaya, 108, 119
Malayan Communist Party (MCP), 58, 60,
    61. See also Malaysia
Malayan Emergency, 58. See also Malaysia
Malaysia, 4, 7, 52–91, 98, 99, 127, 260n77;
    camps in, 5–8, 13, 52–55, 65–73, 85, 86,
    91, 94, 99, 134, 186; Chinese population
    of, 6, 53, 56–67; Cold War, 56–66, 87;
    eastern, 58; Filipino population of, 77,

Ottoman Empire, 9, 77
Oxfam, 139, 141, 182

Pacific Daily News, 40, 44. *See also* Guam
Palawan, 229, 230; camps in, 2, 94, 111, 113,
201–32, 204*map;* environmental haz-
ards in, 222, 230; Iwahig penal colony
on, 203; mining in, 222, 230; political
demonstrations in, 2, 3, 3*fig.,* 201–32;
Vietnamese in, 2–4, 3*fig.,* 203–8, 220–
32. *See also* Philippines; Puerto Princesa
Palawan Times, 216
Palestine Liberation Organization (PLO),
81
Patten, Governor Chris, 197
Peace Corps, 104
People Power Revolution, 118–21, 215. *See
also* Aquino, Corazon "Cory";
Philippines
Philadelphia Inquirer, 115
Philippine-American War, 28
Philippine Baptist Refugee Ministries, 101
Philippine Civic Action Group, 96, 213
Philippine First Asylum Center, 203,
204*map. See also* Palawan
Philippine Free Press, 217, 218*fig.*
Philippine National Red Cross, 101
Philippine Refugee Processing Center
(PRPC), 90–125, 107*map,* 203–6,
263nn2,3; cultural orientation in the,
110–18, 205; English classes of the, 97,
124, 205; humanitarianism of the,
118–20, 201; medical care of the, 117,
124; Vietnamese Amerasians in the,
266n45, 266n49; violence in the,
266n45. *See also* Bataan; Philippines
Philippines, 51, 52, 80, 105–10, 127, 155,
200–32; camps in the, 2–6, 8, 13, 88–125,
158; Catholic Church of the, 6, 96, 201,
212–15, 222, 223; Communist Party of
the, 94; community organizations in
the, 10; first asylum for refugees in, 86,
94; forced repatriation from the, 3, 4,
202, 212–14, 216; government of, 17;
hospitality of the, 113, 215, 217; humanitarianism of the, 113, 124, 201, 212, 214,
220, 230; human rights violations in
the, 94, 95, 124; immigration bureau-

cracy of the, 223, 224; independence of
the, 7, 201, 222, 230; martial law in the,
94; military of the, 209, 213; Muslim
population of the, 77, 78, 87; politics of
the, 221, 230; remittance economy of
the, 219; resettlement in the, 220–29,
231; rural regions of the, 117; screening
process in the, 206, 213, 221; in Southeast Asia, 14*map;* southern, 77, 78. *See
also* Bataan; Mindanao; Palawan;
Visayas
Philippine Star, 212
Poland, 172
political persecution, 2, 10, 12, 57, 155, 196,
236. *See also* Vietnam
Pompeo, Secretary of State Mike, 234
poverty, 103, 113, 118, 154; structural, 236
Powell, Enoch, 143, 144
Power, Samantha, 152
prisoners of war, 37, 38, 46
Project Ngoc, 128, 157, 158, 186–88, 190,
224. *See also* diasporic activism; University of California, Irvine
protest: against forced repatriation, 161–
200; of Vietnamese against the repatriates, 34; of Vietnamese in Guam, 1–4,
2*fig.,* 25, 35–38, 42, 55, 92; of Vietnamese
in Hong Kong, 10, 92, 128, 129, 150,
172–77, 183, 184*fig.,* 188*fig.,* 191–97; of
Vietnamese in Palawan, 2–4, 3*fig.,*
203–8, 220–32. *See also* activism; diasporic activism
Provisional Revolutionary Government
(PRG), 33, 45
Puerto Princesa, 203, 204*map,* 212, 214,
216, 217, 230. *See also* Palawan
Puerto Rico, 24, 249n6
Pulau Bidong, 66–73, 67*fig.,* 68*fig.,* 86, 101.
See also Malaysia

racism, 113–17, 137
Ramos, President Fidel, 201, 213, 214,
215*fig.,* 217, 219
Reagan, President Ronald, 92, 112
Refugee Act (1980), 17, 88, 91, 233
Refugee Concern Hong Kong, 169, 174,
189, 190, 192, 193, 196
Refugee Resettlement Act (1953), 16

229, 237, 245n17, 262n120; community
of, 219, 229, 234; memories of, 63, 101,
186; organizations of, 11, 55, 82–86, 88,
122, 164, 217, 221, 226; responses of, 87,
185, 234; volunteers of the, 210, 211, 217.
See also diasporic activism

Vietnamese Australians, 63, 202, 224, 232.
See also diasporic activism

Vietnamese Overseas Initiative for Conscience Empowerment (VOICE), 220,
223, 232

Viet Nam Thuong Tin, 44, 46, 47*fig.,* 158

Vietnam War. *See* U.S. war in Vietnam

Viet Ville, 216–23, 218*fig.,* 230. *See also*
Philippines

violence: crime of, 101; domestic, 101; gang,
21; imperial, 209; military, 45, 49, 185;
neoliberal, 185, 227; political, 21; protest,
38, 42, 43, 191, 208; racial, 58, 59, 114; on
repatriate flights, 35; of rioting, 137,
283n50

Visayas, 203, 217. *See also* Philippines

Wake Island, 41, 44

Waldheim, Secretary-General Kurt, 93

Wilson, Governor David, 162, 163

Women's Commission for Refugee Children, 175, 176

World Relief Corporation, 101

World Trade Organization, 227

World War II, 16, 24, 58, 81, 82, 96, 105, 147

Yellow Revolution. *See* People Power
Revolution

Founded in 1893,
UNIVERSITY OF CALIFORNIA PRESS
publishes bold, progressive books and journals
on topics in the arts, humanities, social sciences,
and natural sciences—with a focus on social
justice issues—that inspire thought and action
among readers worldwide.

The UC PRESS FOUNDATION
raises funds to uphold the press's vital role
as an independent, nonprofit publisher, and
receives philanthropic support from a wide
range of individuals and institutions—and from
committed readers like you. To learn more, visit
ucpress.edu/supportus.

www.ingramcontent.com/pod-product-compliance
Lightning Source LLC
Chambersburg PA
CBHW020823270326
41928CB00006B/427